HUMAN RIGHTS AND LEGAL HISTORY

Human Rights and Legal History

Essays in Honour of
Brian Simpson

Edited by

KATHERINE O'DONOVAN and GERRY R. RUBIN

UNIVERSITY PRESS

OXFORD
UNIVERSITY PRESS

Great Clarendon Street, Oxford OX2 6DP

Oxford University Press is a department of the University of Oxford.
It furthers the University's objective of excellence in research, scholarship,
and education by publishing worldwide in

Oxford New York

Athens Auckland Bangkok Bogotá Buenos Aires Calcutta
Cape Town Chennai Dar es Salaam Delhi Florence Hong Kong Istanbul
Karachi Kuala Lumpur Madrid Melbourne Mexico City Mumbai
Nairobi Paris São Paulo Shanghai Singapore Taipei Tokyo Toronto Warsaw

and associated companies in Berlin Ibadan

Oxford is a registered trade mark of Oxford University Press
in the UK and in certain other countries

Published in the United States
by Oxford University Press Inc., New York

British Library Cataloguing in Publication Data
Data available

Library of Congress Cataloging in Publication Data
Data available

ISBN 0-19-826496-8

1 3 5 7 9 10 8 6 4 2

Typeset by Hope Services (Abingdon) Ltd.
Printed in Great Britain
on acid-free paper by
Biddles Ltd., Guildford and King's Lynn

Notes on Contributors

J. H. BAKER — Downing Professor of the Laws of England and Fellow of St Catharine's College, University of Cambridge

W. R. CORNISH — Professor of Law, University of Cambridge

Peter FITZPATRICK — Anniversary Professor of Law, Birkbeck College, University of London

J. S. GETZLER — Fellow and Tutor in Law, St Hugh's College, University of Oxford

R. H. HELMHOLZ — Ruth Wyatt Rosenson Professor of Law, University of Chicago

Gareth JONES — Vice-Master of Trinity College, University of Cambridge and formerly Downing Professor of the Laws of England

Christopher McCRUDDEN — Professor of Law and Fellow of Lincoln College, University of Oxford, and Visiting Professor, University of Michigan Law School

Nuala MOLE — Director of AIRE Centre for Advice on Individual Rights in Europe, London

Katherine O'DONOVAN — Professor of Law at Queen Mary College, University of London

James OLDHAM — Professor of Law, Georgetown University Law Center, Washington DC

Gerry R. RUBIN — Professor of Law, Kent Law School, University of Kent at Canterbury

William TWINING — Research Professor, University College, London

Jules WINTERTON — Librarian, Institute of Advanced Legal Studies, University of London

Contents

Introduction
The Editors   1

1. International Law, the Individual, and A. W. Brian Simpson's
Contribution to the Defence of Human Rights
Nuala Mole   13

2. A Common Law of Human Rights? Transnational Judicial
Conversations on Constitutional Rights
Christopher McCrudden   29

3. *Enfants Trouvés*, Anonymous Mothers, and Children's Identity
Rights
Katherine O'Donovan   66

4. In the Highest Degree Ominous: Hitler's Threatened Invasion
and the British War Zone Courts
G. R. Rubin   86

5. Tears of the Law: Colonial Resistance and Legal Determination
Peter Fitzpatrick   126

6. The *ratio decidendi* of the Case of the Prodigal Son
William Twining   149

7. Three Very Remarkable Nineteenth-Century Lawyers:
Lyndhurst, Denman, and Campbell
Gareth Jones   172

8. The Fate of the Civil Jury in Late-Victorian England:
Malicious Prosecution as a Test Case
Joshua Getzler   205

9. The Seventh Amendment Right to Jury Trial: Late-Eighteenth-
Century Practice Reconsidered
James Oldham   225

10. The Author's Surrogate: the Genesis of British Copyright
W. R. Cornish   254

11. Due Process and Wager of Law: Judicial Conservatism in
the Tudor Common Pleas
J. H. Baker   271

12. Brian Simpson in the United States
R. H. Helmholz   285

A. W. Brian. Simpson: A Bibliography
Jules Winterton 293

Index 315

Introduction

The Editors

For those fortunate to be acquainted with Brian Simpson, there can be no disputing that he is a remarkable individual. The biographical outlines are, of course, sketched out in his entry in *Who's Who*. A child of the rectory in Yorkshire, he was educated at Oakham School, Rutland, and was called up for national service between 1950 and 1951. He then entered Queen's College, Oxford, graduating with a first class degree in Jurisprudence in 1954. He followed this by becoming a junior research fellow at St Edmund Hall (1954–5), and then Fellow and Tutor in Law at Lincoln College where he taught across a range of law disciplines for eighteen years.[1]

An inspiring law teacher, he also commenced a distinguished research career where legal theory, legal method, and medieval and, especially, early modern legal history were very rapidly marked out as congenial subdisciplines for his incisive analytical skills. Alfred William Brian Simpson will forever be remembered among academic lawyers as a noted contributor to (and in respect to its second series, co-editor of) the renowned *Oxford Essays in Jurisprudence* (1961 and 1973); author of *An Introduction to the History of the Land Law* (1961; and *A History of the Land Law*, 2nd edn., 1986); *A History of the Common Law of Contract* (1975); and a host of memorable papers in the *Law Quarterly Review*, *Cambridge Law Journal*, and elsewhere. He deepened lawyers' understanding of how the common law developed, declining to adopt monolithic explanations for legal change, and looking for whatever intellectual, professional, cultural, social, or economic factors best fitted the doctrinal or policy developments he was tracking.

A History of the Land Law is a lucid exposition by its young author of terrifyingly complex material, and was received as a *tour de force* when published by Oxford University Press in 1961. This book was the exemplification of elegant and accurate legal writing, and in this respect Brian was perhaps influenced by the cold currents of Austinian language philosophy and the Hartian jurisprudence of the day. His book conveys difficult ideas within a small compass, yet is always utterly clear and accessible to novices and to non-lawyers as well as to jurists. Technical concepts are carefully dismantled and explained so that the work is as much a contribution to analysis as to history. But it is not just analytical or conceptual history; the pressures of social and economic change on legal institutions

---

[1] The editors are grateful to Joshua Getzler for preparing the section of this Introduction which addresses Brian's 'earlier' writings on legal history.

are constantly in view; for example, the nature of military service; the fluctuating power of the King against his Lords; the fiscal strategies of the Crown; the development of commodified agriculture and credit markets, and so on. It is still to Brian's *A History of the Land Law* that students generally turn for admittance into this classical legal world. For example, one of Brian's former students, Mr Justice Longmore reminisces that at Lincoln College he and his fellow-undergraduates were encouraged by John Morris in the latter's lectures on 'Perpetuities' to read various books, including Morris's own. This list ended as follows: 'Then there is Mr Simpson's *An Introduction to the History of the Land Law*. A brilliant book . . . I think.' According to Andrew Longmore, 'Needless to say, that recommendation ensured numerous sales even though it commanded the enormous price of 25 shillings—then the most expensive of the whole Oxford Series but, of course, much the best value.' Indeed, the book[2] in its revised form remains unequalled more than a generation later. It is clear that E. P. Thompson (in 'Custom, Law and Common Right' in his *Customs in Common*[3]) relied on Brian's work as the doctrinal bedrock for his own imaginative inquiry into eighteenth-century property law.

As pop bands know too well, a stunning debut can raise the pressure and the stakes for later work. Brian next broached a major study in the history of contract doctrine. He showed a gleam of what was coming with a fine 1967 article entitled 'The Penal Bond with Conditional Defeasance', and an exploration of covenant and debt as the form of medieval and early-modern contract. The authorial voice was becoming a little less austere though no less scholarly; in his 1967 paper, the evolution of contract was compared to the Abominable Snowman who advances backwards so as to leave confusing tracks for his pursuers; thus did the forms of law confuse those seeking its meaning at a later age. It was that essay which assisted the High Court of Australia twenty years later in its reformulation of the modern penalties' jurisdiction in *Amev-UDC Finance Ltd v Austin* (1986) 162 CLR 171.

In 1975 Brian published the fruits of his first phase of contract research in *A History of the Common Law of Contract: the Rise of the Action of Assumpsit*. This dense text, occupying more than 600 pages, still holds its own as a detailed monographic study, although it stops with the Statute of Frauds in 1677. While there have been harvests of fresh work on the subject since Brian wrote, notably by David Ibbetson in a sustained body of work culminating recently in his *Historical Introduction to the Law of Obligations* (1999),[4] Brian's book, again, was the foundation for much of the exciting

---

[2] The first part, dealing with the early history of tenure and estates, real actions, possessory assizes, ejectment and copyhold, was later revised to take account of the work of Milsom and others on the High Middle Ages.

[3] Thompson, E. P. *Customs in Common* (Harmondsworth: Penguin, 1991) 97–184.

[4] Ibbetson, D., *Historical Introduction to the Law of Obligations* (Oxford: Oxford University Press, 1999).

work that followed. He emphasized well-understood themes such as the importance of forms and procedures in shaping the medieval law and the oscillation of contract rights between proprietary and tortious concepts; but he also brought out less appreciated ideas, such as the archaic concept of contractual exchange as 'reciprocal gifting'; or the Romanist and canonist notion of *causa* or moral consideration for enforcing consensual obligations which went beyond formal pacts and bargains.

Patrick Atiyah paid tribute to Brian's influence in his own blockbuster *The Rise and Fall of Freedom of Contract* (1979).[5] Simpson was invoked with Lon Fuller as a godfather of a new contract school emerging in the late 1970s, whose mission, according to Atiyah, was to expose liberal ideology imbuing the history of contract law; contracts were no longer seen merely as a legal machinery for converting bargains and promises into legal relations. However, there were signs that Brian did not entirely share this explanatory idiom. In 1975 he published an important essay, 'Innovation in Nineteenth-Century Contract Law', in which he argued that the modernization of contract law was driven largely by internal juristic debates. The interesting questions for Brian were literary ones—who was reflecting and writing about doctrine, and who was reading and applying the emergent treatise literature describing the nature of contracts? Which concepts did each writer or judge invent, borrow, or distort from other sources? Suddenly Pothier and the civilian tradition loomed large, rather than wider ideological forces acting upon legal doctrine. Indeed, argued Brian, the search for meaning in legal doctrine was pointless, since so much doctrine was rationally absurd (see, for examples, 'Contract: The Twitching Corpse' (1981)[6] and 'Legal Iconoclasts and Legal Ideals' (1990)[7]). He proceeded to tip cynical acid over ideologically minded interpretations of early modern contract law, and wrote at length to stress the importance of treatise traditions in Anglo-American law ('The Horwitz Thesis and the History of Contracts' (1979)[8] and 'The Rise and Fall of the Legal Treatise: Legal Principles and the Forms of Legal Literature' (1981))[9]. In his glorious burst of work on leading cases in the last fifteen years he has celebrated the importance of the contingent and the peculiar in the making of the common law (*Cannibalism and the Common Law* (1984) and *Leading Cases in the Common Law* (1995)). No doubt Brian would be horrified to realize that his most recent positions, emphasizing chance, inter-textuality and the primacy of language over meaning, place him closer to Jacques Derrida than

[5] Atiyah, P., *The Rise and Fall of Freedom of Contract* (Oxford: Oxford University Press, 1979) at viii.

[6] *Oxford Journal of Legal Studies*, 1 (1981), 265, reprinted in *Legal Theory and Legal History: Essays on the Common Law* (London: Hambledon Press, 1987).

[7] *University of Cincinnati Law Review*, 58 (1990), 819–44.

[8] *University of Chicago Law Review*, 46 (1979), 533, reprinted in *Legal Theory and Legal History*, above n. 6, 203–72.

[9] *ibid.*, 48 (1981), 632, reprinted in *Legal Theory and Legal History*, above n. 6, 273–320.

most Harvard lawyer-Lefties. But happily Brian has neither joined nor founded any School; all of his splendidly varied work has proved to be inimitable as well as inspirational for the legal–historical fraternity.

In respect of his career as a teacher at Oxford, Brian is admired fondly by undergraduates who themselves were to become distinguished in their own branches of the law. For example, Andrew Longmore, now judge in the Queen's Bench Division, recalls that, 'The first question Brian ever asked me was, "Should juries give reasons?" No doubt he asked many of those seeking admission to Lincoln College exactly the same question. The bright and bushy-tailed schoolboy seeking to impress, naturally said that juries should give reasons, not having given any real thought to the question. It took me some years to realise exactly how silly an answer it was, but by that time Brian had been my tutor and taught me how to grow up.'

Reflecting on Brian's breadth of legal knowledge, the judge continues:

'In the course of a single term one might have tutorials in both tort and legal history and at the same time attend his seminars held jointly with Harold Cox, the College's Tutor in Greek Philosophy, for the benefit of both law and Greats' students. It was as if one had been invited to a feast on Mount Olympus or, at least, on the banks of the Ilyssus.'

It seems, however, that life at Lincoln was not wholly devoted to legal scholarship. There were also Brian's marvellous parties.

'Somehow all the most beautiful girls of Oxford would be there and even if it was rather difficult for a mere male to get invited, the rewards were very great. Indeed, so intense was Brian's enthusiasm for spreading the knowledge of the law that it was not just Lincoln's undergraduates who benefited. He volunteered his services to the ladies of Somerville and down they came to Lincoln to sit at the feet of the master, much to the benefit of those of us immured in an all-male college.'

John Tiley, who later became Professor of Taxation Law at Queens' College, Cambridge, was also one of Brian's undergraduate students at Lincoln between 1959 and 1963. He recalls the total attention and engagement with which Brian would conduct his umpteenth (truly well over twentieth) tutorial of the week in the Wesley Room at Lincoln. In this stimulating intellectual environment, imaginative insights were regularly traded between 'doctor and student'. As John observes, 'I suppose we didn't learn how to be practising lawyers (perish that line of thought) . . . and we were not drilled for the exams'. Yet of the common law and how it worked, Brian's students acquired a deep understanding.

'We became', concludes Professor Tiley, 'contemporary legal historians (we had not heard of law and society in those days) rather than lawyers, and that we regarded as entirely appropriate to a university course. Naturally we had to know our black letter law, but Brian always took us further—with that quiet questioning—"I wonder why . . .".'

It is an image shared by Mark Skilbeck, senior partner at Hallet's,

Ashford, who graduated from Lincoln in 1960. Mark's recollections include being taught the rigours of extracting the *ratio decidendi* of a case, but also being encouraged to explore Lord Denning's 'jazz jurisprudence'. More characteristically, Brian 'gave us hysterically amusing and vivid descriptions of the "scene of the tort" where, he often alleged, the *locus in quo* had been visited by his Oxford colleague, Professor R. F. V. Heuston'.' Thus, for Brian's undergraduates, *Bourhill v. Young* and *High Trees* became something considerably more than mere dry case studies.

Many challenges arose in the context of Brian's pastoral and academic responsibilities. As a Proctor at Oxford, he had on one occasion to determine whether a doctoral student was entitled to submit his thesis in Arabic. Perhaps the candidate had been inspired by reading a familiar late nineteenth-century text by a former Vinerian Professor of Law at Oxford? Whatever the origins, the candidate claimed that there was nothing in the regulations to forbid this. Consequently, he argued, what was not forbidden was permitted. The Proctors conferred. Brian, who, it is believed, taught virtually every exemption subject at Oxford *except* constitutional law, disregarded Dicey and found a more satisfactory solution. The official language of the University was Latin. However, English had crept in by usage, custom, and precedent. These were, therefore, the only two permitted languages for theses. *Cecedit quaestio*. The student submitted (in English, we believe).

In 1973 Brian became Professor of Law at the University of Kent at Canterbury (and served as Dean of Social Sciences, 1975–8) where both editors of the present volume recall Brian with great warmth and appreciation for his inspirational friendship (as does Peter Fitzpatrick). In some respects, Kent was, at that time, not so very different in structure from Oxford. There was a strong college-based system of teaching and the collegial atmosphere on campus was pronounced (our colleague, Professor Claire Palley, the distinguished constitutional lawyer, joined the Faculty at the same time and in 1974 became Master of Darwin, the college which Brian joined). As a wonderful raconteur (to which quality his friends and colleagues will readily testify), Brian could hold his small audiences in the senior common-room spellbound with extraordinary accounts either of his own experiences or of some notorious litigant whose history he was then excavating.

In other respects, law at Kent presented a different challenge. For it was during this time in the early- to mid-1970s that the intellectual ferment in United Kingdom law schools aroused by contextual and clinical legal studies (which took issue with so-called 'black-letter' approaches to legal scholarship) was emerging prominently, and the law department at Kent was at the forefront of this development. The department hosted a law clinic whose caseload on occasion took it into difficult territory (challenging interests associated with academic governance), and Brian's skilful diplomacy, tact, and humour as Dean of the Faculty did much to assuage concerns expressed elsewhere.

He conducted Faculty meetings in a similar manner. One vivid memory is of a dark winter's afternoon in 1974. Brian was chairing a Faculty meeting in the Senate building, a single octagon on campus, with the wind howling outside and angry students protesting loudly about a (no doubt justified) grievance. Placards banged on the sides of the outside walls, as the academics inside agonized about the merits of the cause. Brian attempted to move the discussion on in order to complete the agenda, but feelings inside the building continued to run high. Eventually, about five o'clock, Brian left the chair temporarily. On his return, he announced, 'I've rung my wife to cancel the baby-sitter for this evening, so we can go on all night if you wish.' This produced laughter and dissipated the tension. In those days, it was rare for a man to acknowledge that family responsibilities might intrude into the workplace.

It was also at this time that his association with American law schools began to blossom. Following a number of spells as visiting professor at the University of Chicago Law School, he accepted an invitation to join the Faculty of that distinguished institution, later moving to Michigan where he is now based. This phase of his career is well told in the contribution to this volume of his former colleague, Dick Helmholz.

In keeping with his outstanding reputation both in the United Kingdom and abroad, Brian can chalk up both distinguished and somewhat less conventional honours. Fellow of the British Academy, Fellow of the American Academy of Arts and Sciences, magistrate in both Oxford and Kent, and Honorary Deputy District Attorney for Denver!

But while all the above is accurate, it presents, perhaps, only a partial image of Brian. As one of the authors of this Introduction noted in reviewing *In the Highest Degree Odious* (1992).[10]

They say it started serendipitously after a chance remark by De Lloyd Guth at a British legal history conference a few years ago. Apparently Robert Liversidge of *Liversidge v Anderson* fame was still alive and well and living within 60 miles of Vancouver. Brian Simpson's ears pricked up. A veteran of carbolic smoke balls, bursting reservoirs in Lancashire, butchers' assistants falling off the backs of defective carts and, of course, cabin-boy-eating shipwrecked mariners, he excitedly fingered his calling card [emblazoned] with the immortal legend, 'Have Leading Case, Will Travel'. A cross between H. M. Stanley, Howard Carter, Poirot and Indiana Jones, Simpson was off on another quest; and [a] site visit [if] appropriate.

For that is the image now surely familiar to his friends, colleagues, and family. His sense of fun (we thought seriously of sub-titling this volume *Essays in Law, History, Philosophy, and Fun*); his nose for excitement—whether

---

[10] Rubin, G. R., review of *In the Highest Degree Odious*, in *Journal of Legal History*, 15 (1994), 87–8.

as a light-aircraft pilot or as a tall ships' crewman—his qualities as a *raconteur extraordinaire*, his pathbreaking unorthodoxy (among legal historians) in creating the concept of 'Doing a Simpson' (now perhaps part of the orthodoxy of legal methodology), have charmed and entertained all who have had the pleasure of his company or of reading his invariably witty but scholarly and well-informed deconstructions of a leading case, the concept viewed by many as a tribute to the conceit of those nineteenth-century lawyers who proclaimed the triumph of legal 'science'. Yet as Robert Gordon observed in his review of Brian's *Leading Cases*:[11] 'the Simpson of these historical essays is a social satirist with an old-fashioned radical sensibility.' For it is implicit in the above that Brian's scholarship has always been a serious business. Whether it was reconstructing learning exercises in Gray's Inn in the fourteenth century; or writing his history of contract; or taking up the gauntlet thrown down by the 'law and economics' school at Chicago (whose neat solutions to how judgments are reached were, to Brian, as unsubtle as the Horwitzian neo-Marxian analysis of the development of private law); or discovering the truth about shabby government dealings over Defence Regulation 18B; or seeking to identify the legal limits to free expression in respect to pornography (during the period of his membership of the Williams Committee in 1977–9, which advised the government on this matter)—his academic and professional projects were without fail informed by serious purpose—no matter how strongly they might grip the imagination of the general reader (*Cannibalism* (1984) is the obvious example).

Perhaps this is nowhere truer than in his recent work on human rights. Commencing with his historical research into the emergence of the European Convention on Human Rights in 1950, and specifically of the United Kingdom government's role in its creation after the Second World War, Brian is now enjoying yet another phase in his career. It is, moreover, a project in which he is engaging in more than academic discourse. He is also contributing to the improvement and well-being of society by his involvement as a team player in successful legal challenges to the policies and actions of governments infringing individual human rights in disparate areas. In this, as Nuala Mole points out in her contribution, Brian's work has ranged from a legal analysis of the 'deportation' of Archbishop Makarios in 1956 during the EOKA rising in Cyprus,[12] to preparing expert advice for cases destined for the European Court of Human Rights in Strasbourg. He has thus recently contributed most expertly and enthusiastically to the applicants' cases in landmark decisions including *Singh and Hussain v United Kingdom*,[13] and *T v United Kingdom* and *V v United*

---

[11] Gordon, R. W., in 'Simpson's Leading Cases', *Michigan Law Review*, 95 (1997), 2044, at 2054.

[12] Simpson, A. W. B., 'The Exile of Archbishop Makarios III', *European Human Rights Law Review* 4 (1996), 391–405.

[13] (1996) 22 EHRR 1.

Kingdom[14]—all cases involving the sentencing of children and young persons for murder; and *Osman v United Kingdom*[15] on access to courts of law and the 'effective remedy' provision in the European Convention. Brian is indeed a formidable authority on the genesis and application of the Convention and, in respect to British applications at least, his knowledge of the government's own records are a match for, and perhaps surpass, the government's own.

We have thus far referred to Brian's activities in Britain, Europe, and the United States. But other parts of the world, and Africa in particular, also occupy a place in his affections. While at Oxford, he was seconded as Dean of the Faculty of Law at the University of Ghana when that faculty was undergoing a leadership crisis. Brian responded enthusiastically and instituted changes involving staff development (in conjunction with Oxford which provided training for the Ghanaian Faculty); greater involvement of staff in research as well as in teaching; the reorganization of student disciplinary arrangements; and the creation of the office of Dean of Students. One incident is memorable. At a formal university dinner at which guests wore evening dress, a python came in through the window, slithered across the dinner table, and exited out of the door. Nothing daunted, hosts and guests sat quietly and politely, with appropriate post-colonial *sang froid*.

Brian's links with West Africa have been long lasting, as have his friendships—such as with George Ofosu-Amaah who spent a year at Kent during Brian's occupancy of the Chair there. Brian was later awarded an honorary D. Litt. by the University of Ghana in 1993.

But Brian had an earlier experience of Africa. His national service was spent with the Nigeria Regiment, Royal West African Frontier Force from 1950 to 1951. He simultaneously gained a Territorial Army commission (which he held until 1957) in the East Yorkshire Regiment which is now amalgamated with the Prince of Wales's Own Regiment of Yorkshire. The RWAFF at that time was raised by the colonial legislature rather than by the War Office, though it remained under the control of the Army Council. It possessed its own military discipline code contained in an extensive ordinance, albeit one heavily borrowed from the United Kingdom's Army Act 1881.

While Brian was engaged on his military duties, it is reassuring to know that lawyers such as Sir William Dale[16] were busy on his (and on his fellow regimental colleagues) behalf, addressing such legal issues as whether the new Courts Martial Appeal Court created in 1951 should apply to

---

[14] *R v SSHD, ex p V and T* [1998] AC 407. App. No. 24888/94, judgment of the European Court of Human Rights, 16/12/1999.

[15] *Osman v UK*, App. No. 23452/94 CD 140, 22 EHRR (1996).

[16] Dale, W., *Time Past, Time Present: An Autobiography* (London: Butterworth, 1994).

members of the RWAFF when not serving with the British Army in the United Kingdom. In particular, it was considered that: '. . . the possibility of cases arising in which a person subject to the Army Act or Air Force Act and a person subject only to the local legislation are concerned in the same offence should be considered. It may be thought incongruous that the appeals by such individuals should go to different courts. This consideration will be particularly relevant in the case of local forces in which officers are likely to be members of the United Kingdom forces'.[17] Unlike the jurisdictional dispute in *R v Keyn* (1876) which Brian examined in his *Leading Cases*, we are unaware of any collective disciplinary incident during his military service in which the legality of trying military co-offenders separately under different jurisdictional rules became the focus for another of Simpson's leading cases![18]

Given the range of Brian's interests, the editors of this Festschrift were faced with the difficult task of deciding whether to invite contributions which reflect this eclecticism, or whether, as is more fashionable (or expected) of anthologies, to maintain a tight framework around a selected theme. Our confession is that while we seriously endeavoured to commission tributes which engaged with the more recent of Brian's methodological approaches and interests, that is, to encourage contributors themselves either to 'do a Simpson' on a case in modern legal history or to write on a human rights' theme, it was soon recognized that individual tributes in a Festschrift from one scholar to another are invariably as much a personal statement of warmth as they are contributions to learning. As such, each contributor expressed his or her appreciation in the unique and individual fashion which has marked that contributor's work to date, while still conscious of the *spirit* of unity of theme. Thus whereas the themes of the 'leading cases' in modern legal history and of human rights were straightforward to identify, Brian's influence and reputation in other fields of legal study—in particular, legal theory and early modern legal history—are so well-established that these sub-disciplines are also represented by contributions from friends, colleagues, and admirers, themselves considered to be amongst the most distinguished of their profession.

Let us now turn to those individual papers. The thematic sequence, moving from human rights to legal history, is intended to reflect Brian Simpson's recent and abiding interests. The collection opens with a con-

---

[17] Public Record Office, London (PRO), CO 820/74/1, Circular from the Secretary of State for the Colonies, 16 Jan. 1952.

[18] As a postscript it may be worth recording that the year after Brian's national service ended in 1951, an urgent request was sent from the GOC-in-C, West Africa Command, for a judge advocate to attend the court martial for mutiny of 31 African soldiers of the West African Ordnance Corps, RWAFF. No local counsel were available, so E. Garth Moore, a fellow of Corpus Christi College, Cambridge, and frequent contributor to the *Cambridge Law Journal* was sent out. See (PRO) WO 32/15265.

tribution from Nuala Mole (The AIRE Centre for Individual Rights in Europe) which discusses the history of the right of individual petition before the institutions of the European Convention on Human Rights. As Brian's professional colleague in his practice at Strasbourg, and his former Oxford student some thirty years ago, Nuala Mole writes a warm tribute to Brian's legal work.

Three other papers also engage with human rights. Professor Christopher McCrudden, Brian's successor at Lincoln College, Oxford, explores the possible evolution of a transnational 'common law' of human rights, reminding us of Simpson's earlier work on precedent in the common law system. This is followed by the paper by Professor Katherine O'Donovan (QMW, London)—who arrived at Kent in 1973 at the same time as Brian—on comparative human rights, and specifically children's identity rights in French and English law. The theme of wartime civil liberties and government administration, which had been energetically pursued by Brian in his study of the Mosleys, Robert Liversidge, and others under Defence Regulation 18B also informs the paper on the emergency War Zone Courts' scheme by one of the editors of this volume, Professor Gerry Rubin (Kent). That paper provides a bridge between the theme of human rights and that of modern legal history.

Brian's anthropological interests demonstrated in, for example, his study of R. S. Rattray published in *Legal Theory and Legal History* (1987), are recognized in the tribute by a former Kent colleague, Professor Peter Fitzpatrick (Birkbeck College, London), who examines resistance to colonial laws in Papua New Guinea. The paper by Professor William Twining (University College, London) on 'The Ratio Decidendi of the Case of "The Prodigal Son"' is a further reminder of Brian's interest in legal theory and legal reasoning and, in particular, of his celebrated papers in both the first and second series of *Oxford Essays in Jurisprudence*.[19]

Brian's major contribution to legal history is reflected in a number of contributions to this Festschrift. In reverse-chronological order, they commence with an intimate portrait of three nineteenth-century Lords Chancellor, strikingly painted by Professor Gareth Jones (Cambridge University), whose friendship with Brian goes back to their time together as undergraduates at Oxford. It was there Gareth met his wife, a fellow-student to whom he was introduced by Brian.

The significance of the role of the civil jury in the United States can be compared with its fate in England in the two papers by, respectively, an American friend and colleague and stalwart of the biennial British Legal History Conference, Professor James Oldham (Georgetown University,

---

[19] Simpson, A. W. B., 'The *Ratio Decidendi* of a Case and the Doctrine of Binding Precedent', in A. G. Guest (ed.), *Oxford Essays in Jurisprudence: A Collaborative Work* (Oxford: Oxford University Press, 1961); id., 'The Common Law and Legal Theory ', in A. W. B. Simpson (ed.), *Oxford Essays in Jurisprudence: Second Series* (Oxford: Clarendon Press, 1973).

Washington, DC), and Dr Joshua Getzler (Oxford), whose D. Phil. examination Brian conducted some years ago. Indeed, the latter may perhaps allow himself a smile at the reference in Oldham's paper to John Mitford, Lord Redesdale, in view of the major role played by Redesdale's descendant, Lady Diana Mosley, in Brian's study of Defence Regulation 18B (*In the Highest Degree Odious*).

How could a Festschrift for Brian Simpson be complete without analysis of at least one 'leading case'? Happily, Professor Bill Cornish, another close friend of many years and, indeed, colleague of Brian when the latter occupied the Goodhart Chair of Legal Science at Cambridge in 1993–4, analyses the leading case of *Donaldson v Becket*. This was the celebrated eighteenth-century 'battle of the books' conducted during a formative period in the development of copyright law. Stepping back two centuries, the theme pursued by Professor John Baker, another colleague of Brian's while at Cambridge, involves an aspect of the history of the English courts involving judicial rivalry between King's Bench and Common Pleas in the early modern period.

The collection concludes with a semi-biographical contribution from Professor Dick Helmholz (University of Chicago) which reflects upon Brian's North American experience, and a bibliographical listing of Brian's publications by Jules Winterton, Librarian of the Institute of Advanced Legal Studies (University of London). The entries therein vividly remind us both of the breadth of Brian's learning and of the research conducted by him during his remarkable career.

We are concerned, however, not to over-emphasize his contribution to research and publishing at the expense of his other qualities: as a teacher, supervisor, research degree examiner, administrator, government policy adviser,[20] colleague, mentor, father, and grandfather; and now, most recently, human rights activist and practitioner. Both editors are acquainted with the puzzlement which has been shown on occasion by their own children towards their parents' enthusiasm for particular research projects or academic enterprises. In relation to Brian's recent human rights activism, it is perhaps worth recording the view of one of his children who remarked, 'You know, I feel really proud of what Dad's doing'. *Pace* the typical indifference of one's children (at least when they are still relatively young), whether due to their preoccupation with the latest pop icons or through a natural propensity to find nothing of interest in their parents' intellectual pursuits—we ourselves as co-editors (and, we would venture, the other contributors) are pleased to be associated with a

[20] Brian has recounted how a member of the Heilbron Committee on Reform of Rape Laws (1975) on which he was also serving was appointed by the Home Office following a cocktail party conversation. She had told her civil servant fellow-guest that her professional interest was in *rates* whereupon she quickly found herself appointed by the Home Secretary to the *Rape* Committee!

project which pays tribute to the amazing vigour and enthusiasm with which Brian has pursued his intellectual and human rights goals. As Jules Winterton's essay reminds us, Brian's contributions to legal scholarship and to education are not only (how shall we put it?)—*Peerless*![21] It is beyond dispute that they will stand the test of time. Perhaps the last words should be left to the Muse (Ghanaian version):[22]

> *Asinanmu a, Mmra-kyerekyerefoc tuu wo se di wcn anim,*
> *Nyehyee-pa, ne ntotoye pa, a wode dii dwuma yi,*
> *Senea woye maa yen ne Oxford University nyaa agyinatuo*
> *eye nwanwa eye ahodwiri*
> *Senea asaufo be bc bra pa woye maa woyi won so hwefoc.*
> *Obue-Akwan Simpson, yennteam mfre wo kwa.*
> *Woave-ebi ama yen mo-ne-yo!*
> *Wo nnyenyee agye nnin, anyin besi nne*
> *Edi wo ho adansee, ma wo ho da nso*
> *Ma wo homene so, ma yenhye wo abasobc ataadee!*

Nominated by the Law Faculty to be their leader during a crucial period,
The excellent planning and restructuring you infused into your tasks,
And how you forged links with Oxford University,
Have been wonderful, it has been remarkable,
Your suggestion for creating the office of Dean of Students has been successful.
Simpson the Renovator! It is not for naught that we honour you.
Your innovations have taken root and flourished
They bear testimony of your uniqueness

Arise to be robed with fitting honours!

[21] See Simpson, A. W. B., 'Contracts for Cotton to Arrive: The Case of the Two Ships *Peerless*', *Cardozo Law Review*, (1989), 287–333, discussing *Raffles v. Wichelhaus* 33 L.J.N.S. 160.
[22] Written on the occasion of the conferment on Brian of the Honorary Degree of D. Litt. from the University of Ghana, 31 Aug. 1993.

1

International Law, the Individual, and A.W. Brian Simpson's Contribution to the Defence of Human Rights

*Nuala Mole**

As we commence a new millennium, it seems we have come to live in a world in which the press, politicians, and public figures are always ready to make use of the term 'human rights'. It is invoked in encapsulating aspirations of social equality, in expressing a sense of outrage at brutality or cruelty, as well as in emphasizing the importance of the rule of law in achieving justice for individuals and marginalized groups. The proposition that human rights should be observed and respected is virtually unchallenged, but one only has to open a newspaper to see how frequently states disregard in practice even those fundamental rights which are universally recognized.

Legal practitioners who bring complaints of breaches of human rights to international tribunals are only too aware of how much narrower—and legalistic—are the enforceable rights which attract international legal protection.[1] In many cases the only mechanisms available internationally for protecting rights or redressing wrongs are not in truth legal mechanisms but politics dressed up as law. This is certainly true of complaints from the United Kingdom under the United Nations (UN) systems.

In 1945 the UN Charter was signed in San Francisco. It included several references to human rights and created a Commission to act on them. After originally taking the view that the UN Human Rights Commission 'has no power to take any action in regard to any complaints regarding human rights',[2] the UN has since modified its approach. Procedures were created under ECOSOC Resolution 1235 (XLII) which applied to 'situations which reveal a consistent pattern of violations of human rights' (as exemplified by the policy of apartheid), and under ECOSOC Resolution 1503 (XLVIII)) in cases of 'a consistent pattern of gross and reliably

---

* The author wishes to acknowledge the assistance in preparing this paper of Navtej S. Ahluwalia and Catharina Harby.

[1] e.g. the Strasbourg organs have yet to find a violation of the Convention arising from conditions in imprisonment even where there has been, e.g., 760 days of solitary confinement or 15 months in a cell of 6 sq. m.

[2] Resolution 75 (V) 1947.

attested violations of human rights'.[3] But these procedures all depend on the political support of states, and, increasingly, groups of states, for their effectiveness. That political support may not be forthcoming at all or is available only at a political price.

The latter half of the twentieth century has, however, seen the development of a system for the legal protection of human rights which enables the Davids to challenge some of the Goliaths, without having to depend on the support of the other giants to do it. The exercise of the right of individual petition to international bodies has profoundly changed the relationship between the individual and international law. Nowhere has the impact of this change been felt more than in Europe. This paper is one practitioner's view of the enforcement of those rights through the exercise of the right of individual petition under the European Convention on Human Rights (ECHR).

The right of states to intervene on behalf of their own nationals has long been recognized in international law. At the beginning of the twentieth century the legacy of Austinian legal positivism meant that no one in Europe would have anticipated that by the end of the millennium individuals would be able, as of right, to take complaints about the action or inaction of their own states to an international judicial tribunal whose judgment would be binding on the state in question. Still less would it have been anticipated that hundreds of thousands would have done so. Even at the beginning of the second half of the twentieth century, *Oppenheim's International Law*[4] could still aver that states were the only proper subjects of the Law of Nations and that individuals were—at best—only its objects. A decade later, H. L. A. Hart could still write that international law was a primitive legal system where there were primary rules of obligation, but no secondary rules which could efficiently enforce them.

It was therefore even more remarkable that on the other side of the world, in the first two decades of the twentieth century, the five parties to the Convention for the Establishment of a Central American Court of Justice set up an international court which not only had jurisdiction on inter-state disputes but was also able to accept petitions from individuals who wished to complain about the actions of their own, as well as other, governments.[5] In the event only ten such cases were ever taken.[6] They were all declared inadmissible and the system soon fell into disuse. It was, however, the first international court ever established which had a right of access for individuals.

---

[3] For a concise but thorough overview see generally Alston, Philip (ed.), *The United Nations and Human Rights: A Critical Appraisal* (Oxford: Clarendon Press, 1992).

[4] Lauterpacht, *Oppenheim's International Law*, 8th edn (London: Longman, 1955), vol.1.

[5] M. O. Hudson, 'Central American Court of Justice', *American Journal of International Law*, 26 (1932), 759.

[6] There were 5 inter-state cases.

The following decades saw the establishment of various other international non-judicial bodies to which individuals could have recourse. But it was not for another ninety years—with the entry into force of the 11th Protocol to the ECHR in 1998—that the right of direct access to an international court was once more afforded to individuals. Even under the European Convention system, pre-11th Protocol, applicants had first to direct their complaints to the European Commission of Human Rights which decided on the admissibility of the complaint and then went on to examine the merits. The Commission was not a judicial body. It expressed opinions but did not deliver judgments—though towards the end of its life it came to behave more and more like a court. A case might then be referred to the European Court of Human Rights (ECtHR) by either the Commission or the government.[7] Applicants had no right to have their cases referred to the Court.[8] The 11th Protocol has abolished the Commission and established a full-time Court which carries out all the tasks previously shared between the Commission and the Court. Applicants now bring their cases directly before the ECtHR which can and does issue binding judicial pronouncements.

It has taken Europe a long time to arrive at the stage that Central America had reached in the first decade of the twentieth century. The rest of the world is still waiting.

The aftermath of the First World War saw the establishment of the League of Nations and the Permanent Court of International Justice. In 1922, when the German–Polish frontiers were redrawn, an ad hoc system was set up to deal with complaints. Affected individuals could take their complaints to the Council of the League of Nations which established local institutions to consider them. The system expired after fifteen years. Similar systems were established under other Minorities Treaties but after the demise of the Central American Court it was not until November 1998 that a right of individual petition to an international court existed again. Within the UN treaty regime, there are now bodies established under the International Covenant on Civil and Political Rights (ICCPR), the Convention for the Elimination of all Forms of Racial Discrimination (CERD), the Convention Against Torture (CAT), and the Convention for the Elimination of all Forms of Discrimination Against Women (CEDAW), to which individuals may have recourse—but only if the government in question has expressly agreed to accept the right of individual petition. The most recent instance is the right contained in the Optional Protocol to the CEDAW which was adopted on 12 March 1999.

---

[7] Or the government of the state of which the applicant was a national, if that state was a party to the Convention.

[8] Under the 9th Protocol the applicant could request a referral to the Court, but this was not automatically granted and was subject to scrutiny by a Comité de Filtrage. The UK has never been a party to the 9th Protocol.

None of the bodies established under the UN treaty regime are judicial bodies and their findings bind no one, not even the respondent government, as a matter of international law. This was quite deliberate. When the Human Rights Committee was being established, the delegates were most anxious to ensure that it could not be composed of lawyers, fearing this would give the impression that it was a judicial body.[9] Within the Inter-American system, individuals only have the right to complain to the Inter-American Commission; whether or not a case then proceeds to the Court for a binding ruling is out of their control. The African Charter of Human and People's Rights still has no court to complement the work of its Commission.

Even under the various cumulative European Union (EU) treaties—Rome, the Single European Act, Maastricht, and Amsterdam—the aggrieved individual has no right to complain directly to the European Court of Justice (ECJ) about the action—or inaction—of Member States.[10] European citizens may have been given a special status under the Treaty on European Union but if they wish to force a Member State to give effect to their rights under European Community (EC) law, they are entirely dependent on a national judge, who may or may not choose to refer a question to the ECJ in Luxembourg for a 'preliminary ruling' under Article 234 (formerly Art 177).[11] A system exists whereby aggrieved individuals may take their complaints to the Committee on Petitions of the European Parliament, but the Committee is not a court and has no power to make binding rulings.

The UK has not accepted the right of individual petition under any of the UN instruments mentioned above, so no complaints can be made to any of the UN bodies about breaches by the UK of its UN obligations. This refusal to allow alleged transgressions of its international obligations to be considered by the international body of experts appointed to oversee compliance with a treaty has a somewhat hollow ring given the importance which, as Dicey told us, English law has always attached to remedies as a substitute for, if not the essential corollary of, rights.

Article 28 of the Universal Declaration of Human Rights states: 'Everyone is entitled to a social and international order in which the rights and freedoms set forth in this Declaration can be fully realised.'

However, as Horn has put it, 'Human Rights are more similar to one-sided favours given by a state with regard to the individual. Where a state is not ready to recognise a claim right for the individual on the inter-

---

[9] D. McGoldrick, *The Human Rights Committee* (Oxford: Clarendon Press 1994), 44 *et seq.*

[10] There are limited rights to take cases about the acts of the treaty institutions.

[11] The system whereby the Commission may initiate infringement proceedings under Art. 226 (ex-169) is equally dependent on the Commission's view and in any event will only be applied where there is evidence of an administrative practice, not an isolated incident.

national level the individual has no other choice but to submit to such a decision.'[12]

Despite the pre-eminence of fundamental rights, international law—as reflected in the Vienna Convention on the Law of Treaties[13]—permits reservations, declarations, and interpretative statements even to fundamental human rights treaties. The 'General Comment' of the UN Human Rights Committee nevertheless makes it clear that those especially sacred provisions of the International Covenant on Civil and Political Rights that represent either customary international law or, *a fortiori, ius cogens*, may not under any circumstances be the subject of reservations.[14] This is because human rights treaties are for the benefit of individuals not states.[15]

The European Convention goes further. It permits no general reservations at all, no matter what their subject-matter. And even the right to derogate from certain provisions in time of war or national emergency is subject to the scrutiny and rulings of the Court.[16]

It is generally recognized that by far and away the most advanced and developed system for the international adjudication of human rights complaints is that set up under the European Convention on Human Rights (ECHR).

The Convention—like the Universal Declaration of Human Rights—was a creature of the aftermath of the Second World War. The substantive text was largely a British baby, but the institutional structure was heavily influenced by jurists associated with the European federal movement. Altruists will recognize it as an expression of the determination of the states of Europe never again to permit state sovereignty to protect the perpetrators of human rights abuses from international accountability. Cynics may think that the British hoped that by devoting energy to the drafting of a convention which they imagined would have little or no impact on the UK, they would be able to deflect European attention away from the looming spectre of a federal Europe. The Convention's drafting path was therefore—relatively—smooth from the UK's point of view; despite the usual suspects voicing the usual objections. In a volume of essays dedicated to Brian Simpson it would be discourteous (and foolhardy!) for someone without his encyclopedic knowledge of the genesis of the Convention to say more. But it is probably safe to state that only the

---

[12] Horn, F. *Reservations and Interpretative Declarations to Multinational Treaties* (Amsterdam, 1988).

[13] Art. 19.

[14] CCPR/C/21/Rev.1/Add6; (1995) 2 IHRR 10. See also Vienna Convention on the Law of Treaties, Art. 53.

[15] Observations by the UK on General Comment No. 24.; 4th UK Periodic Report (1994) which strongly challenged the General Comment.

[16] *Brannigan and Mc Bride v. UK* 26 May 1993, Series A, No 258–B, 17 EHRR 539.

Colonial Office was really seriously worried that these notions of human rights for all might cause some difficulty.

The right of individual petition was another matter. It was not so easily won. The British and Norwegians were deeply distrustful: 'Personally I object to this right of individuals going to the Commission . . . I foresee shoals of applications being made by individuals who imagine that they have a complaint of one kind or another against the country.'[17]

Having felt very uncomfortable about its inclusion in the Convention at all, when the UK did ratify on 8 March 1951 it did so without accepting the right of individual petition.[18] In 1958 the minister[19] reiterated the British Government's position, 'States are the proper subject of international law and if individuals are given rights under international treaties, effect should be given to those rights through the national law of the states concerned.' Quite so. He went on:

The reason why we do not accept the idea of compulsory jurisdiction of a European Court is because it would mean that British codes of common and statute law would be subject to review by an international court . . . If one subscribes to a convention one then sees that the laws of one's country are in conformity with the Convention, and the individual cases are then tried under the laws of one's own country.[20]

In the minister's Utopia there was clearly no possibility of a situation where domestic law might be lacking. It was not until 1966 that individuals could bring complaints against the UK government to the Strasbourg institutions[21] and that both their right of individual petition and the compulsory jurisdiction of the Court were accepted. Many successive governments have had cause to regret this move.

For about thirty years, individuals only had the right to petition the Commission and not the right to have their cases heard by the Court. In practice this distinction became less important as the years went on and as the procedure before the Commission and the Reports adopted by it came more and more to resemble some kind of first-tier European judicial proceedings and less and less like the administrative filter which had been

---

[17] Ungoed Thomas, Travaux Preparatoires, at 188–90.

[18] It also successfully prevented the rights to property, education, and political freedom being incorporated in the main body of the Convention. Those rights were subsequently included in the First Protocol to the Convention ratified by a Conservative Government in 1952. Some confusion followed the piecemeal ratification of the First Protocol. The Government was apparently unaware until the *Gillow* case (1986 13 EHRR 593) reached the Court that the First Protocol did not apply to the Channel Islands.

[19] Minister of State for Foreign Affairs, Mr Ormsby-Gore.

[20] Hansard No 438, 26 Nov 1958, cols. 333–4.

[21] The acceptance of the right was even then, prudently, delayed to ensure that the statutory reversal (by the War Damage Act 1965) of the House of Lords' decision in *Burmah Oil v. Lord Advocate* 1965 AC 75 could not be challenged in Strasbourg. See, for comparison, *Stran Greek Refineries v. Greece* (1994) 19 EHRR 293.

designed to protect the Court from being flooded with unmeritorious complaints.

The Commission's role was first to establish whether a complaint was admissible, and if so to proceed to examine the merits.[22] The admissibility criteria were (and still are under the 11th Protocol) relatively simple. The complaint had to be brought within six months of the final decision of the national authority, and all domestic remedies had first to be exhausted. Complaints could be rejected *ratione personae* because the complainant was not considered a victim; *ratione loci* because the alleged violation took place outside the jurisdiction of a Contracting Party; *ratione materiae* because it was not a matter covered by the Convention; or *ratione temporis* because the events occurred before the state had become bound. It could also be rejected as being 'manifestly ill-founded'—an unfortunate concept borrowed from French administrative law—in which case the Commission did not then proceed to examine it on the merits. The original role of the Commission—to weed out cases where there was absolutely clearly no violation of the Convention—soon evolved into the *de facto* determination of the merits of the case. A declaration of admissibility was often a virtual guarantee that the Commission would find a violation of some, if not all, of the complaint, but the individual had (and still has) no redress against a decision that the complaint was inadmissible. As time went on, the crucial decision was not whether or not the complaint was ultimately declared admissible, but whether the Commission would decide to declare it inadmissible without communicating the complaint to the respondent government. By far and away the majority of complaints are rejected as inadmissible without the respondent government ever being aware that the complaint has been made. These are the cases that are really considered manifestly ill-founded

For the rest, as van Dijk and van Hoof have so wisely said, 'We find it difficult to accept as a correct interpretation and application of the admissibility requirement the position of the Commission . . . that the term manifestly ill-founded . . . extends further than the literal meaning of "manifestly" suggests at first reading'. They go on to comment wryly on cases where the Commission was seriously divided as to the ill-foundedness: 'If only a bare majority can be obtained for a declaration of manifest ill-foundedness, this in itself makes it evident that the ill-foundedness is not very manifest.'[23]

---

[22] The Commission and Court also had very important powers under rule 36 of Rules of Procedure (now r 39 of the new Court) to 'indicate' to the respondent government any measures which it considered appropriate to be taken (or not taken) whilst the case was under examination. The rule is normally invoked in expulsion cases and the UK's practice is to comply with the request although it does not have the force of law. See *Cruz Varas v. Sweden* (1991) 14 EHRR 1.

[23] van Dijk and van Hoof, *Theory and Practice of the European Convention on Human Rights*, 3rd edn (Dordrecht: Kluwer, 1998).

In the case of *Donnelly v UK*,[24] several lever-arch files of observations had been exchanged between the applicants and the government prior to the admissibility decision and it took the Commission no less that 112 pages of detailed legal reasoning to explain that the case was manifestly ill-founded and that they should therefore not look at the merits. Nevertheless, many complaints pass this hurdle successfully and go on to a full examination.

Most people, including lawyers, who take complaints to the European Commission and Court do so only once in a lifetime. Unlike practitioners before the ECJ, the applicants' representatives in Strasbourg thus rarely have had the chance to become experts in this specialized litigation. And most are unfamiliar with the rapidly increasing body of Convention jurisprudence. The existence of an understanding, expert, and helpful Secretariat is crucial. The team of lawyers who service the work of the Court—particularly those who deal with the cases originating from the UK—has made an often unsung but invaluable contribution to the success of the Strasbourg system.[25] Whilst remaining scrupulously correct in their discretion and impartiality, they go out of their way to ensure that the system is as user-friendly as possible. Their support is particularly important for the novice taking a case for the first time and appearing at a first hearing. A panel of nine or seventeen or nineteen judges arranged in a semicircle on the other side of a vast expanse of immaculately-vacuumed blue carpet is intimidating even to those who are accustomed to the august surroundings of the Lord Chief Justice's court in The Strand. As in the ECJ, the time-constraints are tight. The advocates on each side are allowed only thirty minutes and the speech has to be delivered at a pace which permits the interpreters to do their job properly. Every word counts. The text has to be picked over with a toothcomb by someone who speaks enough French to be aware of possible false linguistic friends or difficult passages and who can tactfully advise counsel to remove untranslatable cricket metaphors. A person with similar linguistic skills needs to listen to the French interpretation during the proceedings, since despite the exceptionally high level of expertise of the interpreters, changes in emphasis or even errors may creep in which can undermine the whole argument. When the Court asks questions the parties are given a brief adjournment of fifteen minutes to prepare their responses and any final arguments that they wish to put.

Legal aid is available from the Court but is only granted once the case has been 'communicated' to the government. It will, however, retrospec-

---

[24] 1972, 4 DR 72.

[25] They have also contributed significantly by writing two of the standard practitioners' works, e.g. Harris, O'Boyle and Warbrick, *Law of the European Convention on Human Rights* (London: Butterworths, 1995) and Reid, Karen, *A Practitioner's Guide to the European Court of Human Rights* (London: Sweet & Maxwell, 1998).

tively cover the preparation of the application. The rates are not generous—2000 FF (about £200) for the preparation of an application and the same amount for attending the hearing (including preparation!), plus a *per diem* of 996 FF to cover accommodation in Strasbourg. As the preparation of the initial application normally takes a minimum of 80 to 90 lawyer-hours this works out at about £2.50 an hour—significantly less than the new minimum wage. In the early days the legal aid payments took the form of a wad of used French francs which was handed over in a brown envelope outside the hearing-room door. The sum is usually just about sufficient to take the applicant's team of lawyers out to a meal before returning to London. Now the payments have been sanitized into bank transfers but the sums have not been increased. The government, on the other hand, has not only a whole team of the Foreign Office's expert legal advisers (and the legal advisers to relevant government departments) at their disposal, but, in the case of the UK, also engages the services of the ablest silks and most expert 'senior-juniors' to defend them. Needless to say, the taxpayer will always pay their salaries and fees, irrespective of whether they win or lose. The applicant's lawyers, on the other hand, frequently put in many months of work for which they know they are unlikely ever to be reimbursed, since their clients are usually without the means to pay fees even if they do not qualify for legal aid. But at least there are no court fees and more importantly, applicants who lose will not be liable for the government's costs. Provided the applicant can afford a lawyer or find someone willing to represent him *pro bono* or on a contingency fee basis, the process itself is free. This may not be of any use to an aggrieved individual who cannot access the process because he lacks the funds (or legal aid) necessary to exhaust domestic remedies.

Prior to the change in the rules of procedure in 1982, applicants' lawyers could only appear before the Court at the discretion of the Commission and then only in the role of offering assistance to the Delegate of the Commission. Even the Delegate of the Commission (as was pointed out in *Lawless v. Ireland*)[26] was not an actual party to the proceedings before the Court, his role being 'ministerial' rather than litigious. Individuals were often not even informed that their case had been referred to the Court. In the case of *Golder v. UK*,[27] Mr Golder only found out that his case had been referred to the Court when he read about it in the newspapers!

This has all changed with the 1982 changes in the Court rules and still more with the coming into force of the 11th Protocol. The applicant is coming closer to enjoying an 'equality of arms' with the government which accords with the standards prescribed for domestic proceedings under the fair trial guarantees of Article 6.

[26] (1961) 1 EHRR 15.   [27] (1975) 1 EHRR 524.

The United Kingdom has been one of the Convention institutions' best customers. Many thousands of complaints have been taken. Although most have been declared inadmissible, some have reached a friendly settlement and others have lost on the merits. Some fifty cases, however, have resulted in findings of breaches of Convention rights by the UK.[28]

They include:

- inadequate safeguards against telephone tapping by the police;
- unfair discrimination against British wives of foreign husbands under the immigration rules;
- unjust restrictions upon prisoners' correspondence and visits;
- judicial corporal punishment and corporal punishment in schools;
- criminal sanctions against private homosexual conduct;
- ineffective judicial protection for detained mental patients, or would-be immigrants, or individuals facing extradition or expulsion to countries where they risk being exposed to torture or inhuman treatment or conditions;
- dismissal of workers because of the oppressive operation of the closed shop;
- interference with free speech by maintaining injunctions restraining breaches of confidence where information had become widely available;
- the right to have a detention order under the Mental Health Act reviewed;
- procedural safeguards for families where children are taken in care;
- access to child care records;
- review of the continued detention of those serving discretionary life sentences;
- access to legal advice for fine and debt defaulters;
- courts-martial procedure;
- availability of legal aid in criminal cases;
- access to civil justice;
- fair trial for children tried in adult courts;
- the right of the Home Secretary to set the tariff in indeterminate sentences

—and so on.

Until the Italians were found in breach for a large number of cases involving the undue length of judicial proceedings, the UK had the dubious distinction of having been found in breach of the Convention more often than any other state. This is a somewhat sad indictment of the minister's confidence in 1958 that domestic law would be effective in protect-

---

[28] Lester and Pannick (eds.) list the key issues in *Human Rights Law and Practice* (London: Butterworths, 1999), at 9.

ing the rights of individuals. Although the Court's jurisdiction is confined to making a finding of a violation and awarding 'just satisfaction'[29] the effect of a judgment will normally be a change in domestic law or the removal of the offending administrative practice. Jacobs and White note that, 'There is hardly an area of state regulation untouched by standards which have emerged from the application of Convention provisions to situations presented by individual applicants.'[30]

In the light of all the foregoing and given that the applicant is inherently disadvantaged in the proceedings, the supporting role of academics who are experts in a particular area of law is often essential to enable the applicant to construct a strong case. Brian Simpson has been an invaluable source of assistance in this respect.

As pointed out in the opening words of this chapter, it is now fashionable to classify a whole range of issues as 'human rights' when they were formerly considered simply as aspects of the rule of law.[31]

As early as 1977, the UK was beginning to realize what impact the Convention might have on domestic law. Brian was appointed Deputy Chairman of the Williams Committee, set up to review the law on pornography after the European Court delivered its judgment in the case of *Handyside v UK* (7 December 1976).[32] Although the Court did not find the UK in breach of the Convention on that occasion, the fact that the case had gone all the way to the Court had highlighted the unsatisfactory state of the law and the authorities were nervous that they might be found in breach next time.

Some fifteen years later, the arbitrary detention of many Iraqis during the Gulf War illustrated that the ghost of *Liversidge v. Anderson*[33] had not been laid. These events coincided with the timely publication of Brian's *In the Highest Degree Odious: Detention Without Trial in Wartime Britain*. In *Odious* he was deeply critical of the arbitrary way in which administrative detention was used before and during the Second World War. Whilst Article 17 of the ECHR,[34] had it existed at that time, might have prevented the Fascists from invoking the right to freedom of expression to disseminate their ideas,

---

[29] Findings of a violation will often not result in the victim being awarded any financial compensation. The Gibraltar shootings cases and *T and V v. UK*, the child murderers, are cases in point. However, the UK government, unlike some others, is punctilious about paying compensation and costs on time.

[30] Jacobs and White, *The European Convention on Human Rights*, 2nd edn (Oxford: Clarendon Press, 1996), at 406.

[31] When Isaiah Berlin, e.g., gave his seminal lecture on 'The Two Concepts of Liberty' in 1958, published in *The Proper Study of Mankind* (Pimlico, 1998) he referred only to individual rights and did not use the term 'human rights' at all.

[32] Report of the Committee on Obscenity and Film Censorship, Cmnd 7772, 1979.

[33] [1942] AC 206.

[34] 'Nothing in this Convention may be interpreted as implying for any applicant, state, group or person any right to engage in any activity or perform any act aimed at the destruction of any of the rights and freedoms set forth herein or at their limitation to a greater extent than is provided for in the Convention.'

there is no doubt that the unattractive nature of their views would not have justified the arbitrary deprivation of their right to liberty and security of the person. Such detention is now outlawed by Article 5 of the European Convention.

In 1996 Brian became one of the first academic contributors to the now well-established journal, the *European Human Rights Law Review*, with a scholarly paper on the detention of Archbishop Makarios during the Cyprus troubles.[35] Like the Bourgeois Gentilhomme's discovery that he was speaking prose, Brian soon found that he had been an authority on 'human rights' for some years!

But his contributions to the field have not been limited to the scholarly writings for which he is well known in legal history and jurisprudence. He has also helped the practical development of Convention case law. His first contribution to the jurisprudence of the ECHR was made in 1994 when he prepared an expert advice for the applicants' representatives on the history of the sentence of detention during Her Majesty's Pleasure for children convicted of murder. The issue in *Singh and Hussain v. UK*[36] was whether or not the sentence was akin to a mandatory life sentence.[37] If so, then following its own jurisprudence in *Wynne v. UK*[38] there was no right under Article 5(4)[39] to periodic review of the detention in the post-tariff phase. If it was more akin to a discretionary than mandatory life sentence, then an Article 5(4) review was required at periodic intervals.

As was to be expected, his advice was scholarly but retained his eminently readable style. He traced the notion of the Monarch's Pleasure back to the Middle Ages. We know that the French judge in the European Court (and can assume others with an interest in history) gained as much pleasure from reading the detailed references to Henry V and the Siege of Falaise which it contained, as from the legal arguments adduced.

Always ready for a new experience, Brain made the journey with the legal team to Strasbourg for the hearing, and was doubly rewarded by having the opportunity to watch the UK government representatives fume as the President of the Court delivered his hour-long judgment in *McCann, Savage and Farrell*, the Gibraltar shootings case.[40] He eagerly collected shoals of newspaper reports of the judgment on the return journey to use as teaching aids for his seminars. It was characteristic of his generosity that

---

[35] 'The Exile of Archbishop Makarios III', EHRLR 4 [1996], 391.

[36] [1996] 22 EHRR 1.

[37] Under the administrative procedures governing such sentences, a 'tariff' period is set to fix the number of years' detention necessary to satisfy the requirements of retribution and deterrence.

[38] [1994] 19 EHRR 333.

[39] 'Everyone who is deprived of his liberty by arrest or detention shall be entitled to take proceedings by which the lawfulness of his detention shall be decided speedily by a court and his release ordered if the detention is not lawful.'

[40] [1991] 21 EHRR 97.

when the bill for costs which had been submitted by the applicants was significantly reduced by the Court he waived the fee which would have been due to him for the Opinion.[41]

His advice assisted the European Court in reaching the conclusion that the sentence was to be assimilated to a discretionary life sentence—such as is imposed for manslaughter—rather than the mandatory life sentence imposed on adults for murder.

His expert advice in that case was subsequently put before the House of Lords in the case of the child murderers, T and V[42] and again before the European institutions when the *T v. UK* and *V v. UK* cases went to Strasbourg. The judgment of the Court in that case (Application 24888/94) was delivered on 16 December 1999. Brian's analysis of the nature of the sentence was once more accepted by the court and the UK was once more found in violation of the Convention. This time, however, the Court made it quite clear that the Home Secretary's role in determining the minimum duration of a convicted juvenile's incarceration (the 'tariff') was incompatible with Article 6 of the Convention. The right to a trial by an independent and impartial tribunal extends to the right to be sentenced by that tribunal and not by a member of the executive.

In 1996, when he had already been working for some time on his magisterial history of the genesis of the ECHR, Brian put his encyclopedic knowledge at the disposal of the applicants again. This time he provided an advice on the drafting history of Article 13 ECHR[43] to the applicants' representatives in the case of *Osman v. UK* (28 October 1998).

That case concerned the striking out of an action in negligence in a case brought against the police by the survivors of a brutal attack on a young boy and his family by a seriously psychiatrically-disturbed schoolteacher. The attack had occurred after a year or more of threatening behaviour of which the police were fully apprised. The Court of Appeal had held that although the proximity and foreseeability elements of the test laid down in *Caparo v. Dickman*[44] were met, it would not be 'fair, just and reasonable' to impose on the police a duty of care towards the child and his family. The applicants argued, *inter alia*, that they had been deprived of the access to court guaranteed under Article 6 ECHR[45] or, alternatively, that since there had been an arguable violation of their right to life under Article 2[46] and

---

[41] He also waived his fee in *Osman*, as did Prof. Jolowicz for his advice on the concept of the duty of care in English law.

[42] *R v. SSHD, ex p V and T* [1998] AC 407.

[43] 'Everyone whose rights and freedoms as set forth in this Convention are violated shall have an effective remedy before a national authority notwithstanding that the violation is committed by persons acting in an official capacity.'

[44] [1990] 2 AC 605.

[45] 'In the determination of [his] civil rights and obligations or of any criminal charge against [him], everyone is entitled to a fair and public hearing within a reasonable time by an independent and impartial tribunal established by law.'

[46] 'Everyone's right to life shall be protected by law.'

of their right to moral and physical integrity under Article 8,[47] they were entitled to an effective remedy under Article 13.

The government argued that the complaint in *Osman* did not concern the determination of a civil right since the UK courts had held that there was no such right in English law. They also argued that the right to an effective remedy contained in Article 13 did not necessitate either a right of access to a judicial tribunal or the right to financial compensation. There was therefore no requirement under the Convention that the victims of police negligence should be compensated through legal proceedings.

The Simpson advice pointed out, in particular, that the UK had strenuously argued precisely the opposite when the corresponding Article under the proposed ICCPR was drafted in 1966.

The United Kingdom considers that an effective remedy must be a legal remedy, and that a claim that a human right has been violated must be determined by a court of law or by a tribunal whose decision has the force of law . . . While it is right that . . . authorities . . . should take action if a violation of a human right has occurred and should for example make *ex gratia* payments by way of compensation in a proper case, such action is no substitute for a right on the part of the individual to have his claim that one of his rights has been violated determined by an independent tribunal.[48]

The European Court, in a decision which has caused considerable controversy,[49] held that the judgment of the Court of Appeal had conferred on the police a procedural bar to an action which would otherwise have lain in negligence.[50] They therefore found a violation of the right of access to court guaranteed by Article 6. As is the wont of the Court, having found a violation of Article 6, it did not consider it necessary to examine the complaint under Article 13 itself which requires a less strict test. However, just as the expert advice Brian had given in *Singh and Hussain* was resubmitted in *T and V*, so too the advice on Article 13 which he had provided in *Osman* was re-submitted to the European Commission (with his permission) in *Z v. UK* and *TP and KM v. UK*, that is *X v. Bedfordshire County*

---

[47] 'Everyone has the right to respect for [his] private and family life, [his] home and [his] correspondence.' The Court considers that the right to moral and physical integrity is protected under the private life rubric of this provision.

[48] Annex H to Applicant's Memorial, *Osman v. UK*.

[49] See e.g. A. J. Weir, *Cambridge Law Journal* 4 (1999); Lord Hoffman, 'Speech to Common Law Bar Association' (London, 25th Nov 1998), published as 'Human Rights and the House of Lords' *Modern Law Review* (1999), 62, 159; Lord Browne-Wilkinson in his judgment in *Barrett v. London Borough of Enfield*. Craig and Fairgrieve, '*Barrett*', 'Negligence and Discretionary Powers', *Public Law* (Winter 1999), 626. All of these eminent jurists had difficulty with the Court's findings that the decision of the Court of Appeal in *Osman* amounted to a procedural bar rather than a definition of the content of the right. None has suggested what remedy should have been available in English law in order to satisfy Art. 13.

[50] The applicants in *Osman* were also assisted by an advice from M. Roger Errera of the French Conseil d'État, Prof. J. A. Jolowicz, and Mme Sophia Spiliotopoulos who, like Brian, all generously donated their expertise.

Council and *M v. Newham London Borough Council* in the domestic courts. *Z* concerned the immunity of social services from liability in negligence for their failure to protect young children from abuse and neglect amounting to inhuman and degrading treatment contrary to Article 3 ECHR. *TP and KM* concerned the removal of a child from her family on the basis of social services' negligent mistaken identification of a suspected abuser.

In *Z* the Commission found, as the Court had in *Osman*, that there had been a violation of Article 6. It found a similar breach in the case of the child applicant in *TP and KM*. However, in the case of the mother applicant in that case, it preferred to find a violation of Article 13 rather than Article 6. In doing so, the Commission echoed the words of the Opinion which Brian had submitted and considered that, 'the notion of an effective remedy entails the payment of compensation where appropriate and a thorough and effective investigation into the allegations'. The Commission rejected the government's submission that recourse to the Ombudsman satisfied the requirement since its powers to make monetary awards were recommendatory only. This was the last UK case in which a Report was adopted by the old Commission and has now been referred to the Court.

These decisions now assume a new importance in the light of the entry into force on 2 October 2000 of the Human Rights Act 1998. Under that statute two mechanisms exist for giving effect to Convention rights domestically. The first is under sections 2 and 3 of the Act which enable UK judges to develop common law remedies to give effect to Convention rights. The second is found in sections 7 and 8 which create a new cause of action for breach of human rights. Whether effect is given to the rights by the development of the common law under sections 2 and 3 or by the use of the new constitutional tort provided for under sections 7 and 8 may prove to be important since section 8(4) requires UK courts to take into account the 'principles' applied by the ECtHR in awarding compensation under Article 41 of the Convention. Since the ECtHR frequently awards nothing even when it finds a violation, litigants may prefer to follow the sections 2 and 3 route[51] and seek the usual damages which English law would award.

The White Paper which preceded the Human Rights Act 1998 was entitled *Bringing Rights Home*, and stated that the Act was intended to, '. . . give people in the United Kingdom opportunities to enforce their rights under the European Convention in British courts rather than having to incur the cost and delay of taking a case to the European Court of Human Rights in Strasbourg'. Considerable efforts are being made by the Judicial Studies Board to ensure that all members of the judiciary are given

---

[51] Discerning 'principles' behind Art. 41 awards may prove a fruitless task in any event. The tables appended to Karen Reid's excellent book on the Convention (see n. 25) give plenty of illustrations but few, if any, principles can be discerned.

at least a cursory introduction to the Convention's principles and case-law, and books on the Convention roll off the presses every week.

Whilst the enactment of the Act should have the happy effect of enabling British judges to 'give further effect' to the Convention, an increased awareness of the ECHR may ironically have the opposite effect to that intended—increasing rather than decreasing the number of cases going to Strasbourg. Practitioners who have researched and presented Convention arguments before the national court but have been unsuccessful may be more inclined to argue their cases before the ECHR than if the Convention had remained unknown to them. The Convention organs have not been short of complaints from the other forty or so Member States of the Council of Europe where the Convention has long been part of domestic law.

Brian Simpson's services to human rights do not stop there. He is more than a helpful legal historian to whom lawyers who are litigating on behalf of applicants in Strasbourg can always turn for an expert Opinion. He has also been instrumental in setting up a scheme which enables bright and altruistic young law students from the University of Michigan to contribute to the work of The AIRE Centre and other organizations working for the legal protection of human rights. The students either work in The AIRE Centre or, whilst attached to academic institutions, undertake research to assist in the litigation which the Centre conducts before the European Court.[52] A highlight for all AIRE Centre interns, not just from Michigan but from all over Europe, is taking up the invitation which he regularly extends when he is in England for them to visit him in Canterbury to make a pilgrimage not only to the beautiful cathedral but also to the home of Thomas Paine, the first writer known to have used the expression 'human rights'.

In January 1999, at an age and stage in his career when many would have opted for the comforts of retirement, he cheerfully joined a team in Albania in the depths of winter and, enduring conditions of some privation, gave up his time to assist the University of Tirana with a pilot academic course on the history, law, and practice of the European Convention on Human Rights. His familiarity with the history of their country and particularly the detailed provisions of the Kanun of Lek Dukagjini[53] impressed both students and faculty almost as much as his detailed knowledge of the genesis of the ECHR. Who knows where the Year 2000 finds him.

---

[52] Under Brian's supervision, Michigan students have undertaken invaluable research for cases such as *D v. UK, Ahmed v. Austria, Osman v. UK, Z v. UK, TP and KM v. UK, Osu v. Italy, Powell v. UK, Gilberson v. France,* and *Cooke v. Austria,* and have written briefing papers for lawyers in both Western, Central, and Eastern Europe, and the former Soviet Union on subjects as diverse as domestic violence, freedom of association, and the rights of nationals from Central and Eastern European countries (especially Roma) under the Europe Agreements.

[53] The complex code which regulates the conduct of blood feuds.

2

A Common Law of Human Rights? Transnational Judicial Conversations on Constitutional Rights

*Christopher McCrudden**

Brian Simpson's unquenchable and infectious intellectual curiosity has resulted in his pursuing as wide a range of scholarly interests as any other legal academic of his generation. Two of these interests are reflected in this article: the role of precedent, and the pursuit of human rights. It is offered as an inadequate 'thank you' for the insights and friendship he has given my family and me over the years.

This chapter considers the meaning and significance of national judges' citation of judgments from other jurisdictions as part of their reasoning in cases with a significant human (or constitutional) rights aspect. The primary focus is on cases under national constitutional or statutory provisions that seek to protect and advance rights of the type typically found in international and regional human rights conventions, such as freedom of speech and freedom from discrimination, amongst many others.

Alongside developments in human rights protection at international and regional levels, there has been a steady growth since the end of the Second World War in the development of human rights protections within national legal systems. This has taken many different forms: adoption of specific legislation to deal with particular abuses, development of home-grown Bills of Rights, application of customary international human rights law in domestic courts, and incorporation of international or regional human rights treaties into national law.

The growth in human rights thinking has been a significantly *legal* phenomenon. The form in which states have chosen to develop their commitment to human rights has as often been 'legal' as 'political'. This is not to say that the motivation for human rights developments, whether at international or national levels, has not been political, only that it has developed primarily in legal forms.

In addition, legal methods of dispute resolution and interpretation have been used as a primary mechanism by which these legally-based human rights values are protected and furthered. At the national level, this has

* I am grateful to participants at workshops at the Centre for Socio-Legal Research, Oxford and at the University of Michigan Law School for helpful comments. Particular thanks are due to Catherine McKinnon, Anne Davies, Eric Stein, William Twining, Spiros Smitis, Nora Demleitner, Joan Larsen, Carl Schneider, Hanoch Dagan, and Jim Hathaway, who commented on earlier drafts. Arad Reisberg translated several articles from Hebrew.

often resulted in judges being thrust (or thrusting themselves) into the front line of the attempted resolution of human rights issues. Such judicial enforcement of human rights is a relatively recent phenomenon, really since the Second World War, linked in part to the increasing popularity of constitutional courts in the last forty years in Europe and beyond. Indeed, the phenomenon of judicial enforcement of human rights often seems to be accepted as axiomatic, now so apparently accepted as part of legal life—in the developed world at least.

Human rights is, however, an immensely controversial area of debate and interpretation. In certain contexts, not all, but certainly many of those that engage domestic courts, there is a profound disagreement about the appropriate reach of human rights protections. The emotional and political force that an allegation of a violation of human rights now has often adds significantly to the salience of this controversy. Controversies about human rights are important not only in the context of national debates, but also between and within regions and states. Whether valid or not, there is also a perception that different jurisdictions take differing ideological positions on human rights in general, and particular human rights specifically.[1] Choosing to emulate a particular country's approach to human rights may be regarded, therefore, as a sign of a particular orientation towards human rights, and therefore controversial in itself.

The phenomenon of borrowing and transplantation from international to national, from national to international, and from national to national jurisdiction is now commonplace. At the level of constitutional human rights protection, Bills of Rights provisions in one country increasingly affect the drafting of equivalent provisions in other countries. Although most post-Second World War constitutions have specifically laid down elements which set them apart, most also have a common core of human rights provisions that are strikingly similar. This is not merely coincidental. They often derive from the Universal Declaration of Human Rights, the European Convention on Human Rights, or more recently the International Covenant on Civil and Political Rights. But constitutional provisions also often derive from other domestic constitutional provisions,[2] in particular those of the United States.[3] India borrowed from

---

[1] e.g., see the discussion of differences between American and German judicial approaches to freedom of speech in Donald P. Kommers, 'The Jurisprudence of Free Speech in the US and the Federal Republic of Germany', 53 *Southern California Law Review* 657 (1980); David S. Bogen, 'Telling the Truth and Paying for it: A Comparison of Two Cases—Restrictions on Political Speech in Australia and Commercial Speech in the US', 7 *Indiana International and Comparative Law Review* 111 (1996); Christopher McCrudden, 'The Impact on Freedom of Speech', in Basil S. Markesinis, *The Impact of the Human Rights Bill on English Law* (Oxford: Oxford University Press, 1998), 85.

[2] Edward McWhinney, *Supreme Courts and Judicial Law-Making: Constitutional Tribunals and Constitutional Review* (Martinus Nijhoff, 1986), 3–9; Jon Elster, 'Forces and Mechanisms in the Constitution-Making Process', 45 *Duke Law Journal* (1995), 364.

[3] See George Athan Billias, *American Constitutionalism Abroad* (Greenwood Press, 1990).

Ireland.[4] Hong Kong borrowed from Canada. South Africa borrowed from Germany, which had borrowed previously from the United States. The new Constitutions of Eastern and Central Europe after the collapse of the Soviet Union were heavily influenced by comparative study of the constitutions of Western Europe and North America.[5] So, too, domestic legislation in certain areas of human rights has tended to be heavily influenced by legislative approaches in other jurisdictions. In attempts to legislate against race and gender discrimination, for example, United States federal legislation has been borrowed in Britain.[6] How such borrowing occurs is complex. Academics, policy researchers, politicians, law reform commissions, and single-issue pressure groups are some of the most important conduits. Though a fascinating issue, this is not, however, the principal topic for this chapter.

Instead it is mostly concerned with what happens *after* human rights legislation, or constitutional human rights provisions have been introduced. How far, if at all, does a country's *judiciary* borrow from other jurisdictions in the interpretation or application of these (now) indigenous human rights norms?

CHALLENGES TO THE LEGITIMACY OF HUMAN RIGHTS ADJUDICATION

In most jurisdictions in which courts play an active role in the legal protection of human rights, there are significant debates about the extent to which the judiciary is either legitimate or competent in carrying out such a role. In part, this debate focuses on whether the purported distinction between legal and political approaches to human rights is convincing. When a judge interprets a human rights provision in a Bill of Rights, for example, is the judge really interpreting law, or making a political judgment? This question goes not only to the issue of judicial independence, but to the larger question of the autonomy of human rights law itself—its separateness from political and economic forces in society. If human rights law is not 'autonomous' (or relatively so), then the judge interpreting it might be said to be acting not as a judge in the traditional sense, but as a politician. If acting as a politician, he or she has (in democratic societies)

---

[4] The use of Directive Principles for state policy (Indian Constitution, Arts. 36–51) was adopted from the Irish Constitution (Art. 45).

[5] Rett R. Ludwikowski, *Constitution-Making in the Region of Former Soviet Dominance* (Duke, NC: Duke University Press, 1993), 2–3. For an illuminating discussion of the Czech and Slovak Constitutions, see Eric Stein, 'Out of the Ashes of a Federation, Two New Constitutions', XLV *American Journal of Comparative Law* (1997), 45.

[6] Christopher McCrudden, 'Racial Discrimination', in McCrudden and Chambers, *Individual Rights and the Law in Britain* (Oxford: Clarendon Press, 1954), 409.

no greater ability or legitimacy than any other political actor, and arguably a good deal less.

A continuing concern for judges interpreting human rights provisions (and lawyers arguing cases), therefore, is how to establish the relative autonomy of human rights law through the sources of authority and style of judgment which judges use in their human rights decisions. What is needed, to use Raz's phrase, are 'distancing devices', i.e. 'devices [judges] can rely on to settle [disputes] . . . in a way that is independent of the personal tastes of the judges'.[7] The aim is to make the interpretation of human rights law as much like the interpretation of 'other' law as possible.

At the risk of over-simplifying a complex process, several sources of authority are common. Judges often have regard, in one jurisdiction or other, to different sources of authority: the authority of the text literally interpreted; of the intention of the legislator; of national history and tradition; of international law norms; of contemporary moral or political theory; of academic jurists; of analogical reasoning; and to the authority of prior judicial decisions. Which of these sources is used is, of course, a crucial question and often an issue of considerable debate and controversy within particular jurisdictions.

At this point, we need to distinguish between two kinds of 'authority' to which judges have regard. Most jurisdictions distinguish between 'binding' and 'persuasive' authority in judicial interpretation. There is, of course, a variety of ways in which decisions might bind; there is also a range of considerations that affect the degree to which, and the way in which, a decision might be persuasive, as we shall see. But, for the moment, these variations within binding and persuasive authority need not detain us. Suffice it to say that binding authority refers to authority that the judge must apply and follow. It implies that there is a hierarchy of sources of authority, some of which the judge must apply and by which he is bound. 'Persuasive authority', on the other hand, exists when, in addition to binding authority, other material is regarded as relevant to the decision which has to be made by the judge, but is not binding on the judge under the hierarchical rules of the national system determining authoritative sources.[8] This chapter focuses on a source of judicial authority in the interpretation of human rights norms which has been relatively ignored in the theoretical literature: the use by national judges in one jurisdiction of judicial interpretations of human rights norms in another jurisdiction as persuasive authority.

---

[7] Joseph Raz, 'On the Authority and Interpretation of Constitutions: Some Preliminaries', in Larry Alexander (ed.), *Constitutionalism: Philosophical Foundations* (Cambridge: Cambridge University Press, 1998), 152 at 190.

[8] H. Patrick Glenn, 'Persuasive Authority', 32 *McGill Law Journal* (1987), 261 at 264: 'Adherence to persuasive authority is therefore a highly sophisticated alternative to notions of binding law and mechanical jurisprudence on the one hand and arbitrary personal licence on the other.'

PERSUASIVE AUTHORITY AND THE HUMAN RIGHTS ACT 1998

This issue is of particular relevance in jurisdictions that have relatively recently incorporated constitutional rights that are significantly judicially enforced. In the United Kingdom, a reconsideration of the use of comparative judicial decisions in human rights cases is therefore particularly timely. The interpretation of the Human Rights Act 1998 will bring with it the issue of how far British courts will (and/or *should*) use jurisprudence from other countries to help in arriving at decisions on the interpretation of the Act.

The Act provides that courts interpreting Convention rights must take the jurisprudence of the European Court of Human Rights into account[9]— but what other courts, if any, beyond that? In part, this will depend on practical factors such as the facility of judges and counsel in foreign languages, and the availability of foreign texts. In part, however, which jurisdictions are chosen will depend on deeper factors. Does the Human Rights Act state human rights principles which are *universal* (in which case potentially all jurisdictions are relevant, but perhaps particularly decisions of international bodies such as the Human Rights Committee interpreting the International Covenant on Civil and Political Rights)? Or does it incorporate a particularly European conception of human rights (in which case one might expect a heavier concentration on jurisdictions that dominate European Court of Human Rights thinking, such as France and Germany)? Or is it thought to contain principles that must be domesticated so as to make it harmonious to *common law* approaches and understandings? Is the [national] court's function, in part, to enable the European Court of Human Rights to better understand how the Convention should be understood when the ECtHR is deciding cases coming from the UK (in which case Commonwealth countries are likely to predominate, particularly Canada, South Africa, New Zealand)?

In the debates on the Human Rights Bill in Parliament, those most in favour of the Bill resisted amendments which would have *required* the United Kingdom courts to apply the decisions of the European Court of Human Rights, rather than merely have regard to them. Their arguments were based to some extent on the undesirability of introducing a strict notion of *stare decisis*.[10] But, in addition, the expansion of the Council of Europe to include Central and Eastern European states and the resulting increased number of judges in the Court from these jurisdictions also

---

[9] Human Rights Act 1998, s. 2(1).
[10] Lord Browne-Wilkinson, e.g.: 'The doctrine of *stare decisis*, the doctrine of precedent, whereby we manage to tie ourselves up in knots for ever bound by an earlier decision of an English court, does not find much favour north of the Border, finds no favour across the Channel, and is an indigenous growth of dubious merit.'

appear to have been influential factors urging a cautious approach to the authority of the European Court of Human Rights. Thus Lord Browne-Wilkinson, for example, arguing against strictly following the case law of the Court, said:

. . . I have found the jurisprudence of the European Court of Human Rights excellent, but a major change is taking place. We are now seeing a wider range of judges adjudicating such matters, a number of them drawn from jurisdictions ten years ago not famous for their observance of human rights. It might be dangerous to tie ourselves to that . . .[11]

The Lord Chancellor (speaking obviously in his Executive capacity) went even further. It was not appropriate for the courts of the United Kingdom to be required to follow the Strasbourg decisions; if anything, the European Court might learn from British courts.

'They [European Court of Human Rights decisions] were a source of jurisprudence indeed, but not binding precedents which we necessarily should follow or even necessarily desired to follow. The Bill would of course permit United Kingdom courts to depart from existing Strasbourg decisions and upon occasion it might well be appropriate to do so, and it is possible they might give a successful lead to Strasbourg.'[12]

The result would have been to leave to the British judiciary decisions as to how much weight to give to the European Court judgments. As Lord Kingsland for the Conservative Opposition said, the government was attempting to '. . . incorporat[e] the substance of the Convention but not its jurisprudence'. He continued:

It is therefore, in my submission, superficially the incorporation of an international treaty but in effect the presentation to this Chamber of a domestic Bill of Rights. . . . In short, as the jurisprudence of the Convention is not binding, judges can really range over the substance of the Bill in any way they want.[13]

What, then, will the Courts take into account in making their decisions? For some of those taking part in the Parliamentary debates, the answer seemed obvious. As Lord McCluskey said: 'In future no lawyer will be able to advise a client on any matter which might involve a public authority without studying not just the European jurisprudence . . . but also American case law, Canadian case law and even Indian case law and

---

[11] House of Lords, 18 Nov. 1998, col. 513. Sydney Kentridge Q.C. in 'Parliamentary Supremacy and the Judiciary Under a Bill of Rights: Some Lessons from the Commonwealth' [1997] *Public Law* 96, at 101–3, stresses the lack of legitimacy for the ECtHR among important sections of British public opinion, and the extent to which decisions by an expanded court with members from Central and Eastern Europe would be even more questioned. 'The point, unfortunate but inescapable, is that the decisions of a court with this enlarged membership are unlikely to win greater respect in this country for the principles embodied in the Convention.'

[12] House of Lords, 18 Nov. 1998, col. 514.   [13] *ibid.*, col. 515.

Australian and New Zealand case law.'[14] If this is what occurs, it will be unsurprising. It is already what has been happening for some years in the period of semi-incorporation of the European Convention on Human Rights before the Human Rights Act was passed. Academic and legal commentators,[15] and the Lord Chancellor,[16] clearly consider such case law to be of continuing relevance to the deep questions the British courts will be called upon to consider in interpreting the Human Rights Act.

Nor is this development confined to human rights cases.[17] We are seeing considerable growth in the frequency of foreign law being cited in British courts more generally. Markesinis notes how 'in recent times some [judges in England] have broken from the ranks and manifested an open interest in . . . foreign law attempting, whenever possible, to make use of [it] in their judgments'.[18] Writing in a recent issue of *Public Law*, Lord Steyn remarked how the 'Law Lords expect a high standard of research and presentation from barristers. . . . For example, if the appeal involves a statutory offence we would expect counsel to be familiar with . . . comparative material from, say, Australia and New Zealand . . .'.[19] Another recent example demonstrates a growth of interest in German law. In *Barry* v. *Midland Bank plc*,[20] Lord Justice Peter Gibson was 'reassured' in his conclusion on the issue before him (an issue involving equal pay issues under European Community law) by the similar conclusion reached by the German *Bundesarbeitsgericht*.

---

[14] *ibid.*, 3 Nov. 1997, col. 1269.

[15] See e.g., Basil Markesinis, 'Privacy, Freedom of Expression, and the Horizontal Effect of the Human Rights Bill: Lessons from Germany', 115 *Law Quarterly Review* 47 (1999); Murray Hunt, 'The "Horizontal Effect" of the Human Rights Act, [1998] *Public Law* 423; David Pannick, 'Comment: Principles of Interpretation of Convention Rights under the Human Rights Act and the discretionary area of judgment' [1998] *Public Law* 545; Lord Lester of Herne Hill and David Pannick, *Human Rights Law and Practice* (London: Butterworths, 1999), *passim*.

[16] Lord Irvine of Lairg, 'Activism and Restraint: Human Rights and the Interpretative Process', 4 EHRLR (1999), 350 at 355: '. . . the jurisprudence of constitutional courts in other jurisdictions is a useful source of guidance to any judge seeking to give meaning to a human rights instrument.'

[17] Allen noted, on the basis of then recent examples, 'a growing disposition in our courts to recognize pertinent foreign judgments as somewhat more than merely "persuasive", and to regard the line between "persuasive" and "binding" as thin and shadowy, or at least as technical and artificial.' C. K Allen, *Law in the Making*, 7th edn. (Oxford: Clarendon Press, 1964), at 284.

[18] B. S. Markesinis, *The Gradual Convergence* (Oxford: Oxford University Press, 1994), 22. For the American influence, see Ian Loveland (ed.), *A Special Relationship?: American Influences on Public Law in the UK* (Oxford: Oxford University Press, 1995). For examples of the use of foreign judicial authority in the House of Lords, see David Robertson, *Judicial Discretion in the House of Lords* (Oxford: Clarendon Press, 1998), 117, 138, 147–9, 203–4, 286.

[19] Lord Steyn, 'The Role of the Bar, the Judge, and the Jury: Winds of Change' [1999] *Public Law* 51, at 58.

[20] [1998] 1 All ER 805.

TRENDS TOWARDS COMPARATIVE HUMAN RIGHTS
JURISPRUDENCE

It is now commonplace in many jurisdictions for courts to refer extensively to decisions of the courts of foreign jurisdictions when interpreting human rights guarantees. Nelken has observed that, 'We increasingly have the sense of living in an interdependent global system marked by borrowing and lending across porous cultural boundaries' and that human rights is one of the areas of law with the greatest ability to travel.[21] Glendon describes a 'brisk international traffic in ideas about rights', carried on by judges.[22] Slaughter says: 'Courts are talking to one another all over the world.'[23] This trend towards the use of comparative material in some contexts can now be found in many jurisdictions: Israel,[24] Australia,[25] South Africa,[26] Canada,[27] India,[28]

[21] David Nelken, 'Disclosing/Invoking Legal Culture: An Introduction, 4 *Social and Legal Studies* (1995), 435 at 440.

[22] Mary Ann Glendon, *Rights Talk: The Impoverishment of Political Discourse* (New York: Free Press, 1991), 158.

[23] Anne-Marie Slaughter, 'A Typology of Transjudicial Communication', 29 *University of Richmond Law Review* (1994), 99.

[24] The most significant study of the citation practices by the Supreme Court of Israel is for the period 1948–94. It finds a significant decline of citation to British and Commonwealth cases, and their replacement by citation to Israeli cases in general, but an increase in the proportion of American cases cited, with significant variation between the judges and between different areas of legal practice (with greater amounts of foreign citation in constitutional and tort law than in other areas in recent years): see Y. Schar, R. Haris, and M. Gross, 'The Character of References in the Supreme Court: A Quantitative Analysis', *Mishpatim* 27(1) (in Hebrew). (I am grateful to Arad Reisberg for translating this article for me.) See also Arturo Bronstein and Constance Thomas, 'European Labour Courts: International and European Labour Standards in Labour Court Decisions and Jurisprudence on Sex Discrimination' (Geneva : ILO, 1995), at 10 (re. Israel): '. . . the National Labour Court has frequently cited decisions by other nations' labour courts, especially where there is no national statutory provision or precedent relating to a particular case . . . [I]t is convenient for its labour court to show that the conclusion it has reached on a new issue is the same, if not similar, to that reached by courts of other nations.'

[25] G. L. Davies and M. P. Cowen, 'The Persuasive Force of the Decisions of US Courts in Australia', 15 *Australian Bar Review* (1996); A. Mason, 'The Influence of International and Transnational Law on Australian Municipal Law' (1996) 7 Pub. L. R. 20.

[26] The South African Constitutional Court, in interpreting the interim Constitution, made extensive reference to German, Canadian, and US decisions in deciding on the constitutionality of capital punishment, *Makwanyane* (1995) 3 SALR 391 (CC). Indeed, the South African Constitution explicitly provides (s. 39) that the Court may consider foreign law. A good example of the comparative method adopted by the Constitutional Court in South Africa is to be found in *DuPlessis v. De Klerk* 1996 (5) BCLR 658 (CC). See Ross Garland, 'The South African Constitutional Court: A Model for the Domestic Application of International and Comparative Human Rights Norms' (Oxford BCL Thesis, 1999); Richard Goldstone, 'The New South African Constitution: The Importance of Comparative Law' (William W. Bishop Lectures, Lecture 1, Michigan Law School, 1998).

[27] The definitive recent study of the use of US precedents in the Supreme Court of Canada is Peter McCormick, 'The Supreme Court of Canada and American Citations 1945–1994: A Statistical Overview', 8(2d) 1997 *Supreme Court Law Review* 527.

[28] On the generally open approach of the Indian judiciary to foreign precedent, see A. Lakshmi Nath, *Precedent in the Indian Legal System* (Eastern Book Company, 1990), at 182.

New Zealand,[29] Zimbabwe,[30] and Ireland. The European Commission for Democracy Through Law (the Venice Commission) now regularly publishes a Bulletin reporting on the case law of constitutional courts and courts of equivalent jurisdiction in Europe as well as in certain other countries of the world.[31] The jurisprudence of the United States has been particularly influential.[32]

But there has also been a persistent undercurrent of scepticism about this trend, and the emergence of a growing debate about its appropriateness in, for example, Israel,[33] Singapore, South Africa, and the United States. Concerns are increasingly voiced by academic commentators: that substantial 'cherry picking' of jurisdictions occurs, and that those jurisdictions chosen will be those which are likely to support the conclusion sought, leading to arbitrary decision-making, not legitimate judging. Summing up the Hong Kong experience up to 1997, Ghai concludes, for example, 'The courts are willing to consider cases from foreign jurisdictions, although as some areas get explored, there is less need for them. However, the approach to the use of foreign cases is not very consistent; they are invoked when they support the position preferred by the court, otherwise they are dismissed as irrelevant.'[34] Although this practice is common within federal states as well, such as those of the United States, it seems more troubling in a situation where the choice of jurisdiction is more politically loaded.

There also appears to be a growing debate within several national judiciaries.[35] One of the best recent examples relates to the Hong Kong

[29] See, e.g. *Martin v. Tauranga District Court* [1995] 2 NZLR 419 (CA) and *R. v. Goodwin* [1993] 2 NZLR 153 (CA) (citing Canadian, British, European Court of Human Rights, US, and Sri Lanka cases). See also ECtHR decisions cited by the Court of Appeal and High Court of New Zealand in *Television New Zealand* [1996] 3 NZLR 24 (CA), *Duff v. Communicado Ltd* [1996] 2 NZLR 89 (HC), and *Att.-Gen. v. Otahuhu Family Court* [1995] 1 NZLR 603 (HC).

[30] Lovemore Madhuku, 'The Impact of the European Court of Human Rights in Africa: The Zimbabwean Experience', 8 *Revue Africaine de Droit International et Comparé* (1996), 932; Anthony R. Gubbay, 'The Protection and Enforcement of Fundamental Human Rights: the Zimbabwean Experience', 19 *Human Rights Quarterly* (1997), 227 at 253.

[31] Council of Europe, European Commission for Democracy Through Law, *Bulletin on Constitutional Case-Law*.

[32] Anthony Lester, 'The Overseas Trade in the American Bill of Rights', 88 *Columbia Law Review* 537 (1988).

[33] See Hanoch Dagan, 'Unjust Enrichment: Between Judaism and Liberalism', in M. Mautner and D. Goodwin (eds), *Law and History* (Jerusalem: Shazar Centre for Israeli History), 165. Dagan notes different effects, depending on which sources are regarded as persuasive. Translated from Hebrew by Arad Reisberg.

[34] Yash Ghai, 'Sentinels of Liberty or Sheep in Woolf's Clothing? Judicial Politics and the Hong Kong Bill of Rights', 60 *Modern Law Review* (1997), 459 at 479.

[35] In addition to the examples given in the text, see the High Court of Australia decision in *Theophanous v. The Herald and Weekly Times*, in which Brennan, J., in dissent, regards the use of US cases as entirely inappropriate in the context of that case. For examples of unease among members of the South African Constitutional Court about the use of foreign case law, see Kriegler, J. in *Bernstein v. Bester* (1996) 2 SALR 751 (CC) at 811; Kriegler, J. and O'Regan, J. in *Fose v. Minister of Safety and Security* (1997) 3 SALR 786 (CC) at 833 and 839 respectively; Kriegler, J. in *Du Plessis v. De Klerk* (1996) 5 BCLR 658 (CC).

judiciary's approach to the interpretation of the Bill of Rights, prior to the hand-over of Hong Kong to China. Ghai, again, has provided an interesting analysis of how references to foreign law became a touchstone in debates between liberal and conservative members of the judiciary. One of the first decisions on the Bill of Rights, by the Hong Kong Court of Appeal in 1991,[36] held that:

> . . . assistance could be secured [in the interpretation of its provisions] from the decisions of common law jurisdictions with an entrenched Bill of Rights (mentioning in particular Canada and the US), the general comments and decisions of the UN Human Rights Committee, and the jurisprudence under the European Convention on Human Rights.[37]

However, in 1993, the Privy Council, in its first consideration of the issues, cast some doubt on this expansive approach.[38] Lord Woolf, delivering the Opinion of the Privy Council, 'supported the use of foreign precedents, but cautioned that they may not always be relevant to the conditions of Hong Kong'.[39] A more dramatic and direct challenge to the use of foreign decisions was mounted by a High Court judge in a 1995 case.[40]

'Resort to foreign judgments', said Justice Waung, should be eschewed, since 'other domestic and international instruments are the product of very different circumstances and situations,' and courts should 'decline to be seduced by the complex foreign jurisprudence and the seemingly inexhaustible literature from the European Court of Human Rights'.[41]

Singapore courts appear particularly resistant to European Court of Human Rights jurisprudence, and seldom cite any persuasive authority from other jurisdictions on human rights issues before them. In one case, the Singapore High Court had to consider whether cases from other jurisdictions were useful in determining the extent of the Singapore law on contempt of court.[42] The Court held that the English cases from the beginning of the last decade onwards were of no assistance in determining the law of contempt in Singapore, which was derived from the common law of England, as the English common law has been modified by statute and by the decisions of the European Court of Human Rights. Recent Canadian decisions did not apply as they were based on the Canadian Charter of Rights and Freedoms which had no parallel in Singapore. Cases from other Commonwealth jurisdictions turned on their own facts, as the judges in these cases were concerned with social, political, industrial, and other economic conditions prevailing in their respective societies at the

---

[36] *Sin Yau-ming* (1991) 1 HKPLR 88.
[37] Ghai, 'Sentinels of Liberty', above n. 34, at 467.
[38] *Att. Gen. v. Lee Kwong-kut* (1993) 3 HKPLR 72 (Waung, J.)
[39] Ghai, above n. 34, at 468.
[40] *R. v. Town Planning Board, ex p Kwan Kong Ltd* (1995) 5 HKPLR 261.
[41] Ghai, above n. 34, at 470–1 quoting p. 300 of the decision.
[42] *Att.-Gen. v. Wain (No. 1)* 1991 SLR 383.

particular time. In determining whether a matter complained of was a contempt of court, it was important, said the Court, that one did not lose sight of local conditions.

In the United States, a tradition of using other courts' jurisprudence might have grown up, for example in the interpretation of the due process clauses of the Fifth and Fourteenth Amendments. As recently as the middle of the twentieth century, in their attempts during the 1940s and 1950s 'to escape from the "idiosyncrasy of a personal judgment", the [US Supreme] Court . . . regarded its function as one of discovering and applying pre-formed moral judgments, rather than of making new moral choices'.[43] As Kadish pointed out, however, the crucial question was *whose* moral judgments would furnish the answer, and where and how they were discoverable. Justice Frankfurter drew on the 'opinions of other countries in the Anglo-Saxon tradition "not less civilized than our own" as reflected in their statutes, decisions, and practices'.[44] In *Adamson v. California*,[45] for example, Frankfurter based his interpretation on 'those canons of decency and fairness which express the notions of justice of English-speaking peoples . . .', a view he repeated in *Rochin v. California*.[46] In *Wolf v. Colorado*,[47] he refers to the 'conception of human rights enshrined in the history and the basic constitutional documents of English-speaking peoples'. Increasingly, however, the appropriateness of doing so became an issue between Frankfurter and Justice Black. In his concurrence in *Rochin*, Black questions 'why we should consider only the notions of English-speaking peoples to determine what are immutable and fundamental principles of justice'.[48] With Black's ultimate ascendancy, and Frankfurter's increasing marginalization on the Court, this technique of interpreting in part by reference to other jurisdictions fell into disuse. Increasingly, emphasis was placed on developing interpretations that grew out of American conceptions of appropriateness.[49]

More recently, a somewhat similar debate has occurred over the use, or non-use, of comparative experience in the capital punishment cases. In the *Furman* case, the first major decision by the Supreme Court in the reconstruction of the death penalty, there is an apparent openness to comparative experience. For Justice Marshall, the abolition of capital punishment would enable the United States to 'join the approximately seventy other jurisdictions in the world which celebrate their regard for civilization and humanity by shunning capital punishment'. For Justice Powell, in dissent, the comparative experience pointed to a different conclusion. Drawing on the English and Canadian experiences, he points to the advantages of

---

[43] S. Kadish, 'Methodology and Criteria in Due Process Adjudication: A Survey and Criteria', 66 *Yale Law Journal* (1957), 319, at 328.
[44] *ibid.*, at 328. See further, p. 333.   [45] 332 U.S. 46 (1947).
[46] 342 U.S. 165, 169.   [47] 338 U.S. 25, 28.   [48] 342 U.S. at 176.
[49] See, e.g. White, J.'s Opinion in *Duncan v. Louisiana* 391 U.S. 145 (1968).

bringing about change through the legislative process: not only is it more democratic, it is also responsive to 'revision and change: mistaken judgments may be corrected and refinements perfected'. The relevant point can be simply stated: the capital punishment cases begin with an apparent openness to the comparative experience; those in favour and those against both used comparative evidence.

However, this approach has been explicitly abrogated. The turning point appears to have been in the late 1980s, and the occasion, the issue of the constitutionality of the application of the death penalty to juvenile offenders. In *Thompson v. Oklahoma*[50] the Supreme Court concluded that the Eighth Amendment's prohibition of 'cruel and unusual punishment' forbade the execution of persons under 16 years of age at the time of their offence. In the course of the plurality's judgment, Justice Brennan argued that to allow the execution of a criminal who was less than 16 years old at the time of the offence would offend civilized standards of decency. He supported this argument by reference not only to the practice of eighteen states in the United States, but also to transnational experience. 'The conclusion [that it would offend civilized standards] is consistent with the views that have been expressed . . . by other nations that share our Anglo-American heritage, and by the leading members of the Western European community', citing as evidence the brief of Amnesty International. In dissent, Justice Scalia not only disagreed with the conclusion, but also strongly disagreed with the use of the comparative method itself.[51] Within two years, however, the issue was re-run in *Stanford v. Kentucky*[52] and the dissenting view on the substantive issue had become the plurality. The Court accepted the constitutionality of the imposition of capital punishment on an offender who was 17 years old at the time the offence was committed. While the dissent relied in part on comparative experience, and on international human rights treaties in support of their view, Justice Scalia, writing for the majority,[53] emphasized that it is 'American conceptions of decency that are dispositive, rejecting the contention of petitioners . . . that the sentencing practices of other countries are relevant . . .'.[54] The United States is now remarkable among precedent-based jurisdictions in citing foreign courts so rarely in human rights contexts.

So, what should we think about these debates? When does such explicit borrowing take place? Why is it resisted in some jurisdictions, or by some judges, and not in, or by, others? What, if anything does the debate tell us about human rights? Remarkably little has been written that is other than descriptive about this phenomenon.

---

[50] 487 U.S. 815 (1987).   [51] Scalia J., at 869, n 4.

[52] 492 U.S. 361 (1989).

[53] A majority of the Court in *Stanford* rejected the use of the comparative approach since O'Connor J. joined that portion of the plurality's Opinion.

[54] n. 1, p. 370.

'USING' TRANSNATIONAL LAW

Before going further, however, some clarification is needed of what is meant by 'using' foreign law, in order to make clear the scope of what I am particularly interested in exploring. I am interested in the use of *foreign* human rights law, not *international* human rights law, nor foreign human rights law that purports to be interpretative of international human rights law (although clearly there is a close connection in some cases). The use to which this foreign law is put, is in the context of the interpretation of a domestic human rights provision, and not of the direct application of the foreign law in the domestic court.[55] The focus, therefore, is on foreign law used transnationally.[56]

The influence of other jurisdictions on a judge may also be general and indirect, as opposed to specific and direct. It is clear that there is a substantial growth of formal and informal contacts between judiciaries in order to discuss human rights interpretation. The Commonwealth Secretariat (together with Interights) has organized several colloquia for judges on human rights issues.[57] The Supreme Court of Israel organizes a yearly seminar, including scholars from other jurisdictions for its judges. Bi-lateral visits of judges from one jurisdiction to another are also increasingly common; for example, judges of the South African Constitutional Court have visited the French courts; and judges of the United States Supreme Court have visited the European Court of Human Rights. Each year, starting in 1996, Yale Law School has hosted a (closed) seminar for senior judges around the world.[58]

No doubt these discussions result in some influences being inculcated—such as a country's culture of rights. But such influences, whilst important, are difficult to pin down and prone to over- (or under-) estimation. Equally difficult to identify with any certainty, are those indirect influences that occur when an idea from one jurisdiction is picked up in a second, and then transferred to the third. The continuing influence of the first is indirect and important, but sometimes untraceable.

A further distinction needs to be made between explicit and non-explicit reference to judicial decisions in other jurisdictions. Jurisdictions tend to

---

[55] See Richard Fentiman, *Foreign Law in English Courts* (Oxford: Clarendon Press, 1998).

[56] Twining defines transnational relations as including 'non-state relations across frontiers'. William Twining, 'Globalization and Legal Theory: Some Local Implications', 49 *Current Legal Problems* (M. Freeman, ed., 1996), vol. II, 1 at 5.

[57] Lord Lester of Herne Hill, 'The Challenge of Bangalore: Making Human Rights a Practical Reality' [1999] EHRLR 273.

[58] 'Global Constitutionalism Seminar', *Yale Law Report*, 45(1) 1998, at 5. In September 1998, e.g., judges from 15 different Supreme Courts, or their equivalents, had their third annual meeting of a 'Global Constitutionalism Seminar' at Yale Law School. 'Third Annual Global Constitutionalism Seminar Draws Justices from Around the World', *Yale Law Report* 46(1) 1999, at 5.

fall into one of three different sorts: those which (in general) do not use foreign human rights law (e.g. the US Supreme Court now seldom cites foreign court decisions in the context of its human rights decisions);[59] those which do use foreign human rights law, but do not do so *explicitly* (e.g. Japan);[60] and those which do so explicitly (e.g. South Africa).

I have mostly confined myself in this chapter to direct, specific, and acknowledged influences. In the main this has involved identifying where judges in one jurisdiction specifically have cited or used as relevant judicial or other legal experiences from another jurisdiction in the course of their judgment. As Slaughter has suggested, it is worthwhile distinguishing between courts drawing on the opinions of foreign courts without attribution, and courts directly citing a foreign decision, 'In [the latter] cases evidence that a foreign court has reached the same conclusion apparently has independent value, leading the listening court not only to borrow the idea, but to publicize its source.'[61]

Lastly, we need to distinguish different *degrees* of influence of cited foreign cases, even where acknowledged. We should differentiate judges

---

[59] Anne-Marie Slaughter, 'A Typology of Transjudicial Communication', above, n. 23, 'The US Supreme Court has not seen fit to reciprocate in kind.' (at 104). Gordon A. Christenson, 'Using Human Rights Law to Inform Due Process and Equal Protection Analyses', 52 *Cincinnati Law Review* (1983), 3 at 5: 'I am curious why our courts shun external sources of law—more specifically, contemporary decisions of foreign and international courts.' He considers that 'most US courts, both state and federal, show less inclination now than at the beginning of the Republic to use sources of foreign, international and customary law to aid interpretation, especially in constitutional cases . . .' (at 6). Richard B. Lillich, 'The Constitution and International Human Rights', 83 *American Journal of International Law* (1989), 851, at 855: 'If American constitutionalism has contributed greatly to the development of international human rights law, the reverse, alas, has yet to occur.' He argues that this should occur, 'if the US, as well as other countries, is to prosper from it over the long haul' (at 860). Bruce Ackerman concurs: 'The typical American judge would not think of learning from an Opinion by the German or French constitutional court' ('The Rise of World Constitutionalism', 83 *Virginia Law Review* 771 (1997), at 772). Statistical studies of the citation practices of courts in the US, both federal and state courts, show a steady decline in the use of foreign cases, see William H. Manz, 'Cardozo's Use of Authority: An Empirical Study', 32 *California Western School of Law* 31 (1995), at 32, n. 1 (summarizing the findings of empirical studies).

[60] 'Japanese judges often study (even if they do not often cite) precedent of the US Supreme Court in constitutional cases, and many influential Japanese legal scholars continue to be well-informed about American laws and judicial decisions touching on constitutional issues.' Lawrence W. Beer, 'Constitutionalism in Asia and the US', in *Constitutionalism In Asia* (Lawrence W. Beer, ed., 1979), at 12. Lawrence W. Beer, 'Constitutionalism and Rights in Japan and Korea', eds Louis Henkin and Albert J. Rosenthal, *Constitutionalism and Rights: The Influence of the US Constitution Abroad* (NY: Columbia University Press, 1990), at 242: pointing to the influence of American law on Japanese law, including presentation of expert testimony on American constitutional law in court. For counter examples, see the Opinion of Kitaro Saito J. in *Koshiyama v. Chairman*, Tokyo Metropolitan Election Commission (1964) in Itoh and Ward Beer, *The Constitutional Case Law of Japan: Selected Supreme Court Decisions, 1961–1970* (Seattle, London: University of Washington Press, 1978), 53, at 55 (citing and discussing Frankfurter's dissent in *Baker v. Carr* 369 US 186 (1962)); Hiroshi Itoh, 'Judicial Activism in Japan', in Kenneth M. Holland (ed.), *Judicial Activism in Comparative Perspective* (NY: St Martins Press, 1991), 189, at 196.

[61] Anne-Marie Slaughter, above, n. 23, at 118.

merely mentioning cases as being of minor relevance, judges actually 'following' them as some sort of authority, and judges 'distinguishing' them. The practice of distinguishing foreign cases raises particularly interesting issues. Even where the *result* of the foreign judicial approach has not been adopted, it has often been influential in sharpening the understanding of the Court's view of domestic law. Such a use of foreign human rights law does not mean that the approach taken in the other jurisdiction will necessarily be adopted, just that it is *considered*. Thus, for example, although the United States Supreme Court decisions are extensively cited in other jurisdictions, they are sometimes of limited influence on the decision actually reached, as opposed to influencing the way in which the issue is considered. In other words, while the United States Supreme Court decisions are often thought to provide a useful structure for analysis, and to identify many of the issues which have to be considered, courts much less frequently adopt the same conclusion that the Supreme Court reached.[62] Why do courts do this? Why, also, do they feel the need formally to distinguish foreign precedent, which is clearly not binding?[63]

ROLE OF PERSUASIVE PRECEDENT REVISITED

One starting point for considering these issues is to begin with the question of why judges have regard to national judicial precedent. I previously identified the distinction between binding and persuasive precedent. However, too much should not be made of the distinction. It is perhaps increasingly too starkly drawn. This is particularly so, it seems, in human rights cases where the role of binding national precedent is often weaker than in other areas of law. More often, even national precedent seems closer to being 'persuasive' than binding.

Several reasons have typically been put forward to explain why courts have regard to national judicial precedent. Of these, the interest in fairness (treating like cases alike) has sometimes been seen as central.[64] But if this is so, Bronaugh observes, it is unclear why a requirement of fairness (treating like cases alike) would result in a decision to restrict the range of

---

[62] David Beatty, 'The Canadian Charter of Rights: Lessons and Laments', 60 MLR 481 (1997), 482, n. 5, 'Although US authorities are frequently referred to by the Court, it has, for the most part, treated them very cautiously and usually as not being very helpful in fashioning solutions that are appropriate for Canada.'

[63] e.g. SA Constitutional Court in *Makwanyane*, above n. 26. In *McGinty v. The State of Western Australia* Dawson J. distinguishes the American approach, describing the US historical context as 'inapt in any consideration of the form of representative government for which the [Australian] Commonwealth Constitution provides. The democratic traditions of both Canada and Australia find their origins in the English model rather than in rebellion against it as is the case in the US' (High Court of Australia, 1995).

[64] See, e.g., Dworkin, *Taking Rights Seriously*, 113. Others are more sceptical, see Anthony Kronman, 'Precedent and Tradition', 99 *Yale Law Journal* (1990), 1029.

similar cases to those within particular national borders. 'The operative aspect of the principle of fairness', he says, 'resides in relevant similarity (and dissimilarity), which can and does obtain across national . . . borders . . .'.[65] Indeed, not only does he argue that following a precedent which derives from outside the jurisdiction is fair, but also that *not* to follow one is *un*fair, assuming that one cannot 'say that the "same things" never happen in other legal systems'.

However, as he rapidly concedes, not only is the 'avoidance of unfairness . . . not decisive in all cases,'[66] but 'meeting the requirements of fairness in full is a practical impossibility'.[67] The vast array of possible relevant persuasive precedents would simply overwhelm the Court.[68] What legal systems do, he suggests, is to set in place 'institutional rules' which circumscribe 'the scope of judicial inquiry and . . . the weight of precedents'.[69] One way of doing this is to limit binding precedent to those arising in *domestic* legal contexts. These, and other ways of circumscribing 'relevance' for practical purposes, are 'judicial creations within a political order'.[70] The '[l]imits which fence inquiry within the political arrangements of the day are not conceptual, but practical'.[71]

It is questionable, however, how far that concession adequately responds to a deeper unease about Bronaugh's central argument.[72] We seem to need a thicker account of the operation of precedent than simply 'similarity'. For the principle of 'fairness' to operate, surely, the decision-maker has to have some duty to treat the similarly-situated parties alike. One traditional source of this duty is the sense of responsibility of a decision-maker for the decision in both cases. If this is accepted, then fairness would not require a Canadian judge to do the same as an American judge even where all relevant respects of the case, say, of C (in Canada) was the same as the case of A (in the US). Why? Because the Canadian court was not responsible for decision A—from which it flows that there is no requirement on the Canadian court to follow A.

An important aspect of our enquiry will be to ask to what extent the source of a duty of fairness in human rights cases extends beyond responsibility of this kind and arises from some other source, such as some more universal set of basic entitlements of all human beings.

Schauer also draws attention to several aspects of precedent which enable us further to clarify aspects of this enquiry. He argues that the operation of a system of precedent 'presupposes an ability to identify the relevant precedent'.[73] This will involve 'some way of determining whether a

---

[65] Richard Bronaugh, 'Persuasive Precedent', in Laurence Goldstein, *Precedent in Law* (Oxford: Clarendon Press, 1987), 217 at 227.

[66] *ibid.,* 227.   [67] *ibid.,* 236.   [68] *ibid.,* 230.   [69] *ibid.,* 236.

[70] *ibid.,* 238.   [71] *ibid.,* 238.

[72] I am particularly grateful to Joan Larsen and Timothy Endicott for clarifying my thoughts on this point.

[73] Fredrick Schauer, 'Precedent', 39 *Stanford Law Review* 571 (1987), at pp. 576–7.

past event is sufficiently similar to the present facts to justify assimilation of the two events'.[74] What is required, therefore, is 'the intervention of organizing theory, in the form of *rules of relevance*, [which] allows us to distinguish the precedential from the irrelevant'.[75] These rules of relevance are themselves 'contingent upon time and culture'.[76] 'The task of a theory of precedent is to explain, in a world in which a single event may fit into many different categories, how and why some assimilations are plausible and others are not.'[77] 'The problem is to determine what constrains a decision-maker's control over the categories of assimilation.'[78]

What sorts of factors are likely to affect these rules of relevance? '[T]he study of the place of persuasive precedent is of the interaction between a moral reason [fairness] and an institutional structure',[79] based on practicality. Jurisprudential writers indicate that factors influencing the rules of relevance consist of a mixture of the principled and the pragmatic. Several interests tend to recur: an interest in stability; an interest in predictability; enabling judges to draw on the knowledge of their peers, thus helping to improve decision-making; efficient decision-making and judicial economy—not having to reinvent the wheel; and reassuring the public that the court's decisions are not arbitrary—to promote public confidence in the law.[80] Of these, the concern to maintain public confidence in the judiciary, and the concern to improve judicial performance are particularly important in the human rights context. Arguably, the 'value-laden nature of constitutional interpretation makes the concern for maintaining public confidence and for improving judicial performance especially compelling in constitutional law'.[81]

For Schauer, the rules for determining relevance may come from the narrower legal world, or they may come 'to legal decision-makers from the larger linguistic and social environment'.[82] Agreeing on the appropriate rules of relevance may be, therefore, particularly problematic. There is more than a theoretical possibility that satisfying the range of concerns will be particularly difficult where one concern derives from the narrower legal world (say, improving judicial performance), and another derives from the larger social environment (say, the unacceptability of resort to precedents from particular countries).

Whilst important, Schauer's account seems flawed in an important respect. We need to challenge his use of the term 'rules' in the context of determining relevance—where 'rules' are taken as setting out hard and fast, binding requirements on judges, as opposed to guiding principles. What we find in practice is that the 'rules' of relevance are extraordinarily fluid in this respect, and in a state of considerable flux, not only *between*,

---

[74] *ibid.*, 577.   [75] *ibid.*, 578.   [76] *ibid.*, 578.   [77] *ibid.*, 579.
[78] *ibid.*, 582.   [79] Bronaugh, 'Persuasive Precedent' (see n. 65), 238.
[80] Note, 'Constitutional Stare Decisis', 103 *Harvard Law Review* (1990) 1344, 1349
[81] *ibid.*, 1351.   [82] Schauer, 586.

but also *within* jurisdictions. And, of course, they may vary over time: what was previously acceptable may become unacceptable. In ancient Rome, apparently, the authority of the poets was regularly drawn on in legal argument because 'before the social sciences poetry was the main source for generalisations about the nature of man and his world'.[83] In the United States, as we have seen, courts now seldom cite foreign judicial decisions; not necessarily the case previously.[84]

Whilst drawing up formal 'rules' of relevance regarding persuasive precedents is probably undesirable and almost certainly unrealistic in many jurisdictions, greater explanation of, and debate about, the practice of transnational citation of human rights jurisprudence is both possible and highly desirable. Interestingly, the courts of some jurisdictions do not disclose that they are influenced by judicial decisions of other countries. But is there perhaps a sense that lack of candour as to the sources drawn upon is appropriate given possible adverse reactions? Is it better to have decisions *informed* by foreign judgments but to avoid the risk of adverse reaction by urging formal attribution?

On the other hand, we usually consider that the, 'requirement that judges give reasons for their decisions—grounds of decision that can be debated, attacked, and defended—serves a vital function in constraining the judiciary's exercise of power. In the absence of an obligation of candour, this constraint would be greatly diluted, since judges who regard themselves as free to distort or misstate the reasons for their actions can avoid the sanctions of criticism and condemnation that honest disclosure of their motivation may entail.'[85]

That view seems to support a conclusion that judges should cite foreign judgments if they have been relied on. The same argument applies to the criteria used to choose which foreign jurisdictions are selected where they *are* acknowledged. Such openness would at least recognize publicly that the issue of persuasive sources, like everything else in the interpretation of human rights guarantees, is itself controversial and thus in need of the most careful justification. It would therefore enable a more public debate to take place about the appropriateness of the approach the court had adopted.[86]

---

[83] G. C. J. J. Van Den Bergh, '*Auctoritas Poetarum*: The fortunes of a legal argument', in Alan Watson (ed.), *Daube Noster: Essays in Legal History for David Daube* (Edinburgh: Scottish Academic Press, 1974).

[84] Clark refers to the 'scant legal literature on the use of foreign and comparative law in US courts because courts rarely cite foreign law'. David S. Clark, 'The Use of Comparative Law by American Courts' (I), 42 *American Journal of Comparative Law* 23 (1994).

[85] David L. Shapiro, 'In Defense of Judicial Candour' 100 *Harvard Law Review* (1987) 731 at 737.

[86] My concern is that both judges and lawyers should take legal arguments more seriously, in Markovits' second sense of valuing legal craftsmanship. See Richard S. Markovits, 'Taking Legal Argument Seriously: An Introduction', in 74 *Chicago-Kent Law Review* 317 (1999).

Even more fundamentally, however, we need to introduce another jurisprudential distinction to understand the different functions that citations of judgments may play in a judge's decision.[87] Summers distinguishes between 'authority' reasons, with which we have mainly been concerned until now, and 'substantive' reasons that are advanced by a judge for or against a legal interpretation.[88] Authority reasons usually take the form: 'Legal conclusion X is correct because court Y (or Judge Z) so decided.' Substantive reasons (which include reasons deriving their justificatory force from beneficial results, other norms, or institutional role), usually take the form: 'Legal conclusion X is correct because of the following [substantive] reason . . . (and Judge Z or Court Y thinks so too . . .).' In examining the use of foreign judgments, we will need to keep in mind these two different uses of precedents and whether foreign judgments are used in the context of conclusions based on authority or substantive reasoning.

FACTORS IN USING COMPARATIVE HUMAN RIGHTS LAW

Is it possible, then, to identify the factors explaining the use of foreign judgments generally, before turning to consider their use in human rights cases in particular? In an interesting article published in 1957, Tripathi examines various apparent reasons for the use by one court of foreign precedents in constitutional decision-making. He concludes, however that:

When a judge looks to foreign legal systems for analogies that shed light on any of the new cases before him, he is looking to legal material which he is absolutely free to reject unless it appeals to his reason. Appeal to one's reason, more often than not, amounts to a confirmation and a strengthening of one's own opinion rather than a shaping of that opinion. Further, in a large majority of cases conflicting foreign precedents may not be hard to find. Taken together all these factors whittle down to insignificance the controlling influence of the 'reasons' that are proclaimed by the judges to direct their choice of foreign precedents. Historical association, cognate nature of the two legal systems, analogy of legal institutions, a supposed need for uniformity, similarity or identity of language, and such other 'reasons' as may be advanced, seem to possess no compelling force of their own; any of them can be played against another; any of them could be preferred to another; any or all of them could be conveniently ignored altogether; and, of course, any of them could be cited in support of a decision where it happens to suit. They are little more than rationalizations of a choice largely shaped by the secret yet unmistakable pressures of psychological motivations. This area of study,

---

[87] I am grateful to William Twining for helpful discussions on this point.

[88] R.S. Summers, 'Two Types of Substantive Reasons: The Core of a Theory of Common-Law Justification' 63 *Cornell Law Review* (1978) 707, 716. See also William Twining and David Miers, *How to Do Things With Rules*, 3rd edn (London: Butterworths, 1991), 265.

namely, the choice of foreign precedents in constitutional law, presents something like the vanishing point of behavioristic jurisprudence.[89]

There are two points of importance in this passage. The first is that Tripathi rightly concentrates on the role of the individual judge in examining the phenomenon. Whilst, as we shall see, there are institutional factors which appear to distinguish the pattern of citing foreign judgments from national court to national court, it is likely that there is as great a variation within—as between—national courts on the issue; different judges appear to adopt significantly different citation practices.[90]

The second, and more controversial point argued by Tripathi is in effect that there are no *rules* of relevance that can be identified, just endless strong judicial discretion. But this is no longer as convincing an explanation as it once may have been, for several reasons. First, the appropriateness of such citation of foreign material is now the subject, as we have seen, of debate between judges in several jurisdictions. Such public judicial debate appears to suggest that there are (or are assumed to be) some *criteria*, if not *rules*, of relevance regulating its use, and that those who use (or do not use) such sources are subject to justifiable *legal* criticism. In *Printz*, for example, Justice Scalia takes Justice Breyer to task for drawing on foreign experience: 'We think such comparative analysis inappropriate to the task of interpreting a constitution, though it was of course quite relevant to the task of writing one.'[91] Secondly, there are also increasing numbers of judges in particular jurisdictions who appear to consider it important to distinguish judgments of foreign courts if they go against the conclusion the judge intends to reach. We are not here, surely, in the realm of strong judicial discretion but nor are we in the realm of rules of relevance strictly defined either. The truth seems somewhere between the two extremes. What, then, are the sorts of factors which lead judges to engage with this foreign material? Several factors seem of particular current importance.

Type of political regime

Not surprisingly, the type of regime from which a foreign judicial decision arises markedly affects the likelihood of its being cited. In the main, the judiciaries of liberal democratic regimes cite each other. Leaving aside all other considerations militating against it, the citation of, for example, Chinese cases by the House of Lords, does not seem likely. The political regime in China within which the judges make their decisions would not be one regarded as sufficiently democratic to be cited approvingly or,

---

[89] Pradyuma K. Tripathi, 'Foreign Precedents and Constitutional Law', 57 *Columbia Law Review* 319 (1957), at 346.

[90] Schar, Haris, and Gross, above, n. 24, at 193 ff.

[91] *Printz v. US* 521 U.S. 898 at 921, 138 L Ed 2d 914, 935 (1997), n 11.

indeed, at all. Such decisions are, in important respects, irrelevant. As Justice Barak of the Supreme Court of Israel has written:

Frequently, before the judge decides on the content and scope of a legal institution found in his system, he will turn to other legal systems for the purposes of comparison. The purpose of this comparison is inspiration. An essential condition for this inspiration is that the legal institutions which are compared are fit for comparison, that is to say, that they are based on common fundamental assumptions and come to realize common goals.[92]

The remaining issues are all subject to this general constraint.

Pedagogical impulse

The strength of the pedagogical impulse within the national judiciary appears to be an important factor. As Slaughter argues, 'The court of a fledgling democracy, for instance, might look to the opinions of courts in older and more established democracies as a way of binding its country to this existing community of states.'[93] Israel provides a particularly interesting example of the use to which foreign persuasive precedents are put in this respect.[94] There has for some time been heavy use of American case law by some members of the Supreme Court of Israel, particularly in the area of freedom of expression.[95] This approach is especially associated with Justice Barak, now the controversial Chief Justice of the Israel Supreme Court. It seems clear that he resorts to American case law because he views it as presenting that conception of democracy which he wishes to see embedded in Israeli society.[96] As Jacobsohn describes it, 'the practice of judicial activism in Israel involves a self-consciously pedagogical commitment premised on the felt need to instil habits of Western democratic participation in a body politic that on the whole is inexperienced in the ways of democracy. The American model can thus serve to facilitate the realization of these democratic aspirations.'[97]

We can also identify a rather different use of foreign judgments in this context, where they are used not to persuade, but as a warning, or as something that illustrates what the domestic judge is trying not to do, and against which he is actively working. In this context, the foreign law is 'the other', which must be avoided. One of the best examples of this is in the

---

[92] *Kupat Am Bank Inc. v. Hendels*, P.D. 34(3) 57 at 67 (quoted in Aharon Barak, 'Constitutional Human Rights and Private Law', 3 *Review of Constitutional Studies* (1996), 218 at 242.

[93] Anne-Marie Slaughter, 'A Typology of Transjudicial Communication', above, n. 23, at 134.

[94] Gary J. Jacobsohn, *Apple of Gold: Constitutionalism in Israel and the US* (Princeton, 1995).

[95] For a discussion up to 1981, see Pnina Lahav, 'American Influence on Israel's Jurisprudence of Free Speech', 9 *Hastings Constitutional Law Quarterly* 21 (1981). See also Jacobsohn, above n. 94, 180. For a statistical analysis, see Schar, Haris, and Gross, above, n. 24, at 213 ff.

[96] Jacobsohn, above n. 94, at 222.   [97] *ibid.*, at 225.

Irish Supreme Court's anxiety to prevent itself being seen as embarking on a road in the 1970s which would lead to the legalization of abortion, echoing what occurred in the United States in *Roe v. Wade*.[98]

Audience

The perceived 'audience' of opinions also plays an important role. 'In the most general terms, a case is cited because it contributes to convincing the relevant audience (which includes, but is by no means limited to, the immediate parties) of the appropriateness of the outcome.'[99] In part, what is at issue here is a fundamental (and difficult) question: to which 'community of respect' does the judge consider him or herself to be appealing? Judges, like the rest of us, want to be seen to be doing a 'good job', but what that involves may well vary depending on the audience. It would not be surprising if those judges cited foreign judgments where they considered this likely to be persuasive to their self-defined audience. As Slaughter has argued: 'references to the activity of fellow courts in other states can act as . . . a security blanket . . . [B]y pointing to the actions of fellow states, a national court can reassure itself (and its government) that it will not disadvantage the nation in dealing with other nations.'[100] For Justice Barak, comparative law 'grants comfort to the judge and gives him the feeling that he is treading on safe ground, and it also gives legitimacy to the chosen solution'.[101]

Where there is a fundamental dispute within the target audience about which countries are appropriate reference points, this will lead the judge to be extremely wary about citing cases from any foreign jurisdiction. Defining what is the relevant group will not only affect whether the judge refers to foreign experience, but also *which* foreign experience is regarded as appropriate. If the primary audience is domestic popular opinion, then whether or not to cite foreign courts in general, or this foreign court in particular, may depend on whether the citation is likely to strengthen, or weaken, its legitimacy with that audience. Where the view among public

---

[98] *McGee v. Att.-Gen.* [1974] IR 284.

[99] Peter McCormick, 'The Supreme Court of Canada and American Citations 1945–1994 . . .', above, n. 27, at 528–9.

[100] Anne-Marie Slaughter, 'A Typology of Transjudicial Communication', above, n. 23, at 116. For a practical example, see Dennis Morris, 'Interpreting Hong Kong's Bill of Rights: Some Basic Questions: Pt IV', 17 *Statute Law Review*, 128 at 144 (1996), 'The Hong Kong courts have not been reluctant to strike down legislation on the grounds of incompatibility with the Bill. In doing so they have been at pains to demonstrate that they have been applying, to the Hong Kong context, interpretative principles drawn from a number of jurisdictions.' Richard Swede, 'One Territory: Three Systems? The Hong Kong Bill of Rights', 44 *International and Comparative Law Quarterly* (1995), 358 at 363. See also Madhuku, above, n. 30, at 943 on Zimbabwe: 'references to comparative international cases are a part of a well designed judicial policy of activism. Judges do not want to be seen to be openly making law. . . . [T]he ECHR has been a great help.'

[101] Barak, above, n. 92., at 242.

opinion is current that human rights are not subject to international debate, either because of unilateralism, relativism, isolationism, or particularism, reference to other foreign courts' decisions is much less likely. McFadden has argued[102] that 'methodological provincialism', as he terms it, may be explained in part by 'a fear that international argument, even if correct, will be unpersuasive'. Louis Henkin has written of his view that, for the United States, human rights have become 'a kind of 'white man's burden', and international human rights have been 'for export only'.[103] He continues:

An abiding isolationism (or unilateralism) . . . continues to appeal to many Americans, even some who readily judge others and are eager to intervene on behalf of democracy and human rights in other countries. There is a reluctance to accept, and have our courts apply, standards perceived to have been created by others, even if they were borrowed from us and reflect our own values.[104]

Where the audience is sufficiently convinced that its role in the world is to lead rather than follow, the use of other courts' approaches is also unlikely. The fact that the United States is the supreme world power politically and economically is surely not irrelevant as a factor explaining the widespread general perception in the United States that United States courts need not bother with foreign judgments. A leadership position in the world may, however, lead to other conclusions. In some contexts, there

[102] Patrick M. McFadden, 'Provincialism in US Courts', 81 *Cornell Law Review* (1995) 4, at 14.

[103] Louis Henkin, 'The US and International Human Rights', in *Justice for a Generation* (papers presented in London, 15–19 July 1985 at the plenary sessions of a meeting between the American Bar Association, the Senate of the Inns of Court and the Bar, and the Law Society of England and Wales), at 377. An early example of unilateralism is John W. Burgess, writing in 1891. After a lengthy comparison of European and American approaches to government and law, he concludes the section on civil liberties:

And while it must be confessed that we can learn much from the European Constitutions in the organization of government and in the details of administration, yet for a clearly defined and well secured civil liberty—one which can defy government, and still be subject to the state, one which can do far more for civilization upon many sides, and upon many of its finer sides, than the best ordered government which the world has ever produced—Europe must come to us, and take lessons in the school of our system. We have not yet by any means perfected our system. Our conceptions in reference to civil liberty are still clouded by crude notions about the federal system, and its requirements as to citizenship, and the immunities of citizenship; but we have done by far the best in this direction which mankind has as yet accomplished; and while we feel the pressure upon all sides to expand the powers of government, in accordance with European practice, let us never forget that constitutional civil liberty is the peculiar product of our own political genius . . .

(in *Political Science and Comparative Constitutional Law*, vol. 1: 'Sovereignty and Liberty' (Ginn and Co.: Boston and London, 1891), 264.

[104] *ibid*. See also Henkin, 'To some extent there is an unwillingness by Americans to admit such influence: that we should be governed by ideas from foreign sources is not congenial to us', in Louis Henkin and Albert J. Rosenthal (eds), *Constitutionalism and Rights: The Influence of the US Constitution Abroad* (NY: Columbia University Press, 1990).

is a recognition that the courts of other countries are part of the audience for the Supreme Court. In *United States v. Alvarez-Machain*,[105] Justice Stevens, dissenting, points to the 'significance of this Court's precedents' in other countries, implying that this brings with it responsibility. He worried about the adverse effect of the majority's decision on the United States' reputation abroad. Pointing to a decision of the Court of Appeal in South Africa, which had drawn on an earlier American decision which the majority now planned to limit, he said: 'The Court of Appeal of South Africa—indeed, I suspect most courts throughout the civilized world—will be deeply disturbed by the "monstrous" decision the Court announces today.'

Existence of common alliances

We can identify several examples where a deliberate 'alliance' appears to be the basis for the citation of foreign sources; where having regard to the judicial decisions of other jurisdictions in the area of human rights is perceived as part of a larger project of economic or social integration, or as a continuation of a common history. Being seen to have regard to these external decisions is thought to be part and parcel of the judiciary's role in bringing about harmonization within the group of countries having an already close relationship or seeking closer integration. Sometimes, the common alliance may be based on historical links, such as a common history of colonial domination by the same power. One of the few judicial statements in the United States in support of the use of foreign judgments was posited on a criterion of relevance based on previous influence.[106] Pakistan's judiciary, 'like that of other post-colonial common law jurisdictions', is said to treat 'case law and other authoritative texts from other common law jurisdictions as strong persuasive authority. Pakistan's constitutional cases are rife with citations to Indian, English, and American cases and treatises.'[107] The Judicial Committee of the Privy Council uses Canadian, New Zealand, United States, Australian, and British cases extensively, but does not confine itself to these jurisdictions. It decided, for example, that the Jamaican Constitution prohibited lengthy delays

---

[105] 504 US 655 (1992).

[106] *US v. Then* 56 F 2d 464, 469 (2d Cir. 1995) (Calabresi, J., concurring):

> At one time, America had a virtual monopoly on constitutional judicial review, and if a doctrine or approach was not tried here, there was no place else to look. That situation no longer holds. Since World War II, many countries have adopted forms of judicial review, which—though different from ours in many particulars—unmistakably drew their origin and inspiration from American constitutional theory and practice. These countries are our 'constitutional offspring' and how they have dealt with problems analogous to ours can be very useful to us when we face difficult constitutional issues. Wise parents do not hesitate to learn from their children.

[107] 19 *Fordham International Law Journal* 40, at 47, n 17.

between the imposition of a sentence of death and its being carried out, using European Court of Human Rights, Canadian, United States, Indian, and Zimbabwean decisions.

Of course, the opposite may also be true: where a state wishes to *disassociate* itself from another state it will be less willing to cite that state's case law. Thus there is often considerable sensitivity in using precedents from a previous colonial power,[108] or the receiving court may be uneasy about being overwhelmed by case law drawn from another more powerful society preventing the emergence of a distinctively new jurisprudence.[109] This may increase the likelihood of citations of multiple foreign courts, in addition to the feared dominant influence, in order to dilute, as it were, the impact of the latter.[110]

The 'common alliance impulse' will be strongest, however, when the integration is set out explicitly as a political programme, with institutional characteristics, such as in Europe.[111] Indeed, the comparative method is explicitly built into the fabric of judicial decision-making. This is particularly the case in the ECtHR and the European Court of Justice. In the former, the approach to a human rights issue taken in Council of Europe member states is often used as one element in the Court's decision whether or not justifications given by a state for an interference with one

---

[108] Cf. the dictum of the Irish judge, Gavan Duffy J., in *Exham v. Beamish* [1939] IR 336 at 348–9, 'In my opinion, this Court cannot be fettered in the exercise of the judicial power by opinions of very different Courts under the old régime . . . Our new High Court must mould its own *cursus curiae* . . .'. See Note, CCXXXIII *Law Quarterly Review*, 1943, 26–7. LaForest J. gave vent to this sense of judicial nationalism when he stated in one of the Supreme Court's early Charter decisions that, 'Canadian legal thought has at many points in the past deferred to that of the British; the Charter will be no sign of our national maturity if it simply becomes an excuse for adopting another intellectual mentor. American jurisprudence, like the British, must be viewed as a tool, not as a master.' See also Berker, C. J. in *In re Corporal Punishment by the State* [1992] LRC (Const) 515 (Namibia Supreme Court) at 536, commenting on the l imited use of foreign precedents, '. . . the Namibian people are now in the position to determine their own values free from such foreign values imposed by their former colonial rulers'.

[109] David Fraser and Alan Freeman, 'What's Hockey Got to Do With it, Anyway?: Comparative Canadian–American Perspectives on Constitutional Law and Rights', 36 *Buffalo Law Review* (1987), 259, at 279: 'The feeling of being smothered is very powerful for Canadians because we are bombarded every day with popular cultural images of American life and politics.'

[110] Davies and Cowen, see n. 25, above, at n. 21.

[111] Jochen Abr. Frowein, 'European Integration Through Fundamental Rights', 18 *Michigan Journal of Law Reform* (1984) 5. As Richards has argued, expressing this view well:

> The test for liberal constitutional institutions in Europe, both at the national and European level, will be the degree to which they foster in the lives of their people a national and European identity expressed through respect for human rights, not in antagonism to them. If American constitutional experience is at all relevant, an institutionally enforceable conception of European human rights may be central to such cultural reconstruction . . .

(David A. J. Richards, 'Comparative Revolutionary Constitutionalism: A Research Agenda for Comparative Law', 26 *New York University Journal of International Law and Politics* (1993) 1, at 59.

of the rights protected by the European Convention will be accepted. In several of the Convention's provisions, interference with a right guaranteed is permitted where, *inter alia*, it is 'necessary in a democratic society'. The European Court of Human Rights draws on the comparative experience of European countries, including judicial experience in deciding what is necessary in a democratic society.[112] While states have a 'margin of appreciation' in determining what is 'necessary in a democratic society', the Court has held that the state's burden of justification will be higher where a substantial number of other states which are parties to the Convention have found it unnecessary to invoke such interference.[113]

In the European Court of Justice, too, the comparative method is highly developed, although the context in which it is used is somewhat different. A brief description of some of the essential features of Community law is necessary at this point. There was no explicit Bill of Rights in the treaties establishing the European Community. In several decisions the European Court of Justice developed a doctrine which gave supremacy to European Community law over the national laws of the Member States of the Community, including any provisions of national constitutions which conflicted with Community law. This gave rise to considerable unease in the highest courts in several Member States, particularly Germany, Italy, and France. They expressed concern that Community law could breach human rights but not be subject to any judicial human rights control either at the national level (because of the supremacy of Community law) or at European level (because of the absence of any explicit protection for human rights in the treaties). The Court of Justice, in response to this concern, interpreted the treaties to include, implicitly, human rights protections that were common to the constitutional law or practice of the Member States and the European Convention on Human Rights.[114] The

---

[112] Although commentators have not infrequently questioned how extensive such comparisons really are. See Rudolph Bernhardt, 'Thoughts on the Interpretation of Human Rights Treaties', in Franz Matscher and Herbert Petzold (eds.), *Protecting Human Rights: The European Dimension* (Cologne: Carl Heymanns Verlag, n.d.) at 67. So, too, Delmas-Marty considers:

> . . . the Court's exercises in comparative law are not sufficiently systematic to extract a rigorous 'common European denominator'. When the Court cites the situation in the 'majority' of the Member States, it is difficult to decide whether the Court is referring to the statistical majority or an ideal majority of those States with a high level of protection of individual rights.

(Mireille Delmas-Marty, *The European Convention for the Protection of Human Rights: International versus National Restrictions* (Dordrecht, London: Martinus Nijhoff, 1992), at 305).

[113] A good example of this process is to be found in the *Dudgeon* case, in which the Court held that the criminalization of acts of sodomy in Northern Ireland could not be upheld as 'necessary in a democratic society', in part because a consensus across Europe had developed in favour of decriminalization, though the Court did not cite explicit authority for this proposition: *Dudgeon v. United Kingdom* (1981) 4 EHRR 149.

[114] J. H. H. Weiler and Nicolas J. S. Lockhart, '"Taking Rights Seriously" Seriously: The European Court and Its Fundamental Rights Jurisprudence', 32 CMLR 51 (1995).

result has been that when the Court of Justice is called upon to consider whether, for example, Community legislation breaches these implicit human rights protections, a comparative approach is adopted.[115]

Usually, this does not result in a particularly detailed explicit analysis (either in the judgment of the Court or in the decision of the Advocate General) of Member States' constitutional provisions or practice. It appears to be the case that this research is in fact done by the Court staff, even though the details of this research may be made public only in a rather brief summary paragraph.[116] Occasionally, however, perhaps to reassure its audience of the methods it adopts generally, a detailed analysis is given of the constitutional law and practice of member states on the issue. The Court of Justice also makes extensive use of decisions by the European Court of Human Rights. This in spite of the fact that the membership of the Community is considerably smaller than the number of states who are parties to the European Convention on Human Rights, although all European Community Member States are also parties to the Convention.

Filling the vacuum created by an absence of indigenous jurisprudence

We can see that in several jurisdictions—South Africa may be one—the purpose of using foreign decisions is to fill a vacuum left by the temporary absence of (preferred) indigenous jurisprudence. In this context, the assumption is that when the national jurisprudence is sufficiently plentiful and sophisticated, the use of foreign law will decline significantly.[117] More youthful constitutions are more likely to be thought to require recourse to foreign jurisprudence. It has been argued that, for some countries (particularly the US), the constitutional tradition is so rich and the accretion of case law is so large that having regard to yet more case law from other countries would be redundant. Mearns has written, for example, that 'an attitude lingers that we [the US] have little to learn from countries whose constitutions have not reached the two-century mark'.[118] But it appears to be the case that, in general, we should expect that the

---

[115] Meinhard Hilf, 'Comparative Law and European Law', in *Encyclopedia of Public International Law*, vol. 1, 695; Pierre Pescatore, 'Le recours, dans la jurisprudence de la Cour de Justice des Communautéennes, a des Norms déduites de la comparaison des droits des états membres', 32 *Revue internationale de droit comparé*, 337.

[116] See Joseph H. H. Weiler, 'Eurocracy and Distrust', 61 *Washington Law Review* (1986), 1103 at 1121–32; C. N. Kakouris, 'Use of the Comparative Method by the Court of Justice of the European Communities', 6 *Pace International Law Review* (1994), 267.

[117] Cf. Albert Kiralfy, 'The Persuasive Authority of American Rulings in England', 23 *Tulane Law Review* (1946) 209, at 210.

[118] Edward A. Mearns, 'Emerging Trends in International Constitutionalism: A Comparative Approach', 28 *Case Western Journal of International Law* (1996) 1.

longer a country is from independence the greater will be the resort to indigenous judicial authority.[119]

The constitution: transformative or conservative?

A useful distinction can be drawn between constitutions that are conceived as transformative in whole or in part, and those that are not so conceived. A constitution is thought to be transformative when its purpose is to change the status quo from what it was at the time of enactment to something more desirable. A constitution would not be transformative where it is thought to reflect the best of what happened at the time of its enactment, and enactment is thought to have been intended to prevent a desirable status quo from being changed *for the worse*. The distinction is intended to reflect two different models which constitutions (and Bills of Rights) might fulfil, although the distinction is seldom as sharp in practice as might be supposed; there may even be deep disagreements over whether the constitution should be regarded as transformative in character. Where the constitution is perceived of as transformative, then it is more likely that foreign experience will be drawn on as examples of how such transformation is possible on particular issues (as has proven to be the case in India).[120] However, where the constitution is perceived to be conservative and where national history and tradition strongly influence what is regarded as the appropriate result, the reception of judicial approaches from other countries is likely to be infrequent.

Theories of law and legal interpretation

The issue of how far, and why, judges in one jurisdiction choose to have regard to, or to ignore, judicial decisions on human rights issues from another jurisdiction appears related also to which theory of law operates. Patrick Glenn develops the point well.[121] He distinguishes between what he regards as two differing underlying views of law: law as national response, and law as enquiry. Law as national response goes hand in hand with the developing idea of the Nation State, and an idea of legal positivism:

---

[119] See, e.g., the analysis of citation to foreign legal sources in Israel in Schar, Haris, and Gross, above, n. 24, at 217 ff (noting the significant decline in the citation of English cases over time since Independence).

[120] Callaghan uses this distinction as a basis for distinguishing between the Indian and the US Constitutions. She argues that, 'while the Indian drafters sought to use the Constitution as a means to transform Indian society, the American drafters sought to maintain the status quo with respect to social conditions' (Maureen B. Callaghan, 'Cultural Relativism and the Interpretation of Constitutional Texts', 30 *Willamette Law Review* (1994) 609 at 610).

[121] H. Patrick Glenn, 'Persuasive Authority', 32 *McGill Law Journal* (1987), 261.

... excluding all but the State itself, and its officers, as sources of law. . . . The idea gains currency that the extent of borrowing of foreign authority is a simple function of the adequacy of local sources and that local sources *can* be adequate if enough law is produced suitable to local conditions.

By contrast he identifies the approach of law as enquiry. This is how he describes it:

... to the extent that the law used by these officers is not definitely made and imposed upon them but is rather chosen by them in an ongoing process, the underlying notion of law is that of enquiry. There is never a closing of sources, never a declaration of satisfaction with existing knowledge, never a pure process of deduction from a single given, never an entire commitment to an exclusive paradigm of law.[122]

It would be unsurprising too if different theories of legal *interpretation* also influenced the reception of foreign judicial decisions. As Weissbrodt has argued as regards the American debate on constitutional interpretation:

There are some scholars, the originalists, who appear to reject any legal development that cannot claim its provenance in the text of the Constitution. As far as they are concerned, arguments about the evolving meaning of such basic principles as due process, cruel and unusual punishment, and freedom of speech may fall on deaf ears. If originalism is combined with a textualist fixation upon the words of the document and a refusal to consider the context or legislative history of those words, the result may be a mind completely closed to the usefulness of global influences or sources.[123]

Foreign law as empirical fact

One device which courts sometimes utilize in support of making controversial decisions is explicitly to draw on empirical and social scientific sources of information as a way of establishing their connectedness with the 'real world'. These attempts at justification of judicial adjudication of individual rights have proven immensely controversial, from the development of the Brandeis brief,[124] through the use of social-psychological evidence in *Brown v. Board of Education*,[125] and on down to the present

---

[122] *ibid.*, at 288.

[123] David Weissbrodt, 'Globalization of Constitutional Law and Civil Rights', 43 *Journal of Legal Education* (1993), 262 at 262.

[124] A 'Brandeis brief' is a 'documentary exposition of social and economic evidence designed to inform the court about the context of the case before it. The procedure is named after a submission by Josephine Goldmark and Louis Brandeis to the [US] Supreme Court' in *Muller v. Oregon*, Carol Harlow, 'Public Interest Litigation in England: The State of the Art', in Jeremy Cooper and Rajeev Dhavan (eds.), *Public Interest Law* (Oxford: Blackwell, 1986), 90 at 136.

[125] 347 US 483 (1954). See Richard Kluger, *Simple Justice* (New York: Knopf, 1976), *passim* on the debate over whether to introduce such evidence in the US school desegregation cases up to and including *Brown*.

day.[126] In the United States, when foreign experience is discussed, it is largely for the purpose of supporting empirically-based conclusions. We can usefully distinguish this 'empirical' fact-finding, as it might be called, from the 'moral' fact-finding of the type in which Justice Brennan engages in the death penalty cases discussed earlier. In the latter, moral significance is attached to the weight of other countries that had abolished capital punishment of juveniles.[127] Foreign law, including foreign judicial decisions, is currently interesting to United States courts, if at all, largely as data rather than as statements of legal or moral values in their own right. The best recent example is in the Supreme Court cases on physician-assisted suicide.[128] So, too, Justice Breyer in *Printz*, in justifying his references to European experience, argues that 'their experience may . . . cast an empirical light on the consequences of different solutions to a common legal problem.'[129] This approach is seen much less often in courts outside the United States.

Perceived judicial competence

A penultimate factor seems to be the extent of judicial fear that lack of competence in the technical legal aspects of the other jurisdiction will lead to mistakes being made, prompting an unease in using such cases as persuasive.[130] Nor is this fear groundless.[131] Recent examples where there has been a serious misreading of foreign experience include the use of (some) US 'affirmative action' cases by the European Court of Human Rights (but not the one directly in point—which indicated the opposite conclusion to that reached by the Court).[132] The increasing frequency of the English courts' resort to foreign cases brings with it, not surprisingly, an increased scrutiny by external commentators of the adequacy of the use to which these cases are put—usually arguing that the courts have misinterpreted

---

[126] See, e.g., Mark A. Chesler, *Social Science in Court: Mobilizing Experts in the School Desegregation Cases* (Madison: University of Wisconsin Press, 1988).

[127] I am grateful to Joan Larsen for pointing out this distinction to me. (For Justice Brennan's rulings see n. 51.)

[128] Christopher McCrudden, 'A Part of the Main?: The Physician-Assisted Suicide Cases and Comparative Law Methodology in the US Supreme Court', in Carl E. Schneider, *Law at the End of Life: The Supreme Court and Assisted Suicide* (Ann Arbor: University of Michigan Press, forthcoming).

[129] *Printz v. US* 521 US 898, at 977; 138 L Ed 2d 914, at 970 (1997).

[130] Cf. the patronizing rebuke in 1910 about the use of American precedents in India: 'We hope the Indian High Courts will not encourage these transatlantic excursions; but if they must go so far abroad, we think Canadian or Australasian decisions would be safer to play with.' Note, 36 *Law Quarterly Review* (1910), 192.

[131] For an extended critique in the European context, see Pierre Legrand 'How to compare now', 16 *Legal Studies* (1996) 232.

[132] *Kalanke v. Freie Hansestadt Bremen* Case C–450/93, 1995 ECR I–3051 which did not cite *Johnson v. Transportation Agency*, 480 US 616 (1987).

the foreign cases in important respects.[133] This is also likely to affect which judicial opinions of a foreign jurisdiction are cited. Foreign judges who are familiar names and 'of whose authority the court can be assured',[134] are more likely to be cited than those who are not. So, too, where lawyers appearing before the court, or clerks assisting the judge, give the judge confidence, then the decisions of foreign systems are more likely to be cited.

Differences in constitutional structure

Finally, to the extent that constitutional issues arise for adjudication, the sources of persuasive precedent are often controversial, and in need of justification. Therefore, the use of *foreign* persuasive authority might seem particularly questionable.[135] Perhaps especially where the issue is perceived as one affected by a nation's exceptionalism, judges may be more resistant to citation of persuasive authority from other jurisdictions.

TRANSNATIONAL JUDICIAL CONVERSATIONS ABOUT HUMAN RIGHTS

We could say, therefore, that (in general) a judge or court in one jurisdiction will not use case-law from another jurisdiction unless it is considered to be comparable, and unless the judge or court feels adequately informed about the other jurisdiction. A judge will probably use such case-law where this is necessary to avoid legal conflicts, where it is expressly mandated so to do, or where it is necessary to fill the vacuum created by a new constitutional settlement. Otherwise, the decision whether to use foreign judicial decisions seems largely in the realm of judicial discretion.

Simply to emphasize these factors, however, would miss a significant element in the emerging debate about when foreign *human rights* decisions are used, and about the appropriateness of this development. So far, in trying to explain what I think is going on, I have identified factors which are applicable to the use of foreign law *generally* as persuasive precedent. Is there something specific to *human rights* that explains the apparently greater use of foreign case law in human rights cases?

---

[133] See, e.g., Ian Loveland, 'The Constitutionalisation of Political Libels in English Common Law?' [1998], *Public Law*, 633.

[134] Kiralfy, above n. 117, at 215.

[135] Christopher Osakwe, 'Introduction: The Problems of the Comparability of Notions in Constitutional Law', 59 *Tulane Law Review* (1985), 875, at 876. See also P. John Kozyris, 'Comparative Law for the Twenty-First Century: New Horizons and New Technologies', 69 *Tulane Law Review* (1994), 165, at 170; and Eric Stein 'Uses, Misuses—And Nonuses of Comparative Law', 72 *Northwestern University Law Review* (1977), 198.

On one explanation, the use of foreign judgments is simply results-driven: advocates and judges simply use foreign decisions that support the result they want in the particular case before the Court. Indeed, there may even be a suspicion that the selective use of foreign judgments is inevitably associated with a rights-expanding agenda. But this would be mistaken. A few examples bear this out. Justice Frankfurter, consistently the Supreme Court Justice most favourably disposed to citing foreign cases, was certainly not pursuing a rights-expanding agenda. The high point of such an agenda in the United States was surely to be found during the 'Warren-era' when the Court seldom used foreign judicial precedents. In the European Court of Human Rights too, the use of the comparative technique has led to judicial timidity as often as judicial activism ('unless there is a consensus, then expansion of rights is inappropriate').

Another possible explanation is that judges consider that they are 'discovering' already-established meanings; that human rights is some form of new natural law. This does not strike me as persuasive; certainly judges do not *say* that is what they are doing. Nor do judges using foreign judgments appear to assume either that in doing so they are engaged only in a process of developing *international* human rights law, as opposed to interpreting indigenous provisions, though clearly the existence of international human rights covenants adds to a perception of human rights as expressing universal principles.[136] Most judges using comparative judicial decisions recognize, indeed *insist* on, the constructed and (to some extent) contingent nature of decision-making on issues of contemporary human rights. Foreign judgments are not thought to be laying down a discovered truth or interpreting higher law, but rather to be struggling through a series of conflicting principles which need to be resolved in conversation with judges in other countries,[137] however different the outcome may be in each country. As La Forest, of the Supreme Court of Canada has written extra-judicially, 'The greater use of foreign material affords another source, another tool for the construction of better judgments. . . . The

---

[136] Gérard V. La Forest, 'The Use of American Precedents in Canadian Courts' 46 *Maine Law Review* (1994), 211 at 216:

> In dealing with cases involving human rights, we make frequent references to international instruments and their application both by international bodies and domestic courts in various countries. This is, in part, a reflection not only of the fact that the Charter and other human rights instruments were adopted against the background of the post-War international recognition of human rights throughout the globe but is also grounded in a belief in the value of comparative analysis. Thus, we frequently cite European sources with regard to . . . human rights . . . .

[137] Stychin has noted how rights discourse 'facilitiates constitutional "conversations" between a plurality of political actors and legal orders' (Carl F. Stychin, 'Relatively universal: globalization, rights discourse, and the evolution of Australian sexual and national identities', 18 *Legal Studies* (1998), 534, at 555).

greater use of foreign materials by courts and counsel in all countries can, I think, only enhance their effectiveness and sophistication.'[138]

For a court to be willing to engage in the comparative task, as Slaughter argues, there is likely to be an 'awareness of a common enterprise, even if only in the sense of confrontation of common issues or problems'.[139] She continues: 'Recognition of this commonality does not obviate cultural differences, but it assumes the possibility that generic legal problems such as the balancing of rights and duties, individual and community interests, and the protection of individual expectations, may transcend those differences.'[140] In the human rights context, Slaughter suggests that there is now an increasing:

recognition of a global set of human rights issues to be resolved by courts around the world in colloquy with one another. Such recognition flows from the ideology of universal human rights. . . . The premise of universalism, however, does not anoint any one tribunal with universal authority to interpret and apply these rights. Collective judicial deliberation, through awareness, acknowledgment, and use of decisions rendered by fellow human rights tribunals, frames a universal process of judicial deliberation and decision.[141]

She argues that, 'Courts engaged in transjudicial communication . . ., conceive of themselves as autonomous actors forging an autonomous relationship with their foreign or supranational counterparts.'[142] Partly as a result, Beatty has argued that '. . . the same set of principles and analytical framework to test the constitutional validity of the various rules and regulations they are asked to review' are in place in Washington, Tokyo, New Delhi, Strasbourg, Rome, Karlsruhe, and Ottawa.[143]

This sense of commonality is not restricted to judges. It appears also to be an increasing feature of the legal profession and human rights groups.

---

[138] La Forest, above, n. 136, at 220.

[139] Anne-Marie Slaughter, 'A Typology of Transjudicial Communication', above, n. 23 at 127. e.g., in one case, the Irish Supreme Court was referred to the decision of the German Constitutional Court in the *Official Propaganda* case and held that although the case was based on a constitution other than the Irish Constitution, it was 'persuasive authority (as a comparative Constitution) on fundamental principles of democracy and equality which, as a basic tenet, are common to both Constitutions' (*In re Bunreacht Na hEireann; McKenna v. An Taoiseach* [1996] 1 ILRM 81 (Supreme Court)).

[140] Anne-Marie Slaughter, 'A Typology of Transjudicial Communication', above, n. 23 at 127.

[141] *ibid.* at 121–2.

[142] *ibid.*, at 123.

[143] David Beatty, 'The Canadian Charter of Rights: Lessons and Laments', 60 *Modern Law Review* 481 (1997):

The Supreme Court of Canada has read the Charter in the same way Bills of Rights have been interpreted all over the world, to include two broad principles of rationality (also known as necessity or avoidability) and proportionality (also known as consistency or equality) which politicians and public officials are obliged to respect . . . [T]he jurisprudence of the Supreme Court of Canada provides . . . evidence that there is a set of neutral . . . principles . . . which lie at the core of the concept of constitutional rights . . .

The role of NGOs in stimulating recognition of the potential relevance of judicial developments in other countries should not be underestimated. One need only look at Internet websites to see the importance of this development. The increased use of foreign judicial decisions is also one among many examples of the vastly increased flow of information and ideas across borders in recent years assisted by the extraordinary technological advances of the past decade.

JUDICIAL GLOBALIZATION AND ITS DISCONTENTS

This 'common enterprise' analysis strikes me as having a considerable degree of accuracy, in describing what many judges engaging in citation of authority across national boundaries in human rights cases think they are doing. In particular, it may help to explain, in part, why United States Supreme Court decisions are particularly thin in discussions of foreign human rights decisions. I suspect, but cannot prove, that the sense of sharing a common enterprise with judges in other jurisdictions is relatively under-developed in that court. A small, though I suggest significant, use of language illustrates the point. Whereas courts in other jurisdictions appear frequently to characterize their domestic rights judgments as 'human rights' decisions, the more common phrase in the United States courts is 'constitutional rights' or 'civil rights'. 'Human rights' seems more associated often with something that happens abroad, not at home.

But is the idea (where it exists) of a common enterprise in human rights adjudication something to welcome? There is concern among some sceptics of such transnational judicial conversations that the phenomenon of national courts getting together on human rights and 'working things out' among themselves is somewhat troubling. If we are concerned about the legitimacy of *national* judges making these decisions—isn't the idea of judges making these decisions *transnationally*, in a cosy dialogue with each other, even more worrying? What follows is the view of Justice Scalia, dissenting, in *Thompson v. Oklahoma*, the death penalty case discussed earlier:

We must never forget that it is a Constitution for the United States of America that we are expounding. The practices of other nations, particularly other democracies, can be relevant to determining whether a practice uniform among our people is not merely a historical accident, but rather 'so implicit in the concept of ordered liberty' that it occupies a place not merely in our mores but, text permitting, in our Constitution as well. . . . But where there is not first a settled consensus among our own people, the views of other nations, however enlightened the Justices of this Court may think them to be, cannot be imposed upon Americans through the Constitution.[144]

[144] *Thompson v. Oklahoma* 487 US at 869, n. 4 (citations omitted).

Later, addressing a conference of judges from the Americas, he argued, '. . . we judges of the American democracies are servants of our peoples, sworn to apply, without fear or favor, the laws that those peoples deem appropriate. We are not some international priesthood empowered to impose upon our free and independent citizens supra-national values that contradict their own.'[145]

To an extent, of course, this interestingly echoes at least two of the concerns expressed over globalization generally, that the global will overwhelm the local and that an unelected international élite will subvert elected representatives, with loss of diversity and a decline in democratic decision-making. We return, therefore, by a somewhat circuitous route perhaps, to one of the issues with which this chapter began: how far, and in what circumstances, judicial, as opposed to political, decision-making is legitimate in this area. Failure to address the democratic concerns about the use of transnational persuasive precedents may undermine support for judicial protection for human rights rather than underpin it. So far, our legal theory seems not sufficiently to have caught up with, and certainly not resolved, this difficulty.

The connection between globalization (or, better, international market liberalization) and transnational human rights dialogue does not end there, for human rights thinking has been seen as one of the tools by which such liberalization can take place.[146] Where a reason for the form of national constitution adopted, or the approach to human rights taken, is in part to provide a ticket for entry into a desirable trading group (which it sometime is),[147] then it is even more likely that comparative experience will be drawn on in its interpretation. That is both a strength and a weakness for the development of a transnational human rights culture, and for the use of foreign precedents. If economic liberalization succeeds in becoming an accepted new economic order, transnational human rights will be strengthened. If economic liberalization fails, however, to gain the support of the population in that country then, to the extent that transnational human rights is seen as part and parcel of that enterprise, it will be concomitantly weakened.

There is a third concern. In the judicial interpretation and application of human rights principles, the voices of the historically disadvantaged and

---

[145] Antonin Scalia, 'Commentary', 40 *Saint Louis University Law Journal* (1996), 1119, at 1122.

[146] See e.g. Jeffrey D. Sachs, 'Globalization and the Rule of Law', *Yale Law School Occasional Papers*, second series, no. 4 (1998).

[147] Rolando Gaete, 'Rites of Passage into the Global Village', VI *Law and Critique* 113 (1995) at 114, 'Human rights have become a banner representing the "civilizing mission" of financial institutions and of the countries that provide most of the funds for these institutions'). Gerhard Casper, 'European Convergence', 58 *University of Chicago Law Review* (1991), 441, at 444–5, 'On the whole, Eastern Europe will follow Western European examples. The Eastern Europeans will find this path pragmatically desirable because of their aspirations to join the Council of Europe and, more importantly, the European Community.'

marginalized are the voices least often heard, nationally and internationally. One way in which that silence is maintained is to make human rights the preserve of lawyers. There is, of course, a crucially important role for lawyers in human rights enforcement and interpretation. But too often, lawyers regard vexed questions of what human rights are as best viewed as technical legal questions, in part to distinguish them from the 'political'.

The silence of those who are most likely to benefit from human rights in debates about the meaning and interpretation of such rights is a complex issue. At the heart of proposals to end this silence lie a series of questions about making modern democracies more inclusive. One way in which some have sought to increase inclusivity in rights interpretations and application is to increase opportunities for the more effective representation of the views of those who are currently excluded. This involves increasing the opportunities for groups to voice an analysis of how policies affect them, and generating policy proposals themselves, in contexts where decision-makers are obliged to show that they have taken these perspectives into consideration. This involves more than merely including individual members of these previously excluded groups in these institutions. It is more a question of the institutions' openness to considerably increased participation in their deliberations by those affected by their decisions.[148] We have seen already that it would be a mistake to suppose that courts are immune from the effects of transnational civil society.[149] In any event, ignoring the problem of participation, whilst at the same time appearing to engage in a closed dialogue with other judges at the supranational level, may weaken the protection of human rights rather than reinforce it. This would be more than a little ironic, given that a principal reason for citing foreign judgments is to *increase* the legitimacy of judicial decision-making in the area of human rights.

CONCLUSION

I am conscious that I have done little more than identify some of the issues that a more complete study of the complex phenonemon discussed in the chapter should examine more systematically. Essentially, I have identified some empirical questions (how far does it happen, and where?), a jurisprudential question (can we identify criteria which help explain why it does or does not happen?), and a normative question (is it legitimate?).

[148] For an interesting perspective on this in the context of judicial decision-making, see Hugh Collins, 'Democracy and Adjudication', in Neil MacCormick and Peter Birks (eds.), *The Legal Mind* (Oxford: Clarendon Press, 1986), 67.

[149] A partial response to Scalia J's concern about a global judicial priesthood may be that the pressure to adopt a comparative approach is not necessarily judicially-led but often lawyer/pressure-group led. Whether this rebuts Scalia's concerns about elitism, or merely enlarges the set of elites involved is a nice question.

None of these basic questions have been adequately answered. The empirical question requires more consistently-gathered evidence than the somewhat anecdotal evidence presented here. The jurisprudential question requires a more thorough examination of how the phenomenon is illuminated by current debates on the theory of judicial interpretation. The normative question requires a closer study of the relationship between the phenomenon and the universality of human rights.

Of the three questions identified, the empirical and the jurisprudential are the most pressing, and probably the most difficult to resolve. What would be an appropriate methodology to adopt as a way of addressing these questions? Three approaches seem particularly worth exploring. The first would involve an application of the increasingly sophisticated field of citation analysis.[150] A second approach would engage in in-depth qualitative case studies of particular national jurisdictions. A third would analyse how the phenomenon of transfer of judgments has occurred or did not occur in the context of particular substantive human rights issues. Clearly the issue is unlikely to go away. We should, at least, therefore, attempt to understand it better.

---

[150] The classic studies in the US have spawned a sub-discipline of legal scholarship (the 'classics' being: John H. Merryman, 'The Authority of Authority: What the California Supreme Court Cited in 1950', 6 *Stanford Law Review* (1954), 613 and 'Toward a Theory of Citations: An Empirical Study of the Citation Practice of the California Supreme Court in 1950, 1960, and 1970', 50 *Southern California Law Review* (1977) 381; and Lawrence M. Friedman *et al*, 'State Supreme Courts: A Century of Style and Citation', 33 *Stanford Law Review* (1981) 773. See, for recent discussions, Richard Posner, 'The Theory and Practice of Citations Analysis, with Special Reference to Law and Economics', *John M. Olin Law and Economics Working Paper No. 83* (2nd series), University of Chicago.

3

Enfants Trouvés, *Anonymous Mothers, and Children's Identity Rights*

Katherine O'Donovan

> . . . early tomorrow morning we will take the children out into the forest to where it is the thickest . . . they will not find the way home again and we shall be rid of them.
> . . .
> When at last they awoke, it was already dark night. Gretel began to cry and said: 'How are we to get out of the forest now?'[1]

Abandoning, or 'exposing', a child under the age of 2 is a specific criminal offence in English law under section 27 of the Offences Against the Person Act 1861. There are also a variety of charges which can be brought against an adult who abandons a child over 2.

In this paper I bring together two areas on which Brian Simpson has written so elegantly: legal history, and human rights. The history of abandonment shows a movement from charitable concern in the Middle Ages, to the criminalization of parents since the early modern era. Today the language of human rights enters a space, somewhere between crime and welfare, in discussions of children, and of the parents who abandon them. We are more likely to speak of the rights of the child. Specifically the language of identity rights may be used in discussion of the abandonment of small children. Concern focuses not so much on protecting life, as on the child's loss of knowledge about genetic family and kin.

The paper arises from my curiosity about a difference between French and English law on abandonment. Under French law it is possible for a woman to accept maternity, but to reject motherhood. This is because there is a step in legal reasoning between giving birth and being registered as a legal mother. No such step exists in English law.

The idea that a woman, after giving birth, might make a rational decision not to become a mother is not entertained in English law nor in the general understanding of womanhood. This idea is, however, present in French law and practice.

And this difference persists despite ratification of the United Nations Convention on the Rights of the Child by both states. In drawing on

---

[1] *Grimm's Fairy Tales* (London: Routledge & Kegan Paul, 1982), 18–19.

aspects of the history of abandonment in both jurisdictions, I am curious as to how different attitudes to abandonment developed, and whether they can be reconciled with an international convention which has received almost universal adherence. Because the story of abandonment in Europe is a topic which touches the deepest emotions, it has drawn on myth and fairytale in the telling.

Returning to the text of 1861, we find that it speaks of endangering the life of, and of permanent injury to the health of the child, suggesting that the parliament of 1860 was concerned about protection from physical harm rather than loss of identity. This raises the question of why an age-limit of 2 was chosen, although the helplessness of infants may be the answer.[2]

Section 27 can be read as new law in 1861, although there was an element of codification of case law. At common law then, if the child survived exposure, conviction of the parent did not necessarily follow. In *R v. Renshaw*,[3] a mother left her child of 10 days at the bottom of a ditch (which had a path running through it). Parke, B. said that:

... there were no marks of violence on the child, and it does not appear in the result that the child actually experienced any inconvenience, as it was providentially found soon after it was exposed, and therefore, although it is said in some of the books that an exposure to the inclemency of the weather may amount to an assault, yet, if that be so at all, it can only be when the Person suffers a hurt or injury of some kind or other from the exposure.

Other reported cases from the mid-nineteenth century emphasize endangerment to life or health.[4] The courts were reluctant to convict, and insisted on some form of injury to the child, even in obvious cases of exposure.[5] When the legislation was presented to Parliament the Solicitor-General stated that it was a consolidating measure and very little debate took place.[6]

Subsequent cases show that 'endangering life' through abandonment has been given importance in convictions.[7] No criminal cases have been reported in the past 30 years, although prosecutions and cautions still

---

[2] Hendrick, H., *Children, Childhood, and English Society, 1880–1990* (Cambridge: Cambridge University Press, 1997), 21, '. . . until well into this century "newborns" were not usually viewed as persons and, therefore, were not always loved as "children".' Other historians suggest that parents 'distanced' themselves emotionally from infants under 2 because of high mortality rates.

[3] (1847) 2 Cox 285; (1847) 9 LT(OS) 395; 11 Jur 615.

[4] *R v. March* (1844) 1 Car & Kir 496; *R v. Cooper* (1849) 1 Den. 459; *R v. Hogan* (1851) 2 Den 277, 169 ER 504.

[5] In *Reg v. Gray* (1857) D & B 303, 169 ER 1017, where an infant was left exposed on open ground, the charge was brought under the statute 7 Wm. IV & 1 Vict., c. 85, but the element of danger to life was held to be lacking because the child was found before any injury was suffered, and because exposure lacked an active element.

[6] Hansard (1860) vol. 159, para. 270, House of Commons, second reading.

[7] *R v. Falkingham* (1870) L. R. 1 CCR 222.

occur.[8] Since 1934, most of these take place under the Children and Young Persons Act 1933, even where the child is under 2.[9]

Definitions of 'abandonment' are to be found in adoption proceedings in addition to criminal cases.[10] A rise in the number of prosecutions and cautions for abandonment can be observed towards the end of the century: from 15 in 1982, to 65 in 1996.[11] However, any conclusions to be drawn from government statistics must be tempered by two factors. First, an alternative prosecution is available under the later Act which is more generally designed for the protection of children under 16.[12] Furthermore, there is social evidence that in the majority of cases of abandonment mother and infant are reunited, and no further legal action ensues. Most cases are treated by the police as social welfare matters, and public expressions of concern are usually for the mother.[13] When asking her to come forward a form of words is generally used which refers to the fact that she may be in need of medical attention.

The Victorians did not express their concern for children in terms of rights. Children's rights are largely a twentieth-century invention.[14] Yet issues of rights are raised by abandonment, and not only rights of safety and protection, but also what are today known as 'identity rights'. Whereas an older child may be able to say where she lives, an infant will not be able to do so. Is this a reason for the apparent recent rise in criminal prosecutions for abandonment?[15] In speculating in this way, a distinction

[8] *R v. White* (1871) 36 J. P. 134; *R v. Williams* (1910) 4 Cr. App. R. 89; *R v. Whibley* [1938] 3 All E R.

[9] *Reg v. Hayles* [1969] 1 QB 364.

[10] Abandonment was defined in *Mitchell v. Wright* (1905) 7 F 568 as, 'leaving the child to its fate'. Although this was a Scottish case, the definition was applied in subsequent English cases. In *Watson v. Nikolaisen* [1955] 2 QB 286, the mother was said not to have abandoned her child where she had made care arrangements.

[11] Home Office, *Criminal Statistics 1996*, Cm 3764, table 5.11.

[12] The Children and Young Persons Act 1933, s. 1 provides:

> If any person who has attained the age of 16 years and has the custody, charge, or care of any child or young person under that age, wilfully assaults, ill-treats, neglects, abandons, or exposes him, or causes him to be assaulted, ill-treated, neglected, abandoned, or exposed, in a manner likely to cause him unnecessary suffering or injury to health . . . that person shall be guilty of an offence.

The maximum penalty is imprisonment for 2 years. Abandonment was interpreted in *R v. Boulden* (1957) 41 Cr App R 105 as leaving a child to his fate.

[13] Interviews with social workers 1998 and 1999. See also, e.g., the report in *Guardian*, 27 Dec. 1996, p.6, of an abandoned baby found in bushes. The police statement was concerned with the mother, 'She may be in need of medical attention and we would ask her to come forward as soon as possible.'

[14] The literature is vast. See, e.g., Fortin, J., *Children's Rights and the Developing Law* (London: Butterworths, 1988), ch. 1; Freeman, M., *The Rights and Wrongs of Children* (London: Frances Pinter, 1983); Alston, P., Parker, S. and Seymour, J., *Children's Rights and the Law* (Oxford: Clarendon Press, 1992).

[15] I use the term 'apparent', as it has not proved possible to disaggregate the prosecutions and convictions under the Children and Young Persons Act, s.1 into those relating to abandonment and those relating to other forms of cruelty.

must be made between a law directed at parental responsibility to make arrangements for children in an orderly fashion (such as in a foundling home or placement in care) on the one hand; and the safeguarding of a child's knowledge of the identity of his or her parents on the other.

Child abandonment has not received much attention from legal scholars. Notwithstanding a growth in writings on the history of childhood, historians have more often commented on the absence of children from the written record.[16] Yet child abandonment played a significant part in early modern experiences. Perhaps the tragedy implicit in abandonment deters investigation, and respect for privacy makes empirical research difficult, particularly where the legal process has not been pursued. That there has long been a human understanding about lost children is evident from folklore and stories ranging from Oedipus, through Romulus and Remus, to Hansel and Gretel.

HUMAN RIGHTS CONTEXT

Children's rights to know their parents, and their own life stories, have become human rights celebrated under Article 8 of the European Convention on Human Rights and under Articles 7 and 8 of the United Nations Convention on the Rights of the Child. The European Court of Human Rights has interpreted Article 8 of the European Convention as recognizing a right to one's own life story. In *Gaskin v. UK* the issue was access to personal files by a person who spent his childhood in care. The right in question was expressed by the Court as follows: '. . . persons in the position of the applicant have a vital interest, protected by the Convention, in receiving the information necessary to know and understand their childhood and early development.'[17]

The files on a childhood in public care were accepted by a majority of the Court as a substitute for parental memory, normally available to children brought up within a family. Although arising from the specific issue of access to files in the hands of a local authority about growing up in care,[18] the potential for wider reading of 'life story' is evident. Information about the applicant had been placed by foster parents and care workers in the files on a confidential basis. However, the majority of the Court held that

---

[16] Laslett, P., *The World We Have Lost* (London: Methuen, 1971), 140. 'These crowds and crowds of little children are strangely absent from the written record.' For recent works on the history of childhood see, Hendricks, above n. 2. The literature has grown, particularly since the *History of Childhood Quarterly* was first published in the 1970s. See also, DeMause, L., *The History of Childhood* (London: Souvenir Press, 1976); Cunningham, H., *Children and Childhood in Western Society* (London: Longman, 1995); Pollock, L., *Forgotten Children*, (Cambridge: Cambridge University Press, 1983). Pollock acknowledges the problem of lack of recorded data on children.

[17] *Gaskin v. UK* (1989) 12 EHRR 36.   [18] *Gaskin v. Liverpool CC* [1980] 1 WLR 1549 (CA).

Article 8 imposed a positive obligation on the state to interpose an independent adjudicator between applicant and state to decide whether the continued confidentiality of information was really necessary. The UK governmental response was the Access to Personal Files Act 1987,[19] which places an obligation on public authorities to provide access to personal information on individuals kept in records.[20]

The United Nations Convention on the Rights of the Child contains a greater commitment to children's identity rights. The *travaux préparatoires* indicate that it was at the behest of the Argentine delegation that Article 8 was included in the Convention. The heroic grandmothers of Plaza de Mayo had, through silent assembly in a public square, drawn attention to the fate of their grandchildren whose parents had 'disappeared' during the military dictatorship.[21] Between 1975 and 1983—a period known as the 'Dirty War'—an estimated 30% of those who disappeared were women, some with children.[22] It is known that 3% per cent of these women were pregnant.[23] The history of what happened to the children remains unclear, but state orphanages, abduction, and illegal adoption all played a part. Some children born in military detention centres were removed from their mothers at birth, without having been registered, or even named. Their origins were deliberately destroyed. This policy of deliberate concealment of births was followed by further steps, often involving the subsequent murder of the mothers.[24]

Research on this period of Argentine history shows the problems associated with reconstructing events, 'Prisoners in advanced stages of pregnancy were kept blindfolded and guarded. In most cases they were subjected to Caesarian operations, after which the mothers were separated from their babies and never seen again.'[25]

In response to these events the grandmothers of Plaza de Mayo formed a pressure group which continues the search for the lost children. Their actions are motivated by the idea that the children who have been located have a right to know who their genetic parents are, and to decide where and with whom they wish to live.

[19] The Act is also a response to the freedom of information campaign. It gives a general right of access to personal information held by authorities, subject to restrictions contained in statutory instruments. See Access to Personal Files (Social Services) Regs 1989, SI 1989/206.

[20] Personal information held by local social services authorities is, subject to regulations, to be accessible to living individuals under s.1, from 15 May 1987. The Act is remarkable for its negativity and restrictions.

[21] The *Guardian* reported on 26 Nov. 1998 that a member of the military junta that ruled the Argentine between 1976 and 1983 had been imprisoned by a Buenos Aires judge, prior to the hearing of charges based on the grounds of the kidnapping of children born to mothers in detention. At least 259 cases are pending.

[22] Van Bueren, G., *The International Law on the Rights of the Child* (The Hague: Nijhoff, 1995), ch. 4.

[23] *ibid.*   [24] Fisher, J., *Mothers of the Disappeared* (Boston: South End Press, 1989).

[25] *ibid.*, 107.

During the drafting of the Convention on the Rights of the Child the Argentine delegation argued for Article 8, which specifically states a right to protection of identity. Initial objections by other states that the elements of identity were covered by other Articles were later withdrawn out of respect and sympathy.[26] However, the conclusion can be drawn that the wording of Article 8 is weak, and results from sympathy rather than legal analysis. Under it, states: 'undertake to respect the right of the child to preserve his or her identity, including nationality, name and family relations as recognized by law without undue interference.'

The remedial duties which states accept under Article 8 are to render appropriate assistance to children 'illegally deprived' of some or all the elements of their identity. The speedy re-establishment of identity is accepted by states as an obligation. However, identity is a concept which may be thought to encompass most or all of the elements of personality. Nowhere in the Convention is identity defined beyond the elements of nationality, name, and family relations mentioned in the first paragraph of Article 8. Commentators regard this list as non-exhaustive, so the concept remains open.[27] As the Convention does not attempt to define 'identity' there is a wide margin for interpretation in the enactment of domestic law.

Article 7 of the Convention does not refer to 'identity'. It refers to the right to a name, registration after birth, the right to acquire a nationality, and as far as possible to know and to be cared for by parents. These are specific rights which might be thought to render a general right to identity otiose. Yet on closer inspection the right, as far as possible, to know one's parents raises many difficulties. Nonetheless, it can provide a legal justification for criminalizing the abandonment of children, separate from issues of survival and danger to health.

ABANDONMENT IN FACT AND FICTION

As children, we all hear fairytales and read our lives into them. But we also want to see and realize our lives as virtual fairytales even as we grow older. We never abandon fairytales.[28]

Analysis of the literary fairytale is part of a larger academic history of storytelling. The oral tradition of European folk-tales was appropriated by the literary fairytale and the recording and writings of Hansel and Gretel, as a tale of abandonment, have a history of their own.[29] The narrative path fol-

---

[26] Cerda, 'The Draft Convention on the Rights of the Child: New Rights', *Human Rights Quarterly* 12 (1990) 115.

[27] Stewart, G. A., 'Interpreting the Child's Right to Identity in the UN Convention on the Rights of the Child' *Family Law Quarterly* 26 (1992), 221.

[28] Zipes, J., *Happily Ever After* (New York and London: Routledge, 1997), 1.

[29] First told to Wilhelm Grimm by Dortchen Wild (later to be his wife), and recorded in the Olenberg MS of 1810, the story was printed in 1812. However, the Grimm brothers

lowed by such stories is said by scholars to provide a way for individuals to think and talk about their own lives. The pursuit of identity and the fulfilment of personal goals are said to be linked to the fairytale genre. Bruno Bettelheim sees folk-tales as enabling children to deal with their inner problems, and as giving structure to their daydreams and existential dilemmas.[30] But the fairytale has also been cast in more sinister light as manipulative of visions of the world. It seems that the fairytale may be interpreted ethnographically as relating to the material conditions of the peasantry, but also psychoanalytically as an imaginative projection of creative writers, thus challenging Bettelheim's therapeutic analysis.[31]

Bettelheim takes a teleological view of childhood: that it is preparation for being an adult. His analysis places child development as central, implying inadequacy according to adult standards and benchmarks.[32] Alison Lurie considers some of Bettelheim's interpretations of fairytales are over-determined by orthodox Freudian analysis, but finds interesting his insight 'that the various protagonists of a story often represent conflicting motives or emotions with a single individual accommodating our identities'.[33]

Doubts have been expressed over Bettelheim's claims that fairytales help humans find their ways through universal existential dilemmas. To Haase, 'Bettelheim's point of view is problematic because what he believes to be universal truths ultimately turn out to be the values of nineteenth-century Europe.'[34] Although some versions of fairytales may contain repressive moral lessons,[35] and claims to prescribe universal normative modes of being human can be condemned as ethnocentric, nevertheless Haase concedes that, if readers avoid 'reading fairytales as models of

acknowledged the similarities with Giambattista Basile's *Ninnillo and Nennella* (1697) and with Charles Perrault's *Le Petit Poucet* (1634). See Zipes, *ibid.*, 41–6.

[30] Bettelheim, B., *The Uses of Enchantment* (Harmondsworth: Pelican Books, 1977). Bettelheim's interpretation of certain fairytales is challenged by Zipes. e.g., to Zipes the story of Little Red Riding Hood is not a way for girls to overcome their fears of rape, but a warning and threat. The particular criticism of Bettelheim is that he did not appreciate that the literary fairytale has passed through the imagination of the writer, who is more than a recorder. Zipes views the Riding Hood tale as a male projection. See Zipes, J. (ed.), *The Trials and Tribulations of Little Red Riding Hood* (London: Routledge, 1993), 349–50.

[31] Zipes, J., *Breaking the Magic Spell: Radical Theories and Fairy Tales* (London: Heinemann, 1979). See also Dundes, A., *Little Red Riding Hood: A Casebook* (Madison: University of Wisconsin, 1989).

[32] For a critique of all theories of childhood as constructed, and of development psychology as based on the idea of the child 'becoming' according to a series of adult benchmarks, see Jenks, C., *Childhood* (London: Routledge, 1996), ch. 2.

[33] Lurie, A., *Don't Tell the Grown Ups* (London: Bloomsbury, 1990).

[34] Haase, D., 'Yours, Mine, or Ours? Perrault, the Brothers Grimm, and the Ownership of Fairy Tales', in Tatar, M. (ed.), *The Classic Fairy Tales* (New York: Norton, 1999) 359.

[35] Bettelheim's interpretation of Hansel and Gretel is of the child freeing himself from the mother, of promitive satisfactions, of oral regression, of the gingerbread house as a symbol of the mother's body, of the good mother who nourishes and the bad mother who makes demands and imposes restrictions, untamed id impulses, the dangers of unrestrained oral greed and dependence. See Bettelheim, above n. 30, pp. 159–66.

behaviour and normalcy, they can become for us revolutionary documents that encourage the development of personal autonomy'.[36]

Various versions of fairytales can be found throughout the world. There are versions of Cinderella from Japan, the Philippines, China, India, the Middle East, France, Germany, and England.[37] Such stories (originating in oral traditions) might claim to be universal. One aspect is the narrative form, which scholars agree gives structure to the ways in which children, and the adults they become, give direction to their lives and understand themselves. When the various versions of fairytales are compared, including those from beyond the Western canon, it can be seen that not only do these moral tales contain varied messages, but they are susceptible to a plurality of interpretations. For the purposes of this essay *Hansel and Gretel* is of interest as ethnography.

The history of abandonment will never be fully written, and scholars freely admit that the demographic data is impossible to reconstruct. We shall never know the extent of, or the outcomes for, lost children. This is why tradition and folk-tales, often finding form in printed creative writings, are a source. Even after allowance has been made for the needs of plot, genre, and message, printed stories are said to provide, 'extremely valuable clues about many details of abandonment', and to 'correspond closely to the facts recoverable from more traditional historical sources'.[38] The fairytale has been analysed as instructional, moral, patriarchal, and as containing a symbolic code and order. It has been rewritten as parody, as a feminist account, or with different stereotypes, in order to present new accounts or new messages. But however it is presented, theorists are agreed on its instructional aspects, both direct and indirect. As Walter Benjamin explains it:

The folk-tale, which to this day is the first tutor of children because it was once the first tutor of humankind, secretly lives on in the story. . . . the wisest thing—so the folk-tale-taught humankind in older times and teaches [sic] children to this day— is to meet the forces of the mythical world with cunning and high spirits.[39]

Not only is there agreement on the sending of messages by stories, but also on the effect of the narrative form in influencing constructions of identity. Hansel and Gretel as a narrative can be analysed on a variety of levels. For Jack Zipes, one of the leading academic commentators on the

---

[36] Haase, above n. 34, 361.

[37] Tatar, M. (ed.), *The Classic Fairy Tales* (New York: Norton, 1999), 101–37.

[38] Boswell, J., *The Kindness of Strangers: The Abandonment of Children in Western Europe from Late Antiquity to the Renaissance* (London: Pantheon, 1988), 429.

[39] Benjamin, W., 'The Storyteller', *Illuminations*, trans. Zohn, Harry (New York: Harcourt, Brace, and World, 1986), 102, cited by Zipes, above n. 28, 135. Perrault, one of the earliest storytellers to commit fairytales to writing in 1697 with his *Histoire ou contes du temps passé*, was quite clear that these were moral, elevating tales, designed to appeal to parents eager for instruction to their children. See, Opie, I. and P., *The Classic Fairy Tales* (New York: Oxford University Press, 1980).

fairytale genre, this tale demonizes women, extols patriarchy, and recon-
ciles children to hierarchy.[40] This view is based on the conclusion to the
tale in which the children are reunited with their father—the (step) mother
having conveniently died.[41] Yet it is Gretel who has the quick wits to push
the witch into the oven, and who persuades the little duck to take them
home across the river, thus saving the pair. As ever, interpretation remains
with the reader or listener. Zipes recognizes this in his discussion of the
psychosociological dimensions: 'the receiver will project conscious and
unconscious feelings onto the tale at an individual level.'[42]

The popularity of Hansel and Gretel as the number one tale in Germany,
where it was first published, and in Europe and North America, is
accounted for through a common denominator of children's experiences
of some form of abuse and continual fear of abandonment throughout
childhood. There was justification for this in the past since the abandonment rate reached 40% of births in parts of Europe in the eighteenth century.[43] John Boswell notes that 'abandonment is such a regular fulcrum for
plots in ancient literature . . . that it is somewhat difficult to imagine its
effectiveness if it were not part of the experience of much of the audience'.[44] In other words, the literary tale has ethnographical roots.

From Oedipus, through Moses, Romulus and Remus, to the Arabian
Nights, the loss and recovery of children are themes in literature. Mistaken
identities, mixing-up of babies in hospitals, and changelings—all catch the
popular imagination. Yet should we distinguish early modern abandon-
ments from those of late modernity? Just as the fairytale is said to enable
children to confront their deepest fears, and have a 'happy-ever-after
resolution', the traditional abandonment stories emphasized triumph
over circumstances and a joyous reunion with parents. The stories, however, seem to be designed to reassure parents, perhaps more than children.
To Boswell the most significant aspect of the medieval abandonment literature is its hopefulness.

It is predicated, like its ancient antecedents, on a universal belief that exposed children not only survive but flourish; not only overcome the difficulties of being
abandoned but rise through them to greatness, becoming popes, missionaries,

---

[40] Zipes, above n. 28, ch. 2.

[41] For a psychoanalytic account of fairytales containing a stepmother see, Schectman, J.,
The Step Mother in Fairytales (Boston: Sigo Press, 1993).

[42] Zipes, above n. 28, 56.

[43] Boswell, above n. 38 cites Delasselle, C., 'Les enfants abandonnés a Paris au xviii siècle'
Annales (1975), 187–218, and Guillaume, P., and Poussou, J.P., *Demographie Historique* (Paris,
1970) as sources for the figure of 40%. It is not possible to summarize all the historical material relied on by Boswell. In any case he is of the view that we shall never know the extent of
abandonment of children in the past. Hunt, D., *Parents and Children in History: the Psychology
of Family Life in Early Modern France* (New York: Harper & Row, 1970), 81, states that reliable
figures for *enfants trouvés* can only be found from the 18th century.

[44] Boswell, *ibid.*, 99.

saints, kings, founders of royal lines, and great heroes, and most often are joyfully reunited with their natal parents in the process.[45]

The societies from which these stories sprang, and the parents obliged by circumstances to abandon their children because of famine and lack of technical means of family limitation, needed to believe that abandonment could lead to a better life. It may be that today some fairy stories serve the functions attributed to them by Bruno Bettelheim,[46] but in the past the abandonment stories served the needs of parents and the wider society. Parents today may not need such myths. Late modern society provides a system whereby parents can be helped and, if necessary, can give their children up to the care of the state. Our attitudes are different.[47] There is an emphasis today on identity and genetic origins which create a new form of analysis, transmuted into 'rights'. Yet the forms in which rights are created depend on existing institutions and mentalities, as will be argued in what follows.

ABANDONMENT AND INFANTICIDE

In English law the abandonment of a child under the age of 2 is, as noted above, a specific crime. Abandonment of older children may lead to a charge under the Children and Young Persons Act 1933, with a lesser penalty.[48] Both the Criminal Law Revision Committee and the Law Commission have recommended the repeal of the specific crime under the 1861 Act, arguing that the 1933 Act deals with abandonment adequately.[49] Although the maximum penalty under the 1861 legislation is greater than under the 1933 legislation, the latter makes abandonment a crime, qualified by unnecessary suffering of injury to health, but without the necessity of proving endangerment to life or permanent injury to health. Its scope is wider than that of the 1861 provision.

In adoption law, abandonment may be grounds for a court order severing the legal tie between birth parents and child.[50] Curiously, it was only as late as 1996 that the courts decided to treat abandonment as a reason for the making of a care order, with consequent parental responsibility to the local authority.[51]

---

[45] *ibid.*, 394.   [46] Bettelheim, above, n. 30.

[47] e.g., in *The Times* (27 Nov. 1998), 23, Grace Bradberry refers to abandonment by mothers as a 'seemingly unnatural act'.

[48] Children and Young Persons Act 1933, s.1. See above, n. 12.

[49] Criminal Law Revision Committee, 14th Report (1980) Cmnd. 7844. Law Commission of England and Wales, *Legislating the Criminal Code*, No. 218 (1993) Cm 2370.

[50] Adoption Act 1976.

[51] *Re M (Care Order: Parental responsibility)* [1996] 2 FLR 84. Parental responsibility as a concept was created by the Children Act 1989, s.2. Local authorities made assumptions about their legal parenthood of abandoned children in the past. This is another reason why such children do not appear often in law reports.

Historical scholars are not precise in their use of the term 'abandonment'. But to leave a child in a forest is surely different from leaving a child in a foundling home—Jean Meyer[52] sees the distinction as centred on anonymity, but this is difficult to sustain, for parents depositing their children in the *tour* of a foundling hospital in France, or in the *ruota* in Italy, will also have benefited from anonymity. And the records of, for example, the Hospital of the Holy Spirit in Rome, or the Innocenti in Florence,[53] and those of many convents across France, show that many parents acted in secrecy. Foundling homes, for which the great majority of abandoned and found children in early modern society were destined, were not known throughout most of the Middle Ages or in the ancient world.[54]

English practice has been to discourage the anonymity of parents, and there is no system whereby a parent can give a child into the care of the state without revealing identity. The Thomas Coram Foundation in London permitted parents to deposit a child anonymously only in its earliest years.[55] Thereafter lengthy interviews with parents were obligatory, and parental identity was recorded.[56] For a mother to retain her anonymity she was obliged to abandon the child in secrecy. It would be easy to conclude that this was because of concern with the child's rights, but there is no evidence to support this. It is arguable that this situation led to infanticide in some cases.

Mothers were promised complete confidentiality and Coram's children were given new names. 'The opportunity of advancement untrammelled by the circumstances of their birth' was the justification.[57] Nevertheless, each child was given a number to ensure that parental identity was not lost. Regarding children as individuals was one of the principles of the institution.[58] Parents were concerned to leave a token whereby they could later identify their child if they returned.[59] The passing of the Foundling Hospital Act 1953 enabled such children, for the first time, to have access to the records on parental identity.

[52] Meyer, J., in P. Laslett (ed.), *Bastardy and its Comparative History* (London: Edward Arnold, 1980).

[53] Gavitt, P., *Charity and Children in Renaissance Florence* (Ann Arbor: University of Michigan Press, 1990). *The Ospedale degli Innocenti* continues its work in Florence today.

[54] Boswell, above, n. 38, 431–3, argues that foundling homes were good neither for children nor for the larger society. In some times and places the mortality rates in foundling homes reached 90%. And the 'kindness of strangers' whereby abandoned children were taken in by those who found them had disappeared. Henry Fielding's *Tom Jones* (1749) provides a fictional example.

[55] McClure, R. *Coram's Child* (New Haven: Yale University Press, 1981), 48–50.

[56] *ibid.*, 51.   [57] Preamble to the Foundling Hospital Act 1953.

[58] McClure, above n. 55, p. 245.

[59] Examples of such tokens can be seen at the Musée de l'Assistance Publique in Paris, and at the London Metropolitan Archive. Often the token, or note, was in two halves, one of which was retained by the parent.

Infanticide is a separate offence from abandonment and, prior to the creation of a specific crime in 1922, with a new text in 1938,[60] was prosecuted as homicide. Infanticide and abandonment are seen as connected, and the practice of conflating the two in historical research has obscured abandonment as an alternative means of child disposal.

The major differences are that the subject of infanticide must be under the age of 1; is dead; and was killed by the mother; whose act is constructed as arising from a medical condition.[61] The history of infanticide as a crime is better documented than abandonment.[62] Because of juries' reluctance to convict mothers of homicide,[63] and because the offence of 'concealment of birth'—also instituted in 1861—was often substituted for a charge of homicide, Parliament created the new offence in 1922.

What this indicates is ambivalence surrounding issues of the protection of infants. Until 1861, it was no crime to abandon a child unless this was a threat to life or health.) This ambivalence probably results from contested views, or uncertainties, about the nature of childhood. Nineteenth-century legislative debates on the criminalization of incest and child prostitution, and the rise of the 'child saving' movement, give testimony to these contests. The history of homicide shows that mothers who killed small children were not convicted by juries, partly because of the mandatory death penalty.[64] Since the enactment of the 1922 Infanticide Act, most women convicted have received non-custodial sentences. There is ample evidence of continuing sympathy and a certain folk understanding on the part of juries. It seems that legal practice has been to balance sympathy for the mother with protection of the child.

The text of the law facilitates this. Curiously the discourse surrounding infanticide does not appear to have entered legal discussions of abandonment, although constructions relating to psychosis have entered the medical discourse of infanticide and the popular discourse of abandonment.

The idea that a woman, after giving birth, might make a rational decision not to become a mother is not entertained in English law nor in the general understanding of womanhood. This idea is, however, present in French law and practice as will be shown later.

Legal policy has not been concerned with the identity rights of children. Interviews conducted with social workers and the police confirm this.[65]

---

[60] Rose, L., *Massacre of the Innocents: Infanticide in Great Britain, 1800–1939* (London: Routledge & Kegan Paul, 1986).

[61] O'Donovan, K., 'The Medicalisation of Infanticide', *Criminal Law Review* (1984), 259.

[62] Wilczynski, A., *Child Homicide* (London: Greenwich Medical Media, 1997).

[63] Royal Commission on Capital Punishment (1866), Report and Minutes of Evidence, *Parliamentary Papers*, vol. 21.

[64] Heath, C., *Some Notes on the Punishment of Death* (London: Society for the Abolition of Capital Punishment, 1908): Ward, T., 'The Sad Subject of Infanticide', *Social and Legal Studies*, 8 (1999) 163.

[65] Interviews conducted in 1997 and 1998.

Yet the impetus to identify the mother is evident in newspaper and other media reports. For example, in a newspaper report of the finding of an abandoned baby in East London in 1998, confidentiality was promised by the police to the mother, and it was made clear that the aim 'is to reunite her with her child'.[66] The police make this their priority when children are abandoned today. Public requests for help in finding and identifying the mother of infants, as noted previously, consistently emphasize her welfare, and the fact that she may need medical help.

No examples have been found where the child's identity rights are mentioned. Nor has emphasis been placed on the infant's survival or health. The question then arises why English law has been anti-anonymity, if this is not about children's rights? One answer may be that there is a paternalist concern for the mother. Although such concern is undoubtedly justified for the child, positioning the mother is more difficult. Some might consider her a single autonomous being once she has given birth. The sub-text to these queries suggests that refusal of motherhood after birth might be a rational choice for some women.

The argument can be advanced that anonymity of mothers is consonant with a concern for the protection of the life and health of a child. Anonymous birth-giving, or anonymous placement of a child in care, enables the protection of both child and mother, but not protection of the individual's right to identity. Survival is self-evidently more important than identity, if only because the former is necessary for the latter. In the discussions which preceded the drafting of the Hague Convention on Inter-Country Adoption (1993), this point concerning the right to life as fundamental, led to the text of Article 30 which subjects the child's right of access to documents of origin to the laws of the states which hold that information. Notwithstanding the provisions of the United Nations Convention on the Rights of the Child, restrictions on the child's rights to information were permitted because of concerns for the mother and infant.[67]

So if refusal of motherhood, after maternity, is not seen as a possible choice, this raises issues about the construction of motherhood. Under French law a woman, after parturition, may leave a maternity hospital without identifying herself; young French women see this as a possibility open to them, and one which makes sense.[68] But the *mentalité* in the British Isles is different. A recent English case, which made national news coverage, illustrates the point. The mother contacted the police, claiming that her 3-year-old daughter had been abducted. After 30 hours of search, the

[66] *Guardian*, 2 Jan. 1998, p. 5.

[67] Convention on Protection of Children and Co-operation in Respect of Inter-country Adoption, 29 May 1993 (Hague Convention). The explanatory report by G. Parra-Aranguren gives details of discussions in the drafting of the Convention.

[68] Interviews with students at the University of Lyon III, Nov. 1999.

child was found abandoned in the middle of a remote wood. Sentencing the mother to five years' imprisonment the crown court judge told her, 'You went against the basis of all maternal emotion and abandoned your child to its fate.'[69] It is true that this case involved a woman who had already been a mother for some time, and on that basis, the court's strictures may be understandable. Nevertheless, the attitude to motherhood is clear, and the evidence is that it is widely shared. The construction of motherhood and 'maternal emotion' is situated in a biological context, and starts from birthgiving. Motherhood and maternity are conflated.

Regard for the genetic identity rights of children is defensible as a human right. But this has not been a noticeable policy of English law. Despite the ratification of the United Nations Convention on the Rights of the Child, English law does not recognize the right of children born through egg, sperm, or embryo donation to know the identities of their genetic parents.[70] Although there is the possibility of recording non-identifying parental details, this has not been widely implemented.[71] Yet these children's genetic parents are recorded in official records, which are secret and not accessible. Such records could be opened up at some time in the future if the law were changed to permit access, as has happened with adoption.[72]

The right of access to their original birth certificates by adopted persons crystallizes on becoming an adult. This right entered English law only in 1975. Prior to then, access was denied.[73] The history of this change in the law has been well-documented. And the outcomes predicted in Parliament at the time of the passing of the legislation have not been realized. It is important to distinguish secrecy and anonymity. Whereas official secrecy was permitted concerning the identity of those who gave up children for adoption in the past, once their details had been officially recorded, the changes enabled the opening of those records to the adopted. In this sense neither anonymity of parents, nor the child's identity rights, have been policies under the adoption laws. Rather secrecy, and internal institutional policies of agencies, have governed the practice of adoption.

---

[69] *Guardian*, 22 May 1999.

[70] The Human Fertilization and Embryology Act 1990 guarantees the anonymity of gametes donors. Not all jurisdictions in Europe take this line. See, Douglas, G., *Fertility and Reproduction* (London: Sweet & Maxwell, 1991), 132–6.

[71] Maclean , S., and Maclean, M., 'Keeping Secrets in Assisted Reproduction', *Child and Family Law Quarterly*, 8 (1996) 243.

[72] I am distinguishing official secrecy from anonymity. Although the discourses which surround gametes donation uses the term 'anonymity', the records are available which could permit a linking of the birth of a child to the earlier donation.

[73] Children Act 1975, s. 26; Adoption Act 1976, ss. 50 and 51. See O'Donovan, K., 'A Right to Know One's Parentage?', *International Journal of Law and the Family*, 2 (1988), 27–45.

ANONYMOUS MOTHERS UNDER FRENCH LAW

French, Italian, Spanish, and Luxembourg law permit a woman to give birth anonymously. In French law this is a right protected by the Civil Code, Art. 341–1, whereby 'at the time of her delivery a mother may demand that the secret of her admission and of her identity be preserved'.[74] Article 341 precludes a child born anonymously ('né/e sous X') from instituting proceedings to establish her or his legal mother. The *action en recherche de maternité* has existed in the French Civil Code since 1804, but in the case of the 'X child' will not be received by the court.[75] The reasons for this exceptional denial of an application, which is open to all other citizens, lie in legal history, including the history of the *tour* of the Middle Ages.

The *tour* was finally abolished in France in 1904,[76] although an example remains on display at the *Musée de l'Assistance Publique* in Paris. The idea of charitable reception of a child of unknown parentage and of the protection of secrecy for the woman lives on. The *tour* consisted of a hole in a wall with a wheel and a door. From outside the wall of a convent receiving foundlings, the door could be opened and the baby placed on a wheel, which then turned inward. From the interior the infant could be collected without the mother being observed by those inside. A bell was rung by the mother on departure to announce the arrival of the baby.[77] Just as the notes attached to children are preserved in the records of the Thomas Coram Foundation,[78] so notes attached to French foundlings can be seen in the Museum of Public Assistance in Paris.[79] Some of these notes are on half a sheet, as mothers tore the paper, conserving the other half as evidence of relationship in the hope of reunion one day.

Under the National Convention of the French Revolution a law was passed on 28 June 1793 to open refuges in every district, 'where the pregnant girl might go in secret to give birth, [and where] she could enter at

---

[74] Articles 341 and 341–1 were first introduced into the Civil Code in 1993. The legislative response to the UN Convention resulted in five bills deposited for Parliamentary discussion between 1991 and 1992. The government commissioned a final report from Prof. J-F Mattei which was presented in November 1993. This report played an important part in the debate which took place over the traditional right in French law of a woman to maintain silence over her own identity when she gives birth.

[75] See Rubellin-Devichi, J., *Droit de la Famille* (Paris: Dalloz, 1999), 1519. The change in the law in 1993 brought about an innovation whereby the *action en recherche de maternité* will be terminated by the court by a *fin de non-recevoir*. This means the action can go no further.

[76] Dreifuss-Netter, F., 'L'accouchement sous X', *Liber amicorum a la memoire de Daniele Huet-Weiler* (Paris: PUS/LGDJ, 1994), 100.

[77] Neirinck, C., 'L'accouchement sous X: Le fait et le droit', *La semaine juridique* 392 (1993): 143.

[78] These can be seen in the archive held at the London Metropolitan Archive, London.

[79] Trillat, B., 'La Loi de l'accouchement anonyme: De l'opprobre à la consecration', *Liber amicorum a la memoire de Daniele Huet-Weiler* (Paris: PUS/LGDJ, 1994), 520.

any time of her pregnancy, according to her wishes'.[80] The rule of secret pregnancy and birth was precise. The law provided that 'it will be provided by the Nation for the need of the mother during her stay, which may last until she is perfectly recovered from giving birth; the most inviolable secret will be preserved on all that concerns her'.[81] It seems that this law was passed at the behest of the women who participated in the first National Convention, for its subsequent history shows that after Robespièrre excluded women from public life in 1793 the law was no longer observed.

The tradition of anonymous birthing was revived in France during the 1870s, after the Franco-Prussian War. Popular sentiment favoured protection of young mothers and their children, particularly where the latter's fate was likely to be infanticide or abandonment. Once more the development of sanctuaries for anonymous birthing was placed on the political agenda. There is a hospital circular on record from December 1899 reminding women about to give birth that they may choose to place their documents of civil status in a sealed envelope to be returned on leaving hospital. Subsequently, where refuges for secret delivery had been established, they were legalized between 1914 and 1924.[82]

The Vichy Government of occupied France in the 1940s followed a pronatalist policy. A law of 2 September 1941 was adopted on the protection of birth. This permitted anonymous birth-giving in public hospitals without cost to the woman, for two months' duration, if necessary. This law was repealed in 1953, but the protection of secret maternity continued.

There is a long French history of sympathy for maternity in distress, allied to the idea of a choice not to enter motherhood.

Similar provisions to those enacted by the Vichy Government entered the Family Code in 1953.[83] Article 47 of the Code provides that the expenses of accommodation and delivery of women who have asked for anonymity shall be borne by the social services of the local *département*.[84] More generally, the principle of medical confidentiality applies where a woman asks for anonymity. That anonymous birthing is assumed as a choice is evident from the Family Code. The entry of a right into the Civil Code in 1993 is the confirmation of what had previously been taken for granted, but not formulated as a right. However the denial of the *action en recherche de maternité* to children 'born under X' is a further step in the recognition of the woman's right. In essence French law, both in relation

---

[80] Neirinck, C., above, n. 74.

[81] Bonnet, 'La loi de l'accouchement secret', *Les dossiers de l'obstetrique* 228 (May 1995), 20; Trillat, B., n. 79, above, at 520.

[82] Bonnet, *ibid*.

[83] Art. 42 by decrets, 29 Nov. 1953; 7 Jan. 1959; Art. 47 (which is still in force) by decret of 6 Jan 1986.

[84] Art. 47 of the *Code de Famille* is still in force today.

to delivery, and to birth registration, allows a woman who has given birth to choose whether to become the mother of the infant. Parentage in French law is a juridical construct.[85]

The debate in the Assemblée Nationale in 1993, which led to the entry of a right to give birth anonymously into the Civil Code, took place in the context of amendment of French law to implement the United Nations Convention on the Rights of the Child. On one side were those who favoured repeal of the existing provisions of the Family Code in order to recognize the child's identity rights under Article 7 of the Convention, in particular the child's right to know its parents. On the other side were those who supported the traditional rights of the mother and favoured the clarifications which eventually resulted in the amendment of the Civil Code.[86] Those who favoured the mother's choice to remain anonymous pointed to the limiting words of Article 7, 'as far as possible'. Article 8 appears to have been treated as irrelevant to the debate.[87]

In 1994, 947 children were 'born to X' mothers in France. A major empirical study of some of the women who have given birth anonymously was undertaken between 1986 and 1989. Entitled *Gesture of Love*, the study argues that the women involved gave up their children to protect them. Catherine Bonnet, the author, concludes that children are safeguarded from infanticide and abuse by anonymity as a choice.[88] Certainly, statistics on abandonment are cited by French scholars to support this view. However, a new debate has now opened on the rights of 'children born to X'.[89]

Bonnet argues that the right to give birth anonymously is a fundamental freedom. She sees this as linked to privacy, to a right to renounce forever the motherhood of a particular child—a right of choice. As French law makes a distinction between maternity and legal motherhood, and treats legal parentage as a juridical concept, such an argument is possible. This may be contrasted with English law which appears to regard initial legal parentage as following automatically from biological fact. However, closer inspection reveals that, although there is no choice for a woman who gives birth to refuse to be registered as the legal mother, she is not

---

[85] Where a single woman gives birth, the entry of her name on the birth register does not automatically establish her motherhood in law. This can be seen as a form of discrimination against single women. See Rubellin-Devichi, J., 'The Principle [of child welfare] in French Law and Practice', *International Journal of Law and the Family*, 8 (1994), 269.

[86] Rubellin-Devichi, J., 'Droits de la mère et droits de l'enfant: reflexions sur les formes de l'abandon', *Revue trimestrielle de droit civil*, 90 (4) (1991).

[87] *ibid.*   [88] Bonnet, C., *Geste d'amour* (Paris: Éditions Odile Jacob, 1990).

[89] Prof. Dekeuwer-Defossez has presented a report, *Renover le droit de la famille* (1999) in response to a commission from the Minister for Justice. Her recommendation is that mothers should retain the right to give birth anonymously, but the records should be open to the child on reaching the age of majority (18 in France). See also Thery, I., Couple, *Filiation et parente aujourd'hui* (Paris: Éditions Odile Jacob, 1998), 178–9, where a family sociologist, in a report for the Ministry of Justice, proposes that art. 341–1 of the Civil Code be repealed.

legally required to be the genetic mother. In the case of egg donation it is giving birth rather than genetics that is definitive of motherhood. The notion of choice to refuse motherhood at the time of parturition, such as exists in French law, has no place.

MAKING SENSE OF OFFICIAL POLICIES

Comparison of English and French law enables us to interrogate the anti-anonymity policy of English law, bearing in mind that distinctions between officially-permitted secrecy, official anonymity, and unofficial anonymity, must be made. English law permits the first, whereas French law permits secrecy and anonymity. If children's identity rights are not central to the English law protecting children from abandonment, why not allow post-partum anonymous surrender of infants?

It can be argued that anonymous, secret, and unofficial abandonment is a consequent route for the desperate. At present, and historically, abandonment is one way of disappearing from the infant's life. The evidence is that this is a growing practice in Britain and elsewhere.[90] It is self-evident that answers to this question must encompass a wide range of factors, including different legal and cultural traditions.

Two explanations from within institutional traditions offer themselves, apart from arguments about children's identity rights which, as explained, are of recent origin. One explanation is derived from the Poor Law, and the other from policies on birth certificates and official statistics. These are not contradictory and may form part of a larger picture.

The reported nineteenth-century cases contain evidence that the criminalization of abandonment related to the Poor Law.[91] 'Burdening the parish' is the opening accusation in the indictments.[92] Making the connection between child and parents was necessary, not for the rights of the child, but for the purse of the rate payers. The records of the Coram Foundation contain accounts which confirm this. In the early years of the foundling hospital complaints were made by the Overseers of the Poor

---

[90] Texas has introduced a bill on legalized abandonment (HB 3423) which was signed by the governor on 19 June 1999. According to the *San José Mercury News*, 16 Jan 2000, California is contemplating such a law as are Florida, Pennsylvania, and Alabama. The discourse in the US is concerned with saving lives and preventing crime.

[91] e.g. in *Reg v. Hogan* 169 ER 504 (1851) the indictment alleged, 'that the prisoner intending to injure the inhabitants of the parish of B. and to burthen them with the maintenance of a bastard child of the prisoner, 4 days old, and not named, and unable to walk or take care of itself, or to make known its wants, did abandon and desert the same child without having any means for its support'. The offence seems to have been the injury to the parish rather than to the child. This can be explained in terms of micro-institutional politics of the Poor Law, but it also illustrates that the rights of the child were not a particular concern, merely its means of support.

[92] See also *Reg v. Phillpot* 169 ER 504 (1853) and *Reg v. Gray* 169 ER 1017 (1857).

that policing the prevention of anonymous abandonment was causing additional expense. The governors agreed to pay for additional watch-men.[93]

Under French law, not only may anonymity be demanded by any woman who gives birth, but even where the mother's name is recorded on the birth certificate, she may, if she is a single woman, choose whether or not to be a legal parent. Furthermore, legal parents who give up their child for adoption can request secrecy of identity, which will be respected beyond the ending of the child's minority. Clearly there are a number of choices for parents, notwithstanding biological facts.

Under English law there is an imperative, sanctioned by the criminal law, to record the name of the woman who gives birth on the child's birth certificate. There is no choice for those seeking anonymity other than to give birth in secret, and this constitutes the offence of concealment of birth under the Offences Against the Person Act 1861. If the child is then abandoned, a further crime may be committed. Infanticide is another way out. An English study of 48 filicides in 1984 reports that 13 were of unwanted children, of whom 9 were neonaticides and killed by their mothers. The pattern of these cases was similar to that reported by Bonnet in France, that is, denial of pregnancy and, sometimes, surprise at the birth.[94]

Birth certificates have a particular status in English law as historical records, such that alteration is almost impossible. This notion of the public record was accepted before the European Court of Human Rights as a defence against applications of transsexuals for a new certificate.[95] Even where medical justification is present, alteration is very exceptional. The official reason relates to accuracy of statistics. Historians may applaud the insistence on accuracy, although doubts about the accuracy of paternity records must necessarily continue.

New birth certificates are also issued on adoption and following court-approved transfers of parentage through surrogate motherhood. However, where new birth certificates are issued in this way on adoption,[96] or parental order,[97] the link between the initial and the later certificate is confidentially maintained.

[93] McClure, above n. 55, at 51. For an account of how the Poor Laws affected the foundling hospital's work, see p. 96 et seq.

[94] Wilczynski, above, n. 62, 44, 48–52.

[95] Rees v. UK Ser A 106 paras 42–6 (1986); Cossey v. UK Ser A 184 para 39 (1990). But compare B v. France Ser A 232–C paras 49–62 (1992). The Divisional Court on 16 Feb 1996 refused an application for judicial review made by two post-operative transsexuals of the decision of the Registrar-General of Births concerning alteration of birth certificates. The Births register is re-stated as a historical record.

[96] The adoption is registered on the Adopted Children Register which provides the link between the original birth certificate and the new birth certificate issued on adoption.

[97] Under s. 30 of the Human Fertilization and Embryology Act 1990, if the court grants a parental order a new birth certificate will be issued. These orders are granted in limited forms of surrogacy arrangements.

CONCLUSION

This essay is not intended as a plea for the introduction of an institution of French law into English law. As has been shown, micro-institutional policies and politics affect the legal response to human difficulties. Throughout history the nature of childhood has been contested. It is evident that differing views remain. Furthermore, taking the child's identity rights seriously as a human right leads to interrogation of the French position. What the essay does show, I hope, is that history and culture lead to the evolution of particular and specific legal institutions. Making cross-cultural comparisons, even between near neighbours, requires care. The interpretation of international human rights texts will take place mainly in such contexts, and within a margin of appreciation. We should not be surprised if different jurisdictions come up with different answers.

4

In the Highest Degree Ominous: Hitler's Threatened Invasion and the British War Zone Courts

G. R. Rubin

> If I understand it correctly, all sorts of people
> can be bumped off without trial.
> (Sir Herbert Williams, MP, House of Commons debates, 23 July 1940).[1]

The Invasion Scenario

> Wild bells ringing in the night from a thousand steeples. Home
> Guardsmen mustering hurriedly in street and field by flash-
> lamp and shrouded lantern. Overhead the monstrous shadowy
> shapes of the giant troop-carriers thronging through the sky.
> What is all this about?
> It is the portrait of invasion, already formed in the minds of
> millions of our people.[2]

Thus wrote an anonymous pamphleteer in 1941. He (or she) was, however, quick to add that the portrait was more fantasy than photography.
Yet the fear of Nazi invasion of the United Kingdom, felt by military men
as well as by civilians, had been very real, especially in the period from

---

[1] 5th series, vol. 363, col. 705.

[2] Anon., *Invasion: A Series of Articles by Expert Strategists* (London: Hutchinson & Co., 1941),
18. It should be stressed that this paper will not be retracing the, by now, well-trodden path
of examining German plans for the invasion of Britain; nor visiting the virtual history exercises of determining how the invasion succeeded or failed; nor, if it had been successful, how
Britain would have been governed under the Nazi dictatorship. There is a wealth of literature on these themes. They include: Cox, Richard, *Operation Sealion* (London: Arrow Books,
1982); Dicks, Terrance, *SS World* (London: Piccadilly, 1998); Roberts, Andrew, and Ferguson,
Niall, 'What if Germany Had Invaded Britain in May 1940?', in Ferguson, Niall (ed.), *Virtual
History: Alternatives and Counterfactuals* (London: Picador, 1997), ch. 5; Fleming, Peter,
Invasion 1940 (see n. 26); Gilbert Adrian, *Britain Invaded* (London: Century, 199)—one of the
more fascinating of the genre; Kieser, Egbert, *Hitler on the Doorstep: Operation 'Sea Lion', the
German Plan to Invade Britain, 1940* (London: Arms and Armour Press, 1997); Lampe, David,
*The Last Ditch: The Secrets of the Nationwide British Resistance and the Nazi Plans for the
Occupation of Britain* (London: Cassell, 1968); Longmate, Norman, *If Britain Had Fallen*
(London: BBC/Arrow, 1975); Macksey, Kenneth, *Invasion: The German Invasion of England,
July 1940* (London: Arms and Armour Press, 1980); Schenk, Peter, *Invasion of England 1940:
The Manning of Operation Sea Lion* (London: Conway Maritime Press, 1990); Shears, David,
'Hitler's D-Day', *Quarterly Journal of Military History*, 6/4 (1994), 40–53; Wheatley, Ronald,
Operation Sea Lion: German Plans for the Invasion of England, 1939–1942 (Oxford: Clarendon
Press, 1958). See also the celebrated film, *Went the Day Well?* (1942, dir. Alberto Cavalcanti;
with Leslie Banks, Frank Lawton, Mervyn Johns, and Thora Hird).

May to October 1940. In those months, Hitler had launched his attack on the Low Countries; his troops had stormed into France; they had forced the British Expeditionary Force to retreat from Dunkirk; they had brought about the capitulation of France on June 17; and then Hitler had embarked on the 'Battle of Britain'—the aerial assault on the United Kingdom which everyone knew was the prelude to invasion.

When I first began to plan this chapter, I had intended to examine one of the anti-invasion schemes (of particular legal significance) hurriedly put together by the British authorities. Then doubts began to creep into my mind as to whether I would be engaging in gainful employment. My proposed topic was a United Kingdom emergency criminal justice scheme created in the summer of 1940 and referred to briefly in Brian Simpson's enthralling study of Defence Regulation 18B (*In the Highest Degree Odious*:[3] shamelessly paraphrased in this chapter's title). Unlike Regulation 18B, the scheme I refer to—'the War Zone Courts scheme'—was intended to come into operation only if and when Hitler's threatened invasion of Britain had begun. We know that the invasion did *not* take place. Consequently, the emergency criminal justice system lay dormant. No War Zone Courts ever sat, and no one was ever prosecuted before, or punished by, them. Like Major Martin, the corpse in Ewen Montagu's wartime account of *The Man Who Never Was*,[4] the War Zone Courts scheme was the 'Criminal Justice System Which Never Was'. Thus unlike the impressive studies of the criminal courts from the fourteenth century onwards, there are, for the War Zone Courts, no statistics, no procedural patterns, no patterns of offences, no profiles of offenders, no criteria for the exercise of the Prerogative of Mercy, no convictions, and no punishment patterns. Was not the investigation of these courts likely to be an empty exercise? But

---

[3] Simpson, A. W. Brian, *In the Highest Degree Odious; Detention Without Trial in Wartime Britain* (Oxford: Clarendon Press, 1992), 190, at 192.

[4] Montagu, Ewan, *The Man Who Never Was* (Harmondsworth: Penguin, 1956). As the book's Foreword explained, it was the 'fantastic but true story of Operation Mincemeat, a brilliant coup by British Intelligence which completely deceived the German High Command and ensured the success of Allied landings in Sicily in 1943'. The operation involved floating the corpse of a fictitious 'Major Martin' in the Atlantic. The body, together with a briefcase, eventually arrived on the Spanish coast. The documents in the briefcase were photocopied by the Spanish authorities and copies passed to the Germans. The body and its possessions were then handed over to the British Consulate. The bogus secret papers and other mundane documents such as theatre tickets, were accepted by the Germans as genuine, and Operation Husky (the Allied invasion of Sicily) was successful. For the official version of the story, see Howard, Michael, *British Intelligence in the Second World War*, vol. 5, 'Strategic Deception' (London: HMSO, 1990, at 89–92). The identity of Martin was revealed in October 1996. The dismal truth was that he was a 34 year-old unemployed labourer, Glyndwr Michael, an illiterate and insane Welshman. Living as a tramp in London, he killed himself by swallowing rat poison. See *Daily Telegraph*, 28 Oct. 1996; *After the Battle* 100 (1998), 62. Montagu, one of the joint planners of Operation Mincemeat while with Naval Intelligence, was a barrister (Middle Temple), KC (1939) and subsequently Judge Advocate of the Fleet and Recorder of Southampton. The film of the events, made in 1955, featured Clifton Webb as Montagu, and Robert Flemyng and Stephen Boyd. It was directed by Ronald Neame.

being ruled by the heart rather than by the head, I resolved to plod on to examine the apparently superfluous activities of the civil servants who earnestly, carefully, and assiduously developed, expanded, and finessed the scheme of War Zone Courts long after serious threats of German invasion had receded. The emergency arrangements uncovered may, of course, strike the reader 60 years after the events as part-serious and part-ridiculous, and as possessing a dim and distant half-reality of 'All Our Yesterdays'. Moreover, the resultant scheme seemed to suggest, in this case at least, that in accordance with Parkinson's law which proclaims that work expands to fill the time available for its completion, the legislative endeavour had a momentum of its own halted only by the likely prospect of Allied victory in Europe after D-Day.

Yet even were one to conclude that the War Zone Courts scheme possessed, in hindsight, a somewhat quaint and unrealistic quality, there is also the perennial question of how liberal-democratic constitutional states address emergency situations. This is the second issue at the heart of this chapter. How much respect for individual civil liberties is maintained when a democratic society is under threat? Does the state succumb to the temptation to replace democratic freedoms by totalitarian rule, albeit temporarily? Constitutional theorists seek to identify a number of principles to be followed when liberal democracies implement emergency legislation (usually to counteract terrorism or a breakdown in the provision of essential services). They include limited (rather than non-existent) legal and political accountability of the executive in respect to the scheme and its implementation. This might embrace effective means of review of its operation, involving perhaps the 'Three Wise Men' principle or even judicial review; perhaps prior consultation with, and regular reporting to Parliament; and objective criteria by which to measure evidence of offending (rather than inferences drawn from, say, life-styles or personal beliefs). The consent of a senior police officer or of the Law Officers might be required before a prosecution is commenced. There should be clear evidence of necessity and institutional arrangements to promote 'reason', such as an open legislature or a press which can debate such matters. Finally, the objective should be to advance the interests of the community as a whole, and not a particular interest group or government.[5] No doubt in wartime a significant 'margin of appreciation' will be accorded a government in planning its emergency powers. As we will see in what follows, despite military pressure for more robust powers over civilians, the

---

[5] For illustrative material, see Finn, John E., *Constitutions in Crisis: Political Violence and the Rule of Law* (New York: Oxford University Press, 1991); Simpson, *Odious* (see n. 3 above), 409–14; Adler, Mortimer, J., 'War and the Rule of Law', in Puttkammer, Ernst W. (ed.), *War and the Law* (Chicago: University of Chicago Press, 1944), 178–98; Walker, Clive, *The Prevention of Terrorism in British Law*, 2nd edn. (Manchester: Manchester University Press, 1992), ch. 13; and see Walker's review of Campbell, Colm, *Emergency Law in Ireland, 1918–1925* (Oxford: Clarendon Press, 1994), in *Legal Studies*, 15 (1995), 315–16.

War Zone Courts scheme, as finally approved in Parliament, possessed some, albeit not all, of the protections outlined above.

A third focus of this study is the debate which has recently been occupying the attention of social and political historians of the 'domestic front' during World War Two. That is, to what extent do popular images of a British people and government, solidly united behind Churchill in the struggle against Nazi Germany, belie a more complex and less flattering picture? In particular, to what extent were the tense years of 1940–1 more accurately characterized by class, race, and gender divisions and by inequalities of opportunity and of sacrifice (cf. the impact of the Blitz) than by the collective and comforting image of the 'People's War'?[6] More specifically, how far were those years marked by government mistrust, whether justified or (deliberately or accidentally) misplaced, of the reliability of the 'ordinary' British people to support the War effort against Nazi Germany and to withstand the privations of war without descending into panic and defeatism? I suggest that it is from the perspective of government elitism and of a belief in the superiority of its own moral courage (when contrasted with its perception of 'the people's' moral vulnerability) that meaning can be attached to the proposals for the War Zone Courts planned by the civil servants and promulgated by ministers. As we shall see, it was not a vision of 'the people' which Parliament universally endorsed.

The basis for the government's conclusion regarding working-class unreliability—seized upon to justify controls under the War Zone Courts scheme—can be questioned. Thus, prior to the Blitz, the Ministry of Information was conscious of the generally healthy state of domestic morale within British society. Consequently, whereas there were grounds to believe that popular confidence in the government did not collapse during this tense period, government confidence in the determination of the

---

[6] For a sample of the literature, see Calder, Angus, *The People's War: Britain, 1939–1945* (London: Panther Books, 1971); *ibid., The Myth of the Blitz* (London: Jonathan Cape, 1991); Jefferys, Kevin, *The Churchill Coalition and Wartime Politics, 1940–1945* (Manchester: Manchester University Press, 1991); Smith, Harold, L. (ed.), *War and Social Change: British Society in the Second World War* (Manchester : Manchester University Press, 1990); Ziegler, Philip, *London at War: 1939–1945* (London: Sinclair-Stevenson, 1995); Kirkham, Pat and . Thoms, David (eds.), *War Culture: Social Change and Changing Experience in World War II Britain* (London: Lawrence & Wishart, 1995). Another perspective explores the extent to which the War years are distinguished by the 'selling out' by Churchill of the British Empire, to the advantage of the US to which Britain became financially and strategically indebted (a complaint associated, in some cases, with the perspective of historians identified with the radical Right in politics). See, e.g., Charmley, John, *Churchill's Grand Alliance: The Anglo-American Special Relationship, 1940–57* (London: John Curtis/Hodder & Stoughton, 1995); *ibid., Churchill* (London: Hodder & Stoughton, 1993); Blake, Robert, and Louis, Wm. Roger (eds.), *Churchill* (Oxford: Clarendon Press, 1993). See also Roberts, Andrew, *Eminent Churchillians* (London: Weidenfeld & Nicolson, 1994). The late Conservative politician and historian, Alan Clark, reasoned that it was in Britain's strategic interest to sign a peace treaty with Hitler in 1940 or 1941 on the footing, *inter alia*, that the Soviet Union was the principal enemy.

people to 'win through' may have been wanting. As the historian of the Ministry of Information has observed, '. . . despite reports [to the Ministry] which generally pointed to a different conclusion, the public's determination and capacity to see things through were seriously doubted'.[7] In a similar vein, Clive Ponting has suggested that the elite, senior officials of the Ministry of Information, such as Kenneth (late Lord) Clark, '. . . had a secret dread that the working class would prove unreliable and defeatist, when the exact opposite was the case'.[8]

Thus, when considering what significance should be given to the imposition of drastic legal controls on the civilian population at the time of Hitler's threatened invasion, one should also have regard to this sub-context of ruling-class fear and distrust at home. As Chamberlain told the War Cabinet on 18 May 1940, it was '. . . "imperative" for Britain to abandon what he described as its "present rather easy-going methods" and adopt a form of government "which would approach the totalitarian" '.[9]

Brian Simpson, in his study of Defence Regulation 18B, likewise demonstrated how government ministers, despite a degree of scepticism, gave consent to MI5's over-reactive insistence on rounding up an 'enemy within'—not all of whom posed dangers to the state.[10] In other words, if anyone had panicked, it was more likely to have been the government and not the general population, and the War Zone Courts scheme should be viewed as a product of that lack of resolve.[11]

What were the legal options contemplated by the authorities as a means of ensuring public order among the civilian population in the event of

---

[7] McLaine, Ian, *Ministry of Morale: Home Front Morale and the Ministry of Information in World War II* (London: George Allen & Unwin, 1979), 61.

[8] Ponting, Clive, *1940: Myth and Reality* (London: Hamish Hamilton, 1990), 157. Lord Clark was, of course, the father of Alan Clark (see n. 6, above).

[9] *ibid.*, 150.

[10] Simpson, *Odious*, see n. 3 above. See also Stammers, Nigel, *Civil Liberties in Britain During the Second World War* (London: Croom Helm, 1983). The vulnerability of civil liberties to encroachment during wartime is exposed in these works. Brian Simpson acknowledges that in practical terms, a strong case could still be made for Reg. 18B at a general level, while its application in individual cases remains more problematic.

[11] This is not to argue that civilian morale, once the Blitz had commenced, was not adversely affected, though the *measurement* of morale was notoriously imprecise and impressionistic. There is extensive evidence of grim determination and cheerfulness during the Blitz and conflicting evidence of despair, resignation, and helplessness. The survival of city centres, public institutions such as cinemas, and public utilities such as transport were consistent with the maintenance of strong morale. See, e.g., Beaven, B. and Thoms, D., 'The Blitz and Civilian Morale in Three Northern Cities', *Northern History*, 23 (1996), 195–203. Nor is it to argue, in the light of the experiences of the French and Belgian military authorities following the German invasion of the Low Countries, that the availability of legal powers against refugees clogging routes through which the Army would have to pass to engage the enemy was not required. Such legislation was indeed appropriate to meet the practicalities of enemy invasion. What is challenged is the underlying assumption among many of the planners and policy-makers that the civilian social fabric was brittle and liable to collapse. In this light, the scheme can be interpreted in part as reflecting the insecurity and fearfulness of *government*, rather than a response to the 'low morale fibre' of the civilian population.

Nazi invasion? In this chapter we will see how, despite elitist views of the unreliability of the general public, the primacy of constitutionalism and of the idea of political accountability seem to have been crucial factors behind the recommendations of senior civil servants to ministers as to the form of law finally adopted. That form was, of course, statute rather than so-called 'martial' law. Parliament seemed also to have been concerned at this grave time of crisis to secure some minimum standards of legal protection for those liable to be sentenced to death by the emergency courts, and to refuse to rubber-stamp the grant of whatever legal powers the executive considered vital in the circumstances.

Finally, the chapter considers the practical arrangements, and also the difficulties, envisaged by the civil servants in implementing the War Zone Courts scheme; *inter alia*: how it was proposed that the judges were to be called into action; what was to happen if parts of a 'War Zone'-designated area were cut off by the enemy; and what arrangements were to be made to carry out executions. In anticipation of these points, I first outline the military situation facing the policy-makers prior to the legislation.

THE MILITARY SITUATION

At the outset of the Second World War, the British military authorities were not anticipating an invading German army.[12] Yet as the Royal Navy in those early weeks had for various reasons lost control of the North Sea—temporarily at any rate—the War Cabinet did ask the Chiefs-of-Staff to reconsider the danger of an invasion force slipping past the Navy and Coastal Command during the longer nights of winter. They replied that small raids were possible and an invasion conceivable, but neither threat was serious.[13]

Until the spring of 1940, the defensive strategy of British Army Home Forces against invasion (under a plan code-named 'Julius Caesar') was based on the assumption of countering a dual sea- and air-borne assault. Nip a parachute assault in the bud and an invasion would be repulsed.[14] In respect to civilians within threatened areas, the plan envisaged that those not in immediate danger should stay where they were, while those in more vulnerable areas would be withdrawn by routes which were thought not to interfere unduly with military traffic.[15] That civilians might be obstructive in one way or another had not yet been considered. For this was the period of the 'Phoney War' during which little military activity of a threatening nature had been experienced. However, the German invasion of Norway in early April 1940 prompted a heightened appreciation of

---

[12] Collier, Basil, *The Defence of the United Kingdom* (History of the Second World War, UK Military Series), (London: HMSO, 1957), 77.

[13] *ibid.*, 83.   [14] *ibid.*, 84.   [15] *ibid.*, 85.

Hitler's next moves. May 10, 1940 was a red-letter day, witnessing the replacement of Chamberlain by Churchill as Prime Minister, Hitler's invasion of the Low Countries and France, and the creation of the United Kingdom Home Defence Executive, designed to co-ordinate the arrangements to be taken against invasion by both the armed service and the civilian departments of government. According to Professor Harry Hinsley, the official historian of British intelligence during the war, the Chiefs-of-Staff were:

. . . already looking beyond the long-expected bombing offensive against the United Kingdom and fearing something still more drastic. And by the end of May, confronted by the proved strength of the GAF [the German Air Force], by the rapid advance of the Germans to the Channel ports, and by the depletion of the RAF and the absence in France of the Army's main fighting strength, they had come to the conclusion that, as was being suggested by a flood of diplomatic and SIS [i.e. M16] reports, an invasion might be attempted at any moment.[16]

There was no disguising the gloom descending on senior military personnel at the awful prospect presented by the German advance in France. On 19 May 1940, Anthony Eden, Secretary of State for War, wrote in his diary:

An interminable day of glorious weather and grim news . . . On our return from the Cabinet, as we walked up the ugly staircase of the War Office to my room, Ironside[17] said to me: 'This is the end of the British Empire'. He [Ironside] did not believe that we could hold out alone for more than a few months.[18]

Perhaps appropriately, 19 May was also the day when a committee met for the first time at the War Office to discuss the legal powers over its citizens which the British authorities would require in the event of the German invasion. This planning process, as we shall see, eventually resulted in the creation of the War Zone Courts: the emergency courts expected to sit in those areas of the country proximate to, but not overrun by, enemy forces.

On 22 May, Parliament enacted the Emergency Powers (Defence) (No. 1) Act 1940 which effectively introduced industrial conscription for the nation. The Act authorized regulations to be issued by Order in Council, requiring persons 'to place themselves, their services, and their property at the disposal of His Majesty . . .'. *The Times* noted that the new measure, '. . . comes near to suspending the very essence of the Constitution as it has been built up in a thousand years. Our ancient liberties are placed in pawn for victory; nothing less than the destruction of Hitlerism will redeem

---

[16] Hinsley, F. H. *et al.*, *British Intelligence in the Second World War: Its Influence on Strategy and Operations*, vol. 1 (London: HMSO, 1979), 165–6.

[17] i.e. General Sir Edmund Ironside, CIGS, who was about to succeed General Kirke as Commander-in-Chief, Home Forces.

[18] Avon, The Rt. Hon. the Earl of, *The Eden Memoirs: The Reckoning* (Cassell: London, 1965), 106. Churchill replaced Ironside with General Sir Alan Brooke, 2 months later. Ironside went into retirement.

them'.[19] Sir John Colville, Churchill's private secretary at 10 Downing Street, commented in his diary that the purpose of the measure was largely that in the event of invasion or if the country were otherwise *in extremis*, the rights of individuals and institutions should not be permitted to stand in the way of the country's safety. He concluded, 'Now if ever *salus populi suprema lex*, and in a totalitarian war even a democracy must surrender its liberties'.[20]

The atmosphere in the United Kingdom in the period from the end of May was deeply apprehensive. On 25 May 1940, Harold Nicolson, Parliamentary Secretary to the Ministry of Information, confided in his diary, 'Go down to the War Office to discuss with Ned Grigg[21] the question of civilian morale in case of invasion . . . the possibility of evacuating the Channel and East Coast towns is now being considered'.[22]

At the same time, intelligence regarding Germany's invasion intentions was being gathered from disparate sources. They included photographic evidence, decrypts of German Enigma messages and other signals' intelligence, diplomatic information, reports smuggled out by an Allied spy at German military intelligence headquarters,[23] Prisoner of War debriefings, messages sent by carrier pigeon from Belgium, even a French peasant writing a desperate message, '*Venez vite, Les Boches sont ici*'.[24] More directly, Hitler issued his War Directive No. 16 on 16 July 1940, coincidentally the very day on which the Home Secretary, Sir John Anderson, introduced in Parliament his Bill to establish the emergency War Zone Courts. Hitler's directive announced:

Since England, in spite of her hopeless military situation, shows no signs of being ready to come to an understanding, I have decided to prepare a landing operation against England, and if necessary to carry it out. The aim of this operation will be to eliminate the English homeland as a base for the prosecution of the war against Germany and if necessary to occupy it completely.[25]

Historians have questioned the seriousness of Hitler's declared intention regarding an invasion of the United Kingdom. But the public mood in Britain was resigned to the prospect. As Peter Fleming has remarked:

[19] *The Times*, 23 May 1940.

[20] Colville, John, *The Fringes of Power: 10 Downing Street Diaries* (New York: W. W. Norton & Co., 1986), 139.

[21] Parliamentary Under-Secretary at the War Office.

[22] Nicolson, Nigel (ed.), *Harold Nicolson: Diaries and Letters, 1939–45* (n.p.: Fontana Books, 1971), 85–6.

[23] On these sources, see Hinsley, *British Intelligence*, ch. 5 (n.16 above). Much of the information was analysed daily by a small Invasion Warning Committee. See the papers of Colonel L. H. B. Sanderson in the Liddell Hart Centre for Military Archives, King's College, London.

[24] Strong, Major-General Sir Kenneth, *Intelligence at the Top: The Recollections of an Intelligence Officer* (New York: Doubleday & Co., 1969), 93.

[25] Trevor-Roper, H. R. (ed.), *Hitler's War Directives, 1939–45* (London: Pan Books, 1966), 74–5.

There were, for once, few doubts about what he would do next. There had been none in Britain since Dunkirk. It was as obvious to her citizens as to her leaders that she was due for the *coup de grace*. There was to the best of their knowledge only one way in which this could be delivered. [26]

Indeed, as Harold Nicolson noted on 20 July,[27] 'I think that Hitler will probably invade us within the next few days. He has 6000 aeroplanes ready for the job.'

Yet the atmosphere was not wholly as one might imagine. 'How strange it all is!' Nicolson continued. 'We all know that we are faced with a terrific invasion. We half-know that the odds are heavily against us. Yet there is a sort of exhilaration in the air.'[28] It was a mood attributed at the time to the relief of knowing that Britain now stood alone, and was responsible only for herself and not for any other country. As we know, it was indeed in the air, in the skies over Southeast England during the Battle of Britain, that Hitler's invasion strategy crumbled. As a 1941 Ministry of Information booklet, recounting the events of that battle, concisely put it, 'Before the German Army could land it was necessary to destroy our coastal convoys, to sink or immobilize such units of the Royal Navy as would dispute its passage, and above all to drive the Royal Air Force from the sky.'[29]

Goering's aerial assault having failed in its mission, Hitler decided on 12 October 1940 to postpone 'Operation Sea Lion', the invasion of England, until the following spring. He nonetheless instructed that the *threat* of invasion should continue in order that military and political pressure on Britain should continue to be felt.[30] Indeed, we shall see that British administrative preparations for the War Zone Courts scheme were carried on well beyond the winter of 1940, by which time the prospect of German invasion was considered to be relatively remote.

BRITISH DEFENSIVE PLANS

The British intelligence authorities' track record in monitoring German invasion intentions has been criticized by some historians.[31] Notwith-

[26] Fleming, *Invasion* (London: Hamish Hamilton, 1958), at 23.

[27] Nicolson (ed.), *Diaries*, 100. The figure was grossly exaggerated.

[28] Fleming refers in his Foreword to 'that tense and strangely exhilarating summer' *Invasion* (see n. 26).

[29] Information, Ministry of, *The Battle of Britain, August–October 1940* (London: HMSO, 1941).

[30] Hinsley, *British Intelligence*, 186 (n.16 above).

[31] Fleming (brother of Ian) is particularly scathing. He states that, 'For three and a half months—from mid-May until the beginning of September [1940]—the British strove hard to divine the Germans' intentions. They failed almost completely to do so . . . East coast or south coast? Heads or tails? It seemed essential to guess right. The British guessed wrong.' See Fleming, *Invasion*, 154–5 (see n. 26); Hinsley's work based on official records suggests that the criticisms may have had some limited, but hardly total, justification. However, the targets of

standing that criticism, the creation of the Home Defence Executive (HDE) on 10 May 1940 signalled the seriousness with which an invasion threat was treated. As Collier observed of the HDE, '. . . not the easiest or the least important of their tasks was that of preparing the commercial and domestic fabric of the nation for the shock of invasion by sea or air, and so avoiding the dislocation which was said to be causing such havoc in Continental countries'.[32] Civil defence arrangements were put in hand. They included the formation of local 'Invasion Committees' which were required to compile 'War Books' for their districts. These would list, *inter alia*, the 'Emergency Transport, Tools, Plant etc' which could be commandeered in the event of invasion, and the 'Sites earmarked for Mass Graves'. These War Books were to be destroyed, 'should hasty evacuation become necessary'.[33] A major development was the appointment of twelve Regional Commissioners, mostly senior politicians, who were granted extensive powers to co-ordinate local civil defence schemes in accordance with military requirements.[34] In the event that communications with Whitehall were severed, the commissioners had wide discretion to take civil defence measures on their own initiative. As we shall see, they were, indeed, given specific functions to perform in the event that War Zone Courts were called upon to function in circumstances where communications with central government had broken down. As Collier points out, 'A great number of counter-invasion schemes had now to be hastily improvised by civil departments and local authorities, passed as satisfactory, and knitted into a coherent whole'.[35]

A thick 'cloud of rumour, exaggeration, and false witness'[36] was abroad—just that atmosphere in which measures to counteract a mythical 'fifth column' of spies, saboteurs, and traitors would find ready and enthusiastic acceptance. Thus emergency regulations were drafted to intern enemy aliens, many of them, of course, refugees from Nazi Germany, or anti-Fascist Italians settled for many years in the United Kingdom. Defence Regulation 18B, as Brian Simpson shows, was directed against British citizens whose loyalty or associations were questioned. Plans were made to deny the enemy on landing the use of ports, railways, telephones, radios, and public utilities; and to prevent access to bulk stores of food, petrol, and other commodities. Open spaces and arterial roads were obstructed to prevent troop-carrying aircraft from landing. Roads and

his criticisms, including Sanderson and Strong, accused Fleming, in turn, of a number of deliberate and misleading distortions in his book. See Sanderson papers and Strong, *Intelligence*, 90–1. If the Germans had succeeded in overrunning Kent, Colonel Fleming would have commanded underground 'auxiliaries' from a base near Canterbury to harass the enemy.

[32] Collier, *Defence*, 103. [33] Fleming, *Invasion*, 82–3 (see n. 26);
[34] O'Brien, Terence H., *Civil Defence* (History of the Second World War, UK Civil Series), (London: HMSO, 1955), ch. X1V.
[35] Collier, *Defence*, 103. [36] *ibid*.

aerodromes were blocked and contingency demolition plans prepared. Signposts for streets, towns, and railway stations were removed; maps, plans, and guidebooks were commandeered or moved inland. Parked vehicles were to be immobilized by the removal of their rotor arms and church bells were to be rung only as a warning that an assault by parachutists or airborne troops had begun. Most importantly, a scheme to recruit local defence volunteers, renamed the 'Home Guard', was devised and then announced on the BBC by Anthony Eden on 14 May. By the end of the month, 300,000 volunteers had enrolled.[37] And an improvised criminal justice system, to be operated in the event of invasion by the enemy, was to be prepared as another one of those anti-invasion measures.

Finally, an overhaul of the British Army's Home Forces' deployment took place. Stress was to be laid on mobile offensive action in response to German landings rather than relying on anti-tank obstacles and forward stop-lines strategically placed through the country.[38] However, whether the Army could perform as well as anticipated would depend partly on whether or not the civilian population in areas experiencing invasion had taken flight on the major roads, hindering the actions of the local mobile reserves. By July 1940, around 80,000 people had moved inland from the Kent coastal towns. That represented two-fifths of the population. The remainder were warned that if the invasion started, they would be expected to remain where they were until further orders, and keep the roads clear.[39] We shall see later that the authorities decided to create a capital offence of 'forcing a picket' and that the War Zone Courts would be expected to try those accused of infringing that new emergency regulation.

PARLIAMENT AND THE WAR ZONE COURTS

Turning now to these emergency courts, the War Zone Courts scheme was a product of ministerial regulations issued under the authority of the Emergency Powers (Defence) (No. 2) Act 1940 passed on 1 August 1940. It was the culmination of extensive discussions which had commenced with a meeting of military personnel at the War Office on 19 May 1940, held to discuss how to introduce martial law in the event of invasion. The debate was broadened out at the insistence of the civilian government departments. For the latter, especially the Home Office, had baulked at the prospect of the military authorities making decisions regarding the exercise of legal powers over the civilian population. In due course, even the military authorities (with minor exceptions) came to accept that political expediency demanded military subordination to the civil power when forming policy on such a sensitive topic. Thus the idea of imposing mar-

---

[37] Collier, *Defence*, 105–7; Avon, *Eden Memoirs*, 103–4; Mackenzie, S. P., *The Home Guard: A Military and Political History* (Oxford: Clarendon Press, 1995), 34.
[38] Collier, *Defence*, 129.   [39] *ibid.*, 144.

tial law or even of subjecting civilians to courts martial once a German invasion had commenced, was settled as politically unacceptable. This did not mean that the civilian officials had greater confidence in the fortitude of the general public than did the military. Nor, of course, did it mean that the military could not resort to martial law if civil authority collapsed in a War Zone. However, what was prescribed was a *statutory* scheme to which *Parliament* could give its assent. The scheme would retain as much of the existing criminal code as possible. It would ensure trial before professional judges and not before panels of military officers, and, in the envisaged contingency, it would seek to ensure as fair an application of the criminal justice system as was consistent with both the need for expedition in the disposal of cases and with the need for deterrence. The resultant courts, expressly stated after much departmental and parliamentary bargaining *not* to be courts martial, were to be set up in areas declared by the Home Secretary to be War Zones consequent on an invasion of the United Kingdom having commenced.

Powers of the war zone courts

They were to be empowered to deal swiftly with all offences, but particularly with serious offences committed by civilians and could, of course, impose the death penalty. Where the military authorities approved, they could also try servicemen.

In outline, the courts were to be presided over by High Court judges assisted by two local magistrates as lay advisers. The court's verdict, however, would rest solely with the president who was bound only to consult with the advisory members. Existing rules of criminal procedure would be radically altered. For example, preliminary examinations by magistrates, remand hearings, and committal proceedings would be dispensed with. This, of course, would permit of the rapid disposal of cases, given the pressing circumstances in which it was assumed trials would be conducted. Nonetheless, the prevailing rules of evidence would broadly remain, and accused persons would be entitled to legal representation. But there would be no provision for juries, nor, in the first legislative draft, would there be a right of appeal. However, this latter omission, in particular, prompted a rebellion in Parliament, even at such a tense moment when the very existence of the country was in doubt. Member after member from all sides of the Commons stood up to denounce the denial of a recognized legal protection for accused persons liable to execution.

Before addressing this 'Commons' revolt',[40] it is significant to note that the Home Secretary, Sir John Anderson, had informed the Commons, on

---

[40] The term is borrowed from Brian Simpson's study of Reg. 18B when the Commons forced the Home Secretary to withdraw the first version of his internment regulation. See Simpson, *Odious*, ch 4 (see n. 3 above).

introducing his Bill on 16 July 1940, that the measure had the support of the Army: the statutory creation of special civilian courts, he argued, would obviate the need for the establishment of *military* courts to try civilians. The latter, it was considered, would merely waste the time of officers preoccupied with more pressing concerns once Hitler's invasion had begun. Anderson explained to the House that, 'There is no question here of any difference of opinion between soldiers and civilians or of any conflict of rival theories. This is something on which there has been general agreement and it is important that that should be made clear.'[41] In the light of these remarks attesting to unanimity between the military and civil power on the construction of the statutory scheme, there seemed good reason to agree with the assessment by one legal periodical on 13 July that, 'The New Bill will at any rate do much to avoid the interminable discussions on martial law which arose in such [Boer War] cases as *Ex parte Marais* [1902] A.C. 109)'.[42]

However, Anderson was, at best, being economical with the truth. Rival theories as to what kind of United Kingdom criminal justice system should prevail in the event of German invasion had in fact been canvassed strongly in the departmental and inter-departmental discussions which had commenced in earnest the previous May. Should there be reliance on the ordinary criminal law supplemented by the existing Defence Regulations introduced since 1939? Should Parliament enact a network of emergency military courts specially designed for invasion circumstances, thereby enforcing statutory martial law regulations? Should the authorities rely solely on the common law doctrine of military necessity to take those steps required to meet a grave emergency?

In the final analysis, the preferred alternative was to create a system of special wartime *civil* courts, underpinned by minor substantive changes in criminal law and punishment, aimed at the rapid dispensing of criminal justice. The intense struggles behind the scenes between the 'civil' and the 'military' factions within government departments were thus well disguised when the Bill was presented to Parliament. In effect, the civil power—in particular, the Law Officers in both Scotland and England, the Home Office, the Scottish Office, the Ministry of Home Security, and the civilian branch of the War Office—successfully argued for measures which seemed to offer a greater prospect of political accountability than the alternatives. The latter were proposals put forward by the military branch of the War Office and by the Judge Advocate General, Sir Henry MacGeagh. They entailed either a hybrid system of civil and military rules or a statutory system of martial law regulations. These latter regulations,

---

[41] H.C. debates, 5th series, 16 July 1940, vol. 363 , col. 66. See also *Punch*, 24 July 1940, 99.
[42] *Law Journal*, 90 (13 July 1940), 11.

which met with the approval of the Adjutant-General, Sir Robert Gordon-Finlayson, were to offer draconian powers to military commanders to maintain public order, while permitting virtually no procedural protections for persons tried by statutory military 'courts',[43] and were justified on the premise that the maintenance of public order among the civil population should be left to the military authorities to handle in their own way.

Representative of the hybrid view is probably this observation of a Scottish Office official:

The more one looks at this troublesome business, the more reason there seems to be for regarding as justified our original contention that the simplest and most satisfactory way of dealing with crime in an area in which military operations are in progress would be to let the military authorities deal out of hand with offences of a military character; and to leave others to the ordinary courts in so far as they can function. Serious crime of no military interest could be sent well 'behind the lines' for attention. Petty crime of no military interest, if it could not be dealt with by civil courts on the spot, could go unpunished without doing anyone much harm.[44]

While this call for martial law, whether formulated in a statutory code or reflected in the common law doctrine of military necessity, was resisted primarily on political grounds, the Home Secretary, in speaking to the Commons on 16 July, emphasized that the statutory scheme would in no way diminish or interfere with the power and the duty of the military authorities to take, under what was sometimes described as 'martial law', such steps as military necessity required.[45] The Attorney-General, Sir Donald Somervell, added that the term 'martial law' was always apt to cause confusion; nonetheless, the doctrine of military necessity would

---

[43] Public Record Office [PRO], London, WO 32/9485, MacGeagh to Gordon-Finlayson, 20 May 1940; *ibid.*, Gordon-Finlayson to MacGeagh, 22 May 1940. The forums, though 'indulged in' by statute, would not be courts in the technical sense, merely panels of officers enforcing their 'martial law' orders. It is noteworthy that MacGeagh considered martial law could be introduced only by prerogative or by legislation; in the former instance, on the basis of necessity. The inference to be drawn is that he did not adhere to a common law (as distinct from a prerogative) basis for martial law. For discussion of these theories see Campbell, *Emergency Law*, 125–30; and the present author's review of Campbell's book in *Law Quarterly Review*, 111 (1995), 520–30.

[44] Scottish Record Office [SRO], Edinburgh, HH 50/70, C.C. Cunningham to David Milne, 19 July 1940. In an unfortunate lapse into political incorrectness, Cunningham concluded, 'If a little drunkenness or some casual wife-beating in these circumstances went unpunished, society would not be permanently injured.' See *ibid*.

[45] H.C. deb., n. 41 above, col. 74. See also (PRO) HO 45/18626/834477, 'Note on Military Courts and Martial Law'. This was a memorandum prepared (probably by Sir Alexander Maxwell, Home Office Permanent Secretary) for Anderson's use during the Commons debate. In the light of Anderson's concession to the common law, the 'military' faction were thus not completely thwarted. What would happen, it was posed, if the War Zone Courts themselves could not operate because of fighting taking place near at hand? That question occupied substantial amounts of time, energy, and paperwork between August 1940 and April 1941.

enable the Army to take drastic action against civilians.[46] Thus the doctrine would permit the Army to take possession of property, occupy any premises, enter on private land, call upon civilians to assist it in civilian work, order civilians to leave any place, and take measures against civilians who obstructed military operations or who assisted the enemy. Indeed, the doctrine would enable the military authorities to 'deal with' civilians, that is, by executing them out of hand or after an inquiry by a committee of officers—a forum erroneously described as a military court.[47] Yet, as an internal memorandum prepared for the debate asserted:

... there is in this country no code of law empowering the military authorities themselves to pass sentences upon civilians who may be guilty of offences. If, under the stress of military necessity, the military authorities take action which would not in ordinary circumstances be authorized by the law of the country, they do so at their own peril in the sense that their actions may subsequently be challenged in the Courts unless an Act of Indemnity is passed by Parliament.[48]

Thus the introduction of a scheme of statutory War Zone Courts would diminish the likelihood of inflicting martial law upon civilians. It would also reduce, for the time being, the uncertainty, on the part of the military authorities, as to whether the actions taken by them against civilians for the purpose of maintaining public order could be justified by the doctrine of military necessity, or whether such steps would subsequently be held by the civil courts to be unlawful in the absence of an Indemnity Act. It seemed likely, for example, that the military authorities, under the doctrine of necessity, would have no power to sentence a civilian offender to a period of imprisonment and that a prison governor would have no answer to a writ of *habeas corpus*. Therefore, since sentences of imprisonment imposed by military authorities might prove to be ineffective, the scheme of civil courts was proposed. Moreover, and contrary to public perceptions, a system of courts martial for the trial of civilians—although then currently prohibited by the terms of section 1(5) of the Emergency Powers (Defence) Act 1939—would *not* answer the aim of securing the rapid disposal of cases against civil offenders at a time of acute urgency. For as Sir Alexander Maxwell, Permanent Secretary at the Home Office, observed, '... contrary to the general belief, procedure by courts martial is elaborate and not particularly swift'.[49] In any case, it was felt, the military authorities ought to be directing their energies against possible German invaders and not against unco-operative British citizens. Indeed, once the

[46] H.C. deb., n. 41 above, col. 138.

[47] (PRO) HO45/18626/834477, 'Note on Military Courts and Martial Law'. A fuller memorandum prepared by Maxwell for the Commons debate is in the same PRO papers: 'Emergency Powers (Defence) Bill', 14 July 1940. And see *ibid.*, 8 for the power of summary execution.

[48] *ibid.*, 'Note on Military Courts', 1; *ibid.*, 'Emergency Powers', 5.

[49] *ibid.*, 'Note on Military Courts', 2. cf., *ibid.*, 'Emergency Powers', 7.

civilian character of the courts had been agreed upon, even the military authorities accepted that the two advisers sitting on the bench alongside the judge should be laypersons rather than military personnel. Thus an early proposal that the special courts should consist of a legal chairman and two military officers appointed by the Regional Commissioner after consultation with the military commander was opposed by the military authorities themselves. The latter concluded that, '. . . it would create a very difficult position if these courts were composed partly of a Chairman not under military control and partly of military officers under military control'.[50]

However, that the survival of the country would ultimately rest in the hands of the military authorities was reflected in the proposal that regulations be issued under the Act enabling the military authorities to have access to the War Zone Courts in order to represent the military point of view and the military implications of any offence in any trial. Indeed, Anderson pointed out that some amendments to the Defence Regulations relating to the *ordinary* criminal law would also be required to take the military requirements into account. Thus if looting were to take place in a War Zone, it would be necessary to have power to inflict the most drastic penalty, even if it were believed that lesser punishments were more likely to be imposed.[51]

Similarly, the action of forcing a safeguard (that is, forcing one's way past a military picket or overpowering a sentry) would be rendered a capital offence under amended Defence Regulations. For cases might arise in which it became necessary for the military authorities to close certain roads or places to civilians. The mobile offensive forces of the Commander-in-Chief, Home Forces, General Sir Alan Brooke, would clearly find such measures useful, especially in the light of the problems which refugees had caused the defending armies vainly trying to stem the German Army on mainland Europe.

The ordinary criminal law, as Anderson reminded the House, had already been supplemented by the Treachery Act 1940 which imposed the

[50] *ibid.*, Maxwell to Sir Findlater Stewart, Home Defence Executive, 16 July 1940. That military officers, while sitting as members of a court of law, should be 'under military control' was not seen as constitutionally problematic. The relationship between 'command influence' and the independence of courts martial has been one of the themes of military justice reforms in the 1990s.

[51] H.C. deb., 16 July 1940, col. 73. After the Bill had passed through the Lords, the former Lord Chancellor, Lord Maugham, pointed out a difficulty with punishing looting. i.e., to prove to whom the property taken had belonged, without which a larceny conviction could not stand. Viscount Simon, then Lord Chancellor, took up the point with Anderson. But the matter was not further pursued. See HO45/18626/834477, Simon to Anderson, 31 July 1940. Recently published figures show that breaking-and-entering offences increased from 11,714 in 1939 to 21,260 in 1945, mainly as a result of looting from bombed or deserted properties (and even from the bodies of those killed in the Blitz). See Central Statistical Office, *Fighting with Figures: A Statistical Digest of the Second World War* (London: HMSO, 1995).

death sentence for acts of espionage or sabotage committed with intent to assist the enemy.[52] Similarly, numerous Defence Regulations relating to signalling, communicating with enemy agents, and spreading false reports had been promulgated, and the severest penalties could follow conviction. However, the spectre of capital punishment imposed by emergency courts without a proper system for appeals clearly alarmed Parliament, and formed one of the planks of parliamentary opposition to the first version of Anderson's scheme.

To recapitulate, the jurisdiction of these special War Zone Courts would be the same as any other civilian court dispensing criminal justice. However, they would be particularly suited to dealing with offences which were important from a military point of view and from the perspective of maintaining order amongst the civilian population. Their procedural advantages over the existing criminal courts were that the prosecuting authorities could dispense with the ordinary peacetime procedure whereby offenders charged with serious offences were brought in the first instance before examining magistrates before their committals for trial at the Assizes or Quarter Sessions. In emergency conditions arising from invasion, '. . . this slow and elaborate procedure would not be practicable'.[53] Thus, in addition to dispensing with a jury trial and with an appeal procedure, the committal stage would also be cut out of the procedure for trial before a War Zone Court. Accused persons would, however, be entitled to the protection of the ordinary rules of evidence (though copies of documents would apparently be acceptable); to legal representation; to full information before trial of the charge and of the nature of the evidence against them; and to a reasonable opportunity to prepare their defence.

Though these courts were to be granted powers to deal with all manner of criminal offences, it was recognized that their caseloads should be limited in order that rapid justice (if that is not a contradiction in terms) should be administered. Thus the emergency courts would also have power to refer to other courts any cases which it was not necessary nor appropriate for the War Zone Courts to try. Minor cases could thus be referred to those local justices untroubled by military operations, while more serious cases, presumably those bearing no relation to military or public order concerns, and which therefore did not justify trial by special proceeding before a War Zone Court, could be referred to any Assizes or Quarter Sessions in an area not yet declared a War Zone. Opposite arrangements were also possible. Thus justices could send cases for trial before a War Zone Court.

The reception given to Anderson's measure, published on 10 July, was not promising. The *Law Journal* on 13 July had already referred to the Bill

---

[52]   H.C. deb., 16 July 1940, cols. 73–4.   [53]   *ibid.*, col. 67.

under the heading, 'Courts Martial for Civilians'.[54] For, as originally introduced, the statute had made provision, *inter alia*, for circumventing the prohibition, in the Emergency Powers (Defence) Act 1939, s. 1(5), of trial of civilians by court martial or by any 'analogous' courts. 'Such courts' (it was not specified which kind) were to be created not by the 1940 Act itself but by regulations authorized by the Act. Their procedure was also to be laid down by regulations which would prescribe whether or not the proceedings were to be subject to review. In other words, it seemed originally that civilians were to be tried by court martial and that there was to be no formal appeal procedure. Moreover, the whole matter of the jurisdiction and procedure of the courts was to be left in the hands of the Executive. The *Law Journal* struck a note of grim resignation in commenting on these features:

However sinister this may sound, it may very well become necessary in the event of a partial or temporary occupation of this country by the enemy, for in that case the civil authority could have but little effect on those areas, and the observance of regulations essential to the safety of the State would have to be enforced by the military authorities.[55]

When the Bill reached the Commons for its Second Reading on 16 July, Anderson had immediately to disavow the aim of establishing courts martial for civilians. [56] 'The purpose of this Bill has, I think, been misunderstood in certain quarters. It is thought by some that the object of the Government is to establish courts martial, or some other form of military tribunal, for the punishment of civil offenders. The exact opposite is the case . . .'—prompting the *Law Journal* to alter its 'Obiter Dicta' headings from 'Courts Martial for Civilians' on 13 July to 'No Courts Martial for Civilians' on 20 July, and finally to 'Courts Not Quite Martial' on 3 August.[57]

The clarification in Anderson's opening remarks did not, however, pacify the House. There were indignant protests when he asked the Commons to pass the Bill through all its stages in the House without delay and as a matter of urgency. As Anderson's biographer, Sir John Wheeler-Bennett, pointed out, '. . . the House would have none of it. Both Parliament and the country were thoroughly alarmed at what appeared to be an attempt on British freedom, and Anderson was much assailed.'[58] Indeed, Wheeler-Bennett quoted from the liberal *News Chronicle*, 'Begging your pardon, Sir John, and with the greatest respect, we would remind

---

[54] *Law Journal*, 90, 13 July 1940, 11.   [55] *ibid.*
[56] H.C. deb., 16 July 1940, col. 65.
[57] *Law Journal*, 90, 13 July 1940, 11; *ibid.*, 20 July 1940, 22; *ibid.*, 3 Aug 1940, 41.
[58] Wheeler-Bennett, John W., *John Anderson, Viscount Waverley* (London: Macmillan, 1962), 246.

you that you are no longer in Bengal',[59] a reference to Anderson's controversial period of office as Governor of Bengal between 1932 and 1937.[60]

Some speakers invoked constitutional principle. Thus Edward Harvey cautioned that the House had, ' . . . stood for law and the sanctity of law through many difficult times'.[61] It should, he said, ensure that any emergency legislation passed at a time of grave national difficulty did not, 'infringe upon those things on which our national life is built'.

But as indicated previously, the House was most agitated by the skeletal nature of the Bill and by the device of the 'Henry VIII clause' reserving the measure's substance to ministerial regulations. Secondly, the House was perturbed that there was to be no appeal mechanism, merely a power exercisable by the presiding judge to respite an execution to enable the Home Secretary to consider whether to recommend the exercise of the Prerogative of Mercy.

On the first matter, on which the Commons made only limited headway, it was not parliamentary legislation but the Defence (War Zone Courts) Regulations 1940,[62] which primarily determined the scheme. Thus the minister had power under the regulations to establish War Zone Courts in any district where he was satisfied that, ' . . . by reason of recent or immediately apprehended enemy action the military situation is such as to require that criminal justice should be administered more speedily than would be practicable by the ordinary courts'.[63] He could then issue an order declaring that area to be a War Zone[64] and the War Zone Courts Regulations would thereupon come into force.[65]

---

[59] *News Chronicle*, 17 July 1940, cited in *ibid*.

[60] Cf., Simpson, *Odious*, 61 (n. 3 above) for a previous Commons reference to Anderson's controversial tenure of office in Bengal.

[61] H.C. deb., 16 July 1940, col. 114. Harvey reminded those speakers who were advocating the introduction of courts martial for civilians rather than the special civilian courts proposed by the government that the House had to maintain its tradition of resisting the extension of martial law as exemplified by its promulgation of the Petition of Right 1628. He went on to cite the celebrated proposition regarding martial law formulated by Sir Matthew Hale which continued, 'Secondly, this indulged [martial] law was only to extend to members of the Army or those of the opposite Army and never was so much indulged as intended to be executed or exercised upon others'.

[62] Defence (War Zone Courts) Regulations 1940, S.R.&.O. 1940, No. 1444, eventually issued at the instance of the Minister of Home Security (i.e., the Home Secretary wearing a different hat) on 7 Aug. 1940. There were, of course, separate regulations for Scotland.

[63] Emergency Powers (Defence) (No. 2) Act 1940, s. 1(1).

[64] Difficulties in delineating war zone boundaries bedevilled much of the civil and military planning. Military commands did not, e.g., correspond to county boundaries whereas the ordinary civilian would be likely to associate war zone districts with conventional local government boundaries when this was not necessarily going to be the case.

[65] The War Zones statute amended the principal Emergency Powers (Defence) Act 1939 to 'make provision for the apprehension and punishment of offenders and for their trial by such courts'. Leslie Hore-Belisha, former Secretary of State for War, described this formulation as a 'strange sequence of thought'. See H.C. deb., 10 July 1940, col. 83; and *Punch*, 24 July 1940, 99.

It was also by virtue of the minister's regulations rather than the statute itself (indeed, the latter made no mention of War Zone Courts at all) that particular courts were to be created. It was regulations which determined their functions and procedure;[66] when they were to commence working, and in which areas; their composition, including the appointment and tenure of their personnel—both judicial (appointed by the Lord Chancellor) and clerical; and their jurisdiction. It was ironic, therefore, for the *Justice of the Peace* magazine to remark, after the Bill had become law, that the statute's '. . . declaratory form is interesting, for it testifies very proper respect for the ancient rights of the British people'.[67] The magazine justified this claim on the ground that whereas the 1939 Act had authorized special courts to be set up by Order in Council, the 1940 Act had repeated this undertaking prior to the regulations being issued.

But this 'proper respect' did not impress everyone. One popular historian, E. S. Turner, called the provision for War Zone Courts, 'The most sinister invasion precaution' devised at the time,[68] and Members of the Commons were not deterred by Britain's parlous state from voicing their strong objections to some of the proposals. Even Leslie Hore-Belisha,[69] former Secretary of State for War who had resigned the previous January, was perturbed. 'As this is an entirely new judicial procedure with many safeguards for the subject, why does not the Right Hon. Gentleman introduce a Bill containing those safeguards?'[70]

Anderson clearly thought the House was being ungrateful. He pointed out that he could have introduced the whole scheme by Order in Council under the 1939 Act. Instead, he brought in a new Bill to authorize the creation of the scheme by regulation. And yet the House was complaining despite his having explained the scheme in outline to the Honourable Members. When the regulations were due to be issued, the House would have an opportunity of debating them. [HON. MEMBERS: 'But not amending them.']^71 He insisted that there was grave uncertainty about the situation and that no one knew exactly for what kind of conditions provision would have to be made. It was therefore necessary to have regard to the flexibility inherent in legislating by regulation. He cited the appointment by the Lord Chancellor of two justices to sit alongside the court president. But that drew the objection of members such as Aneurin Bevan and Emanuel Shinwell that he was referring to issues that would be contained

---

[66] Technically, the Lord Chancellor was granted the power to make regulations regarding practice and procedure in the War Zone Courts.

[67] *Justice of the Peace*, 104, 17 Aug. 1940, 451.

[68] Turner, E. S., *The Phoney War on the Home Front* (London: Michael Joseph, 1961), 250.

[69] Hore-Belisha's reputation as War Secretary, unjustly maligned by senior Army personnel such as Ironside and Dill before and after Dunkirk, has now properly been rehabilitated. See Roberts, *Eminent Churchillians*, 27–34.

[70] H.C. deb., 16 July 1940, col. 68.   [71] *ibid.*, cols. 68–9.

in regulations which were not, of course, before the House.[72] As H. B. Lees-Smith put it, the Minister had given:

... a careful explanation of the intentions of the Bill, though ... not of its actual provisions ... [H]e proposes to establish civil courts with civil judges, who, I gather, would be attached to military headquarters and would move about with the Forces while they administered the civil code. That, I understand, is the intention of the Bill, but the difficulty is that there is nothing of all this in the Bill. It is evident from the Minister's speech that the whole content of this Bill is in the regulations; and the House has not seen the regulations.[73]

The barrister, Kingsley Griffith, was scathing in his criticism of Anderson's performance. 'Are we dealing with this Bill or with the Right Hon. Gentleman's speech? It is all very well for anybody to come before this House and say, "I have a Bill which entitles me to cut off your head, but I can assure you that I am only going to cut your toe nails".'[74] It was no excuse, he added, that the country might face invasion that very night. The government had been aware of the possibility for weeks and should not only have had the 'real Bill' available for debate but should also have prepared the ground with the kind of consultations which had taken place over previous measures—by which he was referring to Regulation 18B.[75] Another speaker complained that as far as his knowledge went, he did not know of any minister in living memory who had introduced a bill of such magnitude, had hoped to carry it through all its stages in a single afternoon, and yet had not once referred to the actual provisions of the Bill.[76]

Alarmed by the accusation that he was 'changing the judicial system of the country by regulations',[77] Anderson responded by pointing out that a statement of powers in outline was a characteristic of any Emergency Powers Bill, as the example of the 1939 Act had demonstrated. Nonetheless, he was prepared to give undertakings that an amendment would be made in the Bill to confirm the civilian status of the proposed courts and that he would undertake consultations with interested parties regarding the terms of the regulations. It was a concession, but not a far-reaching one.

The other matter which principally concerned opponents of the Bill[78] was the absence of a right of appeal. Glenvil Hall, for example, was appalled at the prospect of justices of the peace—who owed allegiance to the 'Patronage Secretary'—advising the judge as to the suitability of the death sentence in any hearing.[79] Sidney Silverman, who was, of course, an

---

[72] H.C. deb., 16 July 1940, cols. 70–1.   [73] ibid., cols. 76–7.
[74] ibid., col. 80.   [75] Simpson, Odious, 61–5 (n. 3 above).
[76] H.C. deb., 16 July 1940, col. 97 (Glenvil Hall, MP).
[77] The charge was made by Cdr. Sir Archibald Southby, Conservative member for Epsom, who preferred to see a system of courts martial for civilians introduced. See ibid., col. 96.
[78] Apart from Southby (n. 77, above), a number of other speakers expressed a desire for a system of courts martial for civilians.
[79] H.C. deb., 16 July 1940, cols. 97–8.

inveterate opponent of capital punishment, put it slightly differently. He objected to making the death penalty applicable, '. . . by what is virtually a one-man court under a regulation which is not before us and for an offence which is not yet specified'.[80]

Newspaper reports of the proceedings in parliament confirmed the difficult ride Anderson had experienced. According to the *New Statesman*,[81] the House of Commons had 'behaved with courage and good sense' in voicing its objections, while according to *Punch*,[82] the Home Secretary had been 'badly heckled' when moving the Bill's Second Reading. Indeed, the Speaker had had to intervene to request a fair hearing for the Minister. Bruised by the experience, Anderson began consulting with Members of Parliament, as he had promised the House. Maxwell, Permanent Secretary at the Home Office, wrote to G. W. Lambert, Assistant Under-Secretary at the War Office,[83] pointing out the very strong demand on the part of Members of Parliament that, were a death sentence to be imposed by a War Zone Court, there should be a reference to some other authority before the sentence was due to be carried out. Even soldiers, he added, had the benefit of the confirmation procedure after a death sentence had been imposed by a court martial. Maxwell indicated that it would be expected that the Home Secretary would normally consider the case in the light of the existence of the Prerogative of Mercy. However, given the emergency nature of the War Zone Courts, there might be a case for asking the judge to certify, that in his opinion, the offender's guilt was clear, the sentence appropriate, and the military situation such as to require the immediate execution of the offender. Perhaps even the *military* authority might submit such a certificate in certain circumstances.

This was not, of course, the kind of sensitive response to parliamentary criticisms expected from the Home Office. In any case, Lambert indicated to Maxwell that the War Office wanted no part in certifying any case for execution. Its concerns were with the exemplary aspect of the sentence and with the avoidance of undue delay between sentence and the ordering of the execution to be carried out.[84] The War Office also regretted that

---

[80] *ibid.*, col. 102. Other speakers voiced similar objections. However, Sir Ralph Glyn took the view that since the principal objective was deterrence, the court's death sentence should be 'promulgated at once, so that everyone in the district may know what warfare means'.Whether promulgation meant only publicity or the immediate carrying out of the death sentence is not clear. See *ibid.*, col. 113. The Att.-Gen., Sir Donald Somervell, also added that until 25 years previously, there had been no right of appeal in England and Wales. [An HON. MEMBER: 'And what a mess they made of it'], and that one had been introduced in Scotland only in 1927. See *ibid.*, col. 143.

[81] *New Statesman*, 24 July 1940, 54.   [82] *Punch*, 24 July 1940, 99.

[83] (PRO) WO32/9485, Maxwell to Lambert, 18 July 1940.

[84] HO45/18626/834477, Lambert to Maxwell, 19 July 1940. Cf., WO32/9485, Lambert to Major-General C. J. Wallace, Director of Personal Services, 18 July 1940; *ibid.*, Lambert to Findlater Stewart, Home Defence Executive, 18 July 1940; *ibid.*, Findlater Stewart to Lambert, 19 July 1940; HO45/18626/834477, Sir Oscar Dowson to Maxwell, 19 July 1940.

sentences to be imposed by the War Zone Courts might, as a result of parliamentary pressure, become subject to review by some other authority.
The deterrent effect of a death sentence, they felt, might be diminished if
there were a general impression abroad that it might not necessarily be
executed.[85] Sir Claud Schuster, long-standing Permanent Secretary to the
Lord Chancellor, Viscount Simon, thought that Maxwell's idea was mis-
conceived.[86] It seemed to impart a process of confirmation, akin to that in
court martial procedure, before an execution was to be carried out.
Schuster had assumed, on the contrary, that what had been desired was
that the Home Secretary should have an opportunity before execution of
considering whether to intervene and whether to recommend the exercise
of the Prerogative of Mercy. The proposal that in the event of the severance
of communications with London, a military commander on the spot
would be expected to consider whether there were extenuating circumstances, was also unacceptable to Schuster. It was contrary to the spirit
upon which the special courts were to be created: that is, that they were to
be civilian, as opposed to military, courts. If a War Zone were cut off from
London, he agreed that the judge should certify that immediate execution
was necessary—but he realized that that proposal might encounter political opposition.

In fact, it encountered the opposition of both the Home Secretary and
the Attorney-General, Sir Donald Somervell.[87] The idea that the judge
should certify the need for immediate execution was dropped, ostensibly
on the ground that certification would abrogate an opportunity for the
exercise of the Prerogative of Mercy. Instead, it was proposed that in all
capital cases, the judge should send a report to the Home Secretary who
should normally reply within a period, to be fixed by regulations, before
the execution was to take place. If no reply were received in time or if the
military situation dictated immediate execution, then the death sentence
was to be carried out.

Quite how this first alternative did not also involve an abrogation of the
Prerogative of Mercy is difficult to see. Indeed, what is clear from these
internal documents is a failure to grasp the essence of the parliamentar-
ians' complaint: that no formal appeal mechanism or even something
comparable to it had been proposed. Given the prospect of death sentences being imposed for offences such as looting, the omission was
viewed as too grave an inroad on basic rights, even in the contemplated
circumstances.

When the Committee stage of the Bill was taken in the Commons on 23
and 24 July, the Home Secretary's complacency was shattered once more.
As the *New Statesman* put it sharply, 'Hats off to the Backbenchers who

---

[85] HO45/18626/834477, Maxwell to Anderson, 20 July 1940.
[86] *ibid.*, Schuster to Maxwell, 22 July 1940.
[87] *ibid.*, Maxwell to Lambert, 23 July 1940.

fought until Sir John Anderson was compelled to agree to vital changes in his Special Courts Bill!'.[88] The Home Secretary conceded that War Zones would only be declared in cases of invasion and that a review, though not, of course, judicial review itself, would operate where a sentence of death had been imposed. As the *New Statesman* observed, 'It was mainly on this last point that the House got excited.[89] Mr Shinwell rightly pointed out that under the Bill as it stood, a starving man who stole a loaf of bread from a shop might be shot out of hand as a "looter".'

Now it is true that members from all sides of the House were acutely aware of the difference between a power to impose a long prison sentence and a power to inflict capital punishment. But they failed to note that Anderson in fact offered his critics very little. He announced:

In regard to the death sentence, there will be a specific provision to ensure that the Regulations shall provide that such a sentence shall not be carried into effect until there has been proper consideration of the question whether the Prerogative of Mercy can be exercized.[90]

That in fact was no different from peacetime practice once all court proceedings had been exhausted. And of course it left the final determination to the Executive rather than to the Judiciary.

For whatever reason, and it may have been a forewarning of trouble ahead in the House of Lords, the Home Office had second thoughts on the matter. It held two more conferences on 25 July and 29 July attended also by representatives from the War Office and Home Forces.[91] The upshot was that an amendment was put forward in the Lords by Viscount Simon.[92] This provided for review in all cases in which a sentence of death had been passed by a War Zone Court and in such other circumstances as might be provided by regulations. The review panel would consist of not less than three persons[93] who held or had held high judicial office. Moreover, it was contemplated that provision should be made in the regulations to enable the Secretary of State to direct that proceedings be

[88] *New Statesman*, 27 July 1940, 79. A number of MPs, four Conservative and one each from the Liberals, Labour Party and Independents, were invited to meet Anderson in his room in the afternoon of 24 July to discuss the amendments. See HO45/18626/834477, letter from Norman Brooke (Anderson's secretary) to the 7 MPs, 24 July 1940.

[89] *New Statesman*, 27 July 1940, 79.

[90] H.C. deb., 5th Series. vol. 363, 24 July 1940, col. 839.

[91] HO45/18626/834477. Maxwell to Anderson, 25 July 1940; *ibid.*, Anderson to Simon, 30 July 1940.

[92] *ibid.*, Simon to Anderson, 29 July 1940. Simon had expressed anxiety about parliamentary reactions to the amendment. He identified 3 possible areas: (a) how did review relate to an appeal procedure; (b) whether there should be 2 or 3 review judges; and (c) in what circumstances other than where a death sentence had been imposed should a review be permitted.

[93] It was Sir Granville Ram, the First Parliamentary Counsel, who had suggested 2 review judges with a third judge as arbiter in the event of a division of opinion. Lord Atkin had suggested to Simon that at least 3 review judges should sit. This was accepted. See *ibid.*, Maxwell to Ram, 30 July 1940.

submitted for review if he thought review was expedient in the interests of justice.

The procedure contemplated left a wide discretion to the review judges. Review would not necessarily be in the nature of a retrial; there would be no obligation on the reviewing judges to hear the prisoner, witnesses, or counsel. In fact, the judges would have complete discretion to do whatever they thought necessary on review, in order to arrive at a proper judicial conclusion.

In non-capital cases, it was considered desirable to allow the president of the War Zone Court a discretion to refer a case for review if he certified that in his opinion the case involved questions of special difficulty of law or fact, or was one which, for any other reason, ought properly to be reviewed. Thus, it would be open to the president of a War Zone Court to refer a case for review on the ground that he himself considered that the sentence which he had imposed might be too severe![94] The implausibility—even if not the impossibility—of such a situation was picked up by Lord Atkin during the Lords' debate. Atkin had made the point strongly on Second Reading[95] that very long sentences of penal servitude ought to be treated for review purposes in the same way as death sentences. Simon acknowledged the point[96] and subsequently wrote to Anderson[97] indicating that when a judge had pronounced a 'swingeing' sentence of penal servitude, that should be taken to mean that he was satisfied with it; in which event, he would not be likely to certify the case as suitable for review.

Consequently, Atkin proposed a further ground for review, viz, where a heavy sentence of penal servitude had been imposed. He suggested a sentence of five years or more penal servitude should attract review. In the event, after consultations between Anderson and various Members of Parliament, the War Zone Court Regulations incorporated the provision that, in addition to the death penalty, a sentence of seven years or more penal servitude would attract automatic review.[98] The irony, of course, is that the particular length of sentence, whether five years or seven years or whatever, was not raised, let alone discussed, in Parliament. It prompted the final revolt on the Bill, albeit one conducted in the polite tones of a Lords debate.

Lord Mottistone, who, as Colonel Jack Seely, had been Secretary of State for War from June 1912 to March 1914,[99] was as deeply concerned as crit-

[94] HO45/18626/834477 Anderson to Simon, 30 July 1940.
[95] H.L. deb., vol. 117, 30 July 1940, col. 25.
[96] ibid., col. 37; ibid., 31 July 1940, cols. 58–9.
[97] HO45/18626/834477, Simon to Anderson, 31 July 1940.
[98] ibid., Anderson to Simon, 3 Aug 1940. See Defence (War Zone Courts) Regulations, art. 12 (1)(a), S.R. & O. 1940, No. 1444.
[99] Anderson had written to Simon on 29 July warning him that Mottistone (M) was intending to raise some questions regarding the duties of the police in those areas where War Zone

ics in the Commons at the Executive's power to legislate by regulation on matters affecting life and death. He regarded with particular distaste the negative resolution procedure whereby once the Order in Council had been laid (authorizing the issue of the regulations), either House would have twenty-eight days within which to resolve that the Order be annulled. Instead of this *sub silentio* procedure, he proposed that when the time came for the regulations to be approved, it should be done by a substantive Motion moved by a minister in both Houses, 'so that the country may fully understand what has been proposed and what has been acted upon'.[100] In the Lords, of course, nothing as *infra dig.* as forcing a division could be contemplated. But the protest reflected the deep-seated anxieties of Members of both Houses, an anxiety covering the span of political opinions represented in both chambers.

The legal press gave the measure as it emerged from Parliament a mixed response. The complimentary remarks of the *Justice of the Peace*[101] on the statute's 'very proper respect for the ancient rights of the British people' have already been noted. But the following week, it went even further in its praise. It viewed the legislative exercise as a, '. . . reinforcement in the people at large of that confidence in the executive essential to the successful prosecution of a war where nerves are as important as navies, and faith in leadership perhaps the final determinant of victory'.[102] It perceived a 'happy partnership' between a people willing to sacrifice both its present convenience and the exercise of its traditional rights, and an executive reciprocating that trust by displaying an intention to attenuate only to the minimal extent necessary the enjoyment of those time-honoured civil liberties.[103] Indeed, here was an Executive willing to listen to reasoned criticism, it trilled, in contemplating the amendments taken on board. Regulations could always be annulled, it soothed, and knowledge of the possibility of annulment would have a restraining effect.

Courts might be established. He had apparently acquired a secret Circular sent to the police from the Home Office. It stated that if the enemy landed in force and occupied an area, the police should not take part, either alone or in conjunction with the Armed Forces, in armed resistance to the landing. Instead, they should arrange an organized withdrawal. A rearguard should remain to maintain order, not to resist the enemy and to surrender any weapons. M complained that this represented a less aggressive role for the police than he desired. See HO45/18626/834477, Anderson to Simon, 29 July 1940. On 1 Aug, M telephoned Churchill about the matter, having decided not to raise the matter in Parliament. Churchill sent the Circular to Attlee and to Anderson with the characteristic comment, 'We cannot surely make ourselves responsible for a system where the police will prevent the people resisting the enemy, and will lay down their arms and become the enemy's servant in any invaded areas.' After much debate and differences of opinion among Cabinet Ministers, Churchill resolved the matter by minuting, 'We do not contemplate or encourage fighting by persons not in the armed forces but we do not forbid it.' See Gilbert, Martin, *Winston S. Churchill*, vol. vi, *Finest Hour, 1939–1941* (London: Heinemann, 1983), 711–12.

[100] H.L. deb., 30 July 1940, col. 63.   [101] *Justice of the Peace*, 104, 17 Aug. 1940, 451.
[102] *ibid.*, 24 Aug. 1940, 468.
[103] Ironically, the scandal of the internment of refugees from Nazi Germany had already been exposed.

But whether the atmosphere in the Commons, in particular, was one of reasoned dialogue or of the expression of anger at the arrogance of the Executive, is a question of interpreting the mood of the time. The *Law Journal*[104] did not repose the same faith in the Executive as its contemporary legal periodical. The Act, it said, had been an 'extremely badly drafted measure in the first instance' and everything depended on the regulations to be made. This was a most unsatisfactory situation, for, 'Governments change, and so do their intentions, and the more that could be got into the Bill itself the better'.[105]

INVASION 1941–1942?

When the 'No 2 Regulations' were finally issued on 7 August, the *Justice of the Peace*, after observing that they constituted a 'well drawn and comprehensive order', remarked that, 'Our firm hope is that [the regulations] will never have to be used but such is the uncertainty of the times that it may receive application even before this article is published'.[106] Simon, in introducing the Bill's Second Reading in the Lords, had been more optimistic. The measure had been drafted, '. . . to provide for an emergency—an emergency that may not arise. We may think that as the weeks pass it is less likely to arise; but an emergency none the less might arise . . .'.[107]

We know from the first part of this chapter, that by 7 August, Hitler had already issued his Directive No. 16. Military historians also tell us that 12 August was *Adlertag*: 'Eagle Day', the commencement of the air assault on Britain, targeted initially on the South Coast airfields and radar stations. Then would follow 'Operation Sea Lion' and by November, Britain would be effectively vanquished.[108] The strategic targets, which later included the sector stations such as Kenley and Biggin Hill, and factories producing new aircraft, did, however, escape total destruction. And then suddenly on 7 September, the Blitz on London commenced, an unremitting air assault on civilians for 57 consecutive nights. It was, ironically, the salvation of the Royal Air Force and, of course, of the country.[109] Hitler announced the postponement of 'Sea Lion' on 12 October, and the British Foreign Office learned of the decision some days later.[110] But since there was not as yet any 'unambiguous indication from a Sigint source that the invasion had been abandoned'[111] (as distinct from assessments based on operational considerations), preparations for the introduction of the War

---

[104] *Law Journal*, 90, 3 Aug. 1940, 41.   [105] *ibid*.
[106] *Justice of the Peace*, 104, 24 Aug 1940, 469.   [107] H.L. deb., 30 July 1940, col. 4.
[108] Hough, Richard, and Richards, Denis, *The Battle of Britain* (London: Coronet Books, 1990), 140.
[109] Fleming, *Invasion*, ch. 15 (see n. 26).
[110] Hinsley, *British Intelligence*, 189 (n.16 above).   [111] *ibid*.

Zone Courts scheme were put in hand. Indeed, military and civil planning for invasion, and the issue of instructions on how to combat it proceeded.

The official position thus seemed to be that while the danger had at least palpably receded, it had not disappeared completely. Indeed, a secret document prepared by MI14 and entitled *Notes on German Preparations for Invasion of the United Kingdom* was printed in April 1941,[112] while members of the Home Guard were issued in September 1941 with pike-like weapons described as 'balanced instruments particularly useful for street-fighting'.[113] Presumably the enemy was not thought only to be spies or downed Luftwaffe pilots. Experiments to set the sea on fire and thereby repel a sea invasion continued into 1941.[114]

The fact was, that diverse sources of information all pointed to the continued existence of German invasion plans and of invasion exercises.[115] At various intervals, however, notes of scepticism were inserted, whether by the Chiefs-of-Staff, or the Joint Intelligence Committee (JIC), or the Combined Intelligence Committee. The scepticism was understandable in the light of Germany's increasing focus on other theatres of war, such as the Balkans, the Middle East, and the Battle of the Atlantic. Yet the issue was swinging like a pendulum. On 10 April 1941, for example, the JIC was concluding that Germany was still giving priority to an invasion of Britain. By 27 April, it had revised its view and decided the danger had receded. Such changes of assessment were not uncommon. And those planning for Britain's emergency courts were not holding their breaths for each change of mood regarding the prospects for invasion.

Following 'Operation Barbarossa' (the German invasion of Russia in June 1941), the British Chiefs-of-Staff concluded that no similar threat

---

[112] Fleming, *Invasion*, 152. (see n. 26); There is a copy in the Sanderson papers at the Liddell Hart Centre.

[113] *ibid.*

[114] *ibid.*, 193. Perhaps reference should be made to the Channel Tunnel. Kenneth Strong of the Combined Intelligence Committee recounted that the committee was expected to take seriously the possibility of the Germans tunnelling their way to the English coast. So air photographs of the Calais area were closely studied for evidence of major digging operations. Even Churchill in 1942 asked for reassurance that work was not in progress and that the Germans would not 'pop up in the middle of Kent'. Some tunnelling experts looked at the workings commenced in the 1880s in the Dover-Folkestone area and concluded that a tunnelling operation from the French side would take 10 years to complete. 'At this', Strong comments, 'interest in the possibility was lost'. See Strong, *Intelligence*, 94. The story has now been more fully told by Keith Wilson who identifies Lord Hankey, a fierce opponent of the idea of a Channel Tunnel, with frightening the authorities in 1941 into checking that the Germans were not undertaking secret burrowing. A platoon of Royal Engineers was then despatched to waste their time placing microphones at different points along the coast at Shakespeare Cliff, Dover. See Wilson, Keith, *Channel Tunnel Visions, 1850–1945* (London: Hambledon Press, 1994).

[115] For this and the following information, see Hinsley, *British Intelligence*, 261–64 (n.16 above). See also Hitler's Directive No. 23, para. 5, 6 Feb. 1941. He instructed that the air and sea war against the UK was to be intensified in order also to 'give the impression that an attack on the British Isles is planned for this year'. See Trevor-Roper (ed.), *Hitler's War Directives*, 104.

would immediately face the United Kingdom. However, the danger, they believed, could recur from the Spring of 1942 and General Sir Alan Brooke, Commander-in-Chief, Home Forces (until Christmas Day 1941) considered that a scenario could be envisaged where British naval defences would not be able to prevent a strong German invasion force from reaching the coast. Thus, 'it would be perfectly possible to lose this country and the War', even without the prior defeat of Fighter Command whose survival in 1940 had been the crucial factor in the postponement of Operation Sea Lion.[116]

Only on 13 February 1942 were those German forces and equipment earmarked for the invasion of Britain redeployed to other tasks. Thus German naval personnel were stood down, and tugs and landing craft sent elsewhere. On 2 March, General Jodl, later hanged at Nuremberg, issued a directive that a year's notice would be given if the invasion scheme were to be revived.[117] The threat was finally over but in the United Kingdom anti-invasion measures were still being enforced, some even after the Normandy landings. Thus local invasion committees were dissolved only in November 1944, road blocks were removed, and railway station signs could reappear.[118] The prohibition on ringing church bells except as a warning of invasion was lifted after Churchill acknowledged in the Commons that the bells had become 'redundant' as a warning signal. He thought that in the event of a serious invasion, the information about it might just leak out.[119]

ADMINISTRATIVE ARRANGEMENTS: HOW TO SET UP WAR ZONE COURTS

The upshot of all this? If the price of freedom is said to be eternal vigilance, in this case the price was having the scheme of War Zone Courts ready for action even though the outcome of the Battle of Britain had ruined Hitler's invasion plan for September 1940. Perhaps more to the point was the fact that the work of busy civil servants must go on and administrative arrangements put in hand. Much of these arrangements might be dismissed as mind-numbingly boring. Indeed they were. The tasks involved compiling lists of suitable War Zone Court assessors (should they all be legally qualified?; what proportion should be women?); and obtaining Treasury consent for the subsistence allowances payable to the court clerks. Since the latter were already in state service, it was some comfort that their sponsoring departments, the Scottish Office and the Home Office, would not require to undergo the Treasury version of Chinese water torture (i.e. having to justify an increase in their establishments

---

[116] Collier, *Defence*, 295–6.
[118] Fleming, *Invasion*, 273. (see n. 26).

[117] Wheatley, *Operation Sea Lion*, 98.
[119] *ibid.*, 89.

funded by the Exchequer). Correspondence with the Office of Works had to be opened to ensure suitable accommodation for courts which might have to undertake a peripatetic role in the circumstances. In the event of court mobilization, the clerks in Scotland were instructed to obtain official papers and ID cards issued by the Scottish Office and were warned to take with them essential stationery supplies 'on a minimum scale'. The instruction left one sheriff clerk in Inverness in a state of subdued perturbation:

I do not anticipate any special difficulty in supplying suitable stationery from this office, but as it may be necessary to complete an extract sentence of death or penal servitude and as these are not in the Sheriff Court list it would be as well if a supply of forms for all types of sentences in the style adopted from those in use in the High Court of Justiciary should be at hand in case of emergency, and I shall be glad if you could arrange that these could be supplied. Probably one dozen of each would be sufficient.[120]

The resolution of legal conundra also forms part of the staple diet of the assiduous civil servant. Thus, back in England on 31 October 1940—ironically the day of the official ending of the Battle of Britain in the eyes of the British government—M. H. Whitelegge, an assistant secretary at the Home Office, was writing a memorandum to L. S. Brass, the assistant legal adviser to the Home Office. He pointed out that regulation 2, para. (1) of the War Zone Courts Regulations appeared to be ambiguous.[121] Was it the intention that the courts should be established right away (in which case their creation was overdue) or, as the opening lines of the paragraph appeared to imply, were they to be set up only when the invasion or other emergency had taken place or was immediately apprehended? Whitelegge seems to have assumed that the clerks and other staff of the War Zone Courts could be appointed at once, while the creation of the courts themselves would have to await the arrival of the emergency or its immediate apprehension. Apparently, the Lord Chancellor's Department had informed the nominated judges, the Presidents-Elect, that they could not officially be appointed until the courts had been set up, and the presidents, in their turn, were adopting the position that in those circumstances, they could not themselves proceed to the informal appointment of anyone else such as clerks to the courts. The matter remained unresolved for some months. After the New Year, it was decided that the appointments should not be made in advance of imminent emergency.[122] Presumably the objective was to avoid creating unnecessary panic.

The actual mechanism was that the Minister of Home Security (the

---

[120] (SRO) HH 50/70, Sheriff-clerk of Inverness-shire to T. McQueen Walker, Scottish Home Department, 5 Sept. 1940. Details of routine administrative arrangements described above are also from Scottish Office correspondence in *ibid*.

[121] (PRO) HO45/19078/863168, Whitelegge to Brass, 31 Oct. 1940.

[122] (PRO) HO45/23079/700178, M. H. Whitelegge, 'War Zone Courts', 25 Jan. 1941.

Home Secretary wearing a different hat), would declare a War Zone and then issue an order establishing a War Zone Court. The Home Secretary (the Minister of Home Security wearing the Home Secretary's hat), would also issue an order formally appointing the clerk to the court and the panel of advisory members.[123] Whitelegge, the civil servant, wondered about the precise conditions which would precipitate the declaration of a War Zone. If the 'enemy action' were merely a 'small-scale affair', or capable of being resolved within a few days, there might be no need to create new courts and to disrupt the ordinary machinery of criminal justice. On the other hand, he thought it might well be safer to trigger the machinery in the light of the 'probability of larger developments in the offing'.

In the event of complete severance of communications with London at an early stage of invasion, Regional Commissioners would assume the functions of government in the region, including those in respect to the creation of War Zone Courts and the appointment of personnel. Uncertainty remained, however, 'as to the precise moment at which they [the judges] are to throw over their normal work and proceed to the War Zone Court district . . .'.[124] It was thought sensible to leave this matter for resolution in the light of the emergency situation which might develop. It was also suggested that on receiving the call, the Presidents should proceed to a central position in their district, 'and not too near the coast', where they would make contact with their clerks.

Further consideration of the administrative arrangements for the courts took place at a conference (the 'Victor' conference) on 6 February 1941 following the conducting of an anti-invasion exercise.[125] At the conference, all the Regional Commissioners insisted that the courts be set up very quickly after invasion had started. The military authorities still believed in a fifth column and that saboteurs would have to be brought rapidly before such courts. The 'leisurely procedure of criminal justice' would not be sufficiently effective in creating a deterrent effect. It also seemed to be the view that as soon as invasion started, War Zone Courts should be created in all regions. For, despite the fact that fighting might only be taking place in one or two areas, there was a prospect that, first, landings from sea or air might be anticipated in other parts of the country; and secondly, in all parts of the country, saboteurs or fifth-columnists might 'spring into activity'. However, the Permanent Secretary at the Home Office, Sir Alexander Maxwell, pointed out that the House of Commons had expressed the desire during the parliamentary stage to limit the operation of War Zone Courts. Not for the first time in this episode was Maxwell reminding others of the principle of parliamentary democracy even during a crisis.

---

[123] On 30 Oct. 1940, Herbert Morrison had replaced Anderson and had filled both ministerial portfolios.
[124] 'War Zone Courts', see n. 122, above.
[125] *ibid.*, Copy of Note by Sir A. Maxwell, 7 Feb 1941.

A further problem was that if there were to be only one judge for a War Zone Court in each region, it might prove impossible for the court to function. Indeed, at the outset of the anti-invasion exercise, it appeared that one of those selected as a War Zone Court judge had been 'captured' at Rottingdean by troops acting as the enemy. Moreover it was noted that a clerk of the peace, appointed as clerk to a War Zone Court, might reside in a town which could be cut off from his court by the enemy. While a deputy clerk could be appointed, it appeared that there was no power in the regulations to substitute another judge. The solution suggested was to confer on the Regional Commissioner an express power to appoint another judge, although arguably this power was inherent when circumstances justified the assumption of governmental powers on the part of the commissioners. The very thought of Regional Commissioners or indeed of anyone else apart from the Lord Chancellor appointing judges under any circumstances was a nightmare too horrible for Sir Claud Schuster to contemplate.[126] Thankfully Schuster's worst nightmare was not realized due to Hitler's thoughtfulness in cancelling his invasion.

In mid-February 1941 a Circular was prepared, making it clear to Presidents, clerks, and advisory members in their letters of appointment that they would have no duties to perform until a War Zone had been declared.[127] A meeting held on 25 February agreed that arrangements should be made for warning the Presidents in two stages, a preparatory or 'threat of invasion' stage; and then a message instructing them to proceed at once to their districts. These messages might be conveyed under the code letters 'X' and 'Y' respectively, and the time for sending them out would have to be judged in the circumstances of the moment. It was not, however, desirable to connect them too rigidly with the military 'stand to' and 'action stations' messages.[128]

The foregoing discussions did yield a positive result. War Zone Courts were finally established, on paper at least, for the various civil defence regions.[129] The order, issued by the Minister of Home Security, divided England and Wales into 12 districts, some of which were to be served with two courts and some with one. While London was deliberately excluded from these arrangements, unfortunately the County of Warwick was clearly thought not to exist as it was omitted from the counties included in the Midlands district, and an amended order had to be prepared.[130]

---

[126] *ibid.*, notes of a conference held on 13 Feb. 1941.

[127] *ibid.*, Circular to Principal Officers from Sir George Gater, Joint Secretary to the Ministry of Home Security, 14 Feb. 1941. Gater had been seconded to the ministry from London County Council.

[128] *ibid.*, 'War Zone Courts, Minutes of a Conference on Feb. 25, 1940'. This was obviously a typing error for 1941.

[129] War Zone Courts Rules 1941 (S.R. & O. 1941, No. 564/L.8, 25 Apr. 1941).

[130] HO45/19078/836168, Whitelegge to Clerks of War Zone Courts, 27 May 1941.

Neither the order appointing the Presidents, nor, of course, any orders declaring War Zones themselves, were issued.[131]

Although they had not yet been formally appointed, the proposed court Presidents had been selected. Who were the judges who would have the power to impose the death sentence following a rapid trial in an emergency court for otherwise non-capital offences such as looting and forcing a safeguard? Within England and Wales, they were, with the exception of two Court of Appeal judges, Goddard and du Parcq, judges of the High Court. It would be tedious to go through the whole list,[132] but there is perhaps some significance in one of the appointments made to the front-line South-Eastern district—covering Kent, Surrey, and Sussex (excluding those areas within the Metropolitan district). One of the judges for this district was Oliver J. who had recently chaired an inquiry into court martial procedure.[133] He had been identified early on by the Judge Advocate General, Sir Henry MacGeagh, as a suitable appointment to enforce the statutory martial law regulations which, as noted previously, MacGeagh had proposed at the early planning stage of the legislative exercise.[134]

Special arrangements were made for transporting the judges to and throughout their districts, given the unreliability of public transport and the probability that both police and military transport were unavailable (though Scottish Command had apparently indicated its willingness to provide transport). Two or three cars and their drivers (volunteers if possible) were therefore to be made available for the judges on the issue of the 'stand to' message and the necessary petrol coupons and priority labels would be arranged. The arrangements for transport were carefully examined because of the expectation that difficulties might otherwise be encountered in getting the judges through certain areas.[135] In the event, a bulk contract for the transporting of judges seems to have been arranged between the Home Office and a firm called 'Daimler Hire' of London who assured the officials that their drivers knew their geography pretty well. The company did, however, ask to be informed of any areas which it would be wise to avoid due to congestion or, perhaps more significantly, due to enemy action.[136]

A more precise system of warning messages was also put in place for the Presidents and their clerks. The codeword 'Greenleaves' would be a

[131] See *Justice of the Peace*, 105, 10 May 1941, 257; *Law Journal*, 91, 10 May 1941.

[132] See list in HO45/23079/700178, 'War Zone Courts: List of Presidents and Clerks'.

[133] *Report of the Army and Air Force Court Martial Committee, 1938*, P.P. 1939–40 (Cmd. 6200), IV, 49. See Rubin, G. R., 'The Status of the Judge Advocate General of the Forces in the UK since the 1930s', *Revue de Droit Militaire et de Droit de la Guerre/Military Law and Law of War Revue*, 33 (1994), 243–71.

[134] WO32/9485, MacGeagh to General Sir Robert Gordon-Finlayson (Adjutant-General), 1 June 1940. MacGeagh's other judicial suggestions were Lawrence, Stable, and Hodgson JJ. The other judge appointed to the South-Eastern district was Cassels J.

[135] HO45/23079/700178, E. Cordes to W. H. Cornish, 12 June 1941.

[136] *ibid.*, minute by J. P. Butler, 18 June 1941.

warning that the judge should be ready to make for his district upon receiving the second signal. That subsequent codeword was 'Inflation' which should be issued when the emergency was considered sufficiently serious for the judge's presence to be required in his district. Third, the codeword 'Swifter' would mean that the whole or part of his district had been declared a War Zone. This signal might or might not be delivered to the judge at the same time as the 'Inflation' message. The cancellation of these messages would be signified by 'Cancel Greenleaves'; 'Cancel Inflation'; and 'Cancel Swifter'—as the case might be.

The judges had been asked to keep the Police Duty Room at the Home Office informed of their present and future addresses. Outside London, the local police would transmit the messages after receiving instructions through the Civil Defence Regional Police Staff Officer and the appropriate Chief Constable. The 'Inflation' message would be accompanied by instructions for the judge's car to proceed to his address unless he had elected to travel to his district in his own car in which event priority labels and petrol coupons would be provided in advance by the Ministry of Home Security.

Of course, not everything goes smoothly in an exercise, let alone during the real thing. When the Ministry of Home Security tried to check up on the address of Mr Justice Croom-Johnson, one of the Northern judges, in March 1941, all it received back was 'care of the Royal Courts of Justice'. A ministry official was advised to try the judge's clerk. He concluded that changes of address were not being notified to the Police Duty Room. He might have added that unchanged addresses were likewise not being notified which would make the transmission of urgent messages somewhat more protracted.

Regarding accommodation in their districts, the original idea was that judges should be accommodated in private houses, an idea soon dropped in favour of judges' lodgings or local hotels. If the former, the employment of domestic staff would be required. If the latter, then a private sitting room would have to be available (presumably contemplating whether to sentence a looter to death should not be done to the accompaniment of knitting needles, the clinks of china teacups, or polite small talk). Whatever was decided, the judge should not, agreed the Home Office, be left to 'fend for himself'.[137]

During the planning phase in July 1940, some Scottish Members of Parliament were doubtful as to the applicability of the Home Secretary's scheme North of the Border. Indeed, the Lord Advocate, Thomas Cooper (later Lord Cooper of Culross), initially concluded that it was unnecessary in Scotland to provide for the establishment of emergency courts on the English model. All that would be required would be statutory provision

---

[137] HO45/19078/836168, Whitelegge to Clerks of War Zone Courts, 27 May 1941.

to enable both the Sheriff Courts and the High Court of Justiciary to function without juries and under an accelerated procedure, while the sentencing powers of sheriffs-substitute might be increased to enable the imposition of sentences of up to two years' penal servitude.[138] It is clear, however, that following discussions with the Home Defence Executive, the War Office, the Home Office, and other interested parties, the principle of uniformity prevailed in the special circumstances contemplated. Thus four War Zone Courts were also set up for Scotland to sit at such places as might be decided in consultation with the military authorities there. They were to be presided over by Lords Russell, Keith, and Patrick, and by Sheriff Sir J. C. Watson, Sheriff of Caithness (whose jurisdiction encompassed Scapa Flow). The clerks appointed were the sheriffs-clerk of Fife, Perth, Kilmarnock, and Inverness—presumably signifying the areas in Scotland considered most vulnerable to invasion. Responsibility for prosecution before the Scottish War Zone Courts would rest with the procurator-fiscal of the district, failing whom a 'special prosecutor' attached to the court, or an officer of His Majesty's Forces, or 'such other person as the Court allows'.[139]

There was one further group of persons within the wartime criminal justice system which required to be informed of the declaration of War Zone areas. These were prison governors who received their instructions from the headquarters of the Prison Commission temporarily housed at Oriel College, Oxford.[140] Once a War Zone had been declared, prison governors were required to ascertain whether they were holding any prisoners for trial in respect of an offence alleged to have been committed in that area. If so, they were to supply particulars to the clerk of the relevant War Zone Court and ask for instructions regarding the disposal of such cases (whether or not proceedings for committal were to follow). It was pointed out that in emergency conditions, it might not be possible to fix at the time of remand or committal the place and time for the production of prisoners, and that any arrangements made might subsequently have to be altered at short notice. It was essential, therefore, that governors should keep in constant touch with the police and with the War Zone Court clerks, and liaise with them about the production of prisoners, and their custody while at court.

But prison governors were also liable to be involved in much more gruesome activities. In the event that a death sentence had to be carried out, the

---

[138] (SRO) HH 50/70, note by C. C. Cunningham, 18 July 1940. The Scottish Office explained to the Home Office that the functions of JPs in relation to criminal law administration in Scotland were negligible. See *ibid.*, Cunningham to Miss J. Williams, 19 July 1940.

[139] *ibid.*, Circular No. 4125, Scottish Home Department. 'Administration of Criminal Justice in Scotland under Conditions of Emergency', 21 Aug 1940, paras. 3(b) and 9.

[140] (PRO) HO 45/19078/836168, 'Prison Commission: Memorandum to all Local Prisons', 14 July 1942.

prisoner was to be conveyed to a prison equipped for carrying out an execution by hanging. The Secretary of State in these cases was required to direct that the prisoner be treated as if convicted on indictment for murder. But if no suitable prison were available for a hanging, then the instructions were that, '. . . the sentence shall be carried out by shooting in like manner as in the case of a person upon whom sentence of death has been passed under the Army Act by a court martial'. [141] This commended itself to Sir Claud Schuster. In writing to Sir Alexander Maxwell, he observed:

> As to execution, you know far better than I do the difficulties in executing by hanging. I had always understood that hanging in modern days was a very highly skilled form of art, requiring very elaborate apparatus; and I greatly fear that if neither the artist nor the apparatus is available, there may be some hideous bungle.[142]

It had originally been proposed that the presiding judge should decide on the method of execution. But at a meeting of the Home Policy Committee of the War Cabinet,[143] the Lord Advocate pointed out that the Scottish judges dissented. The decision on execution, they argued, should be made by the Executive, not by the Judiciary, as the former would be in a better position to know the most practicable course in each case. This suggestion was accepted.

As noted previously, however, the imposition of a death sentence attracted automatic review by a panel of three senior judges. Only once that review had confirmed the original decision and the panel's finding had been communicated to the person whose duty it was to officiate over the carrying out of the execution (usually the sheriff of the county or the prison governor) could the execution go ahead,[144] whether by hanging or, if necessary, by shooting.

After all this frenetic planning regarding the arrangements for the activation of the War Zone Courts and for the transporting of the judges, it hardly needs to be stated that, in the hallowed paraphrasing of Sellar and Yeatman, 'nothing much happened'. Certainly, between May 1941 and May 1942, the contingency legal planners confined themselves to modifying the War Zone Courts rules to take account of some of the suggestions already noted. The result was a revised and consolidated set of rules issued on 15 May 1942.[145]

That civil servants were busy revising these rules as late as that seems therefore to indicate either that intelligence information regarding the

---

[141] *ibid.*, para. 17.   [142] HO 45/18626/8344477, Schuster to Maxwell, 22 July 1940.
[143] WO32/9485, copy of minutes of Cabinet Home Policy Committee meeting, 3 Aug. 1940.
[144] Before provision had been made for a review panel, the Army made it clear that it would be very unhappy to be involved in the custody and execution of a prisoner. It recognized, however, that there might be no alternative in some circumstances. See WO32/9485, Findlater Stewart (Home Defence Executive) to Lambert (War Office), 19 July 1940; HO45/18626/834477, Maxwell to Anderson, 20 July 1940.
[145] War Zone Courts Rules 1942 (S.R. & O. 1942, No. 934/L. 12, 15 May, 1942). See *Justice of the Peace*, 106, 13 June 1942, 279–80; *ibid.*, 4 July 1942, 313; *ibid.*, 11 July, 1942, 327–8.

potential threat of invasion continued to arrive, or that conclusive evidence for the unequivocal abandonment of such plans was still lacking. Indeed, until the United States' naval success in the Battle of Midway in May 1942, the war in the Far East had been a catalogue of disasters, one after another, for the Allies. Until El Alamein in October 1942, the Mediterranean and North African theatres of war were vulnerable, though the outcome of the Battle of the Atlantic and Hitler's strategic error in attacking Russia in June 1941 were arguably the defining moments of the War.[146]

WINDING-UP

Following the opening up of the Second Front with the D-Day landings at Normandy, reviews of the extensive numbers of Defence Regulations were begun in the various ministries. 'C' Division within the Home Office, with responsibility for the War Zone Courts, gave consideration on 21 September 1944 to the question of winding-up the scheme.[147] However, immediate revocation was ruled out at this stage and marked down for repeal upon 'Cease Fire' in Europe.

It should not be forgotten that London was being targeted for attacks by V1 and V2 rockets at this time. The latter, in particular, sorely tested the morale of the capital's inhabitants. The matter was looked at again after the New Year and on 2 February 1945, another Home Office official, J. M. Ross, suggested that the regulations should be revoked at the next Privy Council meeting. Maxwell then intervened to propose a more systematic examination of all the anti-invasion regulations and orders made in 1940 with a view to a comprehensive clear-out rather than *ad hoc* revocation. He wrote to Herbert Morrison on 13 February, informing him that he had discussed with Sir William Brown, Secretary of the Ministry of Home Security, the question of applying a common plan to all clearly recognized anti-invasion regulations. But he obviously had doubts about the wisdom of his own strategy. Thus, if revocations were made at the present time, '. . . such revocations will give a clear indication that the Government regard invasion of this country as now out of the question, and will stimulate MPs to ask why other [presumably less obvious] invasion Regulations are not revoked'.[148]

Maxwell's inclination was therefore to leave in existence until the end of European hostilities all those remaining anti-invasion regulations which

[146] For a recent and scholarly re-appraisal, see Overy, Richard, *Why the Allies Won* (London: Jonathan Cape, 1995).
[147] HO45/23078/700176. But see also, *ibid.*, Sir Frank Newsam to Findlater Stewart, 23 Sept, 1944.
[148] *ibid.*, Maxwell to Morrison, 13 Feb. 1945.

did not cause any actual inconvenience to the public. The reasoning was pragmatic (there is no evidence on Maxwell's part of a sinister illiberal motive; or of a motive which would prepare the ground for a peacetime corporatist or command economy). His argument was: why waste time on an unnecessary revocation exercise? It could await the termination of European hostilities and the anti-invasion regulations could then be revoked together with other regulations earmarked, by a committee chaired by Schuster, for revocation on victory in Europe. On the other hand, Brown, who had been seconded from the Board of Trade, and therefore possibly favoured a laissez-faire approach, believed that the disadvantages of waiting for Stage A (i.e. victory in Europe) outweighed the advantage of saving labour by not attending to revocation at this juncture. Morrison agreed. There should be no delay in revoking unnecessary regulations, though a logical plan to this end should be adopted. Thus not only the War Zone Courts Regulations and other anti-invasion measures, but also regulations not exclusively designed as anti-invasion provisions should be targeted for revocation.

But rapid dismantling and a significant clear-out simply did not go together. The latter absorbed more time than Brown or Morrison assumed would be rerquired (or perhaps Parkinson's Law prevailed once more). The upshot was that a comprehensive revocation order was issued, not immediately but three months later, on the day following VE (Victory in Europe) Day. This covered: the War Zone Courts Regulations; 5 anti-invasion regulations as suggested by the Ministry of Home Security; 7 other regulations which would have been highly relevant in the event of invasion; and Regulation 1B issued in June 1940 in anticipation of the War Zone Courts scheme. The latter was the measure which imposed the death penalty or penal servitude for life for endeavouring to force a safeguard.[149]

---

[149] It was feared that in the event of invasion, refugees might try to advance along a prohibited route blocked by sentries whom they might endeavour to overpower. The anti-invasion regulations to be revoked were Regs 25A and 79B regarding the treatment of animals under invasion conditions; Reg. 84A enabling Regional Commissioners, cut-off from London, to make by-laws equivalent to Defence Regulations which the War Zone Courts could then enforce; Reg. 84AA obliging persons to perform emergency work 'in connection with operations for meeting actual or apprehended enemy attacks on land in the UK'; and Reg. 84AB empowering Regional Commissioners to close shops to facilitate invasion exercises. The 7 other regulations of significance to invasion concerned matters such as removal of direction posts and place-names; control of articles likely to assist the enemy (e.g. high-frequency equipment); detention of suspects by Regional Commissioners; and immobilization of vehicles.

CONCLUSION

The War Zone Courts scheme thus officially came to an end on 9 May 1945.[150] It was an ambitious and desperate expedient. Existing only on paper, a blueprint for a rough-and-ready criminal justice system which purported to make a virtue out of necessity, it was, thankfully, never put to the test. As the creature of administrators planning for a twilight world in which, one might reasonably conclude, backs-to-the-wall resistance against a Nazi invader would be the only issue which mattered, it nontheless co-existed with the still-flickering flame of constitutionalism.

For, while the proposition that everything should be left to the military authorities in those dire circumstances was beguiling, such a prospect was distasteful to the civil servants' cast of mind. It was as if the civil authority enjoyed a *moral* superiority over the military power. Indeed, that was precisely the point in a parliamentary democracy which could be favourably contrasted with the character of the enemy which the United Kingdom was confronting alone.

Yet additionally and paradoxically, there was implicit in the scheme a distrust of the common people which mirrored the state's actions in rounding up alien refugees from Nazi Germany.

Notwithstanding, desperate times required desperate measures and there is little doubt that the country almost tipped over the edge of the abyss. In that respect, the practical need for the rapid disposal of cases and for the creation of further capital offences could be justified, though backbenchers in Parliament across the political divide succeeded—against the initial wishes of a popular coalition government—in ensuring limited protection for the most serious offenders in the form of due process before execution.

Parliament, in short, was still fulfilling its constitutional duty to check the Executive, just at the moment when the nation was teetering on the brink of destruction. Of course, it was a limited constitutional victory. For, apart from the appeal business, the government retained control over every other facet of the (as yet unmobilized) War Zone Courts scheme.

(It is interesting to speculate whether the judges, if called upon, would have been as compliant with government policy as Brian Simpson showed them to be in respect to Regulation 18B.[151])

---

[150] Order in Council Revoking and Amending Certain Defence Regulations, S.R. & O. 1945, No. 540, 9 May 1945.

[151] '[T]he courts did virtually nothing for the detainees, either to secure their liberty, to preserve what rights they did possess under the regulation, to scrutinize the legality of Home Office action, or to provide compensation when matters went wrong.' See Simpson, *Odious*, 418 (n. 3 above).

'The executive controls 99/100ths of this House', complained one back-bencher in July 1940. While government effectively legislated by ministerial regulation, little troubled by Parliament, the tortuous passage of the War Zone Courts scheme through the two Houses reminded everyone that Executive hegemony in Britain, unlike in Nazi Germany, was not total.

5

Tears of the Law: Colonial Resistance and Legal Determination

Peter Fitzpatrick*

I sometimes fear the Duke of Wellington is too much disposed to imagine that he can govern a great nation by word of command, in the same way in which he governed a highly disciplined army. He seems to be unaccustomed to, and to despise, the inconsistencies, the weaknesses, the bursts of heroism followed by prostration and cowardice, which invariably characterize all popular efforts. He forgets that, after all, it is from such efforts that all the great and noble institutions of the world have come; and that, on the other hand, the discipline and organization of armies have been only like the flight of the cannon-ball, the object of which is destruction.

Coleridge, *Table Talk*[1]

Celebration and theory may be one of the less commonly encountered pairings, but they will be combined here with some confidence. To start a little obliquely: there is a suggestive priority in the title to Brian Simpson's collection, *Legal Theory and Legal History*.[2] 'Theory' comes before 'history' even though explicit theory does not figure largely in that volume. Whether, generally, legal theory should have this priority and how it could do so are, of course, matters of incessant debate among historians, and others. The ultimate position on either side of this debate is quite simple, at least as seen from the other.

The deracinated theorist subsumes reality in a transcendent scheme. The promiscuous empiricist is lost in an illimitable specificity—in the wilderness of particular and determinate instances, to adapt a phrase. Intriguingly, in more recent debates we see how each side becomes the other—'becomes' not only in the sense of 'changing into' the other, but also as somehow 'suited to' the other. Postmodern historians, so it is said, adopt a theoretical stance which deliquesces into the infinite possibility of particular interpretations of what is observed or recorded. These historians, in turn, would see a callow empiricism as impelled by some surpassing and putatively determinate grand narrative, usually one of progressive or evolutionary change.

* The author is grateful to Gerry Rubin for his comments on an earlier draft of this paper.

[1] Coleridge, *Select Poetry & Prose* (London: The Nonesuch Press, 1950), 491–2.

[2] A. W. B. Simpson, *Legal Theory and Legal History: Essays on the Common Law* (London: The Hambledon Press, 1987).

History, in terms of my argument here, is placed between such alternating polarities—between the determinant and what is ever 'beyond determination', to take just one way of putting it at this stage. And history is so placed neither as a compromise between these polarities nor as some *tertium quid* such as 'middle-order theory'. Rather, each side of the alternation retains a distinct efficacy whilst being integrally related to the other.

Having just provided an abstractly theoretical prelude to that abrupt synopsis, I will now observe Simpson's stricture against 'imaginative abstract theory' and instead find an equivalent theory in the same place as he finds his—in the law and, more specifically, in its guiding metaphors, constituent logics, and institutional arrangements.[3] Then, joining together the legal and the historical, I will illustrate the dynamic of alternation and interaction in Simpson's legal theory and his legal history—in both their general tenor, and their particular engagement with the colonial situation. What is found in that situation, with Simpson's help, is a denial of the dynamic of alternation and interaction. Instead one finds that a kind of *terminal legality* results which, in its deathly stasis, rejects the dynamic and in so doing itself eventually fails. All of which confirms the intractability of the dynamic if there is to be a living law—to borrow another phrase.

The paper ends with a 'hidden history': a telling 'case' of terminal legality from Papua New Guinea. This is the story of an unremarked revolution when resistance to the system of indentured labour led to the transformation not only of the colonial labour relation, but of the entire legal system. It was the resistances of the colonized, and not imperial importation that initiated a liberal legal and economic order. This was done in part negatively through resistance against the authoritarian system of indentured labour. The resistance, through the cumulation of its 'everyday' forms *and* through extensive organization, created conditions in which that system could no longer operate—and all this unbeknown to the colonist until it was made dramatically manifest. Positively, resistance involved, against great odds, sustained and effective demands on colonial law for it to honour its attenuated promise of liberal legality. No trace of such 'native' origins has appeared in later public discourses of liberal legality within Papua New Guinea.

LAW'S RESPONSIBILITY

We could begin to trace that dynamic denied in the colonial situation through a chasmic divide within the logic of the rule of law. The predominant perception of the rule of law drapes it in a secular solidity. It is intrinsically opposed to the evanescent and responsive. 'In the midst of

[3] For some theoretical elaboration see Peter Fitzpatrick, 'Law in the Antinomy of Time: A Miscellany', in *Time and Law. Is it in the Nature of Law to Last?*, eds François Ost and Mark Van Hoecke (Brussels: Bruylant, 1998).

strangers, law reaches its highest level'; 'the progress of law consists in the destruction of every natural tie, in a continued process of separation and isolation'; or Michelet: 'law, justice, is more reliable than all our forgetful loves, our tears so quickly dried'.[4]

Countless histories and juridical affirmations, then, would have us believe that in some significant sense the rule of law is characterized by certainty, predictability, and order. As against the vagaries of an arbitrary and discretionary power, the rule of law clearly marks out an area of calculability in which the individual can now purposively progress. In order for this law, and 'not men', to rule, it had to be coherent, closed, and complete. If it were not coherent but contradictory, something else could be called on to resolve the contradiction. If it were open rather than closed, then something else could enter in and rule along with law. If it were incomplete and not a whole *corpus juris,* and thence related to something else, then that something else could itself rule or share in ruling with law. For all of which, law had to be self-generating and self-regulating because if it were dependent upon something apart from itself for these things, then, again, those things would rule along with or instead of law. This necessary 'government of doctrines', decreed by Hobbes and seemingly set in a consolidated common law or in the lapidary code, was the very ordering foundation of modern society.[5]

We can, however, take each of these imperative qualities of the rule of law and evoke their opposite 'in' the rule of law itself. For law to rule, it has to be able to do anything—if not everything. It cannot, then, simply secure stability and predictability but must also do the opposite: it has to ensure that law is ever-responsive to change, otherwise law will eventually cease to rule the situation which has changed around it. So, how could the rule of law be complete if it must ever-respond to the infinite variety of fact and circumstance impinging on it? How could it be closed when it must hold itself constantly responsive to all that is beyond what it may at any moment be? And how could law, in extending to what is continually other to itself, avoid pervasive contradiction? Law cannot be purely fixed and pre-existent if it is to change and adapt to society, as it is so often said that it must. Its determinations cannot be entirely specific, clear, and conclusive if it has integrally or at the same time to exceed all determination, to assume a quality of 'everywhereness'.[6] And every tale of law's bringing

---

[4] Respectively, Donald Black, *The Behavior of Law* (New York: Academic Press 1976), 41; Stanley Diamond, 'The Rule of Law Versus the Order of Custom' in *The Social Organisation of Law,* eds Donald Black, and Maureen Mileski (New York: Seminar Press, 1973), 326, quoting von Jhering; and Jules Michelet, *Oeuvres Complétes de Jules Michelet XXI* (Paris: Flammarion, 1982), 268.

[5] Thomas Hobbes, *Leviathan* (Chicago: Encyclopaedia Britannica, 1952), 103 (ch. 18).

[6] Anthony Carty, 'English Constitutional Law from a Postmodernist Perspective' in *Dangerous Supplements: Resistance and Renewal in Jurisprudence,* ed. Peter Fitzpatrick (London: Pluto Press, 1991), 196.

order to disordered times and places in the triumph of modernity or cap-italist social relations and such, can be matched by others where it created uncertainty and inflicted massive disorder in the same cause. So, Hobbes' assured doctrines issue forth from an illimitable sovereign, from the mighty Leviathan which can be neither contained nor tamed. Even Hobbes' attempt to advance 'reason' as encompassing the sovereign's law must fail.[7] Common as the optimistic equation of law and reason may be, the two become incompatible with the adoption of the rule of law. If the dictates of reason, or more specifically the people inventing them, ruled, then the necessarily unique and untrammelled authority of the rule of law would be pre-empted. Leviathan remains savagely violent and irrational.

We can see modern, occidental law similarly stretched between stable determination and responsive change in the persistent squabbles that so enliven jurisprudential thought. These intractably polarized debates alter-nate between law's being autonomous or its being dependent.

Taking the latter first, it is readily said that law is dependent on society, politics, the popular spirit, scientistic administration, the economy, and so on. More recent variants would have law taking identity from the dis-courses or narratives in which it is embedded. In a more diachronic vein, we are told that law has to change along with society or history otherwise it becomes increasingly irrelevant and, eventually, obsolete.

The contrary claims for autonomy, although a little more venerable, have not lost any of the force of their assertion. With them law somehow has to stand apart from the remorseless demands of society, history, and so on. In being so placed, 'absolute and detached from any origin', law not only stands distinctly apart from, say, society, but also orders, shapes, or even creates society—to adopt standard formulations.[8] To the extent that society does not so conform, law yet retains its hold as the measure against which that 'failure' and passing imperfection are to be measured. In this, and indeed in all the various applications and changes throughout its his-tory, a law remains insistently that law. Law's autonomous binding force cannot be contained by what it is or has been, by its history, but extends to all that it will be. Law is eternally present.

Yet for all the enduring dissension, this seemingly chasmic division between conceptions of law erupts within the solitary pursuit of what law may be, in the search for its resolved or resolving unity. When some entity is always attended with opposed perceptions of it, the tempting resolution is to say that these perceptions point to different aspects of that same entity. This is certainly done with law but, more typically, dissension con-tinues but with some mutual and more or less marginal recognition as

---

[7] Hobbes, *Leviathan*, 132 (ch. 26).
[8] For the quotation, see Jacques Derrida, *Acts of Literature* (New York: Routledge, 1992), 194.

between the two dimensions of autonomy and dependence. Nowadays, even the most resolute proponents of dependency would accord law some distinctiveness even if they would, in turn, seek to explain that very distinctness in, say, social or economic terms. Even so, none would argue that the text of the law could be changed simply as an effect of that dependency. And of late, even the most ardent legal positivists would not say that their posited law can remain in a settled stasis but must, rather, give way, and give a way, to what is beyond it. Law must provide a way for what is other to it to enter the never complete or enclosed, always fungible boundary marked out by its own determinative assertion. An easy solution often adopted in both camps is to say that law is discretely autonomous and dependent. In this light, part of any law will be enduringly secure but in other respects the law will be uncertain and subject to change. The poverty of this expedient can be summarily seen in the failure to distinguish between the domains of autonomy and dependence in law, either generally or in any particular instance of it.

Perhaps then the enquiry should be diverted. Rather than seeking law in that which simply conforms to either side or both sides of the opposition, perhaps we could seek a law which 'is' in-between the opposed dimensions, which 'is' the experienced combination of them, and which has its being because each dimension is inexorable yet unable to be experienced by itself. The condition of being 'in law' would then be unresolved and calling for incessant decision and responsible judgment. We may, nonetheless, find prospects for resolution in these dimensions being not only opposed but somehow integral to each other. Clearly, an 'autonomous' completeness of position and a 'dependent' responsiveness to what is beyond position are antithetical things, but there can be neither position without responsiveness, nor can responsiveness exist without a position from which to respond.

So, even though law has to assume an effective position it must also be incipiently ever 'beyond position'. Law must attach to a social reality but it cannot be fully identified with or lost in that reality. Law is, to borrow Cain's pointed phrase, 'necessarily out of touch':[9] it must take on a quasi-transcendence and stand apart from the social, yet if it becomes 'out of touch' with society it ceases to be effective. But effectiveness and ineffectiveness are not simply sociological questions addressed to a pre-existent, 'set-apart' law. Law appears only in the failure, the ineffectiveness of pre-existent determination, for if there were full and effective determination that condition would simply and utterly be, without the necessity of any prescription addressed to it. The very determining force of law, in its vaunted objectivity and autonomy, can only subsist in the prospect of

---

[9] Maureen Cain, 'Necessarily out of Touch: Thoughts on the Social Organisation of the Bar' in *Sociological Review Monograph* (Keele), vol. 23 (1976): 226.

law's always being able to be otherwise than its existent, inevitably compromised, being. And law can only endure as 'the same' by according itself responsively to the infinite possibility which relentlessly impinges on it.

In all, law's responsiveness and its determinacy cannot be separated from each other either entirely or in calculated proportions. Each suffuses the other to their full extent. The responsive cannot be purely beyond and thence merely inaccessible. It must be positioned in possibility, oriented towards determination and becoming present. Nor can determination be at all set or complete. Its assertion is always entirely and infinitely responsive. It cannot be enduringly stilled in or at any point or in any severable part.

TERMINAL LEGALITY

All of which is meant to be portentous, and negatively so. In what now follows, the colonial situation will provide a testing and, ultimately, a fracturing of law in its two integral dimensions. This fracturing results in a terminal failure of law, a failure which is not only richly revealed in Simpson's work on the colonial situation but one which can also be set against his depictions of law's vibrancy in other settings.

Modern imperialism itself had to be responsively accommodating in its expansionary encounters, yet the encountered were somehow to be brought into an enduringly set, imperial, or civilized identity. It would be difficult to imagine a scene more adapted to 'resolution' through law, or at least ostensibly so. To the imperial eye, law was pre-eminent among the 'gifts' of an expansive civilization, one which could extend in its abounding generosity to the entire globe.[10] This was the same law which had assumed a civilizing mission in modernity within the national territory, and for this purpose had become 'a flexible, indefinitely extensible, and modifiable instrument'.[11] The gift was not perceived, however, simply as coming from its immediate national donor. It was the gift of a universal (European) civilization and was itself composed of universal principles.[12]

But if imperial law was a gift of civilization, it was also, like its national equivalent, a 'grim present', as the more perceptive of the colonists recognized.[13] Law, that is, had not only to extend into new-found worlds but

---

[10] Phillip Darby, *Three Faces of Imperialism: British and American Approaches to Asia and Africa 1870–1970* (New Haven: Yale University Press, 1987), 37; Lord Lugard, *The Dual Mandate in British Tropical Africa*, 5th edn. (London: Frank Cass, 1965), 546–7.

[11] Gianfranco Poggi, *The Development of the Modern State: A Sociological Introduction* (London: Hutchinson, 1978), 73–4.

[12] See for a significant example Eric Stokes, *The English Utilitarians and India* (Oxford: Clarendon Press, 1959), 118.

[13] *ibid.*, 299.

had also forcefully to bring them into a determined order. The supreme justification of imperial rule was that it brought order to chaos, reined in 'archaic instincts', and all this aptly enough through subjection to 'laws'.[14] Looked at another way, the violence of imperialism was legitimated in its being exercised through law since, as Fitzjames Stephen would have it, violence was 'forced, disciplined, and regulated in the form of law, [which] played the leading part in the creation of civilization'.[15] For an even more exuberant oracle of the imperial—Kipling—violence was the motor-force of an implacable progress.[16] Pale counterparts in the texts of the law were not without their flaring passion. Thus, a leading authority on international law revealed, with the 'discoveries' in the interior of, 'the Dark Continent . . . the earth-hunger of the Old world had been aroused'; but passion of this kind somehow takes form in a law which can, 'tame . . . [the] wild passion' of the savage on whom it is brought to bear. 'Every civilized and independent political community,' the same authority revealed, 'possesses in greater or less abundance such things as palaces, museums, ships, forts, arsenals, arms, ammunition, pictures, and jewels'.[17] As the prominence of instruments of war in this little list would indicate, this was 'a belligerent civilization', as Fitzjames Stephen proudly proclaimed it.[18]

A stable order is to be miraculously wrought in a disordering violence. Here we find an ambivalence characteristic of occidental self-constitution transposed onto the necessarily obliging savage who has to be a violently disordered being, and thus ever needful of a settled subordination, and at the same time inertly over-ordered, ever awaiting the transforming dynamism of colonization.

The parallel with law in its metropolitan setting now becomes strained. Certainly law was in that setting central to 'the state's social mission' of 'homogenizing and hegemonizing . . . a society conceived as inherently fragmented, atomized, and centerless'.[19] Law played a formative part in this by seeking to effect a direct and primary relation between the state and the individual citizen and, in so doing, to eliminate or dominate all 'intermediate' orders.

In the colonies, however, the savage was the carrier of the irresolution in occidental identity and the constituent negation of its civilization, and so had to be maintained as intractably apart from that identity and that civilization. Such an utterly antithetical being could not be brought within

---

[14] *ibid.*; Edward Said, *Orientalism* (Harmondsworth: Penguin, 1985), 219.

[15] Stokes, *English Utilitarians*, 294.

[16] Ashis Nandy, *The Intimate Enemy: Loss and Recovery of Self under Colonialism* (Delhi: Oxford University Press, 1983), 69.

[17] See Annelise Riles, 'Aspiration and Control: International Legal Rhetoric and the Essentialization of Culture', *Harvard Law Review*, 106 (1993): 723, at 735.

[18] Stokes, n. 15 above, 288.   [19] Poggi, *Modern State*, 121.

the replete realm of civilization, much less integrated into its emphatic instrument, the metropolitan state. The savage was, then, denied a participative legal personality.[20] It was solely the colonist who was to provide civil and civilized order. There were no rights for the savages in this scheme, apart from 'rights' to have things done to them so as to bring them within the ambit of civilization.[21]

The savage, then, had to become the same as the civilized colonists yet remain unalterably different to them. That unsettled ambivalence permeated the whole of colonial settlement. The colonist took on the 'burden' of pervasive powers in the cause of an inclusive civilization, only to use them to exclude, dissipate, and generally 'hold down' the savage as incorrigibly deviant. Comprehensive and draconic legal regimes sought to separate out and stultify not only the colonized but also the traditional or customary institutions and processes imputed to them. All of which was enshrouded in ethical imperatives of 'conservation'—of 'protecting' the native, especially from too disruptive an exposure to the benison of civilization. And any native who assumed a precipitate civility would be checked by a tentacular 'native regulation' or by something more brutally informal. Nothing more readily reveals the native as a projection of an irresolution in occidental identity itself than the hysterical and aggressive response of the colonist to the impertinent *évolué* who successfully takes on civilized abilities, denies deep or intractable difference, and thus exposes the fragility of imperial rule at its seemingly confident core.

What the response to the *évolué* reveals is that the imperial project was decidedly less about a bringing into the fold of civilization and definitively more about a creation and containment as different. The torpid incapacity of the savage was not only one which prevented the assumption of civilized behaviour but also denied the ability to act transformatively at all. The savage could not become anything other than what it had to be in its specular relation to the dynamism of European identity. Despite this, some effective action had to be allowed to the native because of the 'limited penetration' of colonial rule, as it is usually put. Various systems of 'indirect rule' (of 'recognition' of native modes) necessarily proliferated. But, as Simpson's portrait of Rattray in *Legal Theory and Legal History* so poignantly reveals, the reach of the native's effective action was always severely circumscribed.[22] Not only was it characterized as static, repetitive, and mimetic but, for good measure, it was held or attempted to be held within a supervisory system of administration. Custom, for example, was 'recognized' solely in subordination to the law of the colonist and denied such recognition where it was 'repugnant to natural justice, equity,

---

[20] Some colonial powers allowed some rights of metropolitan citizenship but the overall position of the colonized remained very far from even formal equality.

[21] A. P. Thornton, *Doctrines of Imperialism* (New York: John Wiley and Sons, 1965), 158.

[22] A. W. B. Simpson 'R.S. Rattray and Ashanti Law', in Simpson, *Legal Theory*, 407–9, 411–14.

and good conscience'; or contrary to 'the general principles of human-ity'—to take two standard and indicative formulations. Balandier sum-marizes the resulting situation in this way:

Colonization transformed every political problem into a *technical* prob-lem to be dealt by the administration. It contained every expression of communal life and every action that seemed to limit or threaten its grip, irrespective of the forms of the native political society and the colonial regimes that organized their domination.[23]

To which should be added a reminder of the prime place given to law in the imperial project: law as an authoritarian assertion of assured position. Given the separation and containment of the natives and the denial to them of effective modes of engagement—'strictly contractual relations are not possible'[24]—there is no space, as it were, for the development of social relations of a more 'organic' kind, relations which would ease and medi-ate the demands made on an overweening law. The necessity of distance was made a dubious virtue. Like a lawgiver of antiquity, the colonist claimed to bring law from the outside, a civilized law of universal valency, free from polluting involvement with the particularity of the local scene.[25] A similar stance imbued the colonist's claim to be able to stand objectively and transcendently apart from the squabbling diversity of the natives and from there, not just to resolve their differences, but to encompass and determine their very destiny.

The progressive and evolutionary assumptions of imperial rule placed the colonist in a position which enveloped all lesser conditions of exis-tence. From this exalted position, therefore, the colonist could know and speak for the natives better than they could themselves—and thence decide to act with an appropriate force. So, even when a customary legal system was allowed some operative effect, its aberrations and inadequa-cies could be put right by superior prescription. In short, relation could only ever be contemplated and effected within an already given and res-olutely containing frame.

This deathly disregard of the other marks an extremity of legal deter-mination. It could, in one way, be seen as the apotheosis of legality, its perfected achievement. Here is law, supposedly, in its full determinative force. It has no responsive regard for its subjects, or objects, who are, to borrow Maine's and Bagehot's definitive descriptions, 'caught . . . in dis-tinct spots', 'stationary societies' forever 'stopped' in their development.[26]

---

[23] Georges Balandier, *Political Anthropology* (London: Allen Lane, 1970), 160—his emphasis.

[24] J. Maquet, 'Inborn Differences and the Premise of Inequality', in *Race and Social Difference*, eds Paul Baxter and Basil Sansom (Harmondsworth: Penguin, 1972), 232.

[25] Stokes, n. 15 above, 178.

[26] Walter Bagehot, *Physics and Politics, or Thoughts on the Application of the Principles of Natural Selection and Inheritance to Political Society* (London: Kegan Paul, Trench and Trubner n.d.), 29–30; Henry Maine, *Ancient Law* (London: Oxford University Press, 1931), 18–19, 64, 141.

But the stasis and comprehensive containment visited on the savage comprise the very conditions of this law itself. Lacking a responsive dimension, and any vibrant connection to what is beyond their immediate determinations, the laws of imperialism inexorably fail. A premonitory instance of this terminal inadequacy can be discerned in a hiatus vexing the colonial governor of Bombay in the middle of the nineteenth century when he remarked on 'the perilous experiment of continuing to legislate for millions of people, with few means of knowing, except by a rebellion, whether the laws suited them or not'.[27] With an obvious appropriateness, it is the attempt to prolong colonial rule beyond its failure which most sharply reveals terminal inadequacy—nothing in its life became it like the leaving it. Simpson's sardonic study of legal measures taken in 'the death throes of the [British] Empire' captures the desperate intensity of a deracinated regime assuming draconic powers and thereby seeking to reduce its charges to a stilled fixity.[28]

Now to the necessary opposition of 'living law'—before moving finally to the case study of its colonial absence.

LAW'S VIBRANCY

Saying something about the responsiveness or vibrancy of law can be done only obliquely. It could be said (obliquely) that law's vibrancy has been something of a *leitmotif* in Simpson's work. He has freed so much 'from the overburden of legal dogmatics' that there is a happy embarrassment with the richness of it all.[29] I will attempt to concentrate the enquiry by looking at what is perhaps Simpson's most explicit compendium of law's vibrancy, 'The Common Law and Legal Theory'.[30]

There Simpson resurrects a conception of the common law as a type of customary law and sets this against the more modernist, and positivist, rendition of law as a system of authoritative rules. This rendition, so Simpson finds, simply does not fit the common law. Take, with Simpson, 'the act of positing' as a standard grounding or origin of law, one much espoused by legal positivism: if we transpose this act to the judicial decision as the impelling *métier* of the common law, we do not find an assured solidity of origin but something more 'reminiscent of the smile on the face of the Cheshire cat'.[31] A telling perception of deliquescence from another

---

[27] Thornton, *Doctrines*, 181.
[28] A. W. B. Simpson, 'Round Up the Usual Suspects: The Legacy of British Colonialism and the European Convention on Human Rights', *Loyola Law Review* 41 (1996): 629; at 656 for the quote, and more generally 643–82.
[29] Cf. A. W. B. Simpson, *Leading Cases in the Common Law* (Oxford: Clarendon Press, 1995), 29.
[30] A. W. B. Simpson, 'The Common Law and Legal Theory', in Simpson, *Legal Theory*.
[31] *ibid.*, 364, 369.

of Simpson's works: 'How can courts be said to be bound by earlier decisions if they decide which decisions are binding?'[32]

But Simpson's pellucid analysis in 'The Common Law and Legal Theory' has one productive defect. Its point of cohesion lies in its setting the common law as *lex non scripta* against a mythically 'authentic' writing in which rules can be seen as 'an essentially precise and finite notion'.[33] The common law is identified in the initial founding stage of his analysis in terms of what it is not: it is not a code.

But if there is cogency to my earlier account of the rule of law, then the putatively lapidary language of the code is no different to that of the common law. 'The notion of a decision,' says Simpson elsewhere, 'is everywhere problematic'.[34] The decision is made always beyond any pre-existent determination. And the 'act' of making or applying a code is a decision.[35] *Lex* generally, and in some ultimate sense, is *non scripta*.

It is doubtless difficult to make sense of this ultimacy, however. Simpson locates it for the English common law in the consensual community that is or was the cohesive group of lawyers operating the higher courts. The less consensual and the less cohesive the lawyers have become, the greater the, 'interest . . . in the formulation of tests as to how the correctness of legal propositions can be demonstrated, and in the formulation of rules as to the use of authorities—that is to say warrants or proofs that this or that is the law'.[36] All of which Simpson takes to be 'a symptom of the breakdown of a system of customary or traditional law'.[37] But what may here appear to be a symptom of custom's breakdown is but a variation of its form. Custom's association with the cohesively small-scale and with the consensually intimate is a recent and occidental invention. And it is an invention which denies custom's ability to regulate large groups over large areas, a denial conveniently accompanying the assertion of modern 'rational' notions of rule, including imperial rule.

We could expand this gloss on Simpson's resort to customary law, and fold it into the earlier depictions of the rule of law and of the colonial situation, by looking a little more closely at the components of custom. Custom is the fullest manifestation of law in that it presents law's ambivalent dimensions without qualification. Bluntly, custom is said to be immediately responsive. It is so close to what people do that it is characteristically described as being habitual or as corresponding to a people's habits. If it ceases to change with practice, it cannot still be custom. Yet

---

[32] Simpson, *Leading Cases*, 8. [33] Simpson, 'Common Law', 370.
[34] Simpson, *Leading Cases*, 3.
[35] On the irreducibility of the 'madness' of the decision see Jacques Derrida, 'Force of Law: "The Mystical Foundation of Authority"', trans. Mary Quaintance, in *Deconstruction and the Possibility of Justice*, ed. Drucilla Cornell et al. (New York: Routledge, 1992). Derrida's 'love of ruins' here (see 44) could be contrasted with Simpson's meditation on 'legal archaeology' in *Leading Cases*, 12.
[36] Simpson, 'Common Law', 380. [37] *ibid.*, 380.

custom is notoriously taken to be fixed and unchanging. It exists from 'time immemorial'. It is the characteristic way of torpid savages. It is that which is affirmed in the stock response given to the inquisitive anthropologist: 'because it is the way things have always been done.' Yet, in stark contrast to custom's eternal present, revisionist histories now reveal its 'invented' character. Writing of 'custom and government in the lower Congo', McGaffey found that, 'those whose traditions lost a case came back a year or two later with better traditions'.[38]

As this would at least suggest, custom is not a simple rendition of the way things are. It involves a creative decision and, what is more, a normative decision about the way things should be. But if in custom we see law's ambivalent dimensions writ large and unqualified, how can law be maintained in its supposedly intrinsic opposition to custom? Modern law cannot resort to a transcendent positive resolution of its ambivalence—to a deific realm or to some mythic origin—but it does rely on negative moments of alterity. So, we find law elevated in its responsiveness because it is dynamic and progressive in opposition to the fixity of custom. Or it is elevated in its determining force because it is enduringly stable and predictable, in contrast to a custom mimetically tied to ever-changing practice or effected in arbitrary decision. Custom, then, takes onto itself law's own irresolution and law assumes resolution in its opposition to custom.

I now want to 'work' these dimensions of law into a case of resistance to colonial rule.

ENGAGING RESISTANCE

All too often, studies of resistance to colonial rule have been studies of the evanescent and marginal, worlds lost, and passing pathologies of desperate revolt; or they were studies of precarious persistence in stark opposition to the colonial and the modern. Simpson nicely captures an ambivalence of these forays when he describes Rattray's deeply sympathetic attempt to present Ashanti customary law in its vibrant fullness and traditional authenticity. This very attempt, however, would insulate Ashanti customary law from sullying contact and would elevate its completeness and difference.[39]

But effective resistance can only ever be engaged with what it resists. What follows is a study of such resistance to colonial rule.[40]

A basic element of unremarked resistance always inhabited the indentured labour system, the main way of securing labour for capitalist production during most of Papua New Guinea's colonial history. With

---

[38] See Terence Ranger, 'The Invention of Tradition in Colonial Africa', in *The Invention of Tradition*, eds Eric Hobsbawm and Terence Ranger (Cambridge: Cambridge University Press, 1983), 251.

indenture systems, the entry into the contract of employment is supposed to be voluntary; but having entered into the contract the relation then becomes, in the words of a leading official and theorist of colonial rule, 'really rather like slavery'.[41] The same official elaborated the point in this offering to legal science:

The great advantage that the employer has under our indenture system is that it gives him a criminal remedy for a civil wrong; for by our Ordinance a native labourer who, for instance, deserts or neglects his duty, may be punished with fine or imprisonment. These 'penal sanctions' . . . put the employer in a position to exercise great control over his labour force; and they have met with disapproval in many quarters, on the ground that, in the case of a breach of contract, both parties should be left to their civil remedy. Theoretically it is impossible to justify the enforcement of [a] civil claim by criminal procedure, and the first and very natural feeling of anyone who has a regard for justice must be one of resentment against what he would regard as a gross abuse of the criminal law. But actual experience of the administration of a Territory such as Papua will induce him to modify this feeling very considerably and to realise that, if there is to be a contract at all, there must be a remedy for its breach, and that the civil remedy is useless where the defendant has no property of any value, except the few shillings that may be due to him for wages . . . and so may break his contract with impunity.[42]

But such delicate legalisms would not withstand any clear scrutiny. Much of the wage was required by law to be accumulated and paid over on the expiry of the indenture, so any prior breach could often be, and often was, compensated for from a fund of much more than a 'few shillings'. But:

Of course it was not the fact that an indentured labourer had no property that enabled him to break his contract with impunity, it was the fact that he had no economic need to sell his labour-power as a commodity that made the penal provisions that characterized indentured labour necessary. Many free wage-labourers have no property of any value; but they cannot break their contracts with impunity because they must sell their labour-power in order to survive. This gives the employer control over his labour force without the necessity of penal provisions.[43]

Or, as it was put a little more bluntly 'by a village elder to an eminent Australian personality, "Sir, are you telling us that we should go to work every day for forty years so that we can earn what we already have?" '[44]

[39] Simpson, 'Rattray', 415–16.

[40] For an account of the wider setting and a fuller history, see Peter Fitzpatrick, 'Transformations of Law and Labour in Papua New Guinea', in *Labour, Law, and Crime: An Historical Perspective*, eds Francis Snyder and Douglas Hay (London: Tavistock, 1987).

[41] Hubert Murray, *The Scientific Method as Applied to Native Labour Problems in Papua* (Port Moresby: Government Printer, 1931), 9.

[42] Territory of Papua, *Annual Report for . . . 1930*, 10.

[43] C. A. Gregory, *Gifts and Commodities* (London and New York: Academic Press, 1982), 123.

[44] F. L. Beltz, 'Population Growth and the Workforce', paper delivered at the seminar *Population Growth and Economic Development*, University of Papua New Guinea, 1970.

So, more robust legitimations were also created. The same apologist of the indenture system could also remark that for 'people at so low a stage of evolution . . . argument and moral suasion [do not] have very much influence . . . [so] advance must be made with the sanction of Ordinances and Regulations'.[45] People's resistance to labour, which took many forms as we will see, was thus integral to the indentured labour system and to the necessarily authoritarian form of law that was a condition for the system's operation. Sustained resistance also brings about the end of that labour system. The refusal to labour or to keep on labouring requires the colonist to seek inexperienced labour who can be 'voluntarily' engaged from an ever-receding labour frontier. When this comes to an end, the limits of the system of indentured labour are reached.

Perhaps the most surprising thing about this situation is not the massive derogations from liberal legality which it required, but rather the extent to which liberal legality was sustained nonetheless. Indentured labour and the whole system of 'native administration' were based on authoritarian modes of law and the conferring on colonial officials of the broadest discretionary powers and the most arbitrary abilities to affect the lives of their charges. Nor did law apply equally to all. The authoritarian system applied to 'natives' and something close to liberal legality applied to the colonist. The line and justification of division were racial.

The indolent and childlike native had to be continually coerced: again, 'advance must be made with the sanction of Ordinances and Regulations'.[46] But, it should also be stressed, there was a concern that advance be through 'Ordinances and Regulations'. A basic element of legality was operatively insisted on, even if not always consistently and always far from perfectly: any action interfering with the liberty or property of the subject had to be justifiable in law. In this, law played a characteristic dual part as an instrument of political rule and as a practical figure of the wider society which encompassed and bound rulers and ruled. To take a challenging case, in the early days of colonial rule, when observances of legality were at a minimum, colonial officials executed Papua New Guineans for 'serious' offences in front of very large gatherings which they had brought together. The point of this was not merely exemplary of the colonist's power but also of their standards, standards which in the very act of asserting power bound them in popular expectation. This expectation was fostered by the colonist as a strategy of 'pacification'. For example, the declaration of a protectorate over what was then British New Guinea gave the people 'the strongest assurance of Her Majesty's greatest protection of you,' and it warned 'bad and evil disposed men that if they attempt to do you harm they will be promptly punished by the officers of

[45] Territory of Papua, *Territory of Papua, Annual Report for. . . 1919–20*, 111.
[46] *ibid.*, 111.

the Queen'; 'justice' would be done '[s]hould any injury be done to you'.[47] This declaration long retained an extensive popular purchase.

The subjecting of white people to law for offences committed against Papua New Guineans tended to run counter to authority based on racial superiority. It was often the case, and especially in the earlier days of colonial rule, that racially-based authority won out over law and colonists would not be prosecuted for conspicuous offences against 'the natives'. To do otherwise could threaten the whole structure of authority which, especially in those early stages, was fragile. But there were, nonetheless, general rules of the game which set limits on what was acceptable behaviour, and for serious offences—involving for example persistent cruelty or murder—the white population would not object to the severest punishment of one of their number (and in such cases the punishment did tend to be severe).

An instance provided in the 1931–2 New Guinea annual *Report* is not untypical: 'The death of one native was adjudged to be the result of flogging. A European was charged with the murder of this native, found guilty and sentenced to ten years imprisonment with hard labour.'[48] There were two strong forces countering the element of personal racial authority. One was the purposive promotion of legality by colonial officials as a powerful mode of rule. This, in terms of its own rationalities, obliged officials to require white people to behave in the same basic ways as they required black people to do. There was a calculated aspect of reciprocity, or hoped-for reciprocity, in this. For example, on taking over from the Germans in New Guinea, the Australians saw to it that 'compulsory labour has been abolished and ill-treatment of the natives minimalized. It is hoped that the native, with a full realization of the improvement in his conditions, will show a corresponding response'—and be more amenable to being recruited to labour.[49]

The other force countering personal racial authority, widely felt among the colonists, was the necessity for law to act as the good collective capitalist and serve the enlightened self-interest of employers by restraining the more intemperate of their number.[50] Most obviously, particular capitalists had to be restrained from making demands that were too disruptive of those pre-capitalist societies which created and sustained the supply of

[47] B. Jinks, P. Biskup, and H. Nelson, *Readings in New Guinea History* (Sydney: Angus and Robertson, 1973), 38.

[48] Territory of New Guinea, *Report . . . on the Administration on the Territory of New Guinea for Years 1931–1932*, 27.

[49] Territory of New Guinea, *Report . . . on the Administration on the Territory of New Guinea for Years 1914–21*, 22.

[50] Hank Nelson, *Black, White and Gold: Goldmining in Papua New Guinea 1878–1930* (Canberra: Australian National University Press, 1976), 217.

labour (more immediately, but just as essentially, the resistance of Papua New Guineans to ill-treatment by employers and recruiters could be, as we shall soon see, widely disruptive). The 'colonist-as-subject' which these legal measures sought to create was a self-controlled being who would not succumb to 'less-civilized instincts'.[51]

There were, then, general rules and models of behaviour which law partly incorporated and partly sustained and which overrode personal, racially-based authority. But these rules and models did not eliminate or even seek to eliminate that authority. Although they were in ways inconsistent with it, they were also dependent on it.

The main way in which general standards were reconciled with the racially-based power of the employer was not, and could not be, through lowering explicit standards but through the racially differentiated enforcement of the law. Under indentured labour laws, workers were prosecuted ten times more often than employers.[52] This was not because employers did not break the law. Breaches by employers were flagrant, widespread, and usually uncorrected and, especially in the early period of colonial rule, labour-related atrocities were common.[53] There was a system of asking workers on official inspections whether they had complaints, and of recording those complaints. Given the power of employers, it would be a brave worker who complained but, still, officially-recorded complaints by workers, which on the face of them could warrant prosecution, ran into hundreds and sometimes thousands each year—yet prosecutions of employers were few.[54] And it was general practice for officials to allow employers time to rectify breaches of the law. Employers were not loath to complain generally about enforcement which they saw as too rigorous, and planters used their representation in colonial legislatures to press the point. Such complaints were mainly directed at limitations on recruiting, and requirements that workers be repatriated to their home areas. The frequency of these complaints was indicative of some adequate enforcement of the law.

Lacking the generalized, dull compulsion to labour for a wage, to 'voluntarily' submit themselves to capitalist wage-labour and its disciplines, Papua New Guineans had to be subjected through other modes of coercion. Put in such classic terms, the point is somewhat overdrawn for Papua

[51] Cf. I. B. Watson, *Islands within Islands: Australian Planters in the Southwest Pacific 1900–1975* (ms), 110.

[52] This is based on the figures for New Guinea. There are no comparable figures for Papua that I could find.

[53] e.g. Nelson, *Black, White and Gold*; Charles D. Rowley, *The New Guinea Villager: A Retrospect from 1964* (Melbourne: Cheshire, 1972); Ian Willis, *Lay: Village and City* (Carlton: Melbourne University Press, 1974), 70–1.

[54] See e.g. Territory of New Guinea, *Report . . . on the Administration of the Territory of New Guinea for Years 1959–60*, 237–8.

New Guinea, but generally Marx holds good in this. And although some Papua New Guinean cultures were compatible in ways with capitalist work discipline, to the great many it was alien. Colonists' modes of telling the time, marking the passing of days, weeks and months, of weighing and of counting and measuring are not just practical skills but also integral to a strange rationality.[55] Planters continually stressed that close and tireless supervision was necessary. There was a need to be 'seen everywhere'.[56] Minutely specific work-routines and targets had to be set. The necessity for close control was heightened in constant and detailed resistances of the workers—the dilution with water of latex tapped from rubber trees, for example. Given the high turnover of the workforce there was little scope for the development of skills that would lessen the need for such intimate supervision and control. There was also a need for a large coercive power because of that crude imbalance in which the employer or the employer's representative stood against a considerable number of workers.

This position could not be held without the pervasive support of the state. As in other colonies, the plantation itself or the mine was a 'small state' with the employer close to autocratic ruler.[57] Employers or managers not unusually provided comprehensive dispute settlement services within the small state. The ethos of this realm is encapsulated in the neo-Melanesian dictum, *masta i tok, tok i dai* ('the master has spoken, so there is nothing more to be said'). The wider legal and administrative regimes were supportive of and responsive to the rationalities of this small state and even constitutive of it. Legal power was given to employers for a time in German and Australian New Guinea to mete out 'disciplinary punishments'—confinements and fines as well as corporal punishment under the Germans.[58] The worker could only participate in the wider economy through the employer. The worker depended on the employer for the basics of life and, besides tax, often the only outlet for his cash wage was the employer's store. Controls on contracting also underlined the worker's dependence on the employer. There was a standard prohibition on the worker's entering into any other employment contract during the currency of the term of indenture. In Papua, the labour law of 1941 prohibited the worker from entering into any contract at all during this time.

Generally, and in terms of preserving a correct order in the small state, it was for some time an offence for a worker 'to create or foster a bad influence among his fellow workers', and this usually was sufficient ground for

---

[55] P. Smith, 'Education Policy in Papua New Guinea: A Classic Case', paper delivered at the conference *Colonialism in Papua New Guinea*, University of Papua New Guinea, 1984, 4.

[56] Watson, *Islands*, 111.

[57] G. L. Beckford, *Persistent Poverty: Underdevelopment in Plantation Economies of the Third World* (New York: Oxford University Press, 1972), 19.

[58] Territory of New Guinea, *Report 1914–21*, 11–13, 51.

terminating the employment contract. There were standard prohibitions against failure to perform duty, or to perform it diligently and against 'desertion'. The great bulk of cases under the Native Labour Ordinances and Regulations were for these two types of offence. There were massive numbers of these. Acquittals were rare. A surprisingly large number of deserters was prosecuted, but a somewhat larger number went unapprehended. In this, colonial administrations were helped by 'native' officials at the local level who assisted in the enforcement of these (and other) laws, and helped as well by traditional leaders who often had been responsible for having the deserter recruited in the first place. In addition to the sanctions of imprisonment and fines, a deserter stood to lose his or her deferred pay—half of the worker's wages being by law accumulated for payment on expiry of the indenture. Ninety-three per cent of convictions of New Guineans under the indenture labour laws were for desertion or for failure to work or 'perform duty'.

Formally outside of the labour laws, but no less supportive of the small state was a plethora of Native Regulations which, in their ability comprehensively to regulate people's lives, found their characteristic level in tentacular detail. These laws, to take some of the most frequently enforced as examples, restricted singing, dancing, and playing; imposed curfews; prohibited the making and sale of alcoholic liquor; prohibited gambling; and in one large urban area, prohibited the 'riding of a bicycle without a permit in writing'. These things were, as the colonist purported to see them, about public order, morality, and health (the latter's connection with cycling was that a rider's long robes could be caught in the chains). But they were also about the control of labour, about labour discipline, and about restricting the ability of people to gather together in situations of conviviality and potential class and political significance. There were also numerous trials for 'vagrancy' offences where people were penalized for 'having insufficient lawful means of support' and for 'being absent from his tribal area' and being unable to give a good account of 'his means of support'. As applied by the courts, 'means of support' was equated exclusively with being employed by a colonist. For good measure, it was illegal for a Papua New Guinean to remain in a town for more than four days unless employed or with official permission. In short, a 'native' had to be in a so-called 'tribal area' or under the rule of an employer. But these various measures, although probably the most important, were only some of the host of laws which served to shape good colonized subjects and workers, who would deeply feel it to be not their 'place' to be anything but subject to the colonist.

But law did have some contrary promises to keep. Although the full weight of law's 'civilizing mission' was first laid on Papua New Guineans, it was not long before it proceeded to restrain the power of employers and traders whose beatings and shootings of 'natives' came to be the subject of critical and public evaluations in law courts and of increasingly severe sanctions.[59] Operative elements of legality accompanying colonization, including law's comprehensive coverage, were given a testing point of application within the indenture system. Workers were not able to leave employers who struck them or denied them rations to which they were legally entitled—both commonplace sanctions used by employers—but they were expected to resort to law to rectify matters. Law could not countenance assault and the withholding of rations, but if it were too effective in dealing with such things, it would undermine the authority of the employer. In this it would be undermining an authority which it also supported and one, what is more, which supported it: law was integral to a political economy which depended on the violence of the employer.

The 'colonial mentality' is not supposed to be an assertive one. This is usually seen as a matter of passivity, but the perception does not square with the manifold resistances of the colonized. It probably results more from apt calculation. For example, it may well not be advisable to take proceedings against an employer to whose enormous power one would yet remain subject. There were numerous factors which shaped the convenient decision not to resort to law.

It would have been most exceptional for a colonial court to be geographically and culturally accessible to a worker. A more accessible outlet was the inspection by a colonial official of the workplace. This was supposed to take place annually but it was often more infrequent. It was combined with a system of dealing with complaints. But here there may well have been a reluctance to complain to an official who also initiated proceedings against workers, who tended to be understanding of the employer's shortcomings, and who would often be seen by workers in a companionate relation with the employer. The people were little convinced of the separation of powers, conceiving of 'law' as corresponding to all coercive colonial authority, whether it was colonial rule in general or law in particular, and whether it was exercised by officials or by employers.[60] It is, then, all the more remarkable that complaints which would justify prosecution were so many, even if actual prosecutions were so few.

This resistance to the power of employers was undertaken, as I have indicated, against considerable odds, and such heroism was typical. 'Desertions' were especially significant because there were so many pressures to stay. As well as the standard criminal sanctions against desertion, which could lead to imprisonment and then forcible return to the employer, workers stood to lose their deferred pay. They would usually find themselves in a strange and hostile area a long distance from their villages. It was not uncommon for employers to prefer recruits from far

---

[59] See e.g. Nelson, *Black, White and Gold*, 23, 181.

[60] See e.g. Romola McSwain, *The Past and Future People: Tradition and Change on a New Guinea Island* (Melbourne: Oxford University Press, 1977), 58, 80.

places in order to increase the effect of distance and isolation. Even if they succeeded in returning home, there could be trouble with the local leader who may have had them recruited, or with local-level 'native' officials who assisted in the enforcement of these (and other) laws. Given all these factors, the desertion figures were high: on the available figures, almost four per cent of the indentured workforce in New Guinea deserted each year. Mass desertions were not uncommon. Although there was a tendency for the colonists to see mass desertion as a result of irrationality, desertion was predominantly a 'rational' response to bad conditions of employment.[61]

It is indicative of a widespread resistance that two of the most common offences for which Papua New Guineans were tried in the colonial courts were desertion and failure to perform duty or to perform it diligently (or various equivalents to these). It is also suggestive that it was thought necessary to proscribe and quite frequently to prosecute the 'dangerous use of fire'. It was part of the planters' common sense that excessive violence on the part of employers or managers would lead to failure because it provoked the resistance of workers.[62]

There were wider forms of resistance. Strikes were frequent, but as the colonist had an intriguing inability to see a strike, we have to rely on the more sensitive histories to know of them.[63] Such histories are also needed to discern in persistent production by peasants an element of resistance to colonial domination and to wage labour in particular.[64] Although the colonists resolutely persisted in seeing these resistances as aberrant and insignificant, they did have a cumulative efficacy. Ill-treatment of workers led to resistances which adversely affected the supply of labour generally. Employers, at least informally, adapted their behaviour accordingly.[65] Law, as we have seen, supported and defined the resulting standards of behaviour. Resistances informed the law as the embodiment of the enlightened collective capitalist. And it is a cumulation of resistances, such as desertions or refusal to re-engage under indenture, which marks the limits of the indenture system and brings it to an end.

The efficacy of resistance was not confined to diffuse, small-scale instances. It also took extensively coherent forms which were to test the system of legality and indentured labour beyond its limits and then to precipate its termination. One such form was the Rabaul strike of 1929. This was scrupulously restrained, peaceful, and well-organized. It was a strike of almost all the New Guinean workers, including the New Guinean

[61] Nelson, *Black, White and Gold*, 149–50; Territory of New Guinea, *Report . . . on the Administration of the Territory of New Guinea for Years 1933–34*, 34.

[62] Watson, *Islands*, 109.

[63] Nelson *Black, White and Gold*, 23, 58.

[64] See e.g. James S. Fingleton, 'Changing Land Tenure in Melanesia: The Tolai Experience', PhD thesis (Canberra: Australian National University, 1985), 35–7.

[65] See e.g. Watson, *Islands*, 110.

police, in the major town of Rabaul. It was so effectively organized in terms of solidarity that no white resident knew of it until it had happened. The *Rabaul Times* of 4 January 1929, whilst seeking assurance in nervous sarcasm, caught the mixture of surprise and alarm which characterized the response of the colonist:

> . . . before midnight, a number of Kanakas, estimated at from 3,000 to 4,000, marched boldly along the deserted streets, and with them went almost every police boy in Rabaul, these gentry first removing their uniform-laps and accoutrements. Our highly efficient white police did not see the exodus, and it is said knew nothing of it until daylight . . . . The throat of every white resident could have been cut at that time had the boys intended violence. A remarkable and significant feature of the march was that boys from every district were mingled, forgetting their racial hatreds in their antagonism towards the Europeans.[66]

The colonists' response was swift, fearful, and furious. Draconic punishments were inflicted on leaders of the strike, punishments resulting from charges not adequately authorized in law. The bounds of legality were further breached in the temporary suspension of 'sanctions against corporal punishment . . . as employers thrashed their workers'.[67] The constantly voiced concerns of the colonists were that the strike was so well-organized and that people combined across ethnic divisions, something which the Administrator, 'knowing anything of the native mentality', found 'quite inconceivable'.[68]

In all, the colonists' response was revealingly ambiguous. A drastic response was called for to deal with a situation that was threatening in a fundamental way. But to recognize the situation in such terms would undercut the basis of colonial rule, in that New Guineans were not supposed to have abilities of collective organization and political assertion outside 'their' traditional sphere, a torpid domain necessarily seen in terms of simple, almost automatic behaviour. They were hardly expected to be able to transcend that sphere and combine across ethnic divisions. They were supposed to be like children who have to be protected and brought to a civilization which was quite apart, one where they could not act for themselves, at least for the time being. Hence, the other, more settled response to the strike was that it resulted from the malign influence of 'foreign coloured sailors' and of two New Guinean leaders and the rest just followed blindly or irrationally.[69] In this way the necessary illusion that the people could not and would not contribute to their own organization and rule was preserved.

---

[66] From Jinks *et al.*, *Readings*, 245.

[67] Peter Worsley, *The Trumpet Shall Sound: A Study of 'Cargo' Cults in Melanesia* (London: Granada, 1970), 57.

[68] See A. L. Epstein, *Matupit: Land, Politics and Change Among the Tolai of New Britain* (Canberra: Australian National University Press, 1969), 29.

[69] Territory of New Guinea, *Report . . . on the Administration on the Territory of New Guinea for Years 1928–9*, 108–9.

Such an illusion led to, but could not survive, the events in October 1945 surrounding what the colonists called 'Black Monday', a title of unintended aptness. Whatever general social order had been established was severely undermined during the Pacific War. The colonists showed themselves incapable of rule in those large parts of the country occupied by the Japanese, and in the other parts their rule was constantly tested in ways which undermined legality as a basis for the social order. As Worsley notes, 'Legal controls counted for little in such a period'.[70] The state became more and more closely involved in production. Legal restraints were ignored as workers were flogged, over-recruited, forcibly made to labour, and their indentures renewed without their consent. Officials inspecting plantations were no longer to ask labourers if they had any complaints and, if complaints were made, they were to be referred to a higher authority. Complaints made against workers were to be dealt with immediately. This was all in the cause of production for the war effort, which cause the colonists sentimentally assumed was shared by the Papua New Guineans. They were disabused at the war's end with the desertion of almost all the indentured workers on Black Monday. In explicit if belated recognition that work in these conditions of war could not be said to be voluntary, the Australian government soon after cancelled all indentures and all workers were given the option of continuing to work or returning to their villages. No more than five per cent decided to continue.[71]

This sustained mass resistance provoked a dramatic response in the 'new deal' offered by the Australian government to Papua New Guineans after the war. There was a much greater emphasis on the promotion of 'free' labour, and indentured labour was phased out. Taking cues from elsewhere in the imperial world, there was a growing realization that colonial rule would not last forever, even if for the colonists the hope remained that it would still last for a very long time. This hope would not, however, be a long one.

The plot now changes but the story, as I have taken it up elsewhere, remains the same.[72] The events which they set in train culminate in the securing of the colony's independence. But these resistant origins have no part either in postcolonial descriptions of law or in tales of national liberation. The banal thesis of neocolonialism—that the colonial situation persists after 'independence' even if in other forms—should itself be resisted, but it does retain a poignancy in what historical forces are deemed memorable.

---

[70] Worsley, *The Trumpet*, 135.

[71] Richard Curtain, 'Dual Dependence and Sepik Labour Migration', PhD thesis (Canberra: Australian National University, n.d.), 81–2.

[72] Peter Fitzpatrick, *Law and State in Papua New Guinea* (London: Academic Press, 1980).

The colonial situation is now revealed in numerous revisionist histories no longer as the assumed dissemination of an *imperium* marginally resisted but as a scene of endemic contest, one in which colonial rule and its incipient successors were continually shaped and constituted in the engagement with resistances to it.[73] That situation could not, and still cannot, be responded to or even perceived in terms of a civilizing law which had always to be determinedly apart, 'insulated, complete and universal'.[74] Such a law could not but fail in this persistent denial of law's intrinsic need to be responsive; to respond adequately to that which it would determine.

Modern imperialism, in all, marks a terminal extremity of law. Simpson's work, in pointed contrast, is luminous with law's vibrancy.

---

[73] e.g. James Axtell, *The Invasion Within: The Contest of Cultures in Colonial North America*: (New York: Oxford University Press, 1985).

[74] Stella Swain, 'Postmodern Narratives and the Absurdity of Law', in *Just Postmodernism*, ed. S. Earnshaw (Amsterdam: Editions Rodopi B.V., 1997), 22.

6

The ratio decidendi *of the Case of the Prodigal Son*

*William Twining**

MORAL
A Respectable Family taking the air
Is a subject on which I could dwell;
It contains all the morals that ever there were,
And it sets an example as well.
(Hilaire Belloc, 'F is for Family')[1]

Legal scholars and law students are not the only people who should be grateful to Brian Simpson. He has made important contributions to legal history, legal theory, and the study of the common law. He has also been one of the few academic lawyers of his generation to convey to a wider audience the message that the study of law can and should be part of the humanities and of general intellectual culture. Contextual studies of leading cases are Simpson's special genre, as we have seen in the other chapters of this book. These demonstrate how our subject can not only illuminate many things other than law, but can be fascinating and enjoyable as well.

The purpose of this chapter is to add a gloss to Simpson's insights into the role of 'cases' in our legal culture. People sometimes ask: What lessons or morals can be drawn from Brian's accounts of *Rylands v. Fletcher, R v. Dudley and Stephens,* or *Liversidge v. Anderson*? What is the point?

My argument is that it is limiting to think of contextual studies of common law cases or Biblical parables, or the contents of the law reports as being only or mainly like morality tales. 'What is *the* point?' may not be the best question to ask.

Simpson's *Rylands v. Fletcher* essay shows that today's perception of it as the leading case on strict liability in torts is different from perceptions at the time which took it to be a partial response to the immediate problem

* University College London. I have benefited from discussions of this topic with classes in Boston, Miami, and London and with members of the Forensic Expertise Group at the Netherlands Institute for Advanced Study. I am grateful for comments and suggestions by Terry Anderson, Zenon Bankowski, David Miers, Hans Nijboer, and Katherine O'Donovan.

[1] Hilaire Belloc, *Cautionary Verses: The Collected Humorous Poems* (London: Duckworth, 1939; Folio Society, 1997), 76.

of bursting reservoirs.[2] It is also a vivid example of the process by which a decision originating in response to one situation can have little impact on the original problem, but may survive as part of the armoury of the common law, or of its mythology, in quite different social contexts. Like his other studies, it illustrates what the law reports do not tell us. These interpretations are not incompatible with each other, for the essay does not have a single point.

Cannibalism and the Common Law also speaks of many things: disaster cannibalism; nineteenth-century sailing ships; how a case can be staged and managed; relations between elite and popular opinion; moral dilemmas—and so on. It has been suggested that the main point of the book is that leading cases become detached from their original context and take on a life of their own; or that *Dudley and Stephens* was about control of merchant shipping rather than moral condemnation of cannibalism or the defence of necessity; or that it merely provides a vivid illustration of how the main protagonists in a case can all cheat under the veneer of legality. Brian Simpson is a fox rather than a hedgehog. His case studies are centrifugal rather than centripetal. Or to put it differently: *Cannibalism and the Common Law* does not have one *ratio decidendi*.[3]

The concept of the *ratio decidendi* seems rather like the 'moral' of certain kinds of story or 'the point' of a parable. And questions about how to determine a *ratio* are at first sight analogous to questions about interpreting stories and parables. The most obvious link is that they concern *particular* events (real, fictional, stipulated, or hypothetical) that are considered to have *general significance*. But how close are the analogies between reported cases at common law and parables and other kinds of stories? Can consideration of parables (and the vast theological literature about them) throw any light on 'the problem of the *ratio decidendi*'?

I was stimulated to think about the question by an incident in a class on evidence. The case we were studying mainly concerned disputed questions of fact, but as I have argued elsewhere, stories play similar roles in arguments about questions of fact, and questions of law and tend to be subversive of artificially sharp distinctions between fact and law and fact and value.[4] The discussion centred on the relevance of the parable of 'The Prodigal Son', which occupies in theology a place similar to *Donoghue v. Stevenson* in the literature on precedent.[5]

---

[2] A. W. B. Simpson, 'Legal Liability for Bursting Reservoirs: the Historical Context of *Rylands v. Fletcher*', 13 *Journal of Legal Studies*, 249 (1975).

[3] The themes in this paragraph are explored in William Twining, 'Cannibalism and Legal Literature', 6 OJLS 423 (1986).

[4] William Twining, 'Lawyers' Stories' in *Rethinking Evidence* (Chicago: Northwestern University Press, 1994), 228–49; 'Narrative and Generalizations in Argumentation about Questions of Fact', 40 S. Texas L. Rev. 101 (1999).

[5] 'The Prodigal Son . . . . continues to produce more secondary literature than any other parable.' Craig L. Blomberg, 'The Parables of Jesus: Current Trends and Needs in Research',

I am not sure when I was first introduced to the parable of the Prodigal Son, but for as long as I can remember I was vaguely perplexed and even disturbed by it. What does it mean? Is it a *nice* story? Is the point that forgiveness trumps justice? That repentance pays? That one loses out if one stays at home with one's parents? Or merely that reconciliation warrants a celebration? I now realize that I had tended to identify with the elder son who, having stayed at home helping his father and carrying out his filial duties, finds that it is his no-good brother who has been rewarded. The father's reply did not seem to me to meet the charge of unfairness.

I was led to reconsider this view after a discussion in a class on Analysis of Evidence. I regularly use *In Re the Estate of James Dale Warren, Jr* as a vehicle for detailed analysis and construction of arguments about questions of fact.[6] This simulated case concerns a contested Will executed by James Dale Warren, Sr in a nursing home on the afternoon of his death. This new Will purported to leave almost all of his estate to his son, James Dale Warren, Jr, who had been estranged from him for most of his life, but had been recently reconciled with him. He had assiduously attended his father during the last three days before he died. The effect of the Will, if valid, would be essentially to disinherit his only daughter, Susan, and her two children. Susan had lived with her father in his home during his last years until she felt that his medical condition required transferring him to a nursing home. James Sr may have resented the transfer, but otherwise there was little evidence of any serious rift between father and daughter and convincing evidence that James Sr adored his grandchildren for whom his house was the only home they had known. Unfortunately for Susan, she had been involved in a road accident a few days before her father's death and had stayed away for fear that her injuries might upset the old man. Unknown to her, James Jr had stepped into the breach and was in attendance while his father wrote the new Will. Susan contests the Will on two grounds: (1) that the testator lacked testamentary capacity at the time of execution of the new Will; and (2) that the Will was made under the undue influence of James Jr, the principal beneficiary. The main issues are factual.

In the context of a mock trial counsel for each party are asked to develop persuasive 'theories' and 'themes' to support their case.[7] It is hardly

in Bruce Chilton and Craig A. Evans, *Studying the Historical Jesus: Evaluations of the State of Current Research* (Leiden and New York, E. J. Brill, 1994) at 250.

[6] The case is reproduced in full in Terence Anderson and William Twining, *Analysis of Evidence* (London: Butterworths, 1991; Chicago: Northwestern University Press, 1999) at 305–27. This is a hypothetical case that originated as a simulated problem in the American National Trial Competition in the 1980s. It is particularly well-designed in that the documentation is thorough, and the evidence is difficult to analyse, is evenly balanced and raises interesting problems of trial tactics and presentation.

[7] In this context 'theory' means a strategic argument concerning the case as a whole and 'theme' is an element in the argument that is considered sufficiently important to deserve emphasis by repetition. On the relations between theory, theme, and story see Anderson and

surprising that counsel for Susan regularly develop a Dickensian image of grasping relatives fawning over a dying man. It is no more surprising that the other side counters with the parable of the Prodigal Son.[8]

On the occasion in question, in an American law school, before assigning roles I asked the class to discuss what themes might usefully be developed in the case. As usual, the Prodigal Son was the first suggestion. However, at this point the discussion took a surprising turn. Let me try to reconstruct the exchange in the form of an imaginary dialogue:

WLT:	Which side does the parable help?
Student 1:	The son, of course.
WLT:	Why?
Student 2:	Because it is natural for a father to be generous after reconciliation with a long lost son.
WLT:	Is that the moral of the original parable?
Student 3:	It could be about repentance and forgiveness. That still helps James Jr.
WLT:	Are you suggesting that a story from the New Testament is evidence of how fathers behave in 20th-century America?
Student 2:	No. But it does support the proposition that this is reasonable behaviour on the part of the father, therefore he was not behaving irrationally.
WLT:	Is that not inferring an 'is' from an 'ought'?
Student 1:	Well, the story sets out a familiar model of how good fathers do and should behave, like 'best practice'.
WLT:	Again, is that evidence?
Students (chorus):	Yes.
WLT:	Have you read the original text of St Luke's Gospel?
Students 1 and 2 (abashed):	Well, not recently.
WLT:	(*meanly producing the text and circulating copies from the St James' version*):[9] Look, the father, in responding to the elder son's complaint, explicitly says: 'Son, thou art ever with me, and all that I have is thine.' (LUKE 16: 5, 31.) In other words: 'I am not disinheriting you. I am only throwing a party to celebrate.' Surely, that helps Susan.
Student 4:	That's pedantic. The popular image of the story makes it out to be about reconciliation and forgiveness and generosity. It

Twining, op. cit., at 166–8, 278–80 *et passim.* See also, Twining, *Rethinking Evidence*, chs 7 and 8.

[8] In teaching, Anderson and I challenge the appropriateness of both of these images in this context. See *Analysis of Evidence, Teachers' Manual*, at pp. 55–60.

[9] See Appendix.

is the image rather than the text that will have resonance with the jury. So it does help James Jr.

WLT: Is that rational?

Student 1:   Counsel for Susan can point this out, if counsel for James Jr tries to use it . . .

(The dialogue continued).[10]

This is, of course, an idealized construction of the behaviour of both teacher and students. The original incident stimulated me to think further about the roles of theories and themes in argument about questions of fact.[11] I also started thinking more seriously about the parable. I re-read St Luke's Gospel and dipped, though not very deeply, into some of the theological literature about the Prodigal Son and parables generally. This suggested that there might be some illuminating analogies between jurisprudential discussions of precedent and theological discussions of parables. Here I confine myself to possible analogies between debates about 'the point' of parables and about determining the *ratio decidendi* of a case, with particular reference to the Prodigal Son.

CASES AND PARABLES AS TEXTS

On a first reading of a small part of the theological literature it becomes obvious that there appear to be striking analogies between discussions of parables and of cases at common law.[12] Both involve particular instances with potential general significance. Both are associated with 'authority', but in different ways. Theologians as well as lawyers have dabbled in literary theory.[13] There are analogous patterns of difference about emphasis on original intent, text, context, and reader response. Terms such as 'exegesis' and 'hermeneutics' have found their way into juristic literature. However, further consideration suggests the differences may be at least as significant.

The *Oxford English Dictionary* lists 14 primary meanings of the word 'case' (*et casus*), including an event, a chance, an instance or example of the occurrence of an event or the existence of a thing, and the actual state or

---

[10] Subsequently, students alerted to these points have usually shied away from using both the Prodigal Son and *Martin Chuzzlewit* as the explicit basis for themes in presenting their arguments.

[11] On the role of stories in arguments about questions of law and about questions of fact and their interrelationship, see *Rethinking Evidence*, above, n. 4, 228–49.

[12] I have relied heavily in this section on Blomberg, above, n. 5, whose survey concentrates on the period 1980–94. See also Dan Otto Via Jr., *The Parables: Their Literary and Existential Dimension* (Philadelphia: Fortress Press, 1967); J. Ellsworth Kallas, *Parables from the Back Side: Bible Stories with a Twist* (Abingdon, 1992); Joachim Jeremias, *Rediscovering the Parables* (New York: Scribner, 1966); Eta Linneman, *Jesus of the Parables* (New York, 1964).

[13] A useful survey is Anthony C. Thistleton, 'Hermeneutics, Biblical', in *The Routledge Encyclopedia of Philosophy* (London, 1997/8).

position of matters. It lists six uses in Law under the general rubric of 'the state of facts juridically considered', including: (a) a cause or suit; (b) a statement of the facts of any matter *sub judice* drawn up for consideration by a higher court (as in case stated); (c) a cause which has been decided, including a leading case [and] a precedent; and (d) an argument (the sum of grounds on which [one of the parties] rests his claim).[14] Here, then, we are mainly concerned with cases-as-precedents, but also with cases-as-examples (as in Simpson's case studies), and cases-as-arguments.

Cases-as-precedents and parables are both embodied in texts, in the narrow sense of writings in fixed verbal form.[15] When lawyers read or cite cases, we are in fact referring to a particular kind of document or text—a law report. When we read the Parable of the Prodigal Son 'in the original', we are typically reading a translation of St Luke's account of Jesus telling a story. The authenticity, accuracy, and reliability of each text are not the same, but both are treated as authoritative.[16] A law report contains the *ipsissima verba* of each judge; St Luke's account is at best hearsay. Modern law reports follow a standard form; the Gospels are freer-flowing. Nevertheless both texts are treated as primary and authoritative, though in different ways.

Keeping in mind the differences between the texts, it is interesting to compare two standard definitions of parables and cases-as-precedents. C. H. Dodd advanced the following account of New Testament parables, 'At its simplest the parable is a metaphor or simile drawn from nature or common life, arresting the hearer by its vividness or strangeness, and leaving the mind in sufficient doubt about its precise application to tease it into active thought.'[17]

Theologians differ about the nature of parables. In my preliminary reading I have found suggestions that a standard parable, or a particular one, should be viewed as a metaphor, an allegory, an 'example story', a lesson (providing insight rather than a 'moral'), an analogy, an argument, a conundrum, or a morality tale.[18] These are not all necessarily incompatible, but some lead to profound differences of interpretation. If by 'moral-

---

[14] Paraphrased from the *OED*.

[15] Here the important point is that both the New Testament and the law reports are in (relatively) fixed verbal form (though translations differ), but interpretations of parables and cases are not. On the distinction between rules in fixed verbal form (such as statutes) and rules not in fixed verbal form (such as customary or common law rules) see William Twining and David Miers, *How To Do Things With Rules* (4th edn, London: Butterworths, 1999) ('HTDTWR') at 131–2, 137, 218–19.

[16] On the differences between authenticity, veracity, accuracy, and reliability see David Schum, *Evidential Foundations of Probabilistic Reasoning* (Chichester and New York: John Wiley, 1994).

[17] C. H. Dodd, *The Gospel Parables* 5 (Manchester: Manchester University Press, 1932)) quoted by John R. Donahue S.J., *The Gospel in Parable* (Philadelphia: Fortress, 1988).

[18] Several of these, and possible differences between them, are discussed by Blomberg, above, n. 5.

ity tale' is intended a story with a specific 'moral' that can be articulated as a normative proposition, I would contest that interpretation. However, if the term is taken to mean a story that belongs to the general sphere of moral discourse, broadly interpreted, then 'morality tale' can encompass all, or almost all, of these different conceptions.

For example, if the main point of the Prodigal Son is interpreted as providing an insight into the nature of God's love (lesson) or, alternatively, as Jesus' indirect justification for consorting with sinners (argument), both interpretations fit within a broad conception of 'morality tale'. One of the main differences between commentators relates to the appropriateness of thinking of 'the point' as being expressible in the form of a proposition.[19] Similarly, cases-as-precedents, cases-as-examples, and cases-as-arguments are all concerned with normative discourse. To what extent and how a case can be interpreted as authority for, or as an example of, an identifiable, articulated proposition of law is in part what is at issue in 'the problem of the *ratio decidendi*'.

Dodd's definition is contested, but is often treated as fairly representative. It is interesting to contrast this with a well-known American definition of a reported case:

A case is the written memorandum of a dispute or controversy between persons, telling with varying degrees of completeness and accuracy, what happened, what each of the parties did about it, what some supposedly impartial judge or other tribunal did in the way of bringing the dispute or controversy to an end, and the avowed reasons of the judge or tribunal for doing what was done.[20]

These two formulations, if treated as reasonably representative, bring out some differences and similarities between New Testament parables and reported cases. Dodd's account stresses four aspects of parabolic language: (a) its poetic and metaphoric quality; (b) its realism; (c) its paradoxical and engaging quality; and (d) its open-ended nature.[21]

One might say of reported cases that they are (a) prosaic rather than poetic; (b) realistic in the sense of being close to actual events (though not necessarily confined to everyday life); (c) dialectical rather than paradoxical; and (d) although they may engage attention, that is not their primary purpose or characteristic. The most important similarity is that there are leeways for interpreting the general significance of both cases and parables, but within constraints imposed by text and context. Thus the main point of comparison is the room for interpretation of the general significance of an account of a particular event or situation. One might add that narrative plays a major role in both types of account.[22]

---

[19] *ibid*. at 237–40.

[20] Adapted from N. Dowling, E. Patterson, and R. Powell, *Materials for Legal Method* (2nd edn, Chicago: Foundation Press, 1952), pp. 34–5.

[21] Based on Donahue at 6, see n. 17.   [22] *ibid*.; cf. Twining (1994).

The *OED* definition of a 'case' cited above brings out some further differences: the law reports follow a uniform format and typically contain standard ingredients: facts (particular) giving rise to a disputed question of law (general), culminating in a decision (both particular and general) backed by a reasoned justification. Parables differ from cases in that issues are not always sharply framed (what was the issue in The Prodigal Son?); no decision is involved; nor is a reasoned justification for the conclusion necessarily articulated. The absence of precisely-framed issues and of explicit justifications may leave parables a bit more open-ended in respect of interpreting their general significance, but this difference could be exaggerated. Similarly, the fact that a case involves a final decision on a particular dispute does not affect the problem of interpretation of its general significance. Precedents have direct practical effects both on the immediate dispute and beyond it. The practical effects of theological and literary texts are less easy to pinpoint. Both parables and cases are authoritative in quite similar ways at a general level.

THE RATIO OF A CASE AND 'THE POINT' OF A PARABLE

As Simpson rightly pointed out in an early essay, it is important to distinguish between the meaning of the term '*ratio decidendi*' and the problem of determining the *ratio decidendi* of a given case.[23] From the extensive literature on the topic, five different definitions or usages of '*ratio decidendi*' can be singled out:

1. The rule(s) of law explicitly stated by the judge(s) as the basis for the decision (the explicit answer(s) to the question(s) of law in the case).
2. The reason(s) explicitly given by the judge(s) for the decision (the explicit justification for the decision).

---

[23] A. W. B. Simpson, 'The *Ratio Decidendi* of a Case and the Doctrine of Binding Precedent' in A. G. Guest (ed.), *Oxford Essays in Jurisprudence* (First Series, Oxford: Clarendon Press, 1961) 148, at 159, 168. Simpson restricts the concept of *ratio* to binding precedents. This stems from the idea that it is the binding part of a binding precedent. This is a legitimate use, but not the only possible one. The idea of the *ratio* as the proposition of law (principle, rule or rule-fragment) for which the case can be treated as authority, whether binding or persuasive, has two advantages: it (i) separates the puzzling idea of 'bindingness' from other problems of interpreting cases. The meaning of a precedent and its status as precedent can usually be treated as separate issues; (ii) allows for the possibility that the same or closely related methods of interpretation apply both to cases that are binding on the interpreter and to those that are not. Consider the interpretation of Case A, a decision of the Court of Appeal, at a particular moment of time by both the House of Lords and a lower court. The latter is bound, but the former is not; yet the proposition for which it is authority will usually be the same. See, however, some more subtle variants in the standpoints of the House of Lords and lower courts in regard to the Court of Appeal's decision in *Davis v. Johnson* [1979] A. C. 272, discussed in HTDTWR (see n. 15 above) at 266–8. On the difference between Simpson and myself on the issue whether a *ratio* can change over time, see below, n. 28.

3. The rule(s) of law implicit in the reasoning of the judge(s) in justifying the decision (the implicit answer(s) to the question(s) of law in the case).
4. The reason(s) implicitly given by the judge(s) for the decision (the implicit justification for the decision).
5. The rule(s) of law for which the case is or can be made to stand or is cited as authority by a subsequent interpreter (the imputed answer(s) to the question(s) of law in the case).[24]

In ordinary legal usage the term is used quite loosely and, even in jurisprudential debate, each of these usages has its supporters.[25] All five notions have a place in legal discourse and legal reasoning: explicit rule-statements, implicit propositions of law, explicit and implicit justifications for a decision, and imputed propositions of law, are all used by subsequent interpreters of cases-as-precedents and in other contexts. For present purposes it is sufficient to note, first, that the term is ambiguous and does not have one settled usage; and, secondly, that in the first four usages the *ratio* is treated as being embodied in the text and therefore does not change over time, whereas in the last usage the *ratio* can change over time.

Given the ambiguity of the term and the variety of contexts in which it is used there is some doubt as to whether it is a useful concept.[26] I have argued elsewhere that the fifth usage is the most useful because it links the concept of *ratio* more closely to interpretation and use of past precedents: if and only if interpretation of cases involves reading the text of each case in isolation can any of the first four usages fit this context.[27] Since neither theory nor practice precludes interpreting precedents in the context of prior and subsequent cases, legal developments, and other factors, there is no such self-denying rule of interpretation.

The first four usages apply to the context of *justification*, for example from the standpoint of the original judge or someone rationally reconstructing the arguments in the case, but not in most contexts of subsequent *interpretation and use*.[28] The fifth usage is more realistic here because (i)

---

[24] Adapted from HTDTWR (see n. 15 above) at 334, where the definitional question is discussed in more detail.

[25] For references, see *ibid*.

[26] William Twining, 'Il Precedente Nel Diritto Inglese: Una Demistificazione', in *La Giurisprudenza Per Massime e Il Valore del Precedente* (Padova: Cedam, 1988), 461–6 (arguing that the terms *ratio decidendi* and *obiter dictum* obfuscate what is involved in using and interpreting precedents). Sir Rupert Cross arrived at a similar conclusion by a different route, *Precedent in English Law* (2nd edn, Oxford: Clarendon Press, 1968) at 77–8.

[27] *ibid*. Of course, the reasoning of a judge in a prior case cannot only be cited as authority but can also be used as raw material for constructing an argument. In this context citing a passage from a judgment often involves two implicit claims: 'This is a strong argument and look who said it.'

[28] Neil MacCormick refers to the 5th (imputation) definition as *ratio-scepticism*. 'Why Cases Have Rationes and What These Are', in L. Goldstein (ed), *Precedent in Law* (Oxford: Oxford University Press, 1987), 155. He implies that adopting such a usage involves radical indeterminacy or other versions of 'free interpretation'. This is incorrect. Subsequent interpreters often give weight to the text as well as to other factors and such other factors may

different interpreters use cases as part of their arguments on questions of law in significantly different ways: there are, for example, appropriately cautious and bold interpreters;[29] (ii) a single precedent is normally interpreted in the light of other precedents and other contextual factors; (iii) the conditions giving rise to doubt in interpreting a prior precedent also change over time:[30] texts are fixed, but interpretations change.

Within theology there is much debate about whether the interpretation of parables can and should change over time. Clearly the perspectives, techniques, and situations of interpreters vary according to time and place, but the divine origin of the text naturally makes for greater emphasis on 'original intent'. There are fewer possibilities for authoritative interventions between reader and text than in the common law; even an authoritarian church does not typically claim to overrule, reverse, limit, modify, or otherwise change the original text.[31] Despite this powerful constraint, even a cursory glance at the theological literature of any religion shows how much scope there is for differing interpretations of parables and other religious texts. For example, the relevance of changed social and other conditions to such interpretations is, of course, a central issue in Islam and Judaism as well as in Christianity.

The usages of 'ratio' (1, 3, and 5) which identify it with propositions of law (principles, rules, or rule-fragments) suggest a close analogy between precedents and stories with 'morals' that can be expressed as propositions. Both involve the extraction of general normative propositions from

---

limit rather than extend the leeways for interpretation. e.g. there is much less scope for differing interpretations of the *ratio decidendi* of *Donoghue v. Stevenson* in 1999 than there was in 1933 just because other contextual factors, especially later decisions, have narrowed the range of plausible interpretations. We now know that 'the neighbour principle' is too broad and that the duty of care in negligence is not confined to manufacturers of goods. MacCormick's own account is more concerned with justification than with later interpretation and use. Simpson (1961: see above n. 23), attacks as 'perverse' 'the theory that the *ratio decidendi* of a case is a rule which is constructed by a later court when called on to consider the case' (168). This is not the same as definition 5., which relates to the standpoint of an interpreter rather than to someone commenting on another court's interpretation. There is nothing perverse or odd about interpreter D saying: 'Case A has been interpreted differently in cases B and C.' D may prefer one of the two interpretations or construct another; D may argue that each interpretation was plausible at the time, but neither is plausible today, and so on.

[29]   HTDTWR (see n. 15 above) at pp. 336–7.

[30]   *ibid.*, ch. 6.

[31]   Joachim Jeremias (1966; see n. 12 above) concludes, 'The parables have a twofold historical setting. First, the original historical setting, not only of the parables, but of all Jesus' sayings, is their individual concrete situation in his earthly life. Secondly, they went on to live in the primitive Church. We know them only in the form that they were received from the primitive Church, and so we are faced with the task of recovering their original form as far as we can' (at 87). Jeremias suggests that the meaning may have changed because of the evangelizing concerns of 'the primitive Church' and its propensity to add generalizing conclusions. On the tendency of earlier commentators, such as Julicher and Jeremias, to lose interest in the story once they have extracted the point, see Zenon Bankowski, 'Parable and Analogy: The Universal and Particular in Common Law' *Acta Juridica* (1998), 138; see also Zenon Bankowski and Claire Davis, 'Living In and Out of the Law', in *Faith in Law*, Oliver, Douglas-Scott, Tadros eds. (Oxford, 1999).

accounts of particular events. Parables are often treated as morality tales in the narrow sense. This was my assumption before I looked into the theological literature. There one finds that searching for a 'moral' is sometimes challenged as superficial or simplistic. Without going very deeply into the theological debates one can identify a variety of positions on the interpretation of parables. These include propositions that:

1. *A parable may be intentionally polyvalent: the audience is deliberately left to draw its own moral or point from the story.* On this view, it is within the spirit of the genre that different audiences at different times and places should interpret the text differently. This position does not necessarily involve a commitment to radical indeterminacy or to 'the death of the author', because constraints may be put on the range of interpretations: e.g., an interpretation may be treated as only being acceptable if it 'fits' the text or takes due account of what is known of the historical context or the background beliefs of the original audience. On this view, the fact that there are multiple interpretations of the Prodigal Son can be treated as a strength rather than a weakness.

2. *Even if one gives weight to 'original intent', it does not follow that a parable has only one 'point'.* The significance of the Prodigal Son varies, e.g., according to how much one focuses on the prodigal, the father, or the elder son. There is no good reason why a parable or other story need have only one 'point'.[32]

3. *If by 'point ' is meant 'the important or essential thing' (e.g. the point of the matter or 'the salient feature of a story, epigram, or joke ' (e.g., 'he missed the point'),[33] the idea need not be confined to a 'moral'.* For example, the point may be an insight or lesson (e.g., about the nature of God's love); or an argument (the Prodigal Son was Jesus' way of justifying his association with publicans and sinners);[34] or a conundrum (how should the elder son behave?);[35] or a way of challenging some taken-for-granted assumption (the father flouted convention by *running* out and embracing the prodigal *before* he had declared his repentance and by treating him as an honoured guest).[36] *All of these may have an evaluative dimension, but they are not the same as a 'moral' in the form of a moral rule or principle.*

4. *Parables may also be viewed as metaphors or allegories that communicate indirectly, by powerful images, ideas that cannot be adequately expressed in propositional form.*[37] The parable of the Prodigal Son has a powerful hold on

---

[32] Blomberg, n. 5, pp. 237–40.

[33] Adapted from *The Random House Dictionary of the English Language* (unabridged edition, 1966). The *OED* devotes over 10 pages to 'point', cataloguing many nuances and analogies; the closest to the idea in the present context is: '28 . . . The precise matter in discussion to be discussed; the essential or important thing.' Cf. '29b. *to make a point*: to establish a proposition, to prove a contention.'

[34] Linneman, see n. 12 above, at 23.

[35] Kallas, above n. 12, at pp. 79–80.

[36] Blomberg, above n. 5, at pp. 232–3.

[37] *ibid.*, at 237–9

people's imaginations that may be quite different from the impact of an articulated general proposition. Often, to spell out a point or a moral may spoil a story.

This list could be extended considerably.

At first sight, only some of these ideas seem to fit reported cases. But the idea of the *ratio decidendi* is only significant, if ever, in the context of one way of reading and using cases, that of extracting propositions of law from them. One can, of course, read cases for many other purposes: as examples of judicial style or as historical responses to immediate problems (as Simpson does); to identify judicial values or biases; to deconstruct the reasoning; or to provide raw material for substantive arguments.[38] The concept of '*ratio*' has little or no relevance to such readings.

Conversely, one can read and use parables for their 'morals', but many theologians do not consider this to be the primary use. Here the theological literature is suggestive in reminding us that there are other uses of cases in addition to their being treated as authoritative sources of normative propositions.

INTERPRETATION, STANDPOINT, THE POWER OF THE PARTICULAR, AND CONDITIONS OF DOUBT

Ronald Dworkin has developed the idea of interpretation as making a text 'the best it can be'.[39] This fits some contexts better than others. It generally fits the production of a play or conducting a symphony, or texts with alternative endings; it fits legal contexts, especially where the interpreter is participating in the legal system and, for example, is in a relationship of co-operation with the originator of the text or subscribes to the system's basic principles. However, Dworkin's conception of interpretation does not comfortably include a hostile critic of a book or other artifact, a straight historical account of the origin of some text, or an attempt to 'deconstruct' it.

In legal contexts it would be odd to say that a tax consultant representing a taxpayer, or an advocate trying to limit or bury an adverse precedent, Holmes' 'Bad Man', or a member of a Law Commission considering the reform of a controversial statute are trying to make each text 'the best it can be'. What is most appropriate for particular interpreters may be best for their purposes, and perhaps for the system as a whole, but hardly for every text they are called upon to interpret. Hostile interpretations do not

[38] Above, n. 14.

[39] R. Dworkin, *Law's Empire* (London: Fontana, 1986), Ch.2, discussed HTDTWR (see n. 15 above) at 377–9. Dworkin's notion of 'integrity' transfers quite easily from legal to theological interpretation; the idea of precedents being like chapters in a chain novel is less obviously analogous.

necessarily involve uncharitable readings, or distortions, or non-reading of the text—though in practice they often do.[40]

Dworkin's usage probably fits most contexts of theological interpretation of parables. Even so, in order to explain divergent interpretations of parables, one needs to differentiate between standpoints. A preacher using the story as an illustration in a sermon, a Sunday school teacher instructing 10-year-olds, a biographer of Jesus, a theologian trying to construct a coherent interpretation of Luke's Gospel, may have significantly different vantage points, roles, objectives, and interpretive resources. They may also have different theological theories. Similarly, what is the best interpretation of a precedent may be different for a legal historian, counsel for the prosecution in a criminal case, an appellate judge, and the writer of a student textbook according to their context and purposes.

Interpretation is an activity that involves complex relations between interpreter, text (or other object of interpretation) and, indirectly, the originator(s) of the text. Interpretation is relative to the standpoint of the interpreter because the activity takes place in a given historical situation or context. Interpreters can have different vantage points, background assumptions, beliefs, interests, roles, resources, and immediate objectives.

As we have seen, puzzles about the *ratio decidendi* belong mainly to contexts involving reading cases as authoritative sources of law within a legal system rather than for other purposes.[41] In such contexts precedents seem like morality tales in that their significance lies in the general normative answers they give to questions raised by the story. So, for some interpreters, are parables. But, as we have seen, there are disagreements as to when, if ever, it is appropriate to express the moral or point of a parable in propositional form.

Precedents are reported mainly because they raise and purport to answer general questions of law. In the context of interpretation of precedents as authoritative sources of law, it is usually fairly straightforward to identify the question(s) of law raised by the case. The main doubts about interpretation relate to the level of generality at which the question(s) and answer(s) can be most appropriately formulated.[42] The facts, the issue(s)

---

[40] William Twining, 'Other People's Power', 63 *Brooklyn L. Rev.* 189 (1997).

[41] For such purposes, Dworkin's concept of interpretation may be appropriate for most official participants, even if we do not accept, fully or in part, his particular theory of legal interpretation and argumentation. However, as argued elsewhere, it is useful to distinguish puzzlement about role from other puzzlements about interpretation of texts. HTDTWR (see n. 15 above) at 335–7. Thus it is easier to identify what is involved in interpretation of a precedent from the standpoint of an advocate (relevant precedents are either adverse or supportive of an argument) than from the standpoint of a judge just because 'the role of the judge' is more problematic.

[42] Doubts about the most appropriate level of generality of a precedent are not the only ones, but they are the most common. E.g. doubts can arise about the precedent value of a case (is it strongly or weakly persuasive?; Has it been overruled or narrowed down?); and about the appropriateness of the classifying concepts used to categorize the situation (e.g. at

and the answer(s) to the question(s) are all intimately related, for the paradigm example of a single-issue case fits the following format:

Facts: X happened (particular)
Issue: If X happens/ in situations of type X then what? (general)
Answer: Whenever X happens, then Y (general).[43]

X is a constant, i.e. X = X = X. Typically the main doubt in interpreting a case relates to how X is characterized, especially the level of generality of X.

X = X = X suggests one way in which parables and precedents are quite closely analogous. In both, particularity is a key source of their appeal. Why is this? Three different, but possibly complementary, answers may be suggested.

1. *As John Wisdom pointed out in discussing case-by-case argument, there is an important difference between saying 'this is a clear case of X' and giving a general definition of X.*[44] This is because it is often easier to make confident judgments in specific circumstances than to articulate a precise general rule or principle. Case-by-case decision can be easier than the formulation of general rules.

2. *Telling a particular story without articulating its general significance may be a matter of not crossing bridges before one comes to them.* But it may also be a matter of giving more leeway to subsequent interpreters to draw their own conclusions or to make their own choices. At common law the practice of treating the result of a particular case as settled, but not according the same weight to the reasoning and articulated rule-formulations of the judges in the case also has the effect of leaving some leeway for future interpreters, perhaps somewhere between weak and strong discretion.

3. *Explicit, propositional moralizing may be too intellectual and may tend to cut down the scope for the role of intuition and imagination in making judgments.*[45] Child psychologists tell us that indirect story-telling may have a greater impact on children in moral education than explicit moralizing or articulating the morals of stories. Perhaps this was what Belloc was satirizing in his *Cautionary Tales*. Stories are easier to grasp and to remember than abstract principles, but they also, as Dodd suggests, tease the hearer into active thought. They also more readily grip the imagination.

various times there have been differences of view as to whether the facts of *Donoghue v. Stevenson* raised issues of privity or duty of care in negligence or product liability, concepts which do not differ solely in respect of levels of generality).

[43] 'If X' is the protasis, 'then Y' the apodosis of a rule of law. Y typically relates to liability or responsibility (guilty/not guilty; liable/not liable).

[44] See D. C. Yalden-Thomson, 'The Virginia Lectures', in Renford Bambrough (ed.), *Wisdom: Twelve Essays* (Oxford: Blackwell, 1974), discussing John Wisdom's lectures on 'Proof and Explanation' (1957).

[45] See above, nn. 32–7.

Thus the power of the particular narrative lies in: (a) combinations of factors that make for clear cases and confident judgments in particular circumstances; (b) allowing leeways for subsequent interpreters to make their own choices; and (c) avoiding over- intellectualization of judgments.

There are therefore some suggestive analogies between parables and reported cases, including cases-as-precedents. But there are also some very significant differences between interpreting parables and precedents. Such differences become clearer if one considers what are the main conditions of doubt in respect of each genre. When a difficult problem of interpretation arises, it can be helpful to try to diagnose the problem by asking: *what factors are contributing to puzzlement or doubt in this situation?*[46] On the basis of the analysis so far, I suggest that there are at least five reasons why interpreting parables tends to be less straightforward than interpreting precedents. These can be restated as follows:

1. *The text*: there are more problems about establishing biblical texts than modern law reports in relation to authenticity, accuracy, reliability, and translation, especially in respect of what Jesus actually said.[47] Moreover, modern law reports follow a standard format which generally distinguishes clearly between primary material (e.g. the *ipsissima verba* of the judgments) and secondary 'furniture'.

2. *The genre*: precedents are generally reported because they provide authoritative determinations of disputed questions of law. The 'what' of cases-as-precedents is more clearly defined than that of parables as a genre.[48] They have a formal quality as dispositive of previously unanswered questions of law.

3. *Standpoint*: both parables and reported cases are read and used by a variety of kinds of interpreters in a variety of contexts. However, in interpreting and using cases as authoritative precedents the standard participant standpoints of judge, advocate, legal adviser, and expositor generally belong broadly to the same interpretive community, even if their roles, purposes, etc., may be different.[49] Some of these roles and purposes are quite precisely defined. Readers of the Bible and people who cite, retell, or use parables are more numerous and diverse than readers of law reports. They may not have such clearly-defined roles. Perhaps the closest analogies in respect of standpoint are between biblical scholars and jurists in their role of exegetists or expositors of doctrine. But both these standpoints are quite problematic. Furthermore, legal and biblical exegesis are not identical activities. Most of the other legal actors who use precedents—such as judges, advocates, advisers—

---

[46] HTDTWR (see n. 15 above), ch. 6.   [47] Above, p. 154.   [48] Above, p. 155.
[49] I skirt over the issue of whether all those who read and use law reports, especially non-participants who consider them from an external point of view, can be said to belong to one interpretive community.

are typically mainly concerned with the context of interpretation of precedents in legal argumentation concerning the relationship of particular to particular, more than particular to general. This is probably less common in theology.

4. *Issue-posing*: in parables, the question(s) to which it may be treated as giving an answer is often not determinate, e.g., the Prodigal Son could be interpreted as raising such different questions as: What is the nature of God's love? Why was Jesus justified in consorting with sinners? What is the relationship between repentance, forgiveness, and justice? One might say that parables do not fit as easily into a question-and-answer framework as do reported cases; or alternatively, what questions one imputes to a parable depend on one's theory of parables. That cases are selected for reporting because they involved previously unresolved questions of law is not seriously disputed in the theory of precedent.[50] Given that the questions addressed by parables are often less determinate than for precedents, if indeed parables address questions, it is hardly surprising that the range of plausible interpretations for a parable does not operate solely or mainly on a single continuum of levels of generality.[51] Different kinds of questions invite different kinds of answer. And we cannot be as confident about treating parables as raising and answering questions as we can with precedents.

5. *Changing conditions and the status of precedents*: the relevance of changed social and other circumstances (including theories of interpretation) is problematic in theology. Nevertheless the status of the New Testament as an authoritative source is relatively constant. Interpreters of precedents, on the other hand, have to take account of new precedents, other legal developments and other changed circumstances: precedents may be abolished by legislation, overruled, limited, extended, and so on. Changed conditions may raise doubts about the status or scope of a precedent or they may narrow or settle doubts: e.g., the scope and significance of the House of Lords' decision in the recent *Pinochet* case is likely to be much clearer in 5 years time than now, both as a precedent and as a historical event.[52]

---

[50] Katherine O'Donovan rightly points out that in some specialist series of law reports, as in family and medical law, cases may be selected other than for their value as precedents and that the proliferation of reported cases may be attributable to commercial reasons that do not restrict selection to cases of 'precedent value'. My remarks here therefore refer to paradigm examples of general, selective law reports for which the criteria have traditionally been mainly related to their value as precedents.

[51] Above p. 159. Of course, there may be doubts about the scope or level of generality of 'the moral' of a morality tale (see below), but this is not the main source of doubt in respect of parables.

[52] *R v. Bow Street Metropolitan Stipendiary Magistrate, ex p Pinochet Ugarte (Amnesty International intervening) (No 3)* [1999] 2 All E. R. 97.

These five points suggest that interpreting cases-as-precedents—as authoritative sources or supports for propositions of law—is a good deal easier than interpreting parables. There are, of course, some special difficulties in regard to precedents, such as multiple judgment decisions, but by and large the conditions of doubt are more significant in biblical interpretation. This, I hope, may help to demystify precedent.

However, this modest venture into theology also reminds us that there are other significant ways of looking at reported cases in addition to or instead of solely considering them as authoritative precedents. The recent explosion of interest in literary theory within biblical hermeneutics may be more illuminating in regard to other ways of reading the law reports than to reading cases-as-precedents.[53]

THE *RATIO DECIDENDI* OF THE PARABLE

Can lawyers' approaches to interpretation throw any light on a parable? For example, can one argue plausibly that there is a main point or moral of the Prodigal Son that can be extracted by combining juristic method and theological insights? In order to keep this simple, let us assume that the St James' translation of Luke's account of Jesus' parable is an authentic and reliable primary source. My standpoint is that of a lay person, with a common law background, using scholarly commentaries to clarify my understanding of the meaning and significance of the parable out of general interest rather than for some specific purpose.

First, context. The text suggests that Jesus was responding to the Pharisees' complaint that he was consorting with publicans and sinners. The primary audience consisted of scribes and Pharisees and of the people with whom Jesus was consorting. There is some historical evidence about the background beliefs and attitudes of these two audiences. For example, it was not unusual for a younger son to emigrate, taking his share of the inheritance in advance.[54] The Pharisees had clear ideas (rules?) about repentance and forgiveness, so there was nothing new or surprising about a father forgiving his son.[55] But this father's behaviour was unconventional, perhaps shocking, in that he *ran* out to greet his son, embraced him *before* he had expressed contrition, and went *beyond* mere forgiveness to treat him as *an honoured guest* and to order a special feast in *celebration*. It would have been even more shocking if he had reduced the share of the elder son, but he did not do this. Rather he admonished him for putting concerns of merit above the joy of finding a lost sheep. The same chapter in Luke includes two other parables that also deal with the theme of rejoicing over repentance: the parables of the lost sheep and the lost piece of

---

[53] Thisleton, above, n. 13.   [54] Otto Via (1967) at pp. 169–70 (citing Linneman).
[55] Linneman (1964), op. cit., at pp. 74–6.

silver. There is even an articulated moral for the second parable: 'Likewise, I say unto you, there is joy in the presence of the angels of God over one sinner that repenteth.' (LUKE 15: 10).

The textual and historical contexts considerably reduce the scope for interpretation. They tell us about the audience, what they would have taken for granted and what was new. They pinpoint a central question that Jesus was addressing: why are you consorting with sinners? The previous parable explicitly identifies rejoicing at repentance as a central theme. Indeed, one might ask: with all these aids to interpretation, what is the problem? Yet this is the most debated parable in theological literature.[56]

What then are the conditions of doubt? Some of the puzzles and disagreements relate to the status of the text, to its relation to the St Thomas' Gospel, and to the standpoints of different users, such as preachers and evangelists. I have eliminated these as sources of doubt for my purposes and concentrated on scholarly theological commentaries. The range of interpretations is still quite wide. How can this be?

One set of difficulties relates to genre. Is a parable an allegory, a metaphor, an argument, a conundrum, or what? Doubts arising from these nuanced differentiations surround questions like: should a parable be treated as having a single main point or moral?; should such morals be appropriately articulated as 'propositions'?; should the significance of a parable be treated as changing over time, and if so, to what extent?; and, related to that, how much emphasis should be placed on 'original intent'? Here the analogies with legal interpretation are quite resonant.

It seems to me that some of these doubts can be settled quite easily. Take, for example, the suggestion that the moral of the Prodigal Son depends on which of the three main characters is the main focus of attention. The repentance of the son and his hope that he would be accepted back, albeit in a lowly position, contain some lessons for prodigals. But the context suggests that the basic ideas were familiar and that the son's behaviour and attitude did not provide an answer to the question posed by the Pharisees. So I would suggest that this could not be the main point of the story.

The behaviour and attitudes of the father are more striking. In his treatment of the prodigal, he provides a fresh and powerful role-model for compassionate fathers. One may also learn something about the nature of God's love from this. However, the story does not end there and this suggests that, on its own, the father's treatment of the prodigal is not the only point.

The elder son's reaction and the interaction between father and son provide a third focus. I disagree with Kallas' suggestion that the parable ends

---

[56] In contrast, contextual histories of leading cases in the genre originated by Simpson tend to illustrate how far later interpretations may stray from the original context, which may not limit or even affect the scope for interpretation.

with a conundrum: how should the older son (and by analogy the Pharisees) behave?[57] For it seems clear from the context that, *in the circumstances of this case*, the father is implying that the only correct course of action is to join in the celebration wholeheartedly. A strong argument can be advanced to support the suggestion that the elder son represents the Pharisees and that his fault lay in being too legalistic. He had played by the rules and thought that he deserved to be rewarded. One can take the interpretation one step further and suggest that Jesus is implying that salvation depends on faith rather than on works. But this is not the only possible interpretation, and it may be reading too much into the parable. Suffice to say here that even if one accepts that the main point relates to the final exchange between father and elder son, it still leaves open such questions as: what precisely is the best interpretation of this exchange, and can it adequately be expressed in propositional form?

Rather than pursue this hare, let us make a lawyer's move. Let us assume that we are persuaded by the parable about the appropriateness of the behaviour of the prodigal and of his father's treatment of him, and the inappropriateness of the elder brother's response in the circumstances. What if we vary the facts a bit?

Suppose the prodigal had not already repented—would it be appropriate for the father to treat him in exactly the same way, in respect of forgiveness, *and* a special welcome, *and* a celebration? Suppose the father had been even more generous and had given the repentant prodigal part of the elder son's inheritance (or, like James Warren Sr, all of it)? What if the elder son later had further grounds for a sense of grievance, for example, that the younger son continued to be treated with special favour or was perceived to be exploiting his father's generosity? Were the elder son's obedience and good works irrelevant to his prospect of salvation or is it that works alone are not enough? Prior repentance, unconditional forgiveness, and a celebratory party (but no more) are potential limiting factors regarding the scope of possible morals about forgiveness, repentance, and justice.[58] One or more such factors might provide a basis for distinguishing the original situation from some future one. Or they might not. On all these matters the parable is open-ended. In the specific context of justifying consorting with sinners, such issues do not arise. Maybe the original parable presents an easy case. On the facts this was a clear case of X, but it is indeterminate as to the general scope of X.

---

[57] Kallas, above, n. 12.

[58] Cf. the use of such limiters in leading cases: 'the neighbour principle' in *Donoghue v. Stevenson* was presented as setting limits to the scope of the duty of care; similarly, in *Candler v. Crane Christmas*, Denning MR (dissenting) was careful to emphasize proximity, the expert–non-expert relation, and reliance as *potential limiters* as he tried to extend the scope of the duty of care to negligent misstatements involving financial loss. The classic formulation of the rule in *Rylands v. Fletcher* also contains such limiters.

LESSONS

What have I learned from this exercise? First, I have long felt that problems of interpreting legal texts are closer to theology than to literary theory. My first venture into theological scholarship has strengthened this view.

However, the differences between interpreting parables and precedents are as significant as the similarities. Like all analogies this one could easily be pushed too far. Nevertheless, there is scope for further fruitful cross-disciplinary exchanges in this area. Perhaps because of the greater difficulties it has to deal with, the theological literature on parables seems generally more extensive and sophisticated than the juristic literature about precedents, not least in respect of hermeneutics and the relevance of literary theory. The benefits may be reciprocal, because lawyers' treatments on such matters as issue framing, relevance, materiality, and the use of hypotheticals might throw some light on theological puzzlements.

Secondly, this exercise has underlined the difference between routine and problematic readings of texts.[59] The nuanced differences between the various uses of the term 'ratio decidendi' and some of the subtleties of the theoretical literature do not have much bearing on routine reading and using of cases-as-precedents. Similarly, most of us have read or heard parables and other Bible stories without any elaborate theological apparatus. My students adopted a cavalier attitude to the original text. I may have missed the main point of the Prodigal Son until now, if it has one, but it still said something about repentance and forgiveness. When genuine puzzlements or disagreements arise in respect of hard cases, clarification of standpoint, diagnosis of the conditions of doubt, and distinctions between ratio-as-rule, ratio-as-reason, reconstruction of arguments, and imputation are important tools.[60] Similar considerations apply in theology.

Thirdly, my understanding of the Prodigal Son has changed. I no longer consider it to be solely or mainly about reconciliation and forgiveness. Focus on the context narrows the range of plausible interpretations in two main ways. Historical knowledge is helpful in differentiating between what would have been familiar to the original audience and what would have been novel, surprising, or even shocking. The context also helps to identify one, perhaps *the*, central issue: how did Jesus justify consorting with sinners? The answer includes the ideas that the souls of sinners are as important as those of the righteous and that there is special reason for rejoicing when a lost soul is 'found'. However, even if one can formulate a clear central issue, there is still some indeterminacy about the answer to the question and the scope and meaning of the justification. The parable, on its own, leaves open the range of circumstances to which the answer or

---

[59] HTDTWR (see n. 15 above) at 207–8.   [60] *ibid.*, chs 6 and 9.

moral might apply. This is clearly illustrated by the limiters included in the story: prior and genuine repentance by the son; the interests of the elder brother not materially affected by the celebration; and it is not clear whether there were absolutely no conditions attached to forgiveness.

These, in the language of precedent, relate to the level of generality of the governing norm or principle. But, of course, there are other potential levels of meaning and this may be a legalistic and superficial way of reading the story. I had instinctively identified with the older son, who is often interpreted as representing the legalistic Pharisees. Now that I see this, I can empathize more with both the prodigal and the father. However, for me the parable still leaves unanswered some questions about justice.

Finally, despite significant differences between parables and cases-as-precedents, the analogies are illuminating. As mentioned above, the theological literature on parables is sophisticated and quite suggestive. For example, it reminds us that parables, like cases, are read and interpreted in many different contexts for quite varied purposes. Multiple perspectives have been brought to bear on parables. Some are familiar in jurisprudence, others are less so.[61] This exercise has stimulated me to reflect further on cases-as-precedents. It has in some respects confirmed or fortified my prior views, for example, on standpoint, conditions of doubt, and the use of 'what if . . .?' questions. It has also led me to reconsider others: for example, whether attempting to formulate potential interpretations of precedents in propositional form within a framework of question-and answer may not be too intellectual.

There may be many other lessons. But rather than spoil my story by articulating a moral, I leave it to readers to tease out their own conclusions.

---

[61] For useful surveys of the range of perspectives see Blomberg and Thisleton, op. cit.

Appendix

ST LUKE CHAPTER 15
(KING JAMES' VERSION)

1. *Then drew near unto him all the publicans and sinners for to hear him.*

2. *And the Pharisees and scribes murmured, saying, This man receiveth sinners and eateth with them.*

[3.–10. parables of the lost sheep and the lost silver]

11. *And he said, a certain man had two sons:*

12. *And the younger of them said to his father, 'Father, give me the portion of goods that falleth to me.' And he divided unto them his living*

13. *And not many days after the younger son gathered all together, and took his journey into a far country, and there wasted his substance with riotous living*

14. *And when he had spent all, there arose a mighty famine in that land; and he began to be in want.*

15. *And he went and joined himself to a citizen of that country; and he sent him into the fields to feed swine.*

16. *And he would fain have filled his belly with the husks the swine did eat: and no man gave unto him.*

17. *And when he came to himself, he said, 'How many hired servants of my father's have bread enough and to spare and I perish with hunger!'*

18. *I will arise and go to my father, and say unto him, 'Father, I have sinned against heaven and before thee',*

19. *And am no more worthy to be called thy son: make me one of your hired servants.*

20. *And he arose, and came to his father. But when he was a great way off his father saw him, and had compassion, and ran, and fell on his neck, and kissed him.*

21. *And the son said unto him, 'Father, I have sinned against heaven, and in thy sight, and am no more worthy to be called thy son.'*

22. *But the father said to his servants, 'Bring forth the best robe, and put it on him; and put a ring on his hand, and shoes on his feet:*

23. *And bring hither the fatted calf and kill it; and let us eat, and be merry:*

24. *For this my son was dead, and is alive again; he was lost, and is found.' And they began to be merry.*

25. *Now the elder son was in the field: and as he came and drew nigh to the house, he heard musick and dancing*

26. *And he called one of the servants, and asked what these things meant.*

27. *And he said unto him, 'Thy brother is come; thy father hath killed the fatted calf, because he has received him safe and sound.'*

28. *And he was angry, and would not go in: therefore his father came out, and intreated him.*

29. *And he answering said to his father, 'Lo, these many years did I serve thee, neither transgressed I at any time thy commandment: and yet thou never gavest me a kid, that I might make merry with my friends:*

30. *But as soon as this thy son was come, which hath devoured thy living with harlots, thou hast killed for him the fatted calf.*

31. *And he said unto him, 'Son, thou art ever with me, and all that I have is thine.*

32. *It was meet that we should make merry, and be glad: for this thy brother was dead, and is alive again; and was lost, and is found.'*

7

Three Very Remarkable Nineteenth-Century Lawyers: Lyndhurst, Denman, and Campbell

*Gareth Jones**

Brian Simpson has done much to illuminate nineteenth-century legal history. This essay is offered as a modest tribute to a distinguished scholar and a close friend. Its subjects are three lawyers, all born in the late-eighteenth-century but who lived well into Victoria's reign: John Singleton Copley Junior, Lord Lyndhurst (1772–63); Thomas Denman, Lord Denman (1779–1854); and John Campbell, Lord Campbell (1779–1861).

Denman and Campbell were both born in 1779. Lyndhurst, seven years their senior, outlived both of them, dying at the great age of 91. They knew each other well, but were never intimates.[1] Copley and Denman became estranged, divided politically. Denman disliked Campbell. Campbell bored Lyndhurst and resented his mocking condescension, taking his

---

* *A personal note*: I have written on a theme in 19th-century history, the subject of Brian's Selden Society lecture, *Victorian Law and the Industrial Spirit*, and of many of his *Leading Cases in the Common Law*. But if I had been writing an essay 40 years or more ago when Brian and I first met, it would have been on a subject in early modern legal history, which then interested me. At that time, Brian was writing his *History of the Land Law*, preparing materials for what was to be the *History of the Common Law of Contract*, and revelling in the spirited exchanges in the jurisprudence seminars, led by Herbert Hart and Tony Honoré. Two vols of the *Oxford Essays in Jurisprudence*, which Brian edited, were published some years later. My wife and Brian were contemporaries at Oxford. As is fairly well known he introduced me, not only to her, but to Robert Goff. If we were asked why we find Brian such entertaining company we could produce a *catalogue raisonné* of his many talents and virtues. But his most endearing qualities are his loyalty and kindness, his enormous sense of fun (a raconteur of *the* most extraordinary stories!), his sense of adventure, and his insatiable human and intellectual curiosity. Brian's indignation over the capricious operation of the infamous Rule 18B sent him not only in quest of Mr Liversidge but to interview many ageing Fascists: the result, the book, appropriately called, *In the Highest Degree Odious: detention without trial in wartime Britain*. His concern to protect the individual, confronted with the apparatus of State power, has now led him to champion human rights. A new book is forthcoming.
What *will* this extraordinary man do next?

[1] Copley and Denman were members of the Midland circuit and may have been close during those years at the Bar, but their friendship, such as it was, deteriorated: below p. 179. On the other hand, 'Copley and Campbell were friends at the Bar merely in the ordinary sense of legal good fellowship. They were not of the same circuit, they never belonged to the same set; and when Copley married, the slight social relation between them entirely ceased' (Prof. Herman Merivale, writing anonymously, in the *Edinburgh Review*, vol. CXXX, April 1869, reviewing Campbell's *Lives of the Lord Chancellors: Lives of Lord Lyndhurst and Lord Brougham* (London: Murray, 1869), vol. VIII, 556, 557–8. See below pp. 197–8.

revenge, posthumously, in his ill-tempered and inaccurate *Lives of Lord Lyndhurst and Lord Brougham*.[2]

All three served as Attorney-General,[3] which customarily led to high judicial offices: Lyndhurst, three times Tory Lord Chancellor and, for a short time, Master of the Rolls and Lord Chief Baron; Denman, Lord Chief Justice of the King's Bench; Campbell, Lord Chief Justice of the King's Bench and Palmerston's Lord Chancellor. Brougham, in his 6-hour speech in the House of Commons on law reform in 1828,[4] condemned *party* appointments to judgeships in the following words:[5]

The great object of every government, in electing the judges of the land, should be to obtain the most skilful and learned men in their profession, and, at the same time, the men whose character gives the best security for the pure and impartial administration of justice. I almost feel ashamed . . . to have troubled you with such a truism; but the House will presently see the application I am about to make of it. Sorry am I to say, that our system of judicial promotion sins in both these particulars . . . The office of judge is one of so important and responsible a nature, that one should suppose the members of government would naturally require that they should be at liberty to make their selection from the whole field of the profession . . . Is all the field really open? Are there no portions of the domain excluded from the selectors' authority? True, no law prevents such a search for capacity and worth! True, the doors of Westminster Hall stand open to the minister! He may enter those gates, and choose the ablest and best men there . . . But there is a custom above the law—a custom, in my mind, 'more honoured in the breach than in the observance,' that party, as well as merit, must be studied in these appointments. One half of the Bar is thus excluded from the competition; for no man can be a judge who is not of a particular party. Unless he be the known adherent of the government—unless he profess himself devoted to one scheme of policy—unless his party happen to be a party connected with the Crown, or allied with the ministry of the day, there is no chance for him; that man is surely excluded . . . his seat on the bench must depend, generally speaking, on his supporting the leading principles of the existing administration.

But Daniel Duman demonstrated that during the period 1820–50, 48 per cent of *puisne* judges had not been MPs.[6] For example, James Parke, later Lord Wensleydale, was 'never a politician nor the adherent of any political party';[7] his only tenuous connection with 'the existing administration'

---

[2] *Lives of the Lord Chancellors*, vol. VIII. Wetherell said that they added a new sting to death: so records Brougham, in his *Life and Times of Henry, Lord Brougham* (Edinburgh/London: Blackwood, 1871), vol. III, 435; see also Brougham's remarks as reported in the *Athenaeum*, 30 Jan. 1869, 166.

[3] Lyndhurst and Campbell had also served as Solicitor–General.

[4] A speech which led to the legislative adoption of about three-quarters of Brougham's reform proposals.

[5] *Parliamentary Debates* (N.S.), vol. XVIII, cols. 142–4 (7 Feb. 1828).

[6] *The Judicial Bench in England, 1727–1875: The Reshaping of a Professional Elite* (London: Royal Historical Society, 1982), 78.

[7] Ullswater, *A Speaker's Commentaries* (London: Edw. Arnold & Co., 1925), vol. I, 117. Viscount Ullswater was Parke's grandson.

was that he was junior to Gifford and Copley in the trial of Queen Caroline in 1820, eight years before his appointment to the King's Bench. But Brougham was right that the *highest* judicial offices were reserved for *party* men. That it is not to say that they were party hacks or men who were worthy but not distinguished members of the Bar. Quite the contrary; they were leaders of their profession, as the careers of Copley, Denman, and Campbell demonstrate.[8]

AT UNIVERSITY

Campbell was a precocious student; he entered St Andrews when he was 11, and four years later had completed the arts curriculum. Yet he felt that his education was inferior to that of his Oxbridge contemporaries, among whom were Copley and Denman; possibly this made him even more determined to excel in life. He was destined for the ministry. But three years of theology, Hebrew, and exercise sermons at St Mary's College, St Andrews, did not make him less anxious to succeed in a more material world. Like so many Scots he found the road to London too enticing. Copley and Denman were educated at Cambridge and were, respectively, members of Trinity College and St John's college. Copley, undoubtedly the most intelligent of the triumvirate, carried all before him: a first class classicist, second wrangler[9] and fellow of his College. Denman's Cambridge career was not as glittering as Copley's—because he 'despised' mathematics, he did not take the mathematical tripos—which prevented him from competing for the major classical prizes. Consequently, he left Cambridge with an ordinary degree. But he did not give himself over to the pleasures of the flesh, as did so many ordinaries. Indeed, as an undergraduate, he was part of the University's literary elite.[10]

THEIR EARLY YEARS AT THE BAR

Copley, Denman, and Campbell all came to London to begin their careers in the law with limited means. All three became pupils of Mr Tidd, the

---

[8] By contrast, it was thought that it was not 'necessary for the office of *puisne* judge, that a man should be at all the head of his profession in point of practice' (Lord John Russell, in the *Select Committee on Official Salaries*, 144, cited by Duman, above, n. 6, at 80).

[9] At Cambridge University a 'wrangler' is a person placed in the First Class in the Mathematical Tripos. At that time wranglers were ranked in order of merit.

[10] He contributed a translation of the song of 'Callistratus' to *Collections from the Greek Anthology*, which Byron, one of the contributors, praised in *Childe Harold*, third canto, 20th stanza, as 'the best English translation' (Arnould, *Memoir of Thomas, First Lord Denman* (London: Longmans, Green & Co., 1873), vol. I, 17 ('*Arnould*').

special pleader.[11] Denman and Campbell spent three years in his chambers; Copley was with Tidd for seven years. All three joined Lincoln's Inn, described by Campbell as 'the most expensive society, but the most respectable'.[12] Copley was called in 1804, Denman in May 1806, and Campbell six months later.

Copley, Denman, and Campbell had the qualities for success at the Bar: intelligence, capacity for hard work over long hours (in Copley's case, only when hard work was demanded), determined ambition, and fine physical presence. They were big men, in every sense. Disraeli, who did not meet Copley until 1834 or 1835,[13] described his brow as 'majestic'; his deep set eyes, gleaming 'with penetrating fire': a 'high-bred falcon'. 'Indeed nothing could be finer than the upper part of his countenance . . . Nothing could be more beautiful. It was that of the Olympian Jove.' But, he added, 'the lower part of his countenance betrayed the deficiencies of his character; a want of high purpose, and some sensual attributes'.[14] Denman was all too aware of these deficiencies of character; his 'countenance . . . bore a remarkable resemblance to that of Mephistopheles in *Retsch's Outlines of Faust*'.[15]

Denman was 'about five feet eleven inches in height, spare and strong in frame, capable, and fond of vigorous exertion . . .'.[16] His biographer, Sir Joseph Arnould, a jurist and judge of the High Court of Bombay, recounts that, more than once, he walked from Cambridge to London 'in little more than 12 hours'. Campbell was of a similar build. The judge, Sir James Fitzjames Stephen, described him as 'thick-set as a navvy and as hard as nails'.[17] Harriet Beecher Stowe met him in London when he was over 70 years old, and described him as a 'man of most dignified and imposing appearance. Tall with a large frame, a fine high forehead, and strongly-marked features.'[18]

But success came slowly to all of them.

Copley was 32 when he was called to the Bar. It was only a loan of £1,000 from his brother-in-law, Gardiner Greene, a Boston merchant, which

---

[11] The business of a special pleader, who was not a barrister, was to draw up all the written proceedings in a suit at law.

[12] *Life of John, Lord Campbell* (ed. by his daughter, The Hon. Mrs Hardcastle, London: Murray, 1881), vol. I, 60. It is largely based on his writings (*'Life'*).

[13] Below p. 180.

[14] Monypenny and Buckle, *The Life of Benjamin Disraeli, Earl of Beaconsfield* (London: Murray, 1929), vol. I, 333. There are many portraits of Lyndhurst. But his bust, by William Behnes, which stands outside the doors of the Wren Library at Trinity College, Cambridge, 'is considered by those who knew Lord Lyndhurst best to be faultless as a likeness' (Sir Theodore Martin in vol. IV of the *Dictionary of National Biography*, 1113).

[15] Denis Le Marchant, *Memoir of John Charles, Viscount Althorp, Third Earl Spencer* (London: Richard Bentley & Son, 1876), 351. So did many others: see Elizabeth Ilchester, *Lady Holland to her Son, 1821–1845* (London: Murray, 1946), 120; *Arnould* (see n. 10 above), vol. I, 362–3.

[16] *Arnould* (see n. 10 above), vol. I, 25.

[17] Quoted in Atlay, *The Victorian Chancellors* (London: Smith Elder, 1906–08), vol. II, 199.

[18] As E. F. Manson recounts in *Builders of our Law* (London: Horace Cox, 1904), 137.

enabled him to be called. How he supported himself in his early years on the Midland circuit is not known. But on 20 February 1807, three years after Copley's Call, his mother wrote to her daughter, Mrs Greene, 'His prospects are satisfactory, and remove our anxious concern upon that score . . . He has made a great advance and says, he must style himself, as others do, "a lucky dog".'[19]

But it was not until the next decade that Copley's professional career flourished. By the year 1816 he was the acknowledged leader of the Midland circuit.[20] A year later his address to the jury, ridiculing the indictment for high treason of Watson and Thistlewood, secured their acquittal.[21] At the same time it brought his name to the attention of the Tory political grandees. The Tories had few able lawyers in the House of Commons, and Castlereagh, who had sat throughout Watson's trial, proposed Copley's name to the Prime Minister, Lord Liverpool. In 1819 he accepted Liverpool's offer to sit as the member for the rotten borough of Ashburton.

Denman received an allowance of £400 from his father which he supplemented with articles for the Whig journal, the *Monthly Review*, although he rejected his father's advice that he should supplement his income by becoming a law reporter.[22] During his early years on the Midland circuit, which was also Copley's circuit, his family was growing, and his wife found herself 'distressed for money'.[23] It was five years after Call before Denman's practice began to increase, but he was never to command the same large fees as Campbell.

Like the Tories, the Whigs had few stellar lawyers in the House. Denman's political views were well known, and in 1818 he was brought in

[19] Amory, *The Domestic and Artistic Life of John Singleton Copley* (Freeport NY: Books for Libraries Press, 1882), 285.

[20] He had become prominent in 1812 with his successful defence of one of the leading Luddites, John Ingham, who was acquitted on a technicality. But his name was made as counsel for the defendant, who was alleged to have infringed the plaintiff's patent, in *Bovill v. Moore* (1816): see Davies' *Reports of Patent Cases*, 361.

[21] Campbell, who was to vilify him in his *Lives of the Lord Chancellors* (above n. 1), described that address as 'one of the ablest and most effective ever delivered in a court of justice' (*Life* (see n. 12 above), vol. VIII, 17).

[22] Campbell's career, like Alderson's and Blackburn's, refuted Denman's prediction that 'the office of law reporter is much oftener a bar than an introduction to general business' (*Arnould* (see n. 10 above), vol. I, 69–71).

[23] His uncle, Joseph Denman, died in 1812, leaving him estates in Lynn, Norfolk, and Stoney Middleton in Derbyshire; but his interest was a reversionary one. (Stoney Middleton was a small manor house, which Denman lovingly improved over the years. Some of his friends found it unprepossessing; Wensleydale is reported to have said that Denman 'must be very fond of ancestral property to like such a house' (*Arnould*, vol. I, 384 (see n. 10 above).) By that date his financial position had improved so that he could move to 50 Russell Square, then, says Arnould, 'in point of residence, the "*ne plus ultra*" of a successful barrister's ambition': *ibid.*, vol. I, 58. But the burden of supporting a large family meant that he was never affluent. His election as Common Sergeant of the City of London in 1822 was welcome news since it carried with it a stipend of £1,200: see further below p. 182.

for the close borough of Wareham, taking his seat in 1819.[24] The following year was a momentous one. Denman became Queen Caroline's Solicitor-General and, with Brougham, opposed the Bill of Pains and Penalties before the House of Lords.[25] His final speech, lasting 10 hours, was rapturously received. But it enraged George IV who refused him a silk gown until 1828 when Wellington persuaded him to relent. His practice then increased, and in 1830, having refused to stand for Parliament in 1826,[26] he became the Member for Nottingham.

Tidd had paid Campbell £100 a year as his Devil and this financial support, together with subventions from his brother, George, enabled him to build up a 'respectable library' and to meet the cost of his Call to the Bar. After Call, Campbell kept himself going through journalism, writing, under a *nom de guerre*, for the *Oracle* and the *Morning Chronicle* (then a Whig mouthpiece); he reviewed books, translated French newspapers, and reported parliamentary debates and the 'business' of the King's Bench. But as soon as his literary 'fame' was in danger of becoming known to his fellow students, he gave up journalism. His mind was, he wrote, 'relieved from an oppressive sense of degradation'.[27] Law reporting was more respectable. So, three years after his Call, he began his *Nisi Prius Reports*, reporting the decisions of Lord Ellenborough.[28] In one respect Campbell was a less than honest reporter, for he kept a drawer marked 'Bad Law' into which he threw all the cases which seemed to him 'improperly ruled'.[29]

Campbell's early years were also frustratingly slow, so he decided to abandon the Home for the Oxford circuit. But by 1811 he could write to his

[24] In the debate on the first Reform Bill he confessed with, 'some sense of shame that he had not had correct virtue to resist' that invitation to stand: *Parliamentary Debates*, 3rd series, vol. II, col. 1246.

[25] Copley, as Solicitor-General, with Gifford, the Attorney-General, leading for the Crown. Denman praised his 'forcible and skilful' cross-examination (*Arnould*, vol. I, 170 (see n. 10 above)).

[26] His finances were not equal 'even to an undisputed election' (*Arnould*, vol. I, 204 (see n. 10 above).

[27] *Life* (see n. 12 above), vol. I, 122 and 177.

[28] With the exception of the rightly maligned reports of Espinasse (1793–1807) and the more accurate reports of Peake (1790–1812), there were no reports of civil trials. Campbell realised that the Napoleonic War, with the attendant Continental Blockade, would generate novel commercial litigation and that the reporting of Ellenborough's King's Bench decisions would find a ready market. The volumes, covering the years 1808–16, were welcomed and praised by some later judges, like Lord Cranworth, for their accuracy and conciseness: *Williams v. Bayley* (1866) L.R. 1 H.L. 200, 213. But Maule J. condemned them as dangerous precedents because they contained 'too short statements of the case' (Wallace, *The Reporters* (4th edn), 542 n). Maule was no admirer of Campbell, 'He entertained and constantly expressed for him the greatest contempt . . .' (Ballantine, *Some Experiences of a Barrister's Life*, 141).

[29] Campbell's *Nisi Prius Reports* (London: A. Strahan, 1907–16), were innovative in a more admirable sense. He recognized that pleadings and facts 'must often be imperfect, and may sometimes be inaccurate, and consequently subjoined the names of the attorneys on both sides; anyone who doubted the accuracy of the report could then inspect the briefs in the case to verify the report' (*Reports*, vol. I, 4 n.).

father, 'It is no bounce that I had more business last term in the Court of King's Bench than any man of my standing.'[30]

In that year he earned £948, and five years later his professional income was £3,000. Never one to conceal his light under a bushel, he claimed in 1822 that for 'junior business I am now the first, without a rival'.[31] And two years later, he confidently asserted to his brother, 'I think I am in every way a match for Pollock [later Attorney-General and Lord Chief Baron], and as to Brougham and Denman, I shall improve in eloquence more than they will in law, and by and by I do not think that there will be any great inequality between us.'[32]

It is not surprising that his conceit and undisguised ambition made him unpopular with many of his contemporaries. Despite his professional success, Eldon yet again denied him a silk gown.[33] He had to wait until 1827 before he became a King's Counsel. It was Copley, now Lord Lyndhurst and Lord Chancellor, who proposed his name. His political career did not begin until 1830, by which time Lyndhurst had been Lord Chancellor for over three years and Denman was Attorney-General in Grey's administration.

AS POLITICIANS

Lyndhurst and Denman were bitter opponents during the passionate years leading up to the Reform Act of 1832. Campbell, although, like Denman, a Whig, played a more muted role in those debates. After the enactment of the Reform Act, Denman left the House of Commons on his appointment as Lord Chief Justice, but continued to speak in debates in the Lords on reform and the slave trade. Campbell remained in the House of Commons, as Solicitor-General and then Attorney-General, until Denman's resignation seventeen years later. Lyndhurst's finest political hours were in the House of Lords. He became a prominent spokesman for successive Tory administrations.

Lyndhurst

Denman was among those who came to believe that Lyndhurst was a political apostate. In his account of his travels in the United States[34]

---

[30] *Life* (see n. 12 above), vol. I, 270.   [31] *ibid.*, 409.   [32] *ibid.*, 423.

[33] In debates in the House of Commons both he and Denman had sought to reform the Court of Chancery. Eldon was not pleased: see below n. 147.

[34] The family lands on Beacon Hill were sold, without Copley Senior's consent, after he had left Boston. His son, on his visit to the US in 1795–6, was advised to compromise his father's claim. He reluctantly agreed to do so (Amory, 141–2, see n. 19 above; citing Copley's letter, dated 27 Feb. 1796, to his father. The letter sets out in detail the terms of the compromise).

Copley professed himself, 'to have become a fierce Aristocrat! This is the country to cure your Jacobins. Send them over and they will return quite converted.'[35] But Arnould, Denman's biographer, records that on circuit, '. . . a cordial liking sprang up between them increased by the circumstances that they both at that time entertained and frankly avowed sentiments of what in those days was regarded as extreme political Liberalism.'[36]

While Attorney-General, Denman listened to the debate in the House of Lords on the first Reform Bill and heard Lyndhurst's vehement protest, in response to Whig taunts, that he never was a Whig. Althorp records that Denman, standing next to him, pressed his arm and exclaimed:

Villain! No, he was a Democrat. When I was a young man, he took me to a dinner of the friends of the people. The violence of the speeches startled me, and I could not help observing that I thought his friends went too far, for there must be some honest Tories. 'No', he answered, 'it is impossible; an honest Tory is a contradiction in terms . . .[37]

Denman was dismayed by Copley's acceptance of Lord Liverpool's invitation to enter the House as a placeman. He, 'never could forget or forgive this dereliction of principle'.[38] Thereafter their relationship was formal. Greville confided to his diary that he only once saw them shake hands, and then 'with much politeness and grimace'.[39]

Copley was a late starter in politics as he was at the Bar. But legal and political advancement were rapid: Solicitor-General in 1819, and five years later Attorney-General. In 1827 Eldon resigned, and Copley became Lord Chancellor.[40] He held that office until 1830, under, successively, Canning, Goderich, and Wellington. He was Lord Chancellor in Peel's 100-day administration in 1834, and again for the third time when Peel was returned in 1841.

Lyndhurst was a formidable political opponent, rarely appealing to emotion but using the weapons of irony and seering sarcasm with great effectiveness.[41] Like all good lawyers he was, as Le Marchant, a Whig, said:

. . . always a complete master of his argument, his premises being so skilfully laid

[35] Amory, 145 (see n.19 above). Copley was writing to his mother; the letter is dated April 20, 1796.

[36] *Arnould*, vol. I, 62 (see n. 10 above).   [37] Denis Le Marchant, see n. 15 above, 350.

[38] *Arnould*, vol. I, 63 (see n. 10 above).

[39] C. C. F. Greville, *A Journal of the Reign of King George IV and King William IV* (London: Longmans, Green & Co, 1874), ed. H. Reeve; G.G. Moore, vol. II, 331.

[40] He took the title of Lord Lyndhurst of Lyndhurst in the County of Southampton.

[41] Thus, he looked upon 'what proceeded from [Wetherell on the Catholic Relief Bill 1829] rather as the ravings of a disordered imagination, than as emanations from an enlightened and sagacious understanding' (*Parliamentary Debates* (N.S.), vol. XXI, col. 192).

that his conclusions were almost irresistible: nothing could be more clear, distinct, and logical than his handling of a subject—at least according to his view of it; but he grappled with no difficulties he was not sure to overcome.[42-3]

While in Opposition his speeches on the First and Second Reform Bills, which he prophesied would destroy the 'nice balance' of the Constitution and endanger the rights and privileges of the Monarchy and the Church,[44] earned Lyndhurst the deep enmity of the Whigs. When his wrecking amendment to the 1832 Bill successfully postponed discussion of the disenfranchising clauses, a collision with the House of Commons became inevitable and led to the resignation of Grey. Deeply opposed to any reform of municipal government, Lyndhurst was prominent in securing the amendment of the Municipal Corporations Bill 1835[45] and, in the following year, in blocking the Irish Municipal Corporations Bill.[46] His justification for this opposition to the will of the democratically-elected lower House was his arrogant assertion that 'we are no less the representatives of the nation than the House of Commons'.[47]

It was in 1836 that he gave, at Disraeli's suggestion, his first *Summary of the Session*, which was a telling catalogue of ill-considered and abandoned Bills.[48] More restrained than his Reform Bill speeches, it was still acerbic. In the House of Commons the Whigs (against whom it was directed), resented its sarcasm. Even Lord Holland, then the Chancellor of the Duchy of Lancaster, conceded that its impact was powerful, describing it as one of the 'best speeches he had ever heard in Parliament'.[49] In the judgment of Professor Herman Merivale, the son of Denman's great friend, 'None assuredly of our days, perhaps none of any day, have equalled him in the great Parliamentary, as well as forensic, art of unfolding a subject in such a manner as to carry conviction by mere strength of exposition.'[50]

[42-3] Above, n. 15, 351. *The Times* leader writer wrote, on 13 Oct 1863, in similar terms, 'Let the question be ever so intricate or complicated, when Lord Lyndhurst applied himself to expound it, it became clear, simple, and easy. The effect which he produced upon his audience was that there was but one possible view of the subject, and that view was before them.'

[44] *Parliamentary Debates*, 3rd series, vol. VIII, col. 283 *et seq.*

[45] e.g., his amendment that the rights of existing and future freemen and burgesses should be maintained unimpaired, as if the Act had not been passed, was accepted by the Prime Minister, Lord Melbourne: see section II of the Act. For a discussion of the many amendments which he proposed, see Lee, *Lord Lyndhurst: The Flexible Tory* (Niwot (Colo.): University Press of North Carlina, 1994), 197 *et seq.*

[46] During the debate Lyndhurst infuriated O'Connell by saying that the Irish Protestants, 'had to contend with a population alien to Englishmen, speaking, many of them, a different language, professing a different religion, regarding the English as invaders, and ready to upset them on the first opportunity' (*Parliamentary Debates*, 3rd series, vol. XXX, col. 734; vol. XXXIII, col. 297; and vol. XXIV, col. 297).

[47] *ibid.*, vol. XXXIV, col. 888 *et seq.*

[48] Not surprisingly, they were praised by Disraeli, a good friend, in his *A Vindication of the English Constitution* (London: Saunders & Otley, 1835) and by the *Morning Post*. Henrietta Sykes had introduced them to each other: below p. 200.

[49] Quoted by Greville, vol. III, 362, see n. 39 above.

[50] *Edinburgh Review*, Apr. 1869, 556, at 570.

Lyndhurst bore the taunts of want of principle[51] with apparent equanimity. He was greeted with prolonged hoots when he appeared under the gallery of the House of Commons during the debate on the Irish Municipal Corporations Bill in 1837. In his diary Holland records that he was told that he felt these insults 'most grievously';[52] but, commented Greville, he 'neither attempted to stir, nor changed a muscle of his countenance'.[53]

Lyndhurst continued to give his *Summary of the Session* each year until again he became Lord Chancellor in Peel's administration. The years 1835 and 1836 were his last militant political years. His speeches in Opposition had made him popular as well as influential within his own party. There was some talk of his becoming Prime Minister. Disraeli, who thought that it was only Lyndhurst's 'own disinclination' to become Prime Minister which 'stands in his way', exaggerated his political support.[54] Holland was incredulous: it was 'absurd' that he would become leader of his party,[55] a view which some—possibly many—in Lyndhurst's own party shared. The source of Lyndhurst's 'own disinclination' was not only his lack of high political ambition. By nature he was indolent, relying on 'sheer intellectual pre-eminence'.[56] The fiery political exchanges of these years had left their mark. In January 1837 he told Greville, on his return from a delightful four months in Paris:

I suppose the Government will get on; I'm sure that I shall not go on in the House of Lords this year as I did the last. I was induced by circumstances and some little excitement to take a more prominent part than usual last session; but I don't see what I got by it except abuse.[57]

Lyndhurst was true to his words. After the furore of the Irish Bill, the years 1837–40 were quieter years. He was more active in the judicial business of the House, although his *Summary of the Session* of 1839 was enlivened by his description of a discredited government, clinging to office.

In 1841 Lyndhurst became Lord Chancellor for the third and last time in Peel's administration. He and Peel were never intimate. In the House of Lords his interventions were generally confined to matters of legal reform, such as the Copyright Bill 1843 and the ill-fated Charitable Trusts Bill 1845. Peel resigned in July 1846, leaving a party bitterly divided over the repeal

---

[51] In his polemical essay, published days after Lyndhurst's death, 'What Lord Lyndhurst Really Was', Bagehot wrote that he, 'had no more formed opinion that Toryism was true than he had that Mahometanism was true' (*The Collected Works of Walter Bagehot* (London: The Economist, 1965; ed. St John-Stevas), vol. III, 232, at 236).

[52] Kriegel, *The Holland House Diaries 1831–1840* (London: Routledge & Kegan Paul, 1977), 360.

[53] See n. 39 above, vol. III, 389.

[54] Monypenny and Buckle, vol. I, 304 (see n. 14 above).

[55] Kriegel, 235, see n. 52 above.

[56] *Edinburgh Review*, Apr. 1869, 556, at 561 (Merivale).

[57] Greville, vol. III, 378, see n. 39.

of the Corn Laws. Lyndhurst's attempt to reunite it failed dismally. By the end of that decade Lyndhurst was almost blind. But cataract operations in 1850 and 1852 partially restored his sight. A year later he was again speaking in the House of Lords.[58]

Lyndhurst enjoyed being an elder statesman, denouncing Russian aggrandizement in 1853 and speaking passionately in 1859 and 1860 on the state of the national defences. These speeches by an octogenarian were admired for their undiminished force and clarity. The last time he spoke in the House was in 1861 in the debate on Lord Kingsdown's Act for the establishment of the validity of wills of personal estate.

Denman

Denman was saddened that Wellington, whom he personally respected, remained obdurately opposed to Parliamentary reform. When Grey succeeded Wellington in 1831, the Cabinet resolved to introduce the First Reform Bill, and Denman, who had been appointed Attorney-General in the previous November, was entrusted to draft its complex provisions. His speeches, on the second reading, were largely devoted to the refutation of the special objections to its clauses, but the considerable burden of defending its schedules in Committee fell on him.

In March 1832 the Bill passed the Commons, only for the Lords, led by Lyndhurst, to resolve to postpone discussion of the disenfranchising clauses.[59] Grey immediately resigned and Wellington was invited to form an administration. Denman's prospects were now bleak. He wrote cheerfully to his eldest daughter that, despite the loss of the Common Sergeantship which he had resigned on becoming Attorney-General, and the fact that the etiquette of the Bar prevented his going circuit again, he could not doubt that he should 'hold a good station at the Bar'.[60] Denman never returned to the Bar. Wellington found it impossible to form a government. Grey became Prime Minister and Denman once more Attorney-General.[61]

As a schoolboy at Eton, Denman was known for his ultra-liberal views. But in later years he would describe himself as a 'Conservative reformer':[62]

For to hazard all the secured benefits of an established order, from a distaste for those forms which fools alone contest; to reject the freedom which may be enjoyed

---

[58] He refused to be Lord Chancellor in the first Derby administration of 1852.

[59] See above, p. 180.

[60] His wife was not so optimistic, being a 'little hard to pacify just at first' but was then, 'a very Portia' (*Arnould*, vol. I, 362, see n. 10 above).

[61] On 4 June the House of Lords had passed the Reform Bill, the majority of Tory peers having accepted Wellington's advice to give up the struggle.

[62] In a letter dated 4 Sept. 1832, to his close friend John Herman Merivale: *Arnould*, vol. I, 394 (see n. 10 above). To his dying day he venerated Fox's name.

under a constitutional monarchy for the purpose of an experiment . . .—this is a course which would no doubt deserve many other names, but certainly that of folly in a pre-eminent degree.[63]

In the same letter, he reflected on the impact of the Bill. 'For my part I could have been well pleased to follow the great work of Parliamentary Reform with a long repose, that we may set our House in order, not as on the eve of dissolution, but to ensure its being safely and comfortably and socially inhabited.'[64]

In the House of Lords Denman fought passionately for the abolition of all manifestations of the slave trade. It was a cause which aroused his deepest emotions. Denman regarded slavery as 'the foulest stain that ever rested on the character of the country'.[65] His first major speech in the House of Lords was in the debate on the Bill for the Better Suppression of the Slave Trade in 1839. Before speaking he was in a 'state of the utmost anxiety',[66] as he always was when he spoke on slavery. The Bill gave the Crown power to seize vessels suspected of engaging in the slave trade. He dismissed fears that this would lead the country into war with France. Suppression of the slave trade must be a fact as well as a name. 'There must be a right of visitation and search.'[67]

Denman's son, Joseph was then the captain of a cruiser on the West African coast.[68] In 1840 he had first released the slaves and then set fire to the Barracoons where they had been incarcerated. Captain Denman was unsuccessfully sued for the loss suffered by the slave owner. The Court of Exchequer held that, although the slave owner had property in his slaves and could sue in trespass for their seizure, the ratification by the Minister of State of Captain Denman's act rendered it an act of state, for which the Crown alone was liable.[69] His father bitterly commented that it was the first time that the claim of an owner of slaves had been recognized in an English Court of Justice.[70]

---

[63] In a letter to Merivale, dated 24 Aug. 1832 (*Arnould*, vol. I, 389).

[64] In a letter to Merivale, *ibid.*, vol. I, 394.

[65] Parliamentary Debates, 3rd series, vol. III, col. 1496 (18 Apr. 1831).

[66] A letter to his wife, dated 15 Aug. 1839 (*Arnould*, vol. II, 101; see n. 10 above).

[67] Above n. 65.

[68] On the role of Joseph Denman as a slave chaser, see Christopher Lloyd, *The Navy and the Slave Trade* (Ilford, Essex: Frank Cass & Co. Ltd. 1968), 91 ff.

[69] *Buron v. Denman* (1848) 2 Exch. Rep. 167. It was true that mistakes would inevitably be made by raiding parties; therefore it was necessary to indemnify the officers of Her Majesty in the discharge of the duty imposed on them.

[70] *Parliamentary Debates*, 3rd series, vol. XCVI, col. 1055. But the Court was a strong Court: Parke, Alderson, Rolfe, and Platt BB. He had viewed with alarm the judgment in *Reg. v. Serva* (1845) 1 Denison 104–156. The *Felicidade* was a slave-trading vessel, whose crew had killed a boarding party from a Royal Navy cruiser and had been convicted of murder. But the judges gathered as the Court for Crown Cases Reserved, concluded that their convictions could not stand. Denman and Baron Platt dissented. The majority gave no reasons for their decision, and in a pamphlet, reproduced in *Arnould* (see n. 10 above), Appx VII, Denman proposed that in future they should do so.

Denman sensed with alarm that many politicians and members of the public were becoming antipathetic to the anti-slavery movement. The Sugar Duties Bill 1846 proposed to equalise the duties on British colonial and slave-produced sugar. Denman spoke fervently against it, arguing that its enactment would increase the slave traffic. But the appeal to free trade prevailed and the Bill reached the statute book. In 1848 a committee of the House of Commons, chaired by Benjamin Hutt who had slave-trading interests, concluded that the posting of naval squadrons was ineffectual and counter-productive, increasing the suffering of negroes. The slave trade should be left to itself. On 22 and 28 August Denman made two powerful speeches in the House of Lords which swayed public opinion and significantly contributed to the decision not to withdraw the squadrons.[71] Denman's speeches on the slave trade were highly emotional. He admitted that it was 'utterly impossible to talk of slavery and the Slave Trade with any degree of moderation—or indeed with any other feeling than that of the most perfect abhorrence'.[72]

Campbell

Campbell's first attempt to enter the House of Commons was for the notoriously corrupt borough of Stafford in 1826. He contributed to his defeat by declaiming against bribery,[73] but was elected for the same borough at the general election after George IV's death in 1830.[74] Campbell viewed the prospect of electoral reform coolly. In October 1830 he told his brother that, while he supported more members for the great towns and the reform of Scottish representation, it was his view that, 'You cannot generally alter the right of voting without a complete *bouleversement*, and making the House of Commons greatly too strong for the other two branches of the Legislature.'[75] He was a 'decided enemy to Ballot', which 'could not at all check undue influence, except in as far as it promoted falsehood and hypocrisy'.[76] With the enlargement of the franchise, 'there will be more corruption than ever at such a place as Stafford'.[77] Reform of the law against bribery and corruption was more essential.[78]

Campbell played little part in the tumultuous Reform debates in the House of Commons, partly to avoid 'direct collision' with his father-in-law, Scarlett, who had gone over to the Tories.[79] But his letters provide a colourful picture of the debates in the Commons and in the Lords. He was 'quite appalled' by the terms of the proposed Reform Bill of 1831 when it

---

[71] *Parliamentary Debates*, 3rd series, vol. CI, 365–371 is the more important.

[72] *ibid.*, 3rd series, vol. LXXXVIII, 511. Anxious to appeal to the country, he published a number of pamphlets, including *The Slave Trade and the Press*, published anonymously (1847), and *Letters to Lord Brougham on the Extinction of the Trade* (1848).

[73] *Life* (see n. 12 above), vol. I, 432.   [74] *ibid.*, vol. I, 474–5.

[75] *ibid.*, vol. I, 478.   [76] *ibid.*, vol. I, 503.   [77] *ibid.*, vol. I, 514.

[78] *ibid.*, vol. I, 514.   [79] *ibid.*, vol. II, 4–5.

was first introduced.[80] On reflection and possibly influenced by his brother's more radical views, he concluded that it was not revolutionary, but a mere restoration of the constitution—very much an Old Whig view. He was much relieved that it was enacted without the creation of new peers for he doubted whether a numerous creation could be 'considered a constitutional proceeding, and can only be defended as a *coup d'état* to ward off greater evils'.[81]

In November 1832 Sir William Horne succeeded Denman as Attorney-General and Campbell became his Solicitor-General. A month later Campbell was re-elected as the member for Dudley in the reformed parliament and rejoiced that the election was accompanied by neither drunkenness nor bribery.[82] Campbell was dismayed that the Cabinet immediately decided to introduce the Irish Coercion Bill. Despite his having persuaded Grey to remove 'several very obnoxious clauses'[83] from the original draft, he was still appalled by the severity of its provisions; for instance, giving the Lord Lieutenant power to prohibit public meetings and to order the trial of offenders in Courts Martial. He realized the danger of such Draconian measures 'turning the tide of popular opinion'[84] against the government.[85] But in the Committee of the House, which was considering the Bill, he was compelled to defend it—leading O'Connell to denounce him 'as a tool of the "base and bloody Whigs" '.[86]

In 1834, Horne, who had appeared infrequently in the House and whose parliamentary responsibilities had consequently fallen on Campbell, was ousted from office. Campbell succeeded him, '[grieving] on every account to see him [Horne] thus sacrificed, even if it were by his own caprice'.[87] Some said that he shed crocodile tears, and in fact had pressed for Horne's dismissal.[88] Although he was never shy in pressing his claim to office, there is no evidence to substantiate that allegation.[89] Leach, the Master of the Rolls, died in 1834. Grey was anxious that Campbell should remain in the House. So, to his irritation, Campbell was passed over and the Solicitor-General, Pepys, was appointed in Leach's place. Brougham, now Lord Chancellor, partially placated him with the explanation that a common lawyer could not be appointed to the Rolls when the Lord Chancellor was also a common lawyer. Campbell was content to protest, and urged that the

[80] *ibid.*, vol. I, 504.   [81] *ibid.*, vol. II, 12.   [82] *ibid.*, vol. II, 23.

[83] *ibid.*, vol. II, 27.   [84] *ibid.*

[85] The Act, entitled An Act for the More Effectual Suppression of Local Disturbances and Dangerous Associations in Ireland, received the Royal Assent on 2 Apr. 1833.

[86] *Life*, vol. II, 29, 33–4, see n. 12 above.

[87] *ibid.*, vol. II, 40–1.

[88] Denis Le Marchant (see n. 15 above) 62—who, Campbell's daughter claims, 'adduces no authority for the statement which he makes' (*Life*, vol. II, 41 n. 2, see n. 12 above.

[89] Because of this promotion, the 'absurd law' required him to vacate his seat, and to his chagrin he lost Dudley when he offered himself for re-election in 1834. It was 3 months before he returned to the House when he was elected to represent Edinburgh; where 'plain John Campbell', as he was known, represented that city until he was ennobled in 1841.

appointment should not be seen as a precedent. His reaction was not as temperate when he was passed over a second time two years later when Pepys became Lord Chancellor and Bickersteth Master of the Rolls. He claimed that he had an 'unquestionable right' to the Rolls, and went to Melbourne in high dudgeon with a letter of resignation in his pocket. Melbourne flattered him, saying that his services as Attorney-General were indispensable, and offered to raise his wife to the peerage. Campbell convinced himself that installing his wife as Baroness Stratheden of Cupar would remove any suggestion that he had been slighted, and so he stayed.[90] However, this rebuff did lead Campbell to contemplate taking a *puisne* judgeship in 1838 and 1839,[91] but he was again persuaded from abandoning the government.

During his parliamentary years he carried a crushing burden of work. '[A] man', he wrote, 'cannot take a portion of business and no more. He must play the whole game or give it up entirely. Then my station in the House of the Commons depends very much on my station at the Bar. Many, there, look with foolish respect to an eminent counsel.'[92]

As early as 1833 Campbell's practice at the Bar was 'nearly equal' to Scarlett's, with whom he had some 'rather unpleasant collisions'. He claimed that the fault was his father-in-law's who expected the same deference professionally as he did in private life; Campbell naturally claimed that he behaved 'with great moderation and forbearance'.[93] After Scarlett became Chief Baron in 1834 Campbell was the undoubted leader of the Bar. He was learned in the law, hard-working, and had a way with juries. 'To get a verdict, the way is not to consider how your speech will read when reported, but to watch the jury, and to push any advantage you may make, disregarding irregularities and repetitions.'[94] As a judge he was equally adept in controlling his juries. He was never quite as sensitive to the mood of the House of Commons. Few lawyers are; but the House listened to him with respect.

AS JUDGES

Lyndhurst had no ambition to be a great judge. London and Parisian salons and the House of Lords were more seductive than Westminster

---

[90] Denman wrote to his wife to say, 'There is much talk of the Attorney-General being passed over, his indecent boast that he had resigned, and the oddity of his subsequent reconciliation'. Scarlett, now Lord Abinger, was apparently not best pleased when congratulated on his daughter's elevation (*Arnould*, vol. II, 34, see n. 10 above). Pollock was, however, among those who believed that Campbell had been 'bought off' and that the Law Officers and the profession had been insulted. He wrote, contemptuously, that Campbell had failed to, 'distinguish between what you have done and agreeing to accept for your wife a valuable diamond necklace' (Hanworth, *Lord Chief Baron Pollock: A Memoir*; London: Murray, 1929, 205). See also Disraeli's second 'Runnymede' letter.

[91] He had refused one in 1830.   [92] *Life* (see n. 12 above), vol. I, 503.

[93] *ibid.*, vol. II, 31.   [94] *ibid.*, vol. II, 89.

Hall and Lincoln's Inn. But, as a trial judge, he was scrupulously fair-minded. Both Denman and Campbell had judicial ambitions. Denman personified judicial dignity, but he was not a great lawyer and left few memorable judgments. The Bar disliked Campbell but many of its members would have reluctantly endorsed Holdsworth's judgment that he was one of the greatest common lawyers of the Age of Reform.[95]

Lyndhurst

In September 1826 Lyndhurst, then Sir John Copley, had succeeded Gifford as Master of the Rolls, a judicial office which he could hold while retaining his seat in the House of Commons. But his tenure was brief, for he was soon to be Lord Chancellor; not surprisingly, he made no mark on Eldon's Court of Chancery.[96] With the fall of Wellington's administration, Lyndhurst lost the considerable stipend and fees which were the fruits of office. Grey, now Prime Minister, urged by Brougham, surprisingly offered Lyndhurst the office of Chief Baron of the Exchequer. After consulting Wellington, Peel, and Aberdeen, Lyndhurst finally decided to accept the offer, although he knew that he 'should be subjected to so much obloquy and abuse';[97] 'a judicial office, wholly unconnected with politics' was his apologia.[98] Wellington knew that Lyndhurst, 'cannot live without place, as he has no property and he has already expended *three years* beforehand his salary'.[99] £7,000 a year was more attractive than a pension of £4,000.[100] He took his seat on 18 January 1831.[101]

In 1830 little business was done in the Exchequer; in comparison the King's Bench was overworked. There were a number of reasons, said Brougham, why the Exchequer was so unpopular:

Thus, the small portion of business transacted—the suspicion originating in the general mixture of suits, carried on in different ways, that the business is not well

---

[95] Holdsworth, *History of English Law* (London: Methuen, 1965–6), vol. XV, 429.

[96] In his *Lives of the Lord Chancellors*, vol. VIII, 44 (above n. 1), Campbell contemptuously writes, 'no decision of his of the slightest importance is recorded. The gossip of the profession . . . was that "he sat as seldom as possible, and rose as early as possible, and did as little as possible".'

[97] In a letter to his wife he wrote, telling her of Grey's offer, that, it was 'a step backwards', so he was minded to refuse (Lyndhurst Papers, Trinity College, Cambridge, O.16.38/65).

[98] Lyndhurst to Wellington, cited in Martin, *A Life of Lord Lyndhurst* (London: Murray, 1883), 275. The biography is pious hagiography.

[99] Wellington reported Lyndhurst's apologia, made to the Duke of Cumberland, to Eldon. It is cited in Aspinall (ed), *Three Early Nineteenth-Century Diaries*, 'The Le Marchant Diary' (London: Williams & Norgate, 1952), 4 n. 2.

[100] Lady Lyndhurst's influence over Grey may have been instrumental in securing Lyndhurst's appointment: see below p. 199.

[101] Possibly Lyndhurst had led Grey to believe that he would not actively oppose government bills and, in return, may have been offered the reversion to the office of Lord Chief Justice: Greville, above n. 39, vol. II, 329–30 (the 'secret article of the treaty'). But if any bargain was made, it was soon to be broken.

done[102]—the monopoly of attorneys,[103] together with several other causes, occasions his court to be least frequented of any: indeed, it has now scarcely any thing to engage its attention. The judges do not sit for more than half an hour some mornings, and there are hardly ever on the paper more than six or seven causes for trial after term: a dozen would be considered a large entry.[104]

By contrast, the Court of Kings Bench was too popular. The First Report of the Commissioners appointed to inquire into the *Practice and Proceedings of the Courts of Common Law* in 1829[105] made a number of recommendations which were intended to attract suitors into the Exchequer and the Court of Common Pleas.[106] Many were immediately implemented in 1830 in 'An Act for the more effectual Administration of Justice in England and Wales.'[107] A fifth Baron of the Exchequer was appointed.[108] More effective in reducing the arrears was the ending of the monopoly of the four attornies. Section X enacted, 'That all Persons admitted or admissible to practise as Attornies in the Courts of King's Bench and Common Pleas shall be admissible in like Manner as Attornies of the Court of Exchequer, and be admitted and allowed to practise there as such . . .'.

On learning the news of Lyndhurst's appointment Greville predicted that 'the public will gain by the transaction, because they will get a good judge'.[109] That prediction proved to be true. Even Campbell praised Lyndhurst's brief tenure (of just four years) as Chief Baron.[110] Lyndhurst helped to revive what had been a moribund court,[111] although much of his time was occupied leading the opposition to the Reform Bills (his much preferred occupation). 'One of his few oddities on the Bench was this . . .', said Merivale, 'that although he exhibited singular patience, and very rarely interrupted counsel, yet the motion of his lips frequently showed that he was talking to himself.'[112]

Lyndhurst was not a judge who revelled in the niceties of fine legal argument. His judgments do not contain an 'ample exposition of the prin-

---

[102] It was a court of law and of equity, as well as of revenue law.

[103] Four attornies enjoyed a monopoly of business.

[104] *Parliamentary Debates* (N.S.), vol. XVIII, col. 136.

[105] The Commission was established after Brougham's speech on law reform in 1828: above p. 173 and below p. 195. The commissioners were: Bosanquet, Stephen, Alderson, Parke, and Patteson. Campbell was not then one of the Common Law Commissioners; but, although a common lawyer, he became chairman of the Real Property Commissioners: see below pp. 192–3.

[106] Only the recommendations which affected the Court of Exchequer are discussed here, not those proposing reforms of the two other common law courts.

[107] 11 Geo. IV and I Wm. IV (c. 70).   [108] Section I.

[109] Above in n. 39, vol. II, 89.

[110] *Lives of the Lord Chancellors*, vol. VIII, 71–2 (see n. 1 above).

[111] In 1834 Parke, who had been one of the Common Law Commissioners, moved from the King's Bench to the Exchequer, remaining a Baron until 1855. He became the dominant figure in that Court and did much to establish its reputation as a distinguished court of common law. In the same year Alderson left the Common Pleas to become a Baron of the Exchequer, an appointment which also gave that Court greater authority.

[112] *Edinburgh Review*, Apr. 1869, 556, at 564 (Merivale).

ciples applicable to other disputes'. Lyndhurst was not interested in the 'law'; he certainly never pretended to be a 'Chancery man' and to establish himself as a master of equitable doctrines. Campbell claimed that, 'he thought it pleasanter to try larcenies and highway robberies than to listen to seven Chancery lawyers on the same side upon exceptions to the Master's report'.[113] As Chief Baron he was content to assign most of the equity business of the Exchequer to Baron Alderson.[114] And from the Woolsack he delivered few memorable legal speeches.[115] Lyndhurst, wrote Walter Bagehot, was one of those judges:

... who always decide on the particular case before them rightly; who have a nice insight into all that concerns it, are acute discerners of fact, accurate weighers of testimony, just discriminators of argument. Lord Lyndhurst is perhaps as great a judge in this kind as it is easy to fancy. If a wise man had a good cause, he would prefer its being tried before Lyndhurst to its being tried before anyone else.[116]

Denman

On 3 November 1832 Lord Tenterden, Lord Chief Justice of the King's Bench, died. On Brougham's suggestion, Grey proposed Denman as his successor. After a 'short struggle',[117] William IV assented to the appointment which was enthusiastically greeted by the profession and the press.

---

[113] *Lives of the Lord Chancellors*, vol. VIII, 71 (see above n.1).

[114] In 1817 the Chief Baron was allowed to sit alone in equity cases: 57 Geo. III (c. 18), s.1. This was not a success. It was amended in 1833, authorizing the appointment of another Baron to sit in equity when the Chief Baron was sitting on the common law side, at *nisi prius*, in the Privy Council, or when he was ill: 3 and 4 Will. IV (c. 41), s. 25.

[115] *Edinburgh Review*, Apr. 1869, 561–2 (Merivale).

[116] Bagehot, 'Lord Brougham', *The Collected Works of Walter Bagehot*, n. 51, above, vol. III, 159, 180–1 (the essay was first published in July 1857). The Revd. Whitwell Elwin, who was present at Lyndhurst's *Nisi Prius* Court at Norwich, confirmed Bagehot's judgment, recording that he had the 'power of summing up evidence with such terseness, completeness, and exactness from memory alone' (reproduced in Martin, see above, n. 98, 283). Nowhere are these skills better demonstrated than in *Small v. Attwood* (1832) Younge 406. It involved a dispute which centred around the sale, allegedly induced by the seller's fraudulent misrepresentations, of coal and iron mines in Staffordshire. At a 21-day trial, Lyndhurst was confronted with a web of tangled facts, complex calculations, and voluminous documents and depositions. But his judgment, 'was entirely oral, and without even referring to any notes, he employed a long day in stating complicated facts, in entering into complex calculations, and in correcting the misrepresentations of counsel on both sides. Never once did he falter or hesitate, and never once was he mistaken in a name, a figure, or a date' (Campbell, *Lives*, see n. 1 above, at 73). Greville agreed that it was 'one of the ablest judgments ... ever delivered' (see n. 39, above, vol. II, 330). It was subsequently reversed by the House of Lords on technical grounds (6 Clark & Finelly (1838) 232).

[117] *The Life and Times of Henry, Lord Brougham* (Edinburgh & London: Blackwood, 1871), vol. III, 224 (see n. 2 above). Denman had enraged George IV by his sarcastic parallel, at the trial of Queen Caroline, between Caroline and the innocent Octavia, wife of Nero, whose servants were tortured in an attempt to prove her adultery with a slave. His brother, the future William IV—who did not conceal his belief that Caroline was an adulteress—was equally incensed by Denman's apostrophe, addressed to him, 'Come forth, thou slanderer.' William IV was indeed magnanimous ...

Denman was sworn in on 6 November 1832, and presided over that most influential common law court for the next seventeen years.

As an advocate, Denman could not be compared to Scarlett, and as a lawyer he was not as learned as Campbell.[118] Nor was he as intelligent as his contemporaries, Lyndhurst and Brougham. But his tenure as a judge was a successful one. His relationship with the other judges was one of 'uninterrupted harmony',[119] the Bar respected him, and the public regarded him as the personification of judicial dignity. When he took office there was a substantial volume of business in arrears in the King's Bench. Business in the Exchequer was still small, and the work of the Common Pleas was restricted by the fact that only sergeants-at-law could practise before it. Denman resolved to destroy what he called 'that gigantic monster called Arrear'.[120] He did so by working 'like a dragon' and by requiring the Court to sit from early in the morning until late in the evening; remarkably he did so without alienating his colleagues, the profession, or their clients.[121]

Denman was a good trial judge. Although he quickly reached a decision, he had the capacity '[to wind himself] up to the state of patience and quiet which can alone guide [him] through [the heavy calendar] with the least possible annoyance'.[122] He was impartial and unfailingly courteous. Charles Dickens spoke for many lay men when he wrote, 'I would to heaven it were decorous to pay him some public tribute of respect'.[123] Like Lyndhurst, Denman was a judge for the parties: fair, scrupulous, and temperate.[124]

There are few memorable judgments.[125] Denman thought that his reputation as a lawyer would depend on his judgment in *Stockdale v. Hansard* in 1839,[126] which the distinguished American judge and jurist, Joseph Story, had praised.[127]

---

[118] Greville described him as, 'an honourable, high-minded gentleman, but no lawyer, and one of the feeblest Chief Justices who ever presided over the Court of Queen's Bench' (*A Journal of the Reign of Queen Victoria* (London: Longmans, Green & Co., 1885, vol. III, 327)).

[119] In a undated letter to his brother-in-law, Vevers (*Arnould*, vol. I, 420–1, see n. 10 above).

[120] In a letter to his daughter, Theodosia: *Arnould*, vol. I, 423 (see n. 10 above).

[121] Denman calculated that in the 12 years between 1838 and 1850, the date of his retirement, 'no less than 2 additional years of sittings were by this measure given to the public': *Arnould*, vol. II, 94 (see n. 10 above).

[122] In a letter, dated 15 Aug 1841, to Lady Denman: *Arnould*, vol. II, 140 (see n. 10 above).

[123] J. T. Fields, *Memoirs of Dickens*, vol. ii, 85, cited in *Arnould*, vol. II, 149 (see n. 10 above).

[124] Greville, vol. II, 331 (above n. 39).

[125] Two which are still cited, are: *Eastwood v. Kenyon* (1840) 11 Adolphus & Ellis 438, establishing that moral consideration was not valuable consideration sufficient to found a binding contract; and *Williams v. Carwardine* (1833) 4 Barnwell & Adolphus: the motive for an act which amounts to an act of acceptance in law is immaterial.

[126] (1839) 9 Adolphus and Ellis 1.

[127] Denman is writing, in Oct. 1840, to his fellow judge, Coleridge, and mentions Story's approval of the Court's decision: *Arnould*, vol. II, 110–11 (see n. 10 above).

In that case the Court of Queen's Bench held that the existence of a privilege claimed by either of the Houses of Parliament, in particular, by the House of Commons, was a matter of law to be decided by the court and was not to be determined by a resolution of either House. To decide otherwise would make the judge an accomplice in the destruction of the liberties of his country. 'In truth, no practical distinction can be drawn between the right to sanction all things under the name of privilege, and the right to sanction all things whatever, by merely ordering them to be done . . . the power claimed is arbitrary and irresponsible, in itself the most monstrous and intolerable of all abuses.'[128]

In the House of Commons, Campbell, then Attorney-General, vigorously attacked the judgment, 'He was bound to say, then, and to say conscientiously, that in his firm opinion the decision in *Stockdale v. Hansard* was totally contrary to law, and that it involved a usurpation of the privileges of the House of Commons, and a flagrant usurpation of power by the Court of Queen's Bench.'[129]

Denman did not forgive Campbell for this intemperate expression of disapproval. Even more hurtful was his portrayal of Denman as a vainglorious champion of the people. For Denman thought, not without reason, that Campbell was obliquely referring to him, when, in Campbell's *Lives of the Chief Justices*, he talked of a judge who may, '. . . with the best intentions, be led astray into dangerous courses, and may bring about a collision between different authorities in the state which had long moved harmoniously, by indiscreetly attempting new modes of redeeming grievances, and by an uncalled-for display of heroism'.[130]

In 1849 Denman was 70. On circuit and in London he sat very long hours in court: 12-hour sittings were frequent. The strain was great and he suffered his first stroke the day before the beginning of the Easter term. A second stroke followed in July. He could now barely sign his name. Friends, including Brougham, and the eminent physicians, Sir Benjamin Brodie and Dr Thomas Watson, urged him to resign. But the prospect of Campbell succeeding him increased his determination to struggle on. Campbell's bitter attack on his motives in deciding *Stockdale v. Hansard* still rankled 10 years later. The likely succession to the Chief Justiceship became public knowledge and was publicly debated, the *Spectator* suggesting that Campbell was seeking to assassinate Denman by spreading ill-founded stories about his ill-health! Campbell in his turn

---

[128] *Stockdale v. Hansard* (1839) 9 Adolphus and Ellis 1, 147.

[129] *Parliamentary Debates*, 3rd series, vol. XLVIII, cols 365–6 (17 June 1839). The Parliamentary Papers Act 1840 partially vindicated Campbell, for it changed the law on the point which was in issue in *Stockdale v. Hansard*.

[130] Denman took great exception to this passage in Holt's life: *Lives of the Chief Justices* (London: Murray, 1874), vol. II, 402 (*Arnould*, vol. II, 289; see n. 10 above). Campbell was aware of Denman's feelings: *Life*, vol. II, 267–8 (see n. 12 above).

complained that he was, 'assailed by a storm of flippancy, scurrility, and falsehood'.[131]

In March 1850 Denman's health compelled him to resign. He did so somewhat mollified by the letter which he received from Russell, the Prime Minister, who wrote, 'No one can be more persuaded than I am that in the decisions given on Privilege, as in all other cases, none but a conscientious sense of duty was allowed to prevail'. Russell concluded with an assurance that Denman's name stood as a:

... model of uprightness and independence in the judicial office. If, as I infer, you are about to resign, it would surely be better to carry an undivided homage with you into your retirement than to raise a question as to your successor, in which many may think you right, but many others may think you wrong.[132]

Campbell

Campbell was 70 years old when he became Lord Chief Justice. He held this office until 1859.[133] As a judge Campbell's reputation is built upon the thirteen volumes of cases reported by Adolphus and Ellis and Ellis and Blackburn when he was Chief Justice of the Queen's Bench. His judgments are distinguished by a profound knowledge of the unreformed common law. Very few of his decisions were reversed. But his impatience and irascibility sorely tried the patience of some senior counsel. Sergeant Ballantine accused him of a lack of compassion, '. . . he crushed where he ought to have striven to raise'.[134]

In 1859 the Liberal Party regained power. Despite the protests of Sir Richard Bethell, later Lord Westbury, who had been Attorney-General until 1858 and confidently expected to become Lord Chancellor, Palmerston offered the Great Seal to Campbell. Campbell was now in his 80th year, but still vigorous.[135] Apart from his work as chairman of the Real Property Commissioners and his 6 weeks as Lord Chancellor of Ireland in 1841, he had no experience of the procedure or of the substantive doctrines of the Court of Chancery.[136] Campbell accepted the offer with alacrity, and remained on the Woolsack until his death. He was undeterred by the challenge. 'To qualify [myself], during the vacation I looked

---

[131] *Life*, vol. II, 271 (see n. 12 above).

[132] Dated 29 Jan 1850: *Arnould*, vol. II, 290–1 (see n. 10 above).

[133] As Chief Justice he participated in the debates of the House of Lords, particularly on legal issues. He joined Lyndhurst in opposing the Wensleydale life peerage, presided over the Committee whose report was the basis of the Divorce and Matrimonial Causes (Amendment) Act 1857, and inspired the Obscene Publications Act 1857.

[134] Ballantine, *Some Experiences of a Barrister's Life*, 124.

[135] In a letter to his friend, Ellis, written on 24 Nov 1856, Macaulay described him as looking as, 'young as when I first saw him 30 years ago': (T. Pinney ed.), *The Letters of Thomas Babington Macaulay* (Cambridge; Cambridge University Press, 1974–81), vol. VI, 67.

[136] He then became Baron Campbell of St Andrews.

over all the Equity decisions during the last ten years . . . I did not meet any case which I did not understand, or on which, after hearing it well argued, I could not have given a satisfactory judgment.'[137]

His prediction that he had 'no hope of being quoted as a great Equity authority'[138] proved to be correct; but he did clear much of the notorious Chancery arrears, deciding 'off-hand' many of the cases which came before him. His exercise of judicial patronage was scrupulous and courageous; for example, he appointed Blackburn—a most distinguished lawyer—as a judge of the Queen's Bench, 'the fittest man in Westminster Hall, although wearing a stuff gown'.[139]

AS LAW REFORMERS

Lyndhurst

Denman and Campbell were committed law reformers. Lyndhurst, however, was seen by his Whig opponents as contributing 'nothing to the progress of Law Reform . . . In fact, he only retarded it'[140]— which seems not entirely fair. But it is true that he could be mischievous, not resisting the temptation to twist Campbell's tail. So, he mocked Campbell's Bill prohibiting the sale of obscene books, paintings, and prints, predicting that Correggio's *Jupiter and Antigone* would be confiscated, as well as Ovid's *Art of Love*, while Dryden's poem, *Sigismonda and Guiscardo*, 'must be placed in [Lord Campbell's] *Index Expurgatorius*'.[141]

Lyndhurst did not welcome political change. But he did support *some* law reform. In the debate on the Juvenile Offenders Bill 1838 he had drawn a dramatic picture of the horrific treatment of young children in reformatories; and in the same year he proposed, albeit unsuccessfully, the modification of the common law rule which gave a wife, separated from her husband, access to the children only with his permission.[142] In 1853 and 1858 he supported the admission of Jews into Parliament, arguing that the words of the oath, 'without mental reservation and on the true faith of a Christian', were inserted to exclude, not Jews, but Roman Catholics.[143] In 1857, in the debate on the amendment of the divorce laws,[144] his study of the Church Fathers enabled him to refute the Bishop of Oxford who had

---

[137] *Life* (see n. 12 above), vol. II, 383.   [138] *ibid.*

[139] *ibid.*, vol. II, 372, see n. 12 above.

[140] Merivale in the *Edinburgh Review*, April 1869, 556, 564–5.

[141] *Parliamentary Debates*, 3rd series, vol. CXLVI, col. 330 *et seq.*

[142] *ibid.*, vol. XLIV, cols 761–9.

[143] *ibid.*, col. 772 *et seq.* The House of Lords was, to say the least, indifferent. The Bill was 'thrown out' (Contents, 9; Non-contents, 11). See also his speech on the second reading of the Custody of Infants Bill 1839: below n. 154.

[144] *ibid.*, vol. CXXVII, cols. 838 *et seq.*; and *ibid.*, vol. CLI, cols 1070–2.

invoked St Augustine as authority for the dogma of the indissolubility of marriage.[145]

Denman

Between 1818 and 1826, in a hostile House of Commons, Denman introduced a motion for negro emancipation, supported Brougham's motion for an inquiry into slavery in the West Indies,[146] and spoke feelingly of the plight of individuals who had fallen foul of the repressive legislation forbidding seditious meetings and blasphemous libels, which were the two mischiefs which the infamous 'six Acts' hoped to suppress. Both he and Campbell supported Whig motions condemning Eldon's steadfast opposition to any proposal to remove the Chancery arrears[147] or to the reform of common law procedure. He was very anxious to soften the rigour of the bloody criminal law, attempting to secure the abolition of the death penalty for forgery as well as representation by counsel for those accused of felonies. Both proposals were adopted later.[148]

In 1834 Grey, at Brougham's suggestion, decided to strengthen the judicial membership of the House of Lords. Denman was the obvious candidate; on 22 March his title was duly gazetted as Baron Denman of Dovedale. Denman's belief in the rights of the individual was one of the moral principles central to his life. Unlike Lyndhurst Denman was not a man who would sacrifice principle for party dogma. After the passing of the Reform Bill, he wrote:

The greatest of all political evils I have always thought was this—injustice deliberately perpetrated or wilfully persisted in by the State. My own opinion has uniformly been that injustice and wrong, whenever detected, ought to be instantly swept away. Like everything that prevails, it will by degrees strengthen itself by inveterate habits and factitious interests, and even the disinterested will grow in time accustomed and indifferent. Let, then, the first moment be taken when you can bring a sufficient force to bear upon mischief. Shake off the bad principle while

---

[145] *ibid.*, vol. CXLIV, col. 1690 *et seq.*

[146] As has been seen, the slave trade horrified him: above pp. 183–4.

[147] The price they paid was a high one, for Eldon refused them both a silk gown.

[148] Denman's campaign for law reform was conducted outside the House of Commons and the House of Lords as well as within these Chambers. In the *Edinburgh Review* there are critical, if complacent, review essays of Dumont's French edn of Bentham's *Traite des Preuves Judiciares* (Denman spoke fluent French) which had advocated the adoption of the French system of investigation and interrogation of witnesses (March 1824, art. viii, 169–207). For Denman, as for Blackstone, it was a matter of pride that an Englishman enjoyed the security of trial by a lawful jury of his county. Interrogation, he argued, was unfair to the prisoner; 'the mere fact of being accused is, in itself, an overwhelming calamity to an innocent man'. Moreover, in France the 'keen encounter of wits between judge and culprit . . . have a direct tendency to degrade the dignity of justice, because they always disturb its calmness and serenity'.

you may, and scan not too nicely the inconsistencies or even dangers that may result from the success of your exertions'.[149]

He was alive to the connection between ignorance and crime, and 'doubted how far the State was justified in inflicting punishment for an offence against the commission of which it had taken no pains to guard'.[150] In order to 'shake off bad principle', he was ready to support Tory Bills for the repeal of the Test Acts and for Catholic emancipation.

In 1837, despite the bitter opposition of 12 of the 15 judges,[151] Denman and Lyndhurst persuaded the House of Lords to pass Campbell's Prisoners' Counsel Act 1837 which allowed counsel for a person accused of felony to address the jury, and the accused to inspect and take copies of any depositions against him.[152] Its 'practical execution' was essential for 'the honour of the laws, for the due administration of justice, for the realisation of truth, and for the protection of innocence'.[153] In the same year a bill abolishing the death penalty for all cases of forgery passed through both Houses—two measures for which he had fought when first elected to the House of Commons.[154] What is surprising is that he regarded his successful proposal that the courts could sit *in banc* outside the brief legal terms as so significant that he asked for it to be recorded on his tombstone.[155]

Campbell

Campbell was a committed but conservative Whig, frequently upbraiding his brother for what he perceived were his radical views. He confessed to him, 'What I should like above all things, would be to be in the House of Commons, and to bring in Bills for the improvement of the law.'[156] His

---

[149] In a letter to Merivale, dated 24 Aug. 1832 (*Arnould*, vol. I, 388–93; see n. 10 above).

[150] *Parliamentary Debates*, 3rd series, vol. XXVII, col. 1335 *et seq.* (21 May 1835).

[151] In a letter to Brougham, dated 15 Apr. 1851, later published in the *Law Review*, Denman chided his judicial brethren for their reluctance to embrace reform and for their belief in the perfection of the legal system, 'whereas in truth the existing system is for the most part the neglected growth of time and accident' (*Arnould*, vol. II, 319–21; see n. 10 above.

[152] Above p. 194. But in 1838, despite the support of his fellow judges, Denman failed to persuade the House to allow witnesses to affirm instead of taking the oath; he thought a witness should be sworn according to the form which was binding on his conscience. The Law of Evidence (Amendment) Act 1842, which Denman introduced, embodied the Benthamite principle that all interested persons should be allowed to give evidence, leaving it to the jury to estimate its value.

[153] *Parliamentary Debates*, 3rd series, vol. XXXIV, 760–78. In 1839 Denman had also supported, with Lyndhurst, the second reading of the Custody of Infants Bill which gave a wife separated from her husband access to her children (*ibid.*, vol. XLIX, col. 485 *et seq*).

[154] In 1841, moved by the appeal of Caroline Norton, both he and Lyndhurst supported the Custody of Infants Bill.

[155] His eldest son, 'caused the fact to be inscribed on the stone that covers his remains in Stoke Albany churchyard' (*Arnould*, vol. II, 94; see n. 10 above).

[156] *Life*, vol. I, 465–6 (see n. 12 above).

profound interest in law reform remained an abiding one. As a consequence of Brougham's speech in 1828 two commissions were appointed,
one to inquire into common law procedure, and the other to inquire into
the arcane law of real property. Edward Sugden, who had edited Gilbert's
Law of Uses and Trusts, was the obvious choice as the chairman of the Real
Property Commission, but he declined. To Campbell's surprise he was
then invited to chair it. He was the only common lawyer among eight commissioners. But novel challenges never deterred Campbell, and he 'set to
work systematically *ab ovo*'.[157] He wrote the 'Introduction' to the First
Report and that part of it which dealt with 'Prescription and the Statutes
of Limitation'; although still a busy practitioner, he read every case from
the medieval period downwards, the relevant Roman civil law, the law of
modern continental nations, and the law of the American states—a
demonstration of his formidable industry and application.[158] A clutch of
law reform statutes, drafted by the Real Property Commissioners and
enacted in 1833 (3 & 4 Wm. IV), passed quietly, under his guidance,
through largely indifferent Houses, 'without one single syllable being
altered in any of them'.[159] These were not the only law reform statutes
enacted while Campbell was a Law Officer. Others included the
Municipal Corporations Act 1835; the Prisoners' Counsel Act 1837;[160] and
the Wills Act 1837 which prescribed the same formalities necessary for the
validity of Wills disposing of real and personal property.

When Peel and the 'new' Conservative party were returned to power in
1841, Campbell found himself with no judicial appointment and unable to
return to the Bar. In the House of Lords he remained a vocal supporter of
law reform, boring Brougham and Lyndhurst with his ponderous
speeches: the Libel Act 1843[161] and the Fatal Accidents Act 1846,[162] are still
known as 'Lord Campbell's Acts'.

---

[157] *Life*, vol. I, 458.

[158] The First Report was published in 1829, the other three reports over the next 3 years.
But Campbell had 'only the general superintendence' over these last three reports. The
Second Report which proposed a general register of deeds and instruments relating to land
was dear to Campbell's heart, but the proposal was not implemented in his lifetime. The
other recommendations of the commissioners were adopted.

[159] *Life*, vol. II, 29 (see n. 12 above). These included statutes: of limitations; for the abolition
of fines and recoveries; to render freehold and copyhold estates assets for the payment of
simple contract debts; for regulating the law relating to dower (a widow's life estate in half
of her deceased husband's realty); and to allow brothers and sisters of half blood to succeed
one another.

[160] Above p. 195.

[161] It made truth a defence in criminal cases if the publication was for the public benefit,
and, in a civil action, allowed pleas of mitigation that the libel was inserted without malice
and negligence on the part of newspaper owners.

[162] An action for wrongful death by the deceased's representatives.

THEIR LITERARY INTERESTS

Politics and the world of fashion dominated Lyndhurst's life. It is said that until his late years he read but little,[163] although the posthumous sale of his library included classical, English and French authors.[164] Their professional lives left Denman and Campbell little leisure, but they both retained their literary interests. It was Denman's mother who inspired his love of music and poetry.[165] He wrote poetry, and his letters reveal him constantly turning to such favourites as Shakespeare, Dante, Byron,[166] and Wordsworth.[167]

Campbell read widely, and was a prolific writer.[168] He much enjoyed the theatre and had been the drama and literary critic of the *Morning Chronicle*. He was a keen student of Shakespeare, particularly the plays. His book, *Shakespeare's Legal Acquirements Considered*, attempted to demonstrate, from the texts of the plays, that Shakespeare had spent some time as an attorney's clerk before he left Stratford. Critics dismissed it as derivative and unconvincing.[169]

CAMPBELL: THE BIOGRAPHER

It is on Campbell's skill as a biographer, the author of the *Lives of the Lord Chancellors* and *Lives of the Chief Justices*, written during the years when the Whigs were in Opposition, that his literary reputation rests. The first series of the *Lives of the Lord Chancellors* (to 1689) appeared in 1845, the second (to

---

[163] 'Reading, for which he had no time in his early life, as he tells us . . . was, with his farm, the great resource and a new pleasure' (Amory, 405; see n. 19 above).

[164] At a later sale there were Old Master engravings and drawings, and paintings by his father, by Titian, Van Dyke, Tintoretto, Canaletto, and Paulus Potter. But, almost certainly, he inherited them from his father (see Prown, *John Singleton Copley in England*, Washington D.C., Harvard University Press for the National Gallery of Art, 1966), vol. II, 385–405).

[165] *Arnould*, vol. I, 17–23 (see n. 10 above).

[166] Byron's obscene conversation, however, repelled him.

[167] But *Emma* was a 'very silly book'.

[168] His first significant literary foray was the ponderous *Speeches of Lord Campbell* (1842). They include his defence of the Prime Minster, Lord Melbourne, who had been accused by George Norton of criminal conversation with his wife, Caroline. It was the *cause célèbre* of 1836. The evidence was transparently thin and the jury returned, without hesitation, a verdict for the defendant. Campbell was buoyant. After the verdict he returned to the House of Commons to cheers of praise and relief. But the publication of his address to the jury 6 years later was condemned as insensitive, as it would revive painful memories for Mrs Norton and her family. The *Speeches* also contain his argument in *Stockdale v. Hansard* in 1839, over which he had laboured two long vacations. It scrupulously examined the history and boundaries of Parliamentary privilege and concluded that each House of Parliament is judge of its own privileges.

[169] As Campbell admitted: *Life*, vol. II, 362 (n.12 above).

1806) a year later, and the third (to 1827) in 1847—seven volumes in all. A final volume on Lyndhurst and Brougham was not published until after the death of the author and his subjects. The *Lives of the Chief Justices*, a more modest three volumes, was published between 1849 and 1957.

The *Lives of the Lord Chancellors*, over 6,000 pages, written in a short time-span, are an extraordinary achievement. They illustrate Campbell's merits and failings as an author. Campbell is no historian. He rarely uses primary sources and he treats manuscript letters and gossip with the same author-ity. Frequently he plagiarised. There are egregious factual errors, often the product of malice. On the other hand, its pages are 'the repository of a vast mass of tradition, legal and general, which, but for him, might easily have perished'.[170] Some of his portraits are vivid and acute characterisations, enlivened by entertaining anecdotes. Macaulay described the *Lives* as a 'most amusing book'.[171] Not surprisingly the volumes were immediately popular with royalty, politicians, judges, and members of the Bar. Posterity has been less kind. G. P. Moriarty, writing in the *Dictionary of National Biography*, described them as 'the most censurable publications in our literature'.[172] Many contemporaries were astonished to read Campbell's prediction that 'the world may decide that I have finished my biographical labours without forfeiting my claim to impartiality . . .'.[173]

THEIR PERSONAL LIVES

Their home backgrounds were very different. Copley, born in Boston, Massachusetts, was the son of the well-known portrait painter of the same name.[174] Denman's father was a distinguished physician and author of a celebrated textbook of midwifery. So, both fathers were celebrities in their very different ways. Campbell was a son of the manse.

All three were devoted sons, and were to become devoted parents. Copley discharged his father's debts, and was deeply attached to his mother and sisters. Denman's moral rectitude, the hallmark of his charac-ter, seems to have owed much to his mother's stern example and train-ing.[175] Campbell was close to his father (his mother died when he was 13),

[170] Atlay, vol. II, 184–5 (see n. 17 above).

[171] T. Pinney (ed.), *Letters*, vol. V, 96, see n. 135 above; in a letter to Frances Macaulay, dated 2 Mar. 1850.

[172] Moriarty (Oxford: Oxford University Press; reprinted 1921–2), vol. III, 835.

[173] *Lives of the Chancellors*, vol. VII, 696 (see n. 1 above).

[174] Copley Senior's income had dwindled during the turbulent years which led to the Revolution. He had long wanted to visit Europe and decided to leave in June 1774, to be fol-lowed by his wife and 3 of his 4 children.

[175] His biblical knowledge was built on his promise to her to read one chapter of the Bible each day, a promise which he fulfilled even during the busiest period of his life: *Arnould*, vol. I, 8 (see n. 10 above).

and to his brother, George, later Sir George Campbell of Edenwood, who helped him financially in his early years.

Campbell was as determined in the pursuit of love as in the pursuit of professional success, finally winning the hand of Mary Elizabeth, the daughter of Scarlett, later Lord Abinger.[176] Denman's wife, Theodosia Anne Vevers, was 'rich in virtues and graces . . . but with little or no fortune'.[177] Neither played an important part in the professional or political lives of their husbands.

Copley's first wife, Sarah Garay Brunsden, whom he married when he was 47 years old, was very different.[178] Lady Charlotte Bury described her as a handsome woman, with intelligent black eyes, 'so like one of Leonardo da Vinci's pictures'.[179] She loved too much 'the attractions of the world'.[180] The Lyndhurst home in George Street[181] was one of the centres of London fashion.[182] She was manipulative, cultivating the rich and well-born, and was alleged to have had affairs with the Duke of Northumberland and Lord Dudley, while the story of her attempted rape by the Duke of Cumberland was the talk of the salons.[183] But, 'having known what [poverty] is, [she] has resolved to let no momentary fancy expose herself to it again'.[184] When Lyndhurst was in Opposition, Whig grandees were among her guests. Indeed, her influence over Grey may have secured her husband's appointment as Chief Baron of the Exchequer

[176] They had 3 sons and 4 daughters.

[177] *Arnould*, vol. I, 42 (see n. 10 above). She was the mother of his 15 children, 4 of whom died in infancy.

[178] Her earlier marriage, of some 6 weeks, to Lieut-Col. Charles Thomas, had ended with his death at Waterloo.

[179] A. F. Stewart, *The Diary of a Lady in Waiting*, Lady Charlotte Bury (London: John Lane, The Bodley Head, 1908), 200. But Mrs Arbuthnot, the confidante of Wellington, thought that she was a 'singularly vulgar woman, who 2 years ago was trying to get into good society by being *rampante* and cringing to any body she thought more fashionable than others, and now that she is *Madame la Chancellière* she is very grand and means to be dignified, which makes her excessively amusing. I understand that the real fine ladies protest she shall never go into any of their houses' (eds. Bamford and The Duke of Wellington), *Journal of Mrs Arbuthnot, 1820–1832* (London: Macmillan, 1950), vol. II, 127. Lady Holland was a little more charitable, describing her as 'good hearted and good natured', adding with Whig patrician grandeur, 'with odd sallies . . . from coming into the *beau monde* when her ways were formed from another class' (Ilchester, *Elizabeth, Lady Holland to her Son, 1821–1845*; London: Murray, 1946, 91).

[180] Copley's adoring sister, Mary, admitted as much: see Amory (n.19 above), 351.

[181] In 1783 Copley Senior moved to 25 George St (later enlarged by Lyndhurst's purchase of No. 24). It was Lyndhurst's London home throughout his life.

[182] After a great fancy ball at the Hanover Square Rooms, 'Lyndhurst gave a supper in Geo. St to 80 of the supremest ton and beauty'. Disraeli wrote to his sister, 'You can conceive nothing more splendid and brilliant than his house illuminated, with a banquet to a company so fancifully dressed' (Benjamin Disraeli, *Letters: 1835–1837*, ed. J. A. W. Gunn; Toronto/ London: University of Toronto Press, 1982; vol. II, letter no. 408). The letter, written to his sister, Sarah, is dated 27 June 1835. Disraeli had just met Lyndhurst.

[183] Gore, *Creevey's Life and Times, 1768–1838* (London: Murray, 1934), n. 169, 307–9.

[184] Ilchester, *Henry Edward Fox: Journals, 1818–1830* (London: Butterworths, 1923), 359. The diary entry is dated 3 Dec. 1830.

in 1830. She died, suddenly, in Paris in 1834.[185] Mary wrote that 'her brother was devastated'.[186] If so, he was soon comforted. Within months he met Henrietta Sykes, Disraeli's lover. She may have become his kept mistress. She was not alone in thinking that, 'where women are concerned never was there a greater fool'.[187]

Lyndhurst remarried in 1837. His new wife was Georgiana, daughter of Lewis Goldsmith, a double-agent during the Napoleonic War, whom Lyndhurst had met in Paris. She was very different in character from 'Dolly', as Sarah had been affectionately called. Disraeli wrote of their first meeting, 'Without being absolutely pretty, her appearance is highly interesting . . . She is very little, but her appearance is elegant and delicate. She is not at all natural in the vulgar sense, her features being very small . . . Her manner calm and assured, yet tinged with a certain degree of reserve not unbecoming.'[188]

It proved to be a very happy marriage.[189]

CONCLUSIONS

Undoubtedly Denman was the most admirable of our triumvirate, respected for his moral rectitude and personal integrity. Throughout his life he remained faithful to principle.[190] Among his papers there is an autobiographical fragment, which places on record his own estimate of his parliamentary career from 1819 to 1826.[191] He wrote:

I fairly own that I look back on my Parliamentary career with no small satisfaction. I have never wished to recall a sentiment I uttered, or to change a vote I gave. I did my best for the interests of freedom, justice, and truth in every part of the world. For every species of reform, Parliamentary, legal, and economical, I constantly lifted up my voice; to every corruption and abuse I declared the enmity I felt. In all debates on the question of slavery I took that side which must mitigate its horrors and ultimately accomplish its abolition.[192]

As we have seen, the slave trade constantly haunted him. Arnould wrote that, after Denman's wife's death, the 'one subject and one subject only, beyond the limits of his private grief, had still power to move him deeply . . . and that was the terrible, ever-haunting subject of Slavery and the Slave Trade.'[193] The publication in England of *Uncle Tom's Cabin* aroused

[185] Three of their 5 children died in infancy; 2 daughters survived.
[186] Amory, 351 (see n.19 above).
[187] Robert Blake, *Disraeli* (London: Eyre & Spottiswoode, 1966), 118.
[188] Benjamin Disraeli, *Letters, 1838–1841*, vol. III, letter no. 733. He was writing to his sister, Sarah in a letter dated 19 Feb. 1838.
[189] They had one daughter, named Georgiana.   [190] Above pp. 194–5.
[191] Dated 1828.   [192] *Arnould*, vol. I, 121; see n. 10 above.
[193] *ibid.*, vol. II, 332.

Denman's pity and horror. It led him to attack bitterly and publicly his old friend, Dickens, who, he accused, had in 'certain articles in "Household Words"', 'taken pains to discourage the efforts then being made to put down slavery and the Slave Trade, and thus done his best to re-plunge the world into barbarism'.[194]

Denman was a deeply religious, intense man, but perhaps lacking a lightness of touch.[195] He was the personification of Victorian values. It would be unthinkable for him to betray the principles of his youth. So, he condemned Lyndhurst for lacking integrity,[196] and he could not forgive Campbell for questioning his own integrity.[197]

Campbell's 'personality seemed to rouse all the spirit of mischief in Lyndhurst, and on Brougham he acted like a red handkerchief to a bull'.[198] But 'his sublime self-satisfaction carried [him] through the ordeal'.[199] Lyndhurst, even though he 'delighted to play on his weaknesses and render him ludicrous',[200] treated him generously, giving him Silk and suggesting to Palmerston that he be appointed Lord Chancellor.[201] No doubt Campbell was maladroit and tactless; to Greville, lacking 'taste and refinement'—although, Greville reluctantly admitted, he 'is an able lawyer'.[202] Thick-skinned and insensitive, he quarrelled with many in his legal world, not only with Lyndhurst and Denman, but with Pollock, Bethell, Parke, and his vice-chancellors; and, having quarrelled, he rarely forgave.[203] His aggressive self-confidence and unconcealed ambition were unattractive. He was always determined to reach the top of his profession and quite shamelessly pressed his claims to office.[204] Campbell lacked dignity and *gravitas*. His failings are all too evident. But they cannot detract from his great service as a Law Officer, Chief Justice, and Chancellor, legislator and law reformer. He could, moreover, be generous, as his moving tributes to Follett[205] and Denman[206] demonstrate. But his affection was largely reserved for his family. His daughter wrote that 'geniality and tenderness

---

[194] Arnould, vol. II, 332–3. Dickens realised that Denman was a sick man, and wrote, in generous terms, to his daughter, Margaret [Mrs Cropper], to say that he had 'cleared [his] mind of Lord Denman's last opinions of me' (on 21 Jan. 1853; see *Arnould*, vol. II, 333–4, above n. 10).

[195] In the *Dictionary of National Biography*, John Alexander Herbert described him as 'witty and agreeable': vol. V, 815. I do not doubt that he was agreeable. But could so passionately committed a man be witty?

[196] Above pp. 178–81.   [197] Above p. 191.

[198] Atlay, vol II, 209 (see n. 17 above).   [199] *ibid.*, vol. II, 210.

[200] *Athenaeum*, 30 Jan. 1869, 166.

[201] Campbell's vignettes of these Lords Chancellor led Chief Baron Pollock to condemn Campbell, the biographer, as 'base and contemptible. The truth is Campbell was neither honourable nor even honest': Hanworth, 203, see n. 90 above.

[202] C. C. F. Greville, vol. III, 327 (above n. 118).

[203] Brougham, *Life and Times* (Edinburgh/London: Blackwood, 1871), vol. III, 434–5 (see n. 2 above).

[204] Above pp. 185–6.   [205] Cited in Atlay, vol. II, 190 (above n. 17).

[206] *Life*, vol. II, 265 (see n. 12 above). In his diary on 27 Oct. 1849 he wrote: 'He is justly and much beloved, and he is to be treated with the greatest tenderness.'

... distinguished [my father's] private life, and made him beloved by all who belonged to him'.[207] This was a side of Campbell which few outside his family saw.[208]

If Denman was the most admirable of my triumvirate, Lyndhurst would probably have been the most entertaining companion. He lived life to the full, spent too freely,[209] relishing good food, wine, and companionship. Paris was his second home. Returning from that city in January 1837, he told Greville that:

> ... he had never passed such an agreeable time as the last four months; not a moment of *ennui*; had become acquainted with a host of remarkable people of all sorts, political characters of all parties, and the *litterateurs*, such as Victor Hugo, Balzac, the latter of whom ... is a very agreeable man ... He has been leading here 'une vie de garçon', and making himself rather ridiculous in some respects.[210]

Lyndhurst was just as much at ease in the Parisian as in the London *haute monde*. On one such visit, in 1835, he dined with Louis Philippe[211] and 20 years later met Louis Napoleon and the Empress, remaining in 'active conversation, no other person present, for more than an hour'.[212]

His second marriage did not make Lyndhurst respectable, at least for some of his critics, one of whom was William Whewell, later Master of Trinity College, Cambridge, where Lyndhurst had been a Fellow and to which he was devoted. He unsuccessfully opposed Lyndhurst's election as High Steward of the University of Cambridge, not only on the ground that he was a 'political adventurer' but also because the many scandalous rumours about his private life made him 'quite unfitted to hold academic office'.[213] The staid Whewell would have been shocked by the licence and ribaldry of Lyndhurst's conversation and by his appearance, more that of a cavalry colonel than a Lord Chancellor, dressing in 'white Russia duck trousers, strapped under his boots of polished leather and in a becoming frock coat'.[214] For years he remained, in spirit, a Regency buck.

Historians have described Lyndhurst as a 'somewhat enigmatic figure'.[215] He died in the determination that this should be so, for he burnt

---

[207] Mary Scarlett Hardcastle's 'Preface' to the *Life* of John, Lord Campbell (see n. 12 above).

[208] He felt keenly the deaths of his father and brother, and never recovered from the death of his wife in 1860. 'I never expect', he wrote, 'an hour of real happiness in this world, notwithstanding all the devoted affection and never-ceasing solicitude to comfort me of all my children' (*Life*, vol. II, 393; see n. 12 above).

[209] His estate was valued for probate as 'under £18,000': and see Wellington's comment, quoted above p. 187.

[210] Greville, vol. III, 378 (see n. 39 above).   [211] Amory, 132 (see n.19 above).

[212] Cited in Dennis Lee, *Lord Lyndhurst: The Flexible Tory*, 244. Lyndhurst is writing to his friend, Francis Barlow. The letter is dated 3 Dec 1855.

[213] D. A. Winstanley, *Early Victorian Cambridge* (Cambridge: Cambridge University Press, 1940), 100, citing a letter, dated 13 Oct 1840, from Whewell to Julius Charles Hare.

[214] Bagehot, vol. III, 232, at 236 (see above n. 51). At a great fancy ball, in June 1835, he appeared as a Marshal of France!: see the letter of Disraeli, above n. 182.

[215] e.g., Blake, *Disraeli*, 115 (above n. 187).

nearly all his private papers.[216] Condemned for his 'conversion' to Tory principles, a Proteus whose 'path to power was through the wreck of all political consistency',[217] once he entered the House as a Tory he became an unswervingly loyal party man. He would not have gone to the stake for a principle his party had abjured: *against* and then *for* a defendant's right to counsel in felony trials; *against* and within two years *for* Catholic emancipation; *against* any reform of the franchise and within a year *for* some reform; *for* the Corn Laws and shortly afterwards *against* the Corn laws. 'He took up the opinions of the existing Government and advocated them, and to the end of his life would have thought it "nonsense and rubbish" to act otherwise.'[218]

For many Lyndhurst appeared a paid advocate, who could not be trusted to be true to *a* principle. Campbell contemptuously accused him of repudiating 'all the opinions and sentiments which he had before entertained and expressed', and castigated him, while Solicitor-General, for piloting the detested 'Six Acts' through the House of Commons. In a bitter, splenetic passage in his *Lives of Lord Lyndhurst and Lord Brougham*,[219] he remarked that Lyndhurst's conduct had been compared to that, '[of] the mercenary soldier ready to obey every command of his superior officer . . .'.[220]

Lyndhurst did have *some* political convictions. He firmly believed that the House of Lords was a vital part of the constitution; and he opposed the creation of life peers because he feared that governments would create them for political purposes, thereby further eroding that House's authority and independence.[221] But he came to perceive, as he did not in the 1830s, that there were limits to its powers. In 1858 he described its role in these words:

. . . it is also a most important part of our duty to check against the inconsiderate, rash, hasty, and undigested legislation of the other House; to give time for consideration; and for consulting and perhaps modifying the opinions of the constituencies; but I never understood, nor could such a principle be acted upon, that we

---

[216] Campbell, *Lives of the Chancellors*, vol. VIII, 2 (see n. 1 above), where Lyndhurst is said to have told Campbell, 'Materials you shall have *none* from me; I have already burnt every letter and paper which could be useful to my biographer, therefore he is at liberty to follow his own inclination.' The surviving papers are in Trinity College, Cambridge, and the Glamorgan Record Office.

[217] Bagehot, cited in *Arnould*, vol. I, 408 (see n. 10 above).

[218] Bagehot, vol. III, 232, at 236 (see n. 51 above).

[219] *Lives of the Lord Chancellors*, vol. VIII, 30–1 (see n. 1 above).

[220] Campbell went on to quote 3 lines from Lucan's *The Civil War* (Pharsalia): '*Pectore si fratris gladium iuguloque parentis/Condore me jubeas . . . /. . . invita peragam tamen omnia dextra'*. ('Tell me to plunge my sword into my brother's breast/Or in my father's throat . . . /And I shall do it all with this right hand,/ Though it go against the grain'). At least Campbell had sufficient delicacy to omit the words, '*plenaeque in viscera partu Coniugis*' ('or else the belly of my pregnant wife')—Lady Lyndhurst was still alive. (I am indebted to Tony Weir Esq., Fellow of Trinity College Cambridge, for the translation.)

[221] *Parliamentary Debates*, 3rd series, vol. CXXXX, cols. 263–9.

were to make a firm, determined, and persevering stand against the opinion of the other House of Parliament, when that opinion is backed by the opinion of the people, and least of all, on questions affecting, in a certain degree, the constitution of that House and popular rights'.[222]

Lyndhurst's intellectual pre-eminence was widely recognized. Disraeli said he 'rarely originated'.[223] But Disraeli judged him as a politician and, as a politician, he did not seek to 'originate'. But he never ceased to be intellectually curious. 'After he had entered his ninetieth year, he went through the problems of Euclid to ascertain whether he was still capable of effort in mathematics.'[224]

Lyndhurst 'both looked, and was, a great man'.[225] Criticized for his lack of *gravitas*, it was this lack of *gravitas* which even political opponents found endearing. Only the most malicious claimed that he was corrupt.[226] A political opponent who punctured pretension, he was 'perfectly free from all jealousy or petty spite'.[227] He took pains to placate Eldon; he proposed that Campbell should be given Silk; he enjoyed the company of radicals, like Robert Wilson and Roebuck; he and Edward Ellice, a passionate liberal, were 'great friends here [in Paris]';[228] Brougham attacked him in the *Edinburgh Review* and became a close friend; Sydney Smith[229] and Macaulay,[230] loyal Whigs, gratefully acknowledged his patronage.

Lyndhurst was content with the honours he enjoyed and with the influence he exercised in the House of Lords. He was, lamented Henrietta Sykes, 'too unambitious'.[231] His love of society never left him; and society welcomed him for his *joie de vivre* and kindness. At his country home, Turville Park, and in George Street, surrounded by family, he entertained artists, authors, scientists, beautiful and gifted women, as well as politicians. Never bored, cossetted by his devoted wife, sister, and three daughters, supported by his friends, he was in 1863—as in 1791—'naturally a friend to gaiety', continuing despite infirmity to 'love to see what is to be seen'.[232]

---

[222] *ibid.*, vol. CXXXXIX, cols. 1770–1. He was speaking in the debate on the Oaths Bill 1858.

[223] Monypenny & Buckle, vol. I, 329 (see n. 14 above).

[224] Amory, 436 (see n. 19 above).

[225] Bagehot, vol. III, 232 (see n. 51 above).

[226] In 1829 he had successfully initiated criminal libel indictments against newspapers which alleged that he had sold Church appointments and trafficked in political offices: Martin, 245–6 (n. 98 above).

[227] Brougham, cited in Martin, 507 (n. 98 above).

[228] Greville, vol. III, 379 (n. 39 above). The year was 1837.

[229] Trinity College mss, O.16.38/59.   [230] *ibid.*, O.16.38/58.

[231] Blake, *Disraeli*, 118.

[232] In his letter to his mother, dated 26 Feb. 1791, reproduced in Amory (see n.19 above), 117.

8

The Fate of the Civil Jury in Late-Victorian England: Malicious Prosecution as a Test Case

*Joshua Getzler**

The history of the criminal law in Victorian England can be portrayed as a struggle between judge and jury over who can best assess the moral culpability of the defendant. Judges mistrusted the instincts of a jury, especially in the more lurid cases;[1] but the ancient principle that life and liberty should depend on the verdict of one's peers remained unchallenged.

This essay turns attention to the history of the civil jury, asking how the common lawyers of nineteenth-century England regarded the influence of the lay jury on litigation in property, contract, and tort, where fortunes rather than liberty were at stake. The short answer is that the courts all but eliminated the jury from civil trials; but the survivals are instructive, and help explain the motivations for the eviction of the civil jury from the courtroom in the first place.

The decline of the civil jury trial in Victorian England may be regarded as interesting in itself; and it may also serve as an object lesson for modern law reformers. Today the constitutionally-entrenched jury trial in the United States consumes an average of $14,000 per trial in public costs, and has helped create a notably byzantine law of civil wrongs.[2] The new Russian Commonwealth attempted to institute wide access to jury trial in the mid-1990s, but abandoned the experiment when it was found that the jury consumed one quarter of the entire justice budget.[3] Do these modern experiences indicate that the late Victorian exclusion of the jury was

* For helpful discussion and assistance I would like to thank Roderick Bagshaw, Daniel Klerman, Martin Matthews, and the audience at the July 1999 British Legal History Conference in Edinburgh.

[1] Simpson, A. W. B., *Cannibalism and the Common Law* (Chicago: University of Chicago Press, 1984; reprinted Harmondsworth: Penguin, 1986 and London: Hambledon Press, 1994), esp. ch. 9.

[2] Fleming, J. G., *The American Tort Process* (Oxford: Oxford University Press, 1988), 101–39; Robertson, D. W., 'An American Perspective', in B. S. Markesinis and S. F. Deakin, *Tort Law*, 4th edn. (Oxford: Oxford University Press, 1999), 203–37. For the history of attempts to control the American civil jury see Scott, A. W., 'Trial By Jury and the Reform of Civil Procedure', *Harvard Law Review*, 31 (1918), 669; Note, 'The Changing Role of the Jury in the 19th Century', *Yale Law Journal*, 74 (1964), 170.

[3] See further Holmes, S. and Sunstein, C., *The Cost of Rights: Why Liberty Depends on Taxes* (New York: Norton, 1999), 24–8.

well-founded? The costs of jury trial in mounting a civil law system is another important theme.

THE DETHRONEMENT OF THE JURY BY THE JUDICIALIZING OF DECISION-MAKING

The evolution of English private law has been told before as the story of a long decline in jury power, matched by the rise of the judge who comes to control nearly all significant aspects of the civil trial process. According to this model, there first comes the redefinition of adjudication as the matching of fact to fine-spun doctrinal rules, presumptions and precedents, rather than the refining of relevant fact to put to the jury.[4] Forsyth and Thayer, the great Victorian historians of evidence and procedure, demonstrated how procedural devices such as demurrers to evidence, special verdicts, and colourable pleading combined to squeeze out jury discretion as expressed through the general verdict.[5] Judges thereby enlarged their powers to define and ascribe liability and to fix the level of remedy. Trial issues become issues of law not fact.

The emasculation or diminution of the civil jury is then followed in the second stage by its elimination. A series of court reforms from the mid-nineteenth-century, led by the legislature, create a discretion or power to remove the jury almost entirely from the civil trial process. By 1933 it has become sensible to eliminate juries almost entirely because their functions have been denuded.[6]

The dominance of the jury in criminal trials remains, and indeed is enshrined as a foundation of the legal polity. This is because of a perception that findings of wicked conduct occasioning state punishment should be inflicted only through the operation of peer or lay justice.[7] Elsewhere pockets of strong jury control remain only in those tortious areas with stronger moralistic resonance—as where it is an element of the action itself that the defendant must be found guilty of having had a malicious or wicked state of mind when inflicting the injury. The chief examples are defamation, fraud, and abuse of legal process including false imprison-

---

[4] Cf. Milsom, S. F. C., 'Law and Fact in Legal Development', in *ibid., Studies in the History of the Common Law* (London: Hambledon Press, 1985), 171–89; *ibid., Historical Foundations of the Common Law*, 2nd edn (London: Butterworths, 1981), 296–300, 413–24.

[5] Forsyth, W., *History of Trial By Jury* (London: Parker & Son, 1852), 168–91, 259–98; Thayer, J. B., *A Preliminary Treatise on Evidence at the Common Law* (London: Sweet & Maxwell, 1898), 183–262; Thayer, J. B., '"Law and Fact" in Jury Trials', *Harvard Law Review*, 4 (1890), 147.

[6] Devlin, P., *Trial By Jury* (London: Stevens, 1956 & 1966), 130–3. There are now only some two dozen civil trials with jury in England and Wales each year: Zander, M., *Cases and Materials on the English Legal System*, 7th edn (London: Butterworth, 1996), 376–83.

[7] A doctrine undermined by strict liability regulatory offences; see Ashworth, A. S., *Principles of Criminal Law*, 2nd edn (Oxford: Clarendon Press, 1995), 158–67.

ment and malicious prosecution.[8] In each of these spheres a lay, communal judgment is sought to legitimize the possibility of severe legal and moral sanctioning of the defendant, even though there is no criminal dimension of state punishment.

Controversy in recent years has focused on explaining why the civil jury was diminished outside the areas of crime and some of the intentional torts. In the 1970s it was powerfully suggested (e.g. by Nelson, Gilmore, Horwitz, and Atiyah) that the jury was dethroned by elitist judges for ideological reasons.[9] According to this neo-realist interpretation, Victorian judges and jurists looked askance at the jury as a suspect *locus* of populist moral economy and reactionary economic paternalism. Judges could be shown to be influenced by philosophical radicalism and political economy, inclining them to believe in market competition and the natural selection of the economically fit. The argument runs that judges were therefore determined to stamp out the antiquated commercial morality represented by the jury, especially in contract and tort actions. For juries to decide civil law liabilities and so regulate market competition made as much sense to efficiency-minded judges as the old assizes fixing the price of bread. Ideology dictated that the civil jury had to be cut down. Thus did the political economy of the law vanquish the moral economy of the jury.[10]

The ideological explanation equating juries with pre-capitalist nostalgia, and judicial doctrine with free-market theory, has attracted detailed and sometimes devastating empirical criticism. Brian Simpson's 'line by line refutation' of Horwitz's history of modern contract is justly celebrated.[11] Can anything be saved, then, of the striking theory that juries were eliminated from the English civil trial in pursuit of market efficiency? An alternative interpretation is to stress a drive to efficiency not in the type of results sought by courts, but rather in their internal procedures of lawmaking. The judges were not seeking to govern the real, producer economy of competitive markets by issuing rational legal rules, but rather were trying to enhance the legal process itself, as a system to enforce the transactions and protect the interests of litigants. Judges and jurists looked askance at the jury because of its high costs in time and money, and also

---

[8] Supreme Court Act 1981, s. 69(1).

[9] Nelson, W., *The Americanization of the Common Law* (Cambridge, Massachusetts: Harvard University Press, 1975), 165–74; Gilmore, G., *The Death of Contract* (Columbus: Ohio State University Press, 1974; 2nd edn with R. K. L. Collins, 1995), 98–100; Horwitz, M. J., *The Transformation of American Law, 1780–1860* (Cambridge, Massachusetts: Harvard University Press, 1977), 28–9, 84–5, 141–3, 155–9; Atiyah, P. S., *The Rise and Fall of Freedom of Contract* (Oxford: Clarendon Press, 1979), 47–9, 210–11, 390–4.

[10] Cf. Malone, W. S., 'The Formative Era of Contributory Negligence', *Illinois Law Review* (Northwestern University), 41 (1946), 151, 155–69.

[11] Simpson, A. W. B., 'The Horwitz Thesis and the History of Contracts', in *ibid.*, *Legal Theory and Legal History. Essays on the Common Law* (London: Hambledon Press, 1987), 203–72; cf. Simpson, A. W. B., 'Innovation in Nineteenth-Century Contract Law', *ibid.*, 171–202; Barton, J. L., 'The Enforcement of Hard Bargains', *Law Quarterly Review*, 103 (1987), 118.

for the imprecision, uncertainty, irrationality, and unintelligence perceived to infect lay decisions. A jury-based system could not develop precise rules enabling disputes to be determined by actors prospectively without resort to court. By contrast, a judge-based system, stating reasons for assessing fact and developing rulings through repetitive and consistent decision, could provide such hortatory guidance.[12] Juries were therefore targeted, not because they supported a counter-capitalist ideology, but because they could not successfully reason or purpose at all.

The Common Law Commissioners of 1852–3 may have been expressing the opinion of many judges when they reported to Parliament on the perceived inadequacies of the civil jury:

[W]e are not at all blind to the fact that in many instances juries are not so constituted as to ensure such an average amount of intelligence as might be desired . . . in the agricultural districts the common juries are sometimes composed of a class of persons whose intelligence by no means qualifies them for the due discharge of judicial functions. Such persons, unaccustomed to severe intellectual exercise or to protracted thought . . . sometimes pronounce verdicts which bring the institution of juries into disrespect.[13]

Driven by sentiments such as these, judges sought to replace the breadth of jury discretion with more and more elaborate adjectival and substantive law. In 1854 and 1873 statutes permitted reference of matters of account and then 'matters requiring prolonged examination of documents or accounts or any scientific or local investigation' to a curial referee.

However, it was not until 1883 that formal rules permitted judges to exclude the jury from civil trials at discretion, wherever matters were formerly dealt with in Chancery or Admiralty without the assistance of a jury, or in matters where a jury could not conveniently make investigation.[14] Even after that important reform, common lawyers could still assail the unintelligent and unguided populism of jury trial. Dicey, for example, wrote a celebrated attack in 1885:

Trial by jury is open to much criticism . . . the habit of submitting difficult problems of fact to twelve men of not more than average education and intelligence will in the near future be considered an absurdity as patent as ordeal by battle . . . Juries are often biassed against the Government. A technical question is referred for deci-

---

[12] Holmes, O. W., *The Common Law* (Boston: Little, Brown, 1881; ed. M. De Howe, Cambridge, Massachusetts: Belknap Press, 1963), 89–92, 98–103; cf. Thayer, E., 'Judicial Legislation', *Harvard Law Review*, 5 (1891), 172; Green, A. L., *Judge and Jury* (Kansas City: Vernon, 1930), 268–79.

[13] H.C. Parliamentary Papers, xl (1852–3), 701, at 708, quoted in Atiyah, *Rise and Fall of Freedom of Contract*, 390 (see n. 9 above).

[14] Rules of the Supreme Court (1883) ord. xxxvi, r. 26; Devlin, P., 'Jury Trial of Complex Cases: English Practice at the Time of the Seventh Amendment', *Columbia Law Review*, 80 (1980), 43, 95–9. The reform was entrenched by later legislation; see below, text accompanying nn. 17–18.

sion, from persons who know something about the subject, and are impartial, to persons who are both ignorant and prejudiced.[15]

Dicey cannot be accepted as a representative common lawyer; his belief in a technocratic rule of law administered by elites was, at base, an anti-collectivist crusade more than an analytical jurisprudential theory. But the ideology of expertise propounded by Dicey cannot entirely be quarantined from the common-law thought of his time.[16]

What was the practical impact of all this anti-jury sentiment? Jackson has estimated that until the 1883 procedural reform, ninety per cent of common-law civil trials were heard before juries; after the reform, the proportion dipped to fifty per cent and then continued to decline.

The Juries Acts of 1918–33[17] finally decreed that civil trials be conducted without juries unless ordered by the court. Civil jury trials became the exception rather than the rule.[18] Before these reforms, however, and throughout the formative period of the common law of the eighteenth and nineteenth-centuries, juries sat on almost all common-law civil hearings;[19] and judges strove to find methods to hem the jury in and curb its decisional power.

In trials dealing with complex and technical matters the judge might deem the lay jury incompetent to assess the evidence and constitute the court itself as the fact-finder.[20] But the jury role could be diminished by more subtle means than exclusion. The chief method employed was to engage in more and more judicial fact-finding in the guise of testing the propriety of pleadings—and then applying formal legal doctrine to the

[15] Dicey, A. V., *An Introduction to the Study of the Law of the Constitution*, 1st edn (London: Macmillan, 1885; 10th edn, 1959), 394, at 398. Dicey also preferred the judge-made law of the professional courts to the legislation of an untutored and short-sighted Parliament: see *ibid.*, *Lectures on the Relation Between Law and Public Opinion in England During the 19th Century*, 2nd edn (London: Macmillan, 1914; 1st edn, 1905), 361–98.

[16] Cosgrove, R. A., *The Rule of Law: Albert Venn Dicey, Victorian Jurist* (London: Macmillan, 1980). Dicey was more elitist in life than in death; he is buried amongst modest Oxford townfolk and artisans, in St Sepulchre's Cemetery within the site of Lucy's Ironworks, a little north of the University Press in Jericho, Oxford.

[17] The discretion is now stated in the Supreme Court Act 1981, s. 69(1), (3), and (4).

[18] Cornish, W. R., *The Jury* (London: Allen Lane, 1968), 210–42; Devlin, *Trial By Jury*, 130–3; Jackson, R. M., 'The Incidence of Jury Trial During the Past Century', *Modern Law Review* 1 (1937), 132, 138–43. Jackson's findings must now be reviewed in the light of new statistical findings by Michael Lobban suggesting a more gradual decline, 'The Strange Life of the Victorian Civil Jury in England' (paper delivered at the 14th British Legal History Conference, Edinburgh, 16 July 1999). Reasons for the resilience of jury trials on the criminal side are anatomized in Zuckerman, A. A. S., *The Principles of Criminal Evidence* (Oxford: Clarendon Press, 1989), 29–46.

[19] Juries never sat in Chancery suits unless the court remitted a factual question for jury trial: see Devlin, 'Jury Trial of Complex Cases', n. 14 above.

[20] *ibid.*, 65–95; cf. Arnold, M., 'A Historical Inquiry into the Right to Trial by Jury in Complex Civil Litigation', *Pennsylvania Law Review*, 128 (1980), 829, 840–6. The inherent discretion was codified by 19th-century legislation culminating in the Supreme Court Act 1981, s. 69.

established facts. Juries were thereby reduced to deciding narrow questions of fact as determined by the judges, with a seemingly automatic legal result following from the factual findings. Once the judges could decide which narrow factual questions for the jury were relevant (by means of fine-grained legal tests), they, the judges, had won control of the adjudicative process.

There were important exceptions to this general trend, notably the use of special juries to advise the court on some specific area of expertise and so help the court determine which business norms and practices to absorb into legal principle, whether as evidential presumptions subject to rebuttal, or as definite legal rules. The best-known instance was Lord Mansfield's liberal use of special juries of merchants to help develop new doctrines of insurance, bills of exchange, promissory notes, and other areas of commercial law.[21] However, the traditional use of the special jury, with its valued non-legal expertise, did not contradict the wider swing away from the ideal of the untutored citizen jury as a sure fount of justice.[22]

In order to apply the more elaborate and discriminating judicial tests to fact in the course of determining rights, modern courts were required to sit as tribunals of fact, rather than allow the pleading process to narrow the facts in issue down to a stylized point. English law reports after the 1830s show a marked shift in presentation, as the detailed facts of cases slide away from the pleading statements and counsels' arguments, and resurface in the judicial summation of evidence within elaborate reserved judgments. Courts are now sifting through evidence of the parties' conduct to discover who had acted, at which times, with which state of knowledge. For example, in the important 1839 case of *Arkwright v. Gell* dealing with natural property rights, Chief Baron Abinger began his discussion of the case by observing:

A special case was reserved on the trial, for the opinion of the Court, stating a great number of documents and facts, upon which the Court are not merely to give their judgment on matters of law, but to take the office of the jury, by determining whether any and what inferences of fact ought to be drawn from the facts stated. This course leads to one great inconvenience, as it tends to confound the rule of law with an inference of fact only, which inference may have been varied by a very slight circumstance.[23]

---

[21] See Oldham, J. C., 'Special Juries in England: Nineteenth-Century Usage and Reform', *Journal of Legal History*, 8 (1987), 148; *The Mansfield Manuscripts and the Growth of English Law in the Eighteenth Century*, ed. J. C. Oldham, 2 vols (Chapel Hill: University of North Carolina Press, 1992) i, 82–99.

[22] Oldham, J. C., 'The Origins of the Special Jury', *University of Chicago Law Review*, 50 (1983), 137.

[23] (1839) 5 M. & W. 227, 227–8; 151 E.R. 87, 97 (Ex). A similar complaint against conversion of factual inference to *ratio* is articulated in *Harris v. Great Western Railway Co.* (1876) 1 Q. B. D. 515, 521–3 *per* Mellor J.; 529–34 *per* Blackburn J.

This was a special case where the judges formally sat in the office of a fact-finding jury. But the judges' experience of adjudication was not dissimilar where a standard jury did participate. Chief Baron Abinger revealed a growing sense that the courts had bitten off more than they could chew in the field of fact-finding and evidence. Intense pressures on court time, with the heightened litigation of a burgeoning industrial and commercial economy, soon demanded a different style of adjudication and definition of rights.[24]

One solution to this problem was to preserve the common law's concepts of action and intention as the basis of rights, but to simplify them by objectifying the operative intention or consent—what Holmes in *The Common Law* called the 'external standard'.[25]

The final simplification of the law was to allow external standards to predominate over actual intents, agreements, or mind-states of the parties in defining civil rights and duties. The devil only knows the mind of a party; the modern lawyer does not even care to guess, but is interested only in behaviour. This shift allows adjudication to proceed in a more peremptory or summary mode, directly enforcing broad, discretionary policy standards. And in tandem, discouraging parties from litigating chiefly on the basis of instance-specific, detailed factual pleading. Atiyah and Gilmore made much of such trends in nineteenth-century contract doctrine, with Gilmore observing, 'At the height of the classical period it seemed that it was hardly possible to phrase any contract issue other than as a question of law.'[26]

The result of this shift in pleading and proof was a new type of equity in the common law—particular justice and *aequum et bonum* achieved not through fact discretions, but through the working-up of every factual nuance of a case into a discriminating point of law.

The Judicature Acts marked a further change by arming the common law with extended interlocutory powers—enabling courts to process still more fact into law. As a result, special pleading no longer served to reduce the wash of significant evidence going into the courtroom. But the Judicature Acts did not initiate these changes; the common-law courts were reaching for a peculiarly doctrinal style of equity long before 1873.[27]

---

[24] Cf. Atiyah, *Rise and Fall of Freedom of Contract*, 390–1 (see n. 9 above).

[25] 'Objectification' of consent in English legal history is perhaps the leading theme of Holmes, *The Common Law*; see M. De W. Howe, 'Introduction', *ibid.*, pp. xx–xxvii; Hart, H. L. A., 'Diamonds and String: Holmes and the Common Law', in *ibid.*, *Essays in Jurisprudence and Philosophy* (Oxford: Clarendon Press, 1983), 278, 279–83; Horwitz, M. J., 'The Legacy of 1776 in Legal and Economic Thought', *Journal of Law and Economics*, 19 (1976), 621, 626 ff.

[26] Gilmore, *Death of Contract*, 99; Atiyah, *Rise and Fall*, 388 ff., at 405–8 (see n. 9 above).

[27] Cf. Arnold, M. S., 'Law and Fact in the Medieval Jury Trial: Out of Sight, Out of Mind', *American Journal of Legal History*, 18 (1974), 267; Milsom, 'Law and Fact in Legal Development', 171–89; Getzler, J., 'Patterns of Fusion', in Birks, P. B. H., (ed.), *The Classification of Obligations* (Oxford: Oxford University Press, 1997), 157, 170–90.

Occasionally this process was noted and decried by the common lawyers. An example was Mackenzie Chalmers who, despite his position as the leading draftsman of codifying commercial legislation of his time, was also a strong partisan of jury trial.[28] In a speech given to the Oxford Law Club in November 1890, Chalmers pointed out that the elimination of the jury had rendered common law judgments indistinguishable from Chancery. By this he meant the use of fine-spun tests sensitive to every nuance of fact attempting to construct legal rules as a set of finely-tuned moral standards. Chalmers advocated maintaining the civil jury, it seems, on the grounds that a little intuitive and irrational decision-making by the jury on the edge of bright-line legal rules would help protect those rules from fragmenting.[29] In other words, the Aristotelian equity of the jury protected the common law from the natural-law equity of the Chancery.

However, thoughtful pro-jury voices such as Chalmers' were seldom heard in the chorus of anti-jury lawyers of the post-Judicature Act period.

COUNTERSTREAMS TO JURY ABOLITION

It is always useful to look for counterstreams to the orthodoxy: exceptions that probe the edge of a rule. For example, *Rylands v. Fletcher* attracts the historian as a new burst of strict liability in a swelling sea of Victorian fault liability.[30] If we look in the right places, evidence emerges that many Victorian judges apart from Chalmers were ambivalent about hastening the death of the jury, and often tried to reverse the decline of the jury in civil trials. This proclivity to favour jury power was not necessarily driven by trust in lay justice; but rather by a perception that a strong jury role was necessary in order to maintain respect for legality and to protect the Bench from accusations of moral bias or political ambition.[31] With appropriate mutation we may adapt to the Victorian era Maitland's comments on the thirteenth century:

The once popular doctrine which represents the justices as encroaching on the province that belonged to the jurors will not commend itself to students of the . . . century. Neither jurors nor justices had any wish to decide dubious questions.[32]

[28] See Simpson, A. W. B., (ed.), *Biographical Dictionary of the Common Law* (London: Butterworths, 1984), 107–8.

[29] Chalmers, M. D., 'Trial by Jury in Civil Cases', *Law Quarterly Review*, 7 (1891), 15.

[30] Simpson, A. W. B., 'Legal Liability for Bursting Reservoirs: The Historical Context of *Rylands v. Fletcher*', *Journal of Legal Studies*, 13 (1984), 209, revised and reprinted as 'Bursting Reservoirs and Victorian Tort Law: *Rylands and Horrocks v. Fletcher* (1868)' in *ibid.*, *Leading Cases in the Common Law* (Oxford: Clarendon Press, 1995), 195–226; Dalton, C., *Losing History: Tort Liability in the 19th Century and the Case of Rylands v. Fletcher* (MS., 1987).

[31] Cf. the American regard for the civil jury as a constitutionally-entrenched institution of the common law: see Oldham, J. C., ch. 10 in this work.

[32] Pollock, F., and Maitland, F. W., *The History of English Law Before the Time of Edward I*, 2 vols., 2nd edn (Cambridge: Cambridge University Press, 1898, reprinted 1968), i, 631.

In the sixteenth century, Sir Thomas More is recorded as complaining that the judges' fear of decisional power was the chief preserver of the inefficient common-law jury system and, what is more, the chief bar to a rational fusion of law and equity with an inquisitorial method of evidence. More, as Chancellor, asked that the law courts should exercise their discretion to 'mitigate and reform the rigour of the law'. But the judges refused, as More later recounted, because, 'they may by the verdict of the jury cast off all quarrels from themselves upon them, which they account their chief defence'.[33]

As the common law developed in later centuries, lively debate continued over the division of the roles of judge and jury in civil trials in areas including: the definition of tortious negligence liability;[34] the method for construing terms of documents in contract;[35] the fixing of damages rules in tort and especially in contract, as the action on the case gave damages for loss at large, rather than for a liquidated sum;[36] the finding of reputation-harming statements in defamation;[37] and, finally, the method for determining the ingredients of liability for false imprisonment and malicious prosecution.

Malicious prosecution is perhaps the least studied of all these. Yet it was a highly significant arena of debate over jury power, regularly attracting the attention of the Exchequer Chamber and the House of Lords in the classical Victorian age. It is an interesting test-case for the issue of civil jury jurisdiction, because the appellate courts shifted decisional power uneasily back and forth from judge to jury, and along the way raised many arguments about the role of the jury in modern civil law process. The rest of this chapter describes the role of the jury in actions for malicious

---

[33] Roper, W., *The Lyfe of Sir Thomas More*, Hitchcock, E. V. ed.), (London, 1935), 44–5, cited in Plucknett, T. F. T., *A Concise History of the Common Law*, 5th edn. (London: Butterworths, 1956), 687–8. See further Guy, J., *The Public Career of Sir Thomas More* (Brighton: Harvester, 1980); Baker, J. H., 'The Common Lawyers and the Chancery: 1616', in *ibid.*, *The Legal Profession and the Common Law. Historical Essays* (London: Hambledon Press, 1986), 205; Getzler, 'Patterns of Fusion', 175 ff, see n. 27 above.

[34] Thayer, *Treatise on Evidence*, 209–10, 241–53; Milsom, *Historical Foundations of the Common Law*, 296–300, 392–400.

[35] *Bartlett v. Smith* (1843) 11 M. & W. 483; 152 E. R. 895 (Ex.); *Lewis v. Marshall* (1844) 7 Man. & Gra. 743; 135 E. R. 293 (C. P.); *Hutchison v. Bowker* (1839) 5 M. & W. 535; 151 E. R. 227 (Ex.); 9 L. J. Ex. 24; *Neilson v. Herford* (1841) 8 M. & W. 806; 151 E. R. 1266; Thayer, J. B., *A Selection of Cases on Evidence at the Common Law* (revd. edn. by Maguire, J. M., Cambridge, Massachussets: Harvard University Press, 1925), 92–128.

[36] Washington, G. T., 'Damages in Contract at Common Law', *Law Quarterly Review*, 47 (1931), 345 and 48 (1932), 90; Helmholz, R. H., 'Damages in Actions for Slander at Common Law', *Law Quarterly Review*, 103 (1987), 624; Danzig, R., '*Hadley v. Baxendale*: A Study in the Industrialization of the Law', *Journal of Legal Studies*, 4 (1975), 249.

[37] Forsyth, *History of Trial By Jury*, 268–82; Helmholz, R. H. and Green, T. A., *Juries, Libel, and Justice: The Role of English Juries in 17th and 18th-century Trials for Libel and Slander* (Los Angeles: Clark Library, 1984); Mitchell, P., 'Malice in Defamation', *Law Quarterly Review*, 114 (1998), 639.

prosecution. From that study it hopes to extract some general ideas about the role of civil juries.

MALICIOUS PROSECUTION

The action for malicious prosecution is descended from the action on the case for conspiracy to abuse legal process.[38] As a tort action it is peculiar in that it requires *mens rea*, namely malice (a subjective test); and also the *actus reus* of the launching of an unsuccessful criminal prosecution where there was no reasonable and probable cause appearing to the prosecution to justify such an action, either before or during the running of the trial.

This last ingredient amounts to a mixed subjective/objective test, similar to that for modern Provocation: what would a reasonable man, in the place and context of the actor, have done in the circumstances? A prosecution brought with malicious motive but with reasonable cause was not actionable; a reasonable law-enforcing citizen could well hate the defendant and wish him or her harm at the same time as bringing a justified prosecution against him or her. A wholly unreasonable failed prosecution brought without proven malice was not actionable; but extreme lack of reasonable cause could ground a jury finding of malice without more.[39] Outside criminal prosecutions, there were a small number of cases where a failed civil action could result in a tort claim for abuse of process along similar lines (e.g. for maliciously proceeding against a foe in bankruptcy).[40]

The combined *indicia* of liability for abuse of process produced an action that was more than usually difficult to define and apply. Judges disliked the action and greatly resented the jury discretions infecting the process, fearing that juries would find for claimants freshly acquitted of the initial charge, and thus open up a vexatious avenue of revenge against unsuccessful defendants merely striving to advance their own interests by law. In 1599, for example, a court decried the propensity of 'lay gents' of the jury to find for plaintiffs in such actions.[41]

Many judgments hostile to the existence of the malicious prosecution jurisdiction have been made across the centuries, but two stand out. In the

---

[38] Winfield, P. H., *The History of Conspiracy and Abuse of Legal Procedure* (Cambridge: Cambridge University Press, 1921), chs ii and v.

[39] *Turner v. Ambler* (1847) 10 Q. B. 252; 116 E. R. 98; see also *Hailes v. Marks* (1861) 7 H. & N. 56; 158 E. R. 391 (Ex); *Johnson v. Emerson* (1871) L. R. 6 Ex. 329; *Shrosbery v. Osmoston* (1877) 37 L. T. 793 (Ex); *Hicks v. Faulkner* (1881–2) 8 Q. B. D. 167.

[40] *Grainger v. Hill* (1838) 4 Bing. N. C. 212; 132 E. R. 769; *Johnson v. Emerson* (1871) L. R. 6 Ex. 329; *Quartz Hill Consolibidated Gold Mining Company v. Eyre* (1883) 11 Q. B. D. 674 (C. A.); *Cox v. English, Scottish, and Australian Bank Ltd* [1905] A. C. 168 (P. C.); Clerk, J. F. and Lindsell, W. H. B., *The Law of Torts*, 2nd edn (London: Sweet & Maxwell, 1896) 566, at 574 ff; Salmond, J. W., *The Law of Torts*, 1st edn (London: Stevens & Haynes, 1907), 455–68.

[41] *Pain v. Rochester* (1599) Cro. Eliz. 871; 78 E. R. 1096, at 1097.

great case of *Sutton v. Johnstone* in 1786,[42] Lord Mansfield held *obiter* that malicious prosecution ought not to be brought in any case in the wake of an unsuccessfully prosecuted court martial. The civil action ought not to be available to control military jurisdiction because of the need for stern professional discipline in the armed forces, especially during combat. No rule-of-law squeamishness about the military here; rather the opposite:

The salvation of this country depends on the discipline of the fleet; without discipline they would be a rabble, dangerous only to their friends, and harmless to the enemy. Commanders, in a day of battle, must act upon delicate suspicions; upon the evidence of their own eye; they must give desperate commands; they must require instantaneous obedience. In case of a general misbehaviour, they may be forced to suspend several officers, and put others in their places. A military tribunal is capable of feeling all these circumstances, and understanding that the first, second, and third part of a soldier is obedience. But what condition will a commander be in, if, upon exercising his authority, he is liable to be tried by a common law judicature? If this action is admitted, every acquittal before a court martial will produce one.[43]

These high policy considerations might be thought to be confined to cases of 'national security'. But Lord Mansfield held that the final decision as to reasonable and probable cause in all criminal prosecutions, not just courts martial, was reserved to the judge as 'a question of law'.[44] The courts feared an endless regress of actions following a failed prosecution: to permit a fight over the propriety of an earlier prosecution seemed to create a reverse jeopardy where the accuser was punished. One controlling mechanism was to state that the court would not release all the files of the original criminal trial to the aggrieved defendant, to prevent him or her from commencing a malicious prosecution action in its wake—a device especially resorted to where the court regarded the defendant as unrespectable or unworthy.[45]

Our second leading case of *Abrath v. North Eastern Railway Co.* was decided a century after Lord Mansfield's time, in 1883.[46] In *Abrath* a railway company prosecuted a doctor for conspiracy to defraud by collaborating with an accident victim to exaggerate the injuries suffered in a railway accident in order thus to increase the compensation due. The doctor was acquitted of the charge, but lost his own subsequent action for malicious prosecution. *Abrath* is a modern *locus classicus* for the

---

[42] (1786) 1 T. R. 492; 99 E. R. 1215 (Ex. Ch., affd by H. L.). [43] *ibid.*, 549; 1246.
[44] *ibid.*, 545; 1244. To like effect: *Busst v. Gibbons* (1861) 30 L. J. Ex. 76.
[45] See Hay, D., 'Controlling the English Prosecutor', *Osgoode Hall Law Journal*, 21 (1983), 165; *ibid.*, 'Prosecution and Power: Malicious Prosecution in the English Courts, 1750–1850', in Hay, D. and Snyder, F. (eds), *Policing and Prosecution in Britain, 1750–1850* (Oxford: Clarendon Press, 1989), 343–95.
[46] (1883) 11 Q. B. D. 79 (Q. B.); 11 Q. B. D. 440 (C. A.); 11 App. Cas. 247 (H. L.).

doctrine, superseded only in 1962.[47] In *Abrath*, Lord Bramwell, like Lord Mansfield before him, put the objection to malicious prosecution actions in terms of the dangers of jury discretion irrationally favouring the plaintiff. He stated that bodies corporate ought generally to be immune to the action for this very reason:

[E]very one, or every counsel and solicitor listening to me, knows that the only reason why a railway company is selected for an action of this sort is that a jury would be more likely to give a verdict against a company than against an individual. Everybody knows it; and perhaps there is a sort of hope of confusion; it is said 'the man was innocent; somebody ought to be punished for it; here is a railway company; there was an improper motive;' and so there is a jumble; the case gets before a jury, and a railway company is exactly the party to have damages awarded against it. If ever there was a necessity for protecting persons it is in an action for malicious prosecution, and for two reasons. First of all a prosecutor is a very useful person to the community. We have something in the nature of a public prosecutor, but everybody knows that the greater number of prosecutions in this country are undertaken not by the state but by private persons, or, as in this case, corporations.[48]

Lord Bramwell was prepared to go still further and condemn the existence of the doctrine itself:

One may venture to quote Bentham even upon this matter. He said that laws would be of very little use if there were no informers, and that it is necessary for the benefit of the public that people when they prosecute, and prosecute duly, should be protected. And there is an additional reason. A man brings an action for a malicious prosecution; he gives evidence which shews or goes to shew that he is innocent. You may tell the jury over and over again that this is not the question, but they never or very rarely can be got to understand it. They think that it is not right that a man should be prosecuted when he is innocent, and in the end they pay him for it. It is, therefore, all-important that these actions should not be permitted to be brought against persons or bodies or others who are not properly liable in respect of them.[49]

It is worth noting that Lord Selborne L. C. felt compelled to give a second impromptu speech immediately upon hearing Bramwell's, where he made clear that Bramwell's judgment, whilst deserving the usual high respect, was to be regarded by the lower courts as the *obiter dicta* of a solitary judge.[50] We cannot dismiss Lord Bramwell's speech in *Abrath*, how-

---

[47] See *Glinski v. McIver* [1962] A. C. 726 (H. L.) *per* Lords Denning and Devlin. The more recent House of Lords decision in *Martin v. Watson* [1996] A. C. 74 is confined to the question of when a defendant is responsible for launching the initial unsuccessful prosecution and does not investigate the meanings of malice and reasonable cause.

[48] *Abrath v. N. E. Railway Co.* (1886) 11 App. Cas. 247, 252. NB: in modern times at least, the action was also available against a public prosecutor, e.g. a policeman: *Glinski v. McIver* [1962] A. C. 726 (H. L.); Clayton, R. and Tomlinson, H., *Civil Actions Against the Police* 2nd edn (London: Sweet & Maxwell, 1992), ch. 8.

[49] *Abrath v. N. E. Railway Co.* (1886) 11 App. Cas. 247, at 252.   [50] *ibid.*, 256.

ever, solely as the maverick view of a violent partisan of railway companies and of economic development generally. Bramwell could hand down decisions hostile to monopoly capital as well as curbing pro-plaintiff juries;[51] and judges with different political commitments and prejudices to Bramwell's also questioned the justifications for sustaining the malicious prosecution action and the extent of the jury's role in the action.[52]

If the judges were wary of the malicious prosecution action, they were not happy to abolish it or 'scale-back' either. The privilege to bring a criminal prosecution or serious civil action against another person was not to be exercised irresponsibly, without let, for the impact on the reputation, credit, and peace of innocent defendants could be devastating. So the judges continuously spoke of a balance to be struck between due private prosecution of wrongdoing, and safeguarding the innocent from harassment through abuse of legal process.[53] This was an emergent example of the Diceyan model of control of public powers and functions by the technique of private writs. The malicious prosecution action was (and still is) available against officers of the police—though a good defence is that the police and prosecutorial bureaucracy relied in good faith on information collected from informers and witnesses.[54]

The Victorian courts continuously revised and restated the elements of the malicious prosecution action, with hundreds of actions and dozens of appellate hearings taking place across the nineteenth century. Judges were wont to complain when faced with a malicious prosecution case that the law was so difficult and indeterminate that mis-trial through mis-statement of the relevant law, or inaccurate charging of the jury was almost inevitable.[55] The chief problem was to decide the respective roles of judge and jury, first in evaluating the presence or absence of malicious motive, and secondly in assessing reasonable and probable cause. The lack of a reasonable basis for the decision to prosecute could factually imply malice, but need not do so. However, the presence of malice could not of itself imply lack of reasonable basis, since many reasonable private prosecutions would be actuated in part by a motive of harming or punishing the defendant through process of law.[56] Malice as a legally disqualifying

---

[51] Cf. Lord Bramwell's judgment in *Dynen v. Leach* (1857) 26 L. J. Ex. 221 at 223 with that in *Osborn v. Gillett* (1873) L. R. Ex. 88, 94–6.

[52] See *Panton v. Williams* (1841) 2 Q. B. 170; 114 E. R. 66 (Q. B. & Ex. Ch.); S. C. 1 G. & D. 504; 10 L. J. Ex. 545 *per* Tindal C. J.; *Shrosbery v. Osmoston* (1877) 37 L. T. 793 (Ex); *Allen v. Flood* [1898] A. C. 1, at 125 *per* Lord Herschell, 172 *per* Lord Davey (H. L.); Pollock, F., *The Law of Torts*, 6th edn (London: Stevens & Sons, 1901; 9th edn, 1912), 324–8.

[53] See e.g. *Broad v. Ham* (1839) 5 Bing. (N. C.) 722, 727; 132 E. R. 1278, at 1280 *per* Erskine J. (C.P.); *Haddrick v. Heslop* (1848) 12 Q.B. 267; 116 E. R. 869 *per* Lord Denman C.J.

[54] *Glinski v. McIver* [1962] A. C. 726 (H. L.); *Martin v. Watson* [1996] 1 A. C. 74 (H. L.).

[55] See e.g. Bowen L. J. in *Abrath v. N. E. Railway Co.* (1883) 11 Q. B. D. 440 at 455 (C. A.).

[56] *Ravenga v. Mackintosh* (1824) 2 B. & C. 693; 107 E. R. 541 (K.B.); *Hicks v. Faulkner* (1878) 8 Q. B. D. 167;

factor was therefore ultimately defined with perfect circularity as a motive that the law did not like.

An entire book on this convoluted subject was written by Sir Herbert Stephen in 1888, who claimed in the preface that he had been provoked to write in part by the implications of the decision in *Abrath*. Stephen claimed that despite all formal doctrinal postures by the judges, the two key mental *indicia* of malice and reasonable cause were entirely within the purview of the jury as issues of fact. The jury's role was to find malice allied to facts that would not support reasonable and probable cause for bringing a prosecution; the judge was then compelled to draw the factual (but not legal) inference that there was a lack of reasonable and probable cause. Hence the judge tended to ratify the jury's basic factual finding as a matter of course.[57]

It was indeed rare for trial judges to overturn initial jury findings in the spheres of malice and reasonable cause. Most appeals went to misdirection, with disappointed litigants claiming that the judge had arrogated too much or too little power to the jury. In one appeal after another the higher judges expressed their dislike of the judicial role as a fact-trier in this area, but attempted no thorough reform. Some light is thrown on this issue by the 1868–70 case of *Lister v. Perryman*,[58] where the House of Lords were prepared to concede that the judge of a malicious prosecution action was acting as a trier of pure fact and not law, and could not look to any precedents to help him decide the presence of reasonable and probable cause, nor attempt to confine jury discretion with tests screening the evidence. In that case Lister, a local magnate, caused Perryman, a farmer's son, to be imprisoned and prosecuted for felony, accusing him of stealing his favourite rifle. On the way to the police station Lister himself beat up Perryman, who was later acquitted of the felony. The bruised, unfortunate Perryman then sued Lister back for false imprisonment and malicious prosecution without reasonable cause. The factual matter to be tested was whether Lister had been reasonable to rely solely on the hearsay of a servant reporting another's hearsay informing on Perryman. Chief Baron Kelly tried the action and held that as a matter of law there would be no reasonable cause if the jury found as a point of fact that Lister had relied on hearsay alone. Lister sought review of the trial judge's instructions to the jury as an over-direction. The Court of Exchequer reviewing the trial split 2–2.

Barons Pigott and Bramwell held that there could be no automatic rule excluding a hearsay basis for private prosecution. In Bramwell's words, 'it is a question of fact for the jury, whether the channels of information were

---

[57] See e. g. *Rowlands v. Samuel* (1847) 11 Q. B. 39, 41 n.; 116 E. R. 389, 390 *per* Denman C.J.; Stephen, H., *The Law Relating to Actions for Malicious Prosecution* (London: Stevens & Sons, 1888), pp. v–vi, 28–84—an exhaustive treatment of the authorities.

[58] *Lister v. Perryman* (1868) L. R. 3 Ex. 197 (Ex .and Ex. Ch.); (1870) L. R. 4 H. L. 535 (H. L.).

such that the information they conveyed might be reasonably relied upon. Consequently I think there was in this case a misdirection, and that there should be a new trial'.[59] This cogent judgment was trumped by Chief Baron Kelly himself, who sat on the tribunal reviewing his own trial directions and (unsurprisingly) decided that he had been right all along. He stated, in effect, that judges should vigorously control juries and set policy lines in this field:

I agree that we should pronounce no decision which could tend to prevent or impede a firm but honest attempt to obtain justice by one who believes himself to be aggrieved; but on the other hand, I feel that our fellow-subjects are entitled to our protection against the imprisonment of their persons, and the disgrace which necessarily attends a charge of felony, where the accuser has no other ground to act upon than that somebody has told him that he has been told by somebody else of something which may be capable of explanation upon inquiry, though, unexplained, it may be calculated to create suspicion.[60]

Baron Channell concurred with the chief baron, giving an equally divided court; and as was customary a *puisne* justice (Pigott B.) withdrew his contrary judgment in order to give precedence to the chief justice's opinion. It is worth noting that Chief Baron Kelly had been the successful lead counsel in the important 1841 Exchequer Chamber hearing of *Panton v. Williams*, where an anti-jury judge, Chief Justice Tindal, had insisted that the judge, as a question of law, should tell the jury what factual findings would support a reasonable prosecution, and what would exclude a malicious one. Chief Justice Tindal based that decision on Lord Mansfield's anti-jury speech in *Sutton v. Johnstone*.[61]

If matters had rested there, then abuse of process litigation would probably have been subjected in future cases to tight judicial control. But fortunately for legal history, our litigant Lister was not to be defeated so easily, and took his defence up to a heavyweight Court of Exchequer Chamber. He lost. Mr Justice Byles delivered the briefest of judgments for his brothers Justices Blackburn, Keating, Montague Smith, and Lush:

Where there is a ready and obvious method of ascertaining the truth, and the opportunity of so doing is neglected by the defendant . . . we think the absence of inquiry is an element in determining the difficult question of the presence or absence of reasonable and probable cause. What its weight may be must depend on the circumstances of each particular case, but we cannot say that . . . [Kelly c. b.] . . . was wrong in saying that the failure to obtain information from [a witness] would prevent the existence of reasonable and probable cause.[62]

Lister fought on to the House of Lords.

---

[59] *ibid.*, 202.   [60] *ibid.*, 205.
[61] *Panton v. Williams* (1841) 2 Q. B. 170; 114 E. R. 66 (Q. B., Ex. Ch.).
[62] *Lister v. Perryman* (1868) L. R. 3 Ex. 197, 208.

The surprise of the litigation was the forceful decision of the Law Lords overturning all three of the lower courts, and affirming the sovereignty of the jury on the question of reasonable cause. Lord Chelmsford stated that in this area the judge had to take the verdict of the jury on questions of fact and then ratify it or not as a question of fact; the judge could not attempt to state his conclusion as a matter of law without provoking a mis-trial. It was an anomalous case of a factual verdict taking place in two steps, divided between judge and jury. Lord Westbury stated that the judge must be careful to decide reasonable cause as a matter of factual, not legal inference, which Chief Baron Kelly C. B. had failed to do. Lord Westbury went on to state:

I regret, therefore, to find the law to be, that it is an inference to be drawn by the Judge, and not by the jury. *I think it ought to be the other way* (emphasis supplied). I cannot agree with the Judges in the Exchequer Chamber, for they lay down an abstract proposition . . . It is impossible to lay down a general rule, and that proposition of the Court of Exchequer Chamber might in future lead to great inconveniences.[63]

The truly fascinating speech was given by the Lord Colonsay. He also stated that reasonable cause ought to be a jury issue. The learned Scottish lord felt that the English lawyers had got this whole area badly wrong, partly because of the backwardness of their criminal law system.

I . . . find . . . myself placed in what is to me the somewhat novel position of having to deal with the question of want of reasonable and probable cause as a question of law for the Court, and not a question of fact for the jury. I have frequently had to deal with cases of this kind in the other end of the island; but there this question of want of reasonable and probable cause is treated as an inference in fact to be deduced by the jury from the whole of the circumstances of the case, in like manner as the question of malice is left to the jury.[64]

He then held that a Scottish jury could fittingly have found for either plaintiff or defendant in the present case on the question of probable cause; this would be a factual finding impervious to curial control save for patent irrationality:

But in England it is settled law that this is a matter for the Court to deal with. The Court deals with it as an inference to be drawn by the Court from the facts, but whether an inference of law or an inference of fact does not, I think, appear from the reports. I do not see clearly whether it is called an inference of law merely because it is left to the Court, or whether it is left to the Court because it is really an inference of law.[65]

The doctrine according this decision to the court rather than the jury was firmly established by Lord Mansfield in *Sutton v. Johnstone*, '[p]robably . . . from anxiety to protect parties from being oppressed or harassed in conse-

---

[63] *Lister v. Perryman* (1870) L. R. 4 H. L. 535, 538.   [64] *ibid.*, 538–9.   [65] *ibid.*, 539.

quence of having caused arrests or prosecutions in the fair pursuit of their legitimate interests, or as a matter of duty, in a country where parties injured have not the aid of a public prosecutor to do these things for them'. Lord Colonsay then asked which rules and principles of law existed to guide the court's inquiry. 'I did not find that there were any.'[66] The authorities dictated that there was properly to be no authoritative guidance, but rather, 'that it is a mere question of opinion, depending entirely on the view which the Judge may happen to take of the circumstances of each particular case'. The only extant guiding doctrine was that of Chief Justice Tindal in *Panton v. Williams*,[67] which held that the judge must decide how a 'reasonable and discreet person would have acted'. Lord Colonsay indicated that this was inherently a question suitable for a jury; and if a judge was fated to decide it, he must think as a juryman if he could, not as a lawyer.[68]

Lister v. Perryman[69] demonstrated that the division of roles between judge and jury in deciding abuse of legal process was essentially contested territory; and further that at least some of the higher judges favoured a strong or predominant jury role. The majority of the Lords in the later case of *Abrath* were finally content to leave the issue as a question of fact for the sole decision of the jury, monitored only for due weight of evidence by the judge. In a series of appellate decisions that followed,[70] elaborate criteria by which the trial judge could weight the evidence for the jury were supplied, though by this time such jury controls were common enough in mainstream criminal law.[71]

MALICE, PRIVILEGE, AND INTENT REVISITED

When doctrine cannot speak clearly, this may be a warning that the policy-foundations of the laws in question are not agreed or well understood. I have

---

[66] *ibid.*

[67] *Panton v. Williams* (1841) 2 Q. B. 170; 114 E. R. 66 (Ex. Ch., rev. Q. B.); S. C. 1 G. & D. 504; 10 L. J. Ex. 545.

[68] *Lister v. Perryman* (1870) L. R. 4 H. L. 535, 539–540.

[69] Smith, H., *Addison On Torts*, 7th edn (London: Stevens & Sons, 1893), 222–9; Clerk and Lindsell, *Law of Torts*, 564–74; Forsyth, *History of Trial By Jury*, 284–9; Dobbs, D. B., 'Belief and Doubt in Malicious Prosecution', *Arizona Law Review*, 21 (1979), 607; Fribidman, G. H. L., 'Compensation of the Innocent', *Modern Law Review*, 26 (1963), 481, 481–95. For the 19th-century American debate see *Lawyers' Reports Annotated* (L. R. A., N. S.), (Rochester, New York: Lawyers' Cooperative Publishing Co.), 56 (1915 D), 72–80.

[70] *Hicks v. Faulkner* (1881–2) 8 Q. B. D. 167; *Brown v. Hawkes* (1891) 2 Q. B. D. 718 (C. A.); *Cox v. English, Scottish, and Australian Bank Ltd.* [1905] A. C. 168 (P. C.); *Herniman v. Smith* [1938] A. C. 305 (H. L.); *Glinski v. McIver* [1962] A. C. 726 (H. L.).

[71] The US law of malicious prosecution by contrast tends to allocate assessment of reasonable cause entirely to the judge: see Weiner, S., 'The Civil Jury Trial and the Law-Fact Distinction', *California Law Review*, 54 (1966), 1867, 1876–94; Wade, J. W., 'On Frivolous Litigation: A Study of Tort Liability and Procedural Sanctions', *Hofstra Law Review*, 14 (1986), 433; Keeton, W. P. et al., *Prosser and Keeton on Law of Torts*, 5th edn (St Paul: West Publishing Co., 1984), 882.

to conclude that the issues clouding clear judgment in the area of abuse of process went much deeper than the intractable law–fact, judge–jury split. The issues reached into the heart of tort policies in the late Victorian age.

Here we might look to a grand debate that has run for more than a century in the Anglo-American common law tradition, concerning the relationship between actionable tort damage and the absolute nature of common law rights and privileges. The issue is whether rights at common law may be used according to the untrammelled will of the rights-holder—for any motive whatsoever; whether that motive be wholesome and well-intentioned, or immoral and anti-social. At common law (but not in equity) one can generally 'abuse' one's substantive property rights through malicious exercise.

For example, a property-owner may build a 'spite fence', or block a view, or cause degradation of water supply to a neighbour, all for motives other than exploiting his own land, such as a desire to harm another for spite, or to subject that other to intense pressure regarding some other interest. *Bradford Corporation v. Pickles*[72] and *Keeble v. Hickeringill*[73] are classic examples of this phenomenon.[74] Likewise in contract one can exercise one's rights to hurt another, independent of one's desire to make profit— as with strikes, lockouts and other forms of monopolistic competition, as in the celebrated decisions in *Allen v. Flood*[75] and the *Mogul Steamship* case.[76]

Judges and jurists at the turn of the twentieth century were fascinated by the general problem of whether intentional infliction of harm invalidated or de-legitimated the exercise of rights; for example, a good portion of the fourth lecture on tort in Holmes's *The Common Law* of 1881 addresses this issue.[77] Holmes there approved of the English judiciary's conclusion that there was properly no doctrine of abuse of rights in the common law. In this view, to moralize about the exercise of vested legal rights through manipulating discretionary legal remedies was to be resisted as a pre-modern throwback. But by 1894, in Holmes's important essay, 'Privilege, Malice, and Intent',[78] the author was himself doubting this theory. He accepted that where one person intentionally damages another through

---

[72] [1895] A. C. 587 (H. L.).

[73] (1707) Holt K. B. 14, 17, 19, 90; 90 E. R. 906, 907, 908 (one of many reports).

[74] See the elucidation of these last two cases by Simpson, A. W. B., in, respectively, *Victorian Law and the Industrial Spirit* (London: Selden Society, 1995); and 'The Timeless Principles of the Common Law: *Keeble v. Hickeringill* (1707)', in *ibid.*, *Leading Cases in the Common Law*, 45–75.

[75] [1898] A. C. 1 (H. L.).

[76] *Mogul Steamship Co. Ltd. v. McGregor, Gow & Co.* [1892] A. C. 25 (H. L.).

[77] Holmes, *The Common Law*, 104–29.

[78] Holmes, O. W., 'Privilege, Malice, and Intent', *Harvard Law Review*, 8 (1894).

[79] Kelley, P. J., 'A Critical Analysis of Holmes's Theory of Torts', *Washington University Law Quarterly*, 61 (1983), 681; Vandevelde, K. J., 'A History of Prima Facie Tort: The Origins of a General Theory of Intentional Tort', *Hofstra Law Review*, 19 (1990), 447, 471–6, 495–7; and

exercise of an undoubted right, the court must perforce balance between two contending rights-holders, and the law ought not necessarily permit one rights-holder wilfully to injure the holdings of another at least without a good justification. Typically the justifications for such legal side-taking were based on communal expediency—for example, to prevent strangulation of markets by unfair competition and monopolism, or to redistribute economic power to the vulnerable.

It has been suggested[79] that Holmes's 1894 theory of utilitarian justification for harms provided the genesis of an articulate legal realism in the United States—that is, a theory of law that is suspicious of the capacity of formal doctrine to provide meaningful or definite answers, and a concomitant favouring of discretionary balancing tests and overt social engineering. Certainly the United States bench accepted Holmes's theory that intentional infliction of harm was a *prima facie* tort that needed some utilitarian policy justification to escape liability; to that extent some version of realism was entrenched in American law.[80] It was an irony that the Supreme Court tended to reject the liberal justifications for competitive harms propounded by Holmes and did not follow him in allowing trade unions the right to strike and so injure their employers' businesses in order to bargain for wages in the industrial marketplace.[81]

The English courts in the great case of *Allen v. Flood* decided against adopting the *prima facie* tort doctrine.[82] Despite campaigns by moralizing jurists such as Devlin, Fleming, and Finnis in the twentieth century,[83] the doctrine of *Allen v. Flood* still commands adherents.[84] What is less often noticed is that the majority of the judges sitting on *Allen v. Flood* wanted to attach liability to intentional abuse of contract rights to cause harm and so adopt the Holmesian *prima facie* tort theory. It was a narrow liberal majority in the Lords that rejected the idea, precisely because they mistrusted the jury, especially the prejudices that middle-class juries might bring against insurgent trade unions. So much may be collected from the lead-

Horwitz, M. J., *The Transformation of American Law 1870–1960: The Crisis of Legal Orthodoxy* (New York: Oxford University Press, 1992), 123–42.

[80] Ames, J. B., 'How Far an Act May be a Tort Because of the Wrongful Motive of the Actor', *Harvard Law Review*, 18 (1905), 411; American Law Institute, *Restatement of Torts (2nd)*, *1977* (St Paul: A. L. I. Publishers, 1979), art. 870, comments a–c, e; Vandevelde, K. J., 'The Modern Prima Facie Tort Doctrine', *Kentucky Law Journal*, 79 (1990–1), 519.

[81] Vandevelde, 'A History of Prima Facie Tort', 476–95.   [82] [1898] A. C. 1.

[83] Devlin, P., *Samples of Lawmaking* (London: Oxford University Press, 1962), 11–13; Fleming, J. G., *The Law of Torts*, 9th edn. (Sydney: Law Book Co., 1998), 471–3, at 751 ff.; Finnis, J., 'Intention in Tort Law', in D. G. Owen (ed.), *Philosophical Foundations of Tort Law* (Oxford University Press, 1995), 229, 237–42; and see also Fridman, G. H. L., 'Malice in the Law of Torts', *Modern Law Review*, 21 (1958), 484; Heydon, J. D., *Economic Torts*, 2nd edn. (London: Sweet & Maxwell, 1978), 128 ff.; Markesinis and Deakin, *Tort Law*, 466–70.

[84] Weir, T., *Economic Torts* (Oxford: Clarendon Press, 1997); Carty, H., 'Intentional Violation of Economic Interests: The Limits of Common Law Liability', *Law Quarterly Review*, 104 (1988), 250; for another view, Howarth, D., 'Is There a Future For the Intentional Torts?', in Birks (ed.), *Classification of Obligations*, 233.

ing speech by Lord Herschell, who stated:

I can imagine no greater danger to the community than that a jury should be at liberty to impose the penalty of paying damages for acts which are otherwise lawful, because they choose, without any legal definition of the term, to say that they are malicious. No one would know what his rights were. The result would be to put all our actions at the mercy of a particular tribunal whose view of their propriety might differ from our own. However malice may be defined, if motive be an ingredient of it, my sense of the danger would not be diminished.[85]

In other words, it was a desire to restrain the class power of the jury as much as a belief in the amorality of positive legal rights that led to the rejection of the abuse of rights doctrine in England.[86] But much extant common law—such as malicious prosecution itself could not easily be fitted into this newly-stated positivist doctrine, as Holmes himself conceded.[87]

It was a bothersome contradiction to hold that in some areas of life persons were free to abuse their substantive rights and maliciously or intentionally do down their fellows; yet in other cases to enjoin persons from abusing their adjectival right and mulct them for unsuccessfully invoking the courts to vindicate their interests.

The pain of this contradiction was lessened by pushing the test of malicious prosecution and abuse of interests away from the judges and into the sphere of jury discretion.

We can see now why English judges, forced to balance between the right to prosecute and the right not to be legally harassed, might tend to favour an enlarged jury sphere to try malicious prosecution. Let the jury decide and give no reasons; no light is shed and the contradiction is dimmed.

There were other areas of sharply contentious public policy where judges might seek to evade clear decisional power, either by the technique of enhancing the jurisdiction of the jury, or by constituting the judges themselves as triers of fact, sheltering behind rationally empty tests of reasonableness and interest-balancing. The modern theory (or circular nontheory) of negligence is a prime example.[88] It was rare for explicit tests of social utility to be invented as the Americans did; realism did not suit the English legal mind with its devotion to the sharp separation of law and politics.

For these good legal and political reasons, the Victorian judges were not always hostile to civil jury power; indeed, to avoid spelling out the political implications of their work they were often happy to become civil juries themselves.

---

[85] [1898] A. C. 1, 118.
[86] See further Hoffmann, L. H., '*Rookes v. Barnard*', *Law Quarterly Review*, 81 (1965), 116.
[87] Holmes, *The Common Law*, 112–13; Vandevelde, 'A History of Prima Facie Tort', 457–62.
[88] Cf. Weiner, 'The Civil Jury Trial and the Law-Fact Distinction', 1876–94.

9

The Seventh Amendment Right to Jury Trial: Late-Eighteenth-Century Practice Reconsidered

James Oldham

In the United States trial by jury, however controversial in application, remains a treasured part of most citizens' concept of liberty. Everyone is familiar with the safeguards that trial by jury supplies to criminal defendants. Nearly everyone knows that the right to a jury trial also applies to civil cases, although it can be waived. The source of the right in civil cases in federal courts is the Seventh Amendment, and in state courts the right is preserved by comparable provisions of state constitutions.

The Seventh Amendment provides that in suits at common law involving more than twenty dollars, the right to jury trial shall be preserved. This seems simple and straightforward, but what does it mean? What right to jury trial? What did the framers have in mind by their simple formulation? One possibility is that they intended to preserve the jury trial practices that existed in suits at common law in the United States when the Seventh Amendment was adopted. But as Edith Henderson observed in her study of the background of the Seventh Amendment, there were enormous and unsystematic variations among the original thirteen states, and although 'a general guarantee of the civil jury as an institution was widely desired ... there was no consensus on the precise extent of its power'.[1] Indeed, the Seventh Amendment can be viewed as a formulation that was deliberately imprecise in order to cover divergent practices.

Unavoidably, it fell to the Supreme Court to fashion a test that could be used to measure the scope of the protection embodied in the Seventh Amendment, or in state imitations. The Court did so in 1812 in an Opinion by Justice Story, who wrote, 'Beyond all question, the common law here alluded to [in the Seventh Amendment] is not the common law of any individual state, (for it probably differs in all), but it is the common law of England, the grand reservoir of all our jurisprudence.'[2] Story added that his proposition must be so obvious, 'to every person acquainted with the history of the law' that it needed no explanation.[3] He did not peg the test

---

[1] Edith Henderson, 'The Background of the Seventh Amendment', 80 *Harv L Rev* 289, at 299 (1966).
[2] *US v. Wonson*, 28 F Cas 745, at 750 (CCD Mass. 1812).   [3] *ibid.*

to 1791, the year when the Seventh Amendment was adopted (later clarified in an Opinion of the Court).[4]

The rule thus fashioned by the Supreme Court has come to be called, 'the historical test'. A commonly-quoted, succinct version of the test is the following 1935 formulation, 'In order to ascertain the scope and meaning of the Seventh Amendment, resort must be had to the appropriate rules of the common law established at the time of the adoption of that constitutional provision in 1791.'[5]

This test survives to the present day, despite unrelenting criticism. Illustrative of the views of the critics is the following summary by Martin Redish, '[B]lind adherence to history would seem to place modern judicial administration in an historical straight jacket, controlled by the policies of a society of 200 years ago. Traditional constitutional analysis has never been so limited. Ever since Chief Justice Marshall admonished that it "is a constitution we are expounding", courts generally have been willing to read the broad language of the Constitution to account for changing social conditions.'[6]

In three recent cases, the Supreme Court had the opportunity to revisit the historical test for the scope of the Seventh Amendment right to jury trial.[7] In the first of these—*Markman v. Westview Instruments, Inc.*—the Court emphatically declined the opportunity, unanimously re-affirming the historical test but finding no jury trial necessity on applying the test to the facts of the case. Based on my understanding of English trial practice in the late eighteenth century, the Court's application of the historical test to the facts of *Markman* seems to me to be wrong. I rely predominantly on two manuscript sources—the trial notes of Lord Mansfield, Chief Justice of the Court of King's Bench from 1756 to 1788, and a sampling of Plea Rolls from the Court of Common Pleas from the 1770s and 1780s.[8]

The discussion to follow is in four parts. The first summarizes the Court's application of the historical test in *Markman v. Westview*

---

[4] *Thompson v. Utah*, 170 US 343 (1898).   [5] *Dimick v. Schiedt*, 293 US 654, at 657 (1935).

[6] Martin H. Redish, ' Seventh Amendment Right to Jury Trial: A Study in the Irrationality of Rational Decision Making', 70 Northwestern L Rev 486, at 487 (1975), citing *McCulloch v. Maryland*, 17 US (4 Wheat) 316, at 407 (1819). See also Kenneth S. Klein, 'The Myth of How to Interpret the Seventh Amendment Right to a Civil Jury Trial', 53 Ohio State LJ 1005 (1992); Fleming James, Jr, 'Right to a Jury Trial in Civil Actions,' 72 Yale L J 655 (1963). For a thorough, oft-cited study of the attitudes and circumstances surrounding the adoption of the Seventh Amendment (a study ultimately arguing for a 'dynamic' rather than 'static' reading) see Charles W. Wolfram, 'The Constitutional History of the Seventh Amendment,' 57 Minn L Rev 639 (1973).

[7] See *Markman v. Westview Instruments, Inc.*, 517 US 370 (1996); *Feltner v. Columbia Pictures Television, Inc.*, 118 S. Ct. 1279 (1998); *City of Monterey v. Del Monte Dunes at Monterey, Ltd.*, 1999 WL 320798.

[8] I have transcribed and published Lord Mansfield's trial notes, and I will use that published source. See J. Oldham, *The Mansfield Manuscripts and the Growth of English Law in the Eighteenth Century*, 2 vols, Chapel Hill and London, 1992. The sampling of Common Pleas Plea Rolls was done in 1996 and 1997 at the Public Record Office in London.

Instruments, Inc. The second invokes the eighteenth-century English man-uscript sources to assess whether the historical test was soundly applied in Justice Souter's unanimous Opinion for the Court in *Markman*. The third re-opens a question addressed in legal scholarship in the 1980s and in some decisions by lower federal courts—whether it is constitutional to permit a 'complexity exception' to the Seventh Amendment jury trial guarantee. Fourth, the two recent, post-*Markman* Seventh Amendment cases by the Supreme Court are taken up.

THE *MARKMAN* DECISION

In *Markman*, the plaintiff owned a patent on a method for tracking inven-tories in dry-cleaning establishments. He sued Westview Instruments for patent infringement and won a jury verdict. Central to the dispute was the meaning of the term 'inventory' in the patent claim, as to which the plain-tiff presented his own testimony and that of an independent expert wit-ness. The trial judge, however, granted a deferred motion for judgment on a matter of law, concluding that the term 'inventory' could not support the meaning contended for by the plaintiff. Markman appealed, claiming that the trial judge had improperly supplanted the jury. The US Court of Appeals for the Federal Circuit affirmed the trial judge, as did the US Supreme Court after a grant of *certiorari*. Among the issues before the Supreme Court was the application of the historical test for Seventh Amendment rights to the specific facts.

While the Supreme Court's *Markman* decision was pending, Court-watchers commented on the case. One writer expressed hope that the jus-tices would reach beyond narrow patent law 'and make some major corrections', specifically, 'the Supreme Court should reject the 1812 hold-ing in *Wonson* requiring federal courts to look to 18th century English law as a constitutional touchstone'.[9] The Court, however, did not take that path. After quoting the text of the Seventh Amendment, Justice Souter began his constitutional analysis with the following:

Since Justice Story's day, [and] *United States v. Wonson* . . . we have understood that '[t]he right of trial by jury thus preserved is the right which existed under the English common law when the Amendment was adopted' . . . In keeping with our long-standing adherence to this 'historical test' . . . we ask first, whether we are dealing with a cause of action that either was tried at law at the time of the Founding or is at least analogous to one that was . . . If the action in question belongs in the law category, we then ask whether the particular trial decision must fall to the jury in order to preserve the substance of the common-law right as it existed in 1791.[10]

---

[9] Jerome L. Wilson, 'Dusting Off the Right to Trial by Jury', *Legal Times*, 1 Apr 1996, 24–5.
[10] *Markman v. Westview Instruments, Inc.*, see n. 7 above; citations omitted.

Justice Souter had no trouble with the first part—patent infringement actions were brought at common law in the late eighteenth century. He next posed the second question in a way that foretold the outcome, '[W]hether a particular issue occurring within a jury trial (here the construction of a patent claim) is itself necessarily a jury issue, the guarantee being essential to preserve the right to a jury's resolution of the ultimate dispute.'[11] He concluded that the answer to the second question was 'no', largely for the following reasons: (1) late-eighteenth century English patent law was primitive and did not include the requirement that there be a stated patent 'claim'; (2) even accepting the point that the patent specification in late-eighteenth century England could be viewed as closely analogous to the claim in twentieth century American patent law, there is not much to go on, since the specification itself was relatively new, and 'the mere smattering of patent cases that we have from this period shows no established jury practice sufficient to support an argument by analogy that today's construction of a claim should be a guaranteed jury issue';[12] (3) no demonstration was offered the Court that the role of juries in interpreting patents was different from their role with regard to other written instruments, 'and we do know that in other kinds of cases during this period judges, not juries, ordinarily construed written documents'.[13]

According to eighteenth-century English trial practice, Justice Souter's second reason is incorrect, and, on the facts of *Markman*, the third reason is unpersuasive. As to reason two, there were many more patent cases in England in the second half of the eighteenth century than a 'smattering'; indeed, Justice Buller of the Court of King's Bench remarked in *Turner v. Winter* in 1787 that '[m]any patent cases have arisen within our memory',[14] and Chief Justice Eyre of the Court of Common Pleas observed in 1795 that 'we have had many cases upon patents'.[15] It is true that there was not an abundance of *reported* patent cases from the late-eighteenth century at the 'appellate' level, but this was in no way indicative of the depth of experience at the trial level.[16]

---

[11] *Markman v. Westview Instruments, Inc.*, at 377.   [12] *ibid.*, at 379–80, n. omitted.

[13] *ibid.*, citing Devlin, 'Jury Trial of Complex Cases: English Practice at the Time of the Seventh Amendment', 80 Colum L Rev 43, 75 (1980). On the complex case question, and Lord Devlin's point of view, see below, text accompanying nn. 84–134.

[14] 1 T.R. 602, at 606.

[15] *Boulton v. Bull*, Davies Pat Cas 162, at 204 (1795).

[16] Souter J. referred to a total of 22 (reported) cases, relying on H. Dutton, *The Patent System and Inventive Activity During the Industrial Revolution, 1750–1852* (1984), 71. Dutton was counting printed reports, all or almost all of which would have described arguments on motions or on questions of law before the full Bench of the relevant common-law court, and the judges' decisions. But only a fraction of the cases at the trial level went forward to full court proceedings on motions or on reserved questions of law. There were clearly many dozens of patent trials in the English common law courts during the second half of the 18th century. In Lord Mansfield's surviving trial notes (only about half of the notes that he kept survive), e.g., there are 9 unreported patent trials, and this was in only one of the three common-law courts, albeit the busiest. Unfortunately, the Supreme Court's understatement of the true volume of

In addition to citing Lord Devlin as authority for the third reason,[17] Justice Souter referred to the 1786 decision in King's Bench in *Macbeath v. Haldimand*[18] because there, the construction of written documents and letters was said by Justices Mansfield and Buller to be for the court, not for the jury. Nevertheless, on close inspection, Justice Souter's reliance on *Macbeath* seems misplaced. What was at issue was the legal import of the letters and documents on an agency question—letters and documents about which there was no factual disagreement. Even so, there was something of a difference of views among the judges. Justice Willes said that since the case came forward after a verdict (instead of after a non-suit), and since the letters had been before the jury, construction of them was 'proper for the consideration of the jury', though he agreed that 'construction of deeds is a matter of law'.' Buller then stated, 'I do not agree with my brother Willes as to the construction of letters. If they be written in so dubious a manner, as to be capable of different constructions, and can be explained by other transactions, the whole evidence must be left to the jury to decide upon; for they are to judge of the truth or falsehood of such collateral facts which may vary the sense of the letters themselves: but if they be not explained by any other circumstances, then, like deeds or other written agreements, the construction of them is a mere matter of law.'[19] And in *Markman*, the plaintiff argued that the term 'inventory' was capable of different constructions, so that the whole evidence should have been left to the jury to decide, as was done by the trial judge.

After disposing of the constitutional issue in *Markman*, Justice Souter moved on to other arguments in the case, pointing out that complicated patent issues can be handled better by judges than by lay juries.[20] This 'functional' consideration is taken up below,[21] but first, in order to understand more fully the historical test, let us consider eighteenthth-century English trial practice in order to learn what cases customarily went to juries.

EIGHTEENTH-CENTURY ENGLISH TRIAL PRACTICE

The first and most important point is that the parties, through their counsel, had a great deal of control in shaping the course their dispute would take within the courts, and the overwhelming majority sought damages in jury trials. The forms of action were varied. Although actions were still

patent litigation in 18th-century England may be hard to set right, as is shown in commentary on the case. See G. J. Michelson, 'Did the *Markman* Court Ignore Fact, Substance, and the Spirit of the Constitution in its Rush Toward Uniformity?', Loyola of Los Angeles L Rev 30: 1749, 1765 (1997), where the author states, citing Dutton incorrectly, that, 'patent law in England at that time [the end of the eighteenth century] was scarcely describable; from 1750–99 there were only eighteen patent decisions in England', citing Dutton.

[17] See n. 13, above.   [18] 1 TR 173 (1786).   [19] 1 TR at 180–2.
[20] 517 US, at 388.   [21] See text at nn. 84–134.

brought on ancient writs such as Debt, Assault and False Imprisonment, or Trespass *vi et armis*, the most popular form of action by the 1770s was Trespass on the Case. This catch-all category encompassed all contract and quasi-contract actions, ordinarily actions in assumpsit (see ch. 11) or on the 'common counts'—goods sold and delivered, work and labour performed, money had and received, etc.—as well as a host of other private civil actions. This can readily be seen in Lord Mansfield's trial notes.[22] Also, the Common Pleas Plea Rolls for the 1770s show the use of Trespass on the Case for suits on written obligations (bills of exchange, promissory notes),[23] for defamation,[24] for enticing away one's servants,[25] for recovering a bankrupt's goods,[26] to resolve water rights disputes,[27] and for other actions.

The Common Pleas Plea Rolls contain three main types of entries: (1) fictitious actions entered on the court records as default judgments;[28] (2) default judgments with unascertained damages to be determined by a writ of enquiry;[29] and (3) actions in which the defendant 'puts himself upon the country', that is, denies the plaintiff's claim and requests a jury trial. Other entries appear, though much less frequently, for executions of previously-entered judgments. There are examples of pleadings that show a demurrer and joinder, where there would be no jury trial, but these are

[22] See The Mansfield MSS, above n. 8. Most of the cases presented in the chapters on commerce and contract (ch. 5, contract and quasi-contract; ch. 6, insurance; ch. 7, negotiable instruments; ch. 8, usury; ch. 9, prize; ch. 10, trade; and ch. 11, intellectual property) were filed in Trespass on the Case. This was the form of action for all civil cases of defamation and libel. Other examples in Lord Mansfield's trial notes include: actions for private nuisance (ch. 15); for damage caused during public riots (e.g., *Patrick v. Kennett* and *Peachey v. Kennett*, pp. 1028–9); damage caused by a sheriff by letting a prisoner escape from arrest (*Medlycott v. Elton*, 1044); negligence (ch. 18); breach of promise of marriage (ch. 22); threatening a worker boycott (*Leake v. Smith*, 1345); malicious prosecution (*Farmer v. Darling*, 1403, at 1404); and for false arrest (*De Hahn v. Slater*, 1413).

[23] See, e.g., *Robert Withey v. John Browne*, Middlesex, Trinity 1770, (PRO) CP 40/3693, fo. 34 (promissory note); *John Bushby v. John Carruthers*, Cumberland, Trinity 1770, (PRO) CP 40/3694, fo. 835 (bill of exchange).

[24] See, e.g., *William Baseley v. John Banner*, Warwickshire, Trinity 1770, (PRO) CP 40/3693, fo. 322.

[25] See *George Whiffin v. Michael Foster*, Surrey, Trinity 1770, (PRO) CP 40/ 3693, fo. 508. A like action between Whiffin and Foster was tried in the Court of King's Bench on 31 July 1770. See The Mansfield MSS at 1336.

[26] *Mathew Buscall and John Rose, assignees of the estate of Joseph Thickpenny, Bankrupt v. George Hogg*, Trinity 1770, (PRO) CP 40 3693, fo. 366.

[27] *Hugh Meares v. George Ansell*, Surrey, Trinity 1770, (PRO) CP 40/ 3693, fo. 1121. The water rights dispute between Meares and Ansell also produced two trials in the Court of King's Bench. See The Mansfield MSS at 182–3, 1161–6.

[28] Ordinarily these were either executory debts or agreements about the right to possess real property. The fictitious judgments could then be executed in case of non-performance by the defendants.

[29] The Writ of Enquiry was directed to the sheriffs of the county where the suit was brought instructing the sheriffs to call a jury to determine what the damages would be. These juries were sometimes convened at public buildings such as Guildhall, but as often they met at taverns or other informal venues. See generally n.152, below.

quite rare. For example, in the Plea Rolls for Trinity Term 1770, there is only one case on demurrer, compared with 181 cases sent to jury trial.[30] Yet in the late eighteenth century, the demurrer was virtually the only pre-trial method in the common law courts to take a case forward for decision without calling a jury.[31]

In other words, almost all cases in the common law courts were tried before juries. There was no pre-trial discovery,[32] nor was there any pre-trial conference or other occasion or procedure (other than the demurrer) that would allow a judge to determine before trial that a case presented no issue to be decided by a jury, or that an issue in a case should be withheld from the jury.

Once the jury was convened and the trial began, however, the picture changed. It was open to the judge to enter a non-suit against the plaintiff. The jury could be requested to give a special verdict.[33] Also, it was common to allow the jury to give a verdict for the plaintiff that would be subject to a 'case stated', that is, the verdict would stand or fall according to the judgment given by the full court on a reserved question of law after argument the following term. And after the trial concluded, motions for new trials could be argued, as could motions in arrest of judgment.

There is no need to go through these devices in detail.[34] I will, however, give some examples from Lord Mansfield's trial notes, which can then be used in considering the Seventh Amendment's 'historical test'. Three aspects of Lord Mansfield's trial notes are of interest—the frequent entry of a non-suit, the jury verdicts subject to a 'case stated', and what happens in the cases where Mansfield indicates that he was dissatisfied with the verdict.

In legal literature, the eighteenth-century non-suit is described as a technical procedure requiring that the plaintiff's name be called at the end of his evidence when that evidence seemed inadequate, and a non-suit would be entered only if he failed to answer.[35] The plaintiff could decide

---

[30] These figures were obtained by an inspection of the Plea Rolls and a tabulation of the entries. The comparable figures for Trinity Term 1774 are 4 cases on demurrer, compared with 197 cases sent 'to the country'.

[31] See n. 117, below, for one special pleading alternative for trying title in a trespass case.

[32] This was sometimes arranged by consent. See, e.g., *Martin v. Pewtress*, The Mansfield MSS at 1199, 1200 n. 2 (discovery arrangements described, as entered in the King's Bench Rule Book for the plea side).

[33] Even if requested by the judge, the jury could insist on returning a general verdict. See G. Duncombe, *Trials per Pais*, 5th ed, London 1718, at 233.

[34] Others have done so. See E. Henderson, 'The Background of the Seventh Amendment',above n. 1, at 300–17; Austin W. Scott, 'Trial by Jury and the Reform of Civil Procedure', 31 Harv L Rev 669, at 678–90 (1918). See also The Mansfield MSS at 150–1, 156–60.

[35] See Henderson, 'The Background of the Seventh Amendment', above n. 1, at 300; Scott, 'The Reform of Civil Procedure', above n. 34, at 687. The judgment in a 'compulsory nonsuit' would be, 'That the plaintiff has not prosecuted his suit . . . let the defendant depart without delay.' Henderson, above n. 1, at 300. Examples of such entries, or close cousins, can be seen in the Common Pleas Plea Rolls, but they are extremely rare. See, e.g., (PRO) CP 40/3714, Trinity 1774, fo. 956.

whether to be present or not, and this fact led Austin Scott to state that '[a]t common law nonsuits were wholly voluntary'.[36] Edith Henderson, however, wrote that '[i]f the plaintiff should somehow obtain a verdict in a case proper for nonsuit, defendant could move, before the judges *en banc*, to have the verdict set aside and judgment of nonsuit entered'.[37] One of Henderson's authorities is a Mansfield case, and it demonstrates the technique. In *Abbot v. Plumbe*,[38] the plaintiff obtained a verdict, and Mansfield 'saved the question of the sufficiency of the evidence'.[39] The following term, counsel for defendant obtained a rule (that is, an order) for the plaintiff to show cause why a non-suit should not be granted. On argument, the plaintiff's evidence proved insufficient, and the rule was made absolute (that is, the non-suit was granted). The insufficiency in the plaintiff's evidence was the absence of the subscribing witness on the bond that was the source of the plaintiff's claim, or of proof that the witness was unobtainable. The court held that the 'technical rule' that the subscribing witness be produced could not be dispensed with. In practical effect, this case works out to be identical to the 'case stated', in which a verdict for the plaintiff is made subject to argument and decision on a reserved question of law.

Lord Mansfield's trial notes show a much less technical, much more free-floating use of the non-suit than the procedure described by Henderson and illustrated by *Abbot v. Plumbe*.[40] In many cases, it became clear as the plaintiff's evidence unfolded that he had no case, and the non-suit was entered with the plaintiff's consent. For example in *Sharpe v. Maidman*,[41] Mansfield wrote at the end, 'They could not prove delivery. Plaintiff non-suited, of themselves. I said nothing.' And in *Trinder v. Smith*,[42] the *London Chronicle* reported that 'the action was based on the supposition that the defendant was liable to pay the tradesmen for the costs of the expenditures for the voyages because the defendant had insured his money lent on the mortgage', but after Mansfield observed 'that there was not the least pretence for such action, Mr Trinder very genteelly gave it up'.[43]

In other actions, Lord Mansfield perceived that as a matter of law, the plaintiff had no case, and he declared a non-suit. Probably this was done

---

[36] Scott, above n. 34, at 687.   [37] Henderson, above n. 1, at 300–1.
[38] 1 Doug 216 (1779).   [39] *ibid.*
[40] This is true as well of other procedures. One case, e.g., shows the introduction of a demurrer after the plaintiff's testimony was presented. *Cocksedge v. Fanshaw*, 11 Dec 1777, The Mansfield MSS, at 705.
[41] 5 July 1759, The Mansfield MSS, at 256.   [42] 23 Feb 1763, *ibid.*, at 268.
[43] *ibid.*, n. 1. We must remember, of course, that there was very little pre-trial preparation in these cases, and that the barristers and parties were often uncertain about what directions the evidence would take. Other examples of non-suits with the plaintiff's consent are: *Leake v. Howard*, 23 Feb 1757, *ibid.*, at 419 (Mansfield's note: 'Non-suit on the evidence [of] Calvert by their own consent'); *Green v. Rucker*, 8 Dec 1759 ('Plaintiff satisfied to be nonsuited'). In one case, it came out that the plaintiff had sued the wrong person. *Christie v. Baker*, 6 Dec 1782, *ibid.*, at 1310.

with the plaintiff's consent. Whether or not consent was always 'genteel',it is hard to imagine in Mansfield's courtroom that a refusal to consent would be voiced. Thus, in a suit by a creditor for payment for necessaries supplied to defendant's wife, the plaintiff was non-suited because, according to the *London Chronicle*, it appeared to the court that defendant and his wife 'had been many years separated, and that separation notoriously known'.[44] In another action by the payee against the acceptor of a bill of exchange, Mansfield, according to his own notes, 'nonsuited the Plaintiff by reason of the indorsement on the back, which I thought discharged the Acceptor'.[45] Later, on a motion for new trial, the judges determined that 'instead of a nonsuit, the question should have been left to the jury, it being a question of intention arising out of the circumstances', but as two of the three judges hearing the motion thought the jury should have received strong directions to find for the defendant, and in view of the small amount involved, a new trial was denied.[46]

As may have been true in the previous case, Mansfield occasionally noted that, in declaring a non-suit, he also invited the plaintiff to move for a new trial in order to argue his case before the full Court of King's Bench. Thus in *Luke v. Edwards*,[47] the plaintiff, an overseer of the poor, sued for false imprisonment, and Mansfield wrote, 'Plaintiff [was] nonsuited, because I thought the evidence proved a legal imprisonment. Liberty to move for a new trial without costs.'[48] Furthermore, although the non-suit was usually declared at the close of the plaintiff's evidence, there are examples of non-suits after both parties presented testimony, or even after argument (at trial) on a point of law.[49]

The two other features of Lord Mansfield's trial notes of relevance are the directed verdict and the 'case stated'. Henderson reached conclusions about English trial practice by researching printed sources, and while much of her description is correct, the trial notes suggest some differences. For example, I question her assertion that the English cases 'do not sustain' the view that the directed verdict as practised in the late eighteenth century was not binding on the jury.[50] The only authority she gives for her

---

[44] *Williams v. Dyer*, 15 Feb. 1766, *ibid.* at 282. A similar case was *Norton v. Compton*, 19 Feb 1773, *ibid.* at 308, where the plaintiff was non-suited in an action to recover for the sale of goods to defendant's wife, but 'the evidence showed that the wife had eloped from the defendant before contracting the debt'.

[45] *Ellis v. Galindo*, 23 July 1783, *ibid.* at 629.   [46] *ibid.*, at 630, n. 2.

[47] 14 Aug 1764, *ibid.*, at 963.

[48] *ibid.* For another such case, see *Melchart v. Halsey*, 14 June 1770, *ibid.* at 297.

[49] See *Norton v. Williams*, 15 July 1783, *ibid.* at 444; *Taylor v. Woodmass*, 23 Feb 1764, *ibid.* at 503 (Mansfield note: 'scandalous on the part of Plaintiff'); *Farquaharson v. Hunter*, 5 Mar 1785, *ibid.* at 591 (Mansfield comment: 'Defendant produced the bills of sale in which there is no contract to indemnify, & put it upon the Plaintiff to prove the promise, & entered into a full argument whether this promise could be considered as an insurable interest in Plaintiff. I thought it could not. So Plaintiff was nonsuited').

[50] 80 Harv L Rev, at 302.

claim is the *Macbeath* case, discussed above.[51] But in that case, the motion for new trial failed because a majority of the judges thought, as was noted earlier, that the construction of the uncontested written documents in the case was for the court, not the jury. I do not see how the case stands for the proposition that the trial judge's directed verdict was binding. That this was not the case is clearly demonstrated in Lord Mansfield's trial notes. For example, in *Brammall v. Jones*,[52] the plaintiff recovered a verdict of over £337 for his claim to part of the proceeds from the condemnation of a ship, and Mansfield wrote at the end of his notes, 'Verdict against my direction, but as Defendant had a bond [of] indemnity I doubt whether it should be set aside.' Mansfield's comment, of course, implies that he had the power to set aside the verdict, but this would have been done by the full court on a motion for new trial.[53] This is what happened in *Shirley v. Wilkinson*.[54] This was an action to collect on an insurance policy, and at the first trial, Mansfield noted, 'I thought the suppression of what the Captain wrote in his letter of the 20th of July material and that the policy was void, but the Jury, nine of whom I know, found otherwise.' Despite Mansfield's view of the case, the jury verdict awarded the plaintiff substantial damages at the second trial as well as at the first.

In some cases, Mansfield noted his dissatisfaction with the verdict, but apparently let it stand without any invitation to move for a new trial. Thus in *Olney v. Allen*,[55] a suit for payment for taking care of defendant's cattle, Mansfield noted, 'Damages contrary to my directions', adding that 'I looked at Plaintiff's books, though I made no mention of it', and then Mansfield explained why he thought the verdict wrong. Yet the verdict stood. So did the verdict in *Harris v. Worsley*,[56] a medical malpractice action, where, after recording a verdict for the plaintiff for two guineas, Mansfield wrote, 'To the astonishment of every body. [It was] clear Defendant had treated her right upon a suspicion of a fracture & Plaintiff had not suffered.'

In several cases, Mansfield not only declared the verdict wrong, but expressly ruled out a new trial. This could be because there had already been one or two new trials,[57] but not always. Thus in *Walnutt v. Pomfret*,[58] the plaintiff won a verdict of £111 in an action for wages due to his wife, and Mansfield wrote, 'I directed the Jury from the injustice of the demand

---

[51] Text at nn. 18–19.   [52] 23 May 1782, The Mansfield MSS, at 368.

[53] Thus in *Rigard v. Wright*, 25 July 1763, *ibid.* at 264, Mansfield wrote, 'I am much dissatisfied with the verdict & I certified.' By this he meant that he certified the case as proper for a motion for new trial. See also the cases discussed *ibid.* at 89–90.

[54] The first trial was 24 July 1781, *ibid.* at 563; the second, 20 Dec 1781, *ibid.* at 569.

[55] 4 Aug 1783, *ibid.*, at 354.   [56] 26 July 1773, *ibid.* at 1239.

[57] e.g., after the third trial of *Bruckshaw v. Hopkins*, 13 June 1776, *ibid.* at 994, Mansfield wrote: 'A wrong verdict, but [it] should not be set aside.'

[58] 3 Dec 1776, *ibid.* at 316.

upon the state of it to find against Plaintiff, but they found for the wages & then named the sum. There can be no new trial.'

I question another of Henderson's claims—that the 'case stated' device, '[u]sed only when there was no substantial factual controversy ... reduced the jury's role to a formality', so that 'the jury scarcely participated at all'.[59] This is not even remotely what is shown in Lord Mansfield's trial notes, and Mansfield was a great believer in the 'case stated'.[60] There are dozens of examples of the procedure in the trial notes. In them, the testimony is as full and the role of the jury is as substantial as in other cases. The verdicts are as realistic an assessment of the plaintiff's damages as they ever are. Well-known illustrative cases in the trial notes include *Luke v. Lyde*[61] and *Moses v. Macferlan*.[62] In almost all cases the verdict for the plaintiff is quantified and entered, subject to the case stated; only in one instance did Mansfield note, 'The verdict [is] to be entered according to the Opinion of the court.'[63]

Variations on the 'case stated' procedure appear in the trial notes. The counterpart when the verdict was for defendant was to argue the question of law on a motion for new trial. Thus in *Evans v. Saunders*,[64] a tenant was sued for, among other things, taking away fixtures, and after the verdict for defendants, Mansfield wrote, 'I was of opinion [that] the tenant might [take] away the frame [and] plate glass of the hothouse. I told Mr Howarth [plaintiff's counsel] if he found reason, he might move the court [for a new trial], instead of a case.' And finally, in *Ross v. Johnson*,[65] Mansfield expressed his disapproval of the use of a non-suit by consent to accomplish a case stated—as reported by Burrow,[66] Mansfield 'declared his disapprobation of non-suits, founded upon objections which had no relation to the merits of a cause'.

With these trial practices in mind, let us now return to the 'historical test' of the Seventh Amendment and to Mr Justice Souter in the *Markman* case. Recall that Justice Souter put his second question as whether a specific issue can be removed from the jury when the basic structure of the jury trial remains in place. How would this have worked had *Markman* come before Mansfield in the Court of King's Bench in, say, 1785?[67]

In *Markman*, the trial judge granted a motion for judgment as a matter of law, but only after a jury verdict for the plaintiff had been given. *Markman*

---

[59] 80 Harv L Rev, at 305–6.

[60] On Mansfield's use of the 'case stated', see The Mansfield MSS at 101, n. 179. In *Vallejo v. Wheeler*, 1 Cowp. 143, 153 (1774), Lord Mansfield observed that, 'it is not easy to collect with certainty from a general verdict, or from notes taken at Nisi Prius, what was the true ground of decision', so that in the case before him, 'as in all doubtful cases' he, 'wished a case to be made for the Opinion of the Court'.

[61] 10 Aug 1759, The Mansfield MSS, at 251.   [62] 11 Feb 1760, *ibid*. at 258.

[63] *Barzillai v. Lewis*, 5 Mar 1782, *ibid*. at 576.   [64] 10 July 1781, *ibid*. at 1171.

[65] 16 Dec 1771, *ibid*. at 1201.   [66] 5 Burr, at 2857.

[67] Mansfield ceased being active on the Bench in 1786, although he did not resign until 1788. He died in 1793.

was thus comparable in form to some of the non-suits ordered by Lord Mansfield, described above. As I have stated, however, I believe the motion in *Markman* was improperly granted by the trial judge, since there was conflicting testimony about the meaning of the term 'inventory,' and in late-eithteenth-century England, this conflict would certainly have been sent to the jury for resolution. It might have been sent with strong instructions, but, except for one theoretical possibility (discussed below), it would have been sent.[68] It was customary to send 'the whole matter' to the jury. And if the jury disregarded the trial judge's directions, a new trial might be granted, but as we have seen, not necessarily.

On the specific question in *Markman*, I have no doubt that the issue of the patent claim construction would have gone to the jury. As has been noted, the issue was not like that in *Macbeath* where there were uncontested written documents in evidence that had to be construed. The issue was much closer to that in an influential late-eithteenth-centurycentury patent infringement action tried before Lord Mansfield in 1778, *Liardet v. Johnson*.[69] In *Liardet*, the plaintiff had patented a method of making stucco, and defendant claimed that he was not guilty of infringement since the patent specification did not properly describe how to make the stucco. Mr Justice Buller's notes of the case (when it came on for argument on motion for new trial) survive at Lincoln's Inn, and Buller noted that Lord Mansfield 'left to the jury . . . all objections made to exactness, certainty and propriety of the Specification, & whether any workman could make it by [the Specification]'.[70]

The *Liardet* case was relied on by Markman in argument to the Supreme Court, but Mr Justice Souter was not persuaded. He concluded that *Liardet* 'does not show that juries construed disputed terms in a patent', and that '[f]rom its ambiguous references' (i.e. the quote above from Buller's notes) 'we cannot infer the existence of an established practice . . .'.[71]

The one theory that might lead to a different conclusion about the issue in *Markman* is the possibility that the evidence on what is ostensibly a fact question (the meaning of 'inventory') was so clear that, in the opinion of the judges, reasonable minds could not differ on the question, so that the question thereby became one of law rather than fact. This notion is familiar to the modern lawyer. It was also recognized in eighteenth-century

---

[68] Even in *Ellis v. Galindo*, above n. 45, Lord Mansfield acknowledged that he should not have kept from the jury (by a non-suit) a dispute about a bill of exchange (a subject within Mansfield's special expertise as a founder of commercial law), since the legal effect of the indorsement by the payee on the acceptor might possibly depend on the intent of the parties under all the circumstances

[69] 21 Feb 1778, The Mansfield MSS at 749. See generally J. Adams and G. Averley, 'The Patent Specification: The Role of *Liardet v. Johnson*', *Journal of Legal History*, 7 (1986): 156.

[70] *ibid.*, at 756. The argument was held on 8 May 1778, the day after Buller took his seat as a judge on King's Bench.

[71] *Markman*, see n. 7 above, at 380, n. 5.

England, but only rarely, and controversially. Lord Mansfield generally avoided the issue by leaving things to his juries, while at the same time giving strong instructions to the juries to come out the way he thought the verdicts should go. In one series of cases, however, Lord Mansfield could not avoid the law–fact question. The cases dealt with the question of what was a 'reasonable' time in commercial cases for merchants holding nego- tiable paper to take certain actions. As an example, using modern termi- nology, how long could a holder of a cheque reasonably wait before depositing the cheque in his bank? This issue arose in the eighteenth cen- tury because all banks operated then as partnerships, and their businesses frequently failed. When a bank failed, disputes arose over whether mer- chants holding cheques that had not yet been deposited in the bank and cleared had any claim against the bank. This depended on whether the time during which the merchant held the cheques was reasonable or not. Did the merchant have to get to the bank for a deposit on the same day he received the cheques? Could he wait until the next day? Longer?

It should be obvious that whether the reasonableness of time is a ques- tion of fact or law is not easy to answer. In the cases that came before the Court of King's Bench in the 1780s, as I stated in *The Mansfield Manuscripts*, 'different special juries in each case stubbornly rejected the weight of the evidence on what was a reasonable time after receipt for merchants to deliver drafts to their banks for payment'.[72] The first case was tried twice, and after the first trial in the second case, *Appleton v. Sweetapple*,[73] Mansfield stated, 'It is a Question of law and fact proper for the determi- nation of the jury.'[74] Eventually, in the case of *Tindal v. Brown*,[75] Mansfield was brought around sufficiently to declare that, although the question of reasonableness may depend on facts such as the distance the parties live from each other, 'wherever a rule can be laid down with respect to this rea- sonableness, that should be decided by the court, and adhered to by every- one for the sake of certainty'.[76] Mr Justice Buller in his Opinion in *Tindal* had no doubt—he said that the series of cases reflected 'great discredit on the courts' and did 'infinite mischief in the mercantile world' and could 'only be remedied by . . .considering the reasonableness of time as a ques- tion of law and not of fact'.[77]

In an article published in the *California Law Review*, Stephen Weiner wrote about the law–fact distinction in civil jury trials.[78] He devoted much

---

[72] The Mansfield MSS, at 158.   [73] 8 July 1782, *ibid.*, at 375, 3 Doug 137 (1782).
[74] 3 Doug, at 138.
[75] 24 May 1785, The Mansfield MSS at 633, 1 TR 167 (1786).   [76] 1 TR, at 168.
[77] *ibid.*, at 169. Despite all of the judges' opinions, the jury in the new trial granted in *Tindal v. Brown* came out the same way as all the other juries. A third new trial was ordered, and the 'right' result (the one the court wanted to reach) was obtained by means of a special verdict. See The Mansfield MSS at 159–60.
[78] Stephen Weiner, 'The Civil Jury Trial and the Law–Fact Distinction', Cal L Rev 54: 1867 (1966).

attention to 'reasonableness' questions. He demonstrated the widely-held view that 'reasonable care' in negligence cases is considered a jury question, while as to commercial cases, '[i]n sharp contrast to the negligence cases . . . judicial authority is badly divided concerning the role of judges and jury in applying the reasonable time standard'.[79] In both the negligence and commercial contexts, Weiner addressed the Seventh Amendment question. He noted that '[t]here is authority suggesting that the constitutional right to a jury trial would be violated were the courts to take away from juries the issue of what constitutes reasonable care'.[80] And with regard to commercial cases, he approached the Seventh Amendment question by analysing *Tindal v. Brown* and antecedent cases, concluding that '[s]ince the weight of authority strongly suggests that an English judge in 1791 would not have submitted the issue [reasonable time] to a jury, there is no seventh amendment violation if a modern federal judge follows the same course'.[81]

If nothing else, the issue in the King's Bench cases from the 1780s illustrates the awkwardness of locking the scope of the Seventh Amendment right to jury trial to the state of things in England in 1791. As Weiner noted, describing a reporter's footnote to a 1796 King's Bench decision, 'prior to *Tindal v. Brown*, which "settled" the matter, what was a reasonable time . . . was considered a question of fact for the determination of the jury'.[82]

For present purposes, however, the 'reasonable time' cases demonstrate that in 1791, there were situations in which the judges would take possession of an ostensibly factual issue and convert it into a legal issue. They did so as a matter of commercial policy, and because of their conviction that any reasonable person assessing the evidence in the cases could come to but one conclusion.[83]

In *Markman*, then, a conclusion that reasonable minds could not differ on what 'inventory' meant in the patent claim would have been a legitimate resolution, both under modern law and within the English legal framework of 1791. Although there is some suggestion of this view in the majority Opinion by the Federal Circuit in *Markman*, the Opinion seized the opportunity to paint on a larger canvas and to claim for the court the construction of the patent claim. The broader issues were also those dealt with by the Supreme Court.

---

[79] Stephen Weiner, 'The Civil Jury Trial and the Law–Fact Distinction', Cal L Rev 54: 1867 (1966) at 1876–8, 1896.

[80] *ibid.*, at 1889.   [81] *ibid.*, at 1907–8.   [82] *ibid.*, at 1908, n. 207.

[83] This is, of course, extremely odd, since over 6 special juries in 3 different cases unanimously came to what the Court regarded as the incorrect conclusion. Nearly all of the special jurors were merchants, and it seems astonishing that such a collection of unreasonable merchants could be assembled. Nevertheless, these things happen. Holmes J. argued that as judges gained experience, they should be prepared to convert questions of fact into questions of law once they fully understood the questions and the way they should be decided. See O. W. Holmes, *The Common Law* (Boston, 1881), 123–4.

THE 'COMPLEXITY EXCEPTION'

In the decision of the Federal Circuit in *Markman*, Judge Mayer declared, 'Today's decision . . . threatens to do indirectly what we have declined to do directly, that is, create a "complexity exception" to the Seventh Amendment for patent cases.'[84] Judge Mayer's remark relates to a larger debate in Seventh Amendment cases, inspired by a footnote in a 1970 Supreme Court decision, *Ross v. Bernhard*,[85] a shareholder derivative suit in which the Court held that the shareholder plaintiffs did have a right to a jury trial. *Ross* involved a strand of the historical test for Seventh Amendment coverage different from that presented in *Markman*— whether a suit should be called predominantly equitable or legal in nature. If equitable, it will be aligned with suits tried in the Court of Chancery in the eighteenth century in England, and no jury will be required. If legal, a jury will be a matter of right, assuming the case resembles sufficiently jury trials in the English common law of 1791 (as *Markman* did not, according to the Court).[86] The analysis of whether a case is legal or equitable focuses on the nature of the action and the remedy sought. The line of cases decided by the Supreme Court has been criticized as being over-inclusive and ahistorical, extending jury trial unnecessarily to new causes of action (mainly those created by statute).[87]

In deciding that a jury trial was required in *Ross*, the Supreme Court observed in a footnote, 'As our cases indicate, the "legal" nature of an issue is determined by considering, first, the pre-merger (of law and equity) custom with reference to such questions; second, the remedy sought; and, third, the practical abilities and limitations of juries.'[88] The third criterion was an open invitation for a claim that cases that are too complex need not be subjected to jury trial. That claim was made before the US Court of Appeals for the Third Circuit in 1980,[89] and in gathering ammunition, the parties commissioned legal historians Morris Arnold and Patrick Devlin on opposing sides to undertake studies of the question.

---

[84] 52 F 3d 967, at 993 (concurring in the judgment).   [85] 396 US 531 (1970).

[86] In n. 10 to his *Markman* Opinion, Souter J. wrote, 'Because we conclude that our precedent supports classifying the question as one for the court, we need not decide either the extent to which the Seventh Amendment can be said to have crystallized a law/fact distinction . . .or whether post-1791 precedent classifying an issue as one of fact would trigger the protections of the Seventh Amendment if (unlike this case) there were no more specific reason for decision.'

[87] The leading Supreme Court case on this aspect of the historical test is *Beacon Theaters, Inc. v. Westover*, 359 US 500 (1959). For representative scholarly commentary and criticism, see M. Redish, 'Seventh Amendment Right to Jury Trial', above n. 6, at 488–508, 514–30; D. L. Shapiro and D. R. Coquillette, 'The Fetish of Jury Trial in Civil Cases: A Comment on *Rachal v. Hill*', Harv L Rev 85: 442 (1971).

[88] 396 US, at 538.

[89] *In re Japanese Electronic Products Antitrust Litigation*, 631 F 2d 1069 (3d Cir 1980).

Parts of these studies were published in the *Pennsylvania Law Review* and the *Columbia Law Review*,[90] and Lord Devlin followed up with another article in the *Michigan Law Review* three years later.[91]

The argument for a generalized complexity exception to the Seventh Amendment jury trial guarantee was built upon Chancery cases. The ordinary course when a factual dispute arose in a case before the Court of Chancery was for the Lord Chancellor to refer the question to one of the common law courts for jury trial resolution, suspending the Chancery case to await the verdict, afterwards continuing the case 'on the equity reserved'. Lord Devlin claimed, however, that long before 1791 it was well established that factual issues arising in a Chancery case need not be sent to the law courts for jury trial resolution if the questions were too complicated, for example, in cases seeking an accounting. This practice, viewed as part of the overarching authority of the Chancellor to prevent injustice, validated the complexity exception without the necessity of showing that the Chancellor actively prevented common law jury cases from proceeding because the subject-matter was beyond the jury's grasp. Nevertheless, Devlin argued that two pre-1791 cases showed that the Chancellor did indeed occasionally enjoin the common law courts in this way. Devlin's interpretation of those two cases—*Clench v. Townley* and *Blad v. Bamfield*[92]—was the principal focus of Arnold's opposing article. Arnold argued that *Clench*, when fully understood from manuscript sources, did not support what Devlin claimed, and Arnold discounted *Blad*, as standing 'for the simple proposition that suits involving foreign relations ought to be tried in prerogative courts'.[93]

The Third Circuit Court of Appeals was not persuaded 'that complexity alone ever was an established basis of equitable jurisdiction'.[94] On the court's analysis, this would have to be proved by establishing 'the authority of a chancellor to remove difficult issues from juries in suits at law', and there was but 'meager support' for such authority (one possible interpretation of *Clench*). The suits in equity seeking an accounting were inconclusive ('[w]e are aware of no case . . . in which a chancellor ordered an accounting in a suit involving nothing more than liability for money damages in trespass or tort'),[95] and the cases sent by Chancery to the law courts

---

[90] P. Devlin, 'Jury Trial of Complex Cases: English Practice at the Time of the Seventh Amendment', Columbia L Rev 80:43 (1980), see n. 13, above; M. Arnold, 'A Historical Inquiry into the Right to Trial by Jury in Complex Civil Litigation', Pennsylvania L Rev 128:829 (1980).

[91] P. Devlin, 'Equity, Due Process and the Seventh Amendment: A Commentary on the *Zenith* Case', Michigan L Rev 81:1571 (1983).

[92] Respectively, Carey 23 (1603); 3 Swans. 604 (1674).

[93] 128 Penn. L Rev at 846. The debate was expanded by two lawyers who had worked with Lord Devlin on behalf of IBM. See J. S. Campbell and N. Le Poidevin, 'Complex Cases and Jury Trials: A Reply to Professor Arnold', Pennsylvania L Rev 128: 966 (1980); M. S. Arnold, 'A Modest Replication To a Lengthy Discourse', *ibid.*, 986 (1980).

[94] 631 F 2d at 1083.   [95] *ibid.*, at 1080.

for advisory jury verdicts were brushed aside as 'irrelevant to our inquiry' ('[t]hese cases say nothing about the chancellor's authority to provide for non-jury trials in suits at common law').[96]

The court also declined to adopt the broader argument advanced on the basis of Lord Devlin's research—that the chancellor was, 'aware of the limited capabilities of juries and, as evidenced by his practices in accounting and advisory jury cases, often viewed these limitations as an impediment to justice'; thus, he 'would have exercized his control over his jurisdiction to decide the [complex] case in Chancery'.[97] Observing that this approach had not been taken in any previous federal court decision, the court chose 'not to pioneer in this use of history'.[98] Yet in effect the court did just that by using the clause of the Fifth Amendment that prohibits the state from depriving citizens of property without due process of law, instead of the historical exercise of the chancellor's jurisdiction under the Seventh Amendment. On the premise that, 'the law presumes that a jury will . . . resolve each disputed issue on the basis of a fair and reasonable assessment of the evidence and a fair and reasonable application of relevant legal rules', the court concluded that, 'due process precludes trial by jury when a jury is unable to perform this task with a reasonable understanding of the evidence and the legal rules'.[99]

In his later article, Lord Devlin celebrated this aspect of the Court of Appeals' decision, and he elaborated on the similarities between equity as practised in the Court of Chancery and due process. He also placed heavy emphasis on an 1804 Irish Chancery case, *O'Connor v. Spaight*,[100] decided by Lord Redesdale, who in his pre-titled life as John Mitford had written *A Treatise on the Pleadings in Suits in the Court of Chancery*.[101] In the treatise, Mitford explained that courts of equity had assumed jurisdiction 'in a variety of complicated cases of account [and other matters]', and 'seem by degrees to have been considered as having on these subjects a concurrent jurisdiction with the courts of common law . . .'.[102] And in *O'Connor*, Lord Redesdale (Mitford) stated, 'The ground on which I think this is a proper case for equity, is, that the account has become so complicated that a court of law would be incompetent to examine it upon a trial at *Nisi Prius*, with all necessary accuracy. . . . This is a principle upon which courts of equity constantly act . . .'[103]

---

[96] *ibid.*, at 1081. The court explained that '[t]he Chancellor's authority to direct an issue to a jury derived from his control over the method of finding facts in suits already within his jurisdiction', citing an article by John Langbein, 'Fact Finding in the English Court of Chancery: A Rebuttal', Yale L J 83: 1620 (1974).

[97] 631 F 2d at 1083.   [98] *ibid.*   [99] *ibid.*, at 1084.

[100] 1 Sch & Lef 305 (1804).

[101] First published in London in 1780, and substantially revised for a 1789 edn. See Devlin, 81 Mich. L Rev 1571, n.3.

[102] J. Mitford, *A Treatise on the Pleadings in Suits in the Court of Chancery* (2nd edn., Dublin 1789), 111, quoted by Devlin, 81 Mich. L Rev at 1629.

[103] 1 Sch. & Lef. at 309, quoted by Devlin at 81 Mich. L Rev 1628.

In his *Columbia Law Review* article, Devlin dealt briefly with *Gyles v. Wilcox*,[104] decided by Lord Hardwicke in 1740, a case that seems to me to have more persuasive force than the one-half page devoted to it.[105] Devlin mentioned only one of the two published reports, and omitted any reference to the arbitration feature of the case.[106] *Gyles* was a copyright infringement case brought for injunctive relief under the Statute of Queen Anne.[107] Fletcher Gyles was a bookseller who published an edition of Matthew Hale's *Pleas of the Crown*. Wilcox then published a volume called *Modern Crown Law*, which Gyles claimed was nothing but his book with a few obsolete statutes omitted and with all the Latin and French quotations translated into English. Lord Hardwicke, in Atkyns' report, observed that the question was whether Wilcox's work was a fair abridgement, which it would not be if merely 'colourably shortened'. He then stated:

Mr Attorney General has said I may send it to law to be determined by a jury: but how can this possibly be done? It would be absurd for the chief justice to sit and hear both books read over, which is absolutely necessary, to judge between them, whether the one is only a copy from the other. The court is not under an indispensable obligation to send all facts to a jury, but may refer them to a master, to state them, where it is a question of nicety and difficulty, and more fit for men of learning to inquire into, than a common jury.

This I think is one of those cases where it would be much better for the parties to fix upon two persons of learning and abilities in the profession of the law, who would accurately and carefully compare them, and report their opinion to the court. The House of Lords very often, in matters of account which are extremely perplexed and intricate, refer it to two merchants named by the parties, to consider the case, and report their opinions upon it, rather than leave it to a jury; and I should think a reference of the same kind in some measure would be the properest method in the present case.[108]

Accordingly, a reference to arbitration was endorsed.[109]

The *Gyles* Opinion, of course, is not dispositive of whether there was, in equity, a generalized 'complexity exception' to the practice of sending factual questions to law for jury determination. In an 1803 case involving tithes owing on land, Lord Eldon observed that, 'Beyond all question, it

---

[104] 2 Atk. 141 (1740), Barn. C. 368, with further proceedings reported at 3 Atk 270 (sub nom *Gyles v. Wilcocks*).

[105] See 'Jury Trial of Complex Cases', above n. 90, at 73.

[106] At 80 Columbia L Rev 77–80, Devlin discusses the arbitration features of the Common Law Procedure Act of 1854 and subsequent reform legislation, mainly as they related to actions of account.

[107] 8 Anne ch. 19 (1710).

[108] 2 Atk, at 144. Only the first two paragraphs of this passage were quoted by Lord Devlin. 80 Columbia L Rev at 73.

[109] In a brief note at 3 Atk 269, the agreement to arbitrate is indicated. With consent of the parties, Lord Hardwicke issued an order referring all matters in dispute to the award and determination of Mr Cay and Mr Thomas Stephens, with the customary terms of such an order set out. On this procedure, see H. Horwitz and J. Oldham, 'John Locke, Lord Mansfield, and Arbitration During the Eighteenth Century', *Historical Journal*, 36:137 (1993).

belongs to the constitution of a Court of Equity to decide upon matters of fact, if they think proper', but he added that 'Courts of Equity have for a great number of years, where questions of fact have been disputable, thought it a more proper exercise of their jurisdiction, to have them determined by a jury.'[110] Nevertheless, Lord Hardwicke's language in *Gyles*, the pre-eminence of Hardwicke as both Chief Justice of the Court of King's Bench and as Lord Chancellor, and the fact that the case was *not* the typical problem of accounts combine to make the case a strong precedent. Also forceful is the version of Hardwicke's Opinion in Barnes' report of *Gyles*. According to Barnes, Hardwicke acknowledged that, 'Whether the second Book is the same Book with the former is a Matter of Fact, and a Fact of Difficulty to be determined.' Then:

It has been hinted, that as this is a Matter of Fact the Court may send it to be tried before a Jury, but the Court is not confined to send all Matters of Fact to be tried in that Way. Where the Matter indeed consists of a single Fact, or of two or three Facts, the Court does take that Method to determine them, but where the Facts are of an extensive Nature, as Matters of Account, or the like, the Court does not take

---

[110] *O'Connor v. Cook*, 8 Ves. Jr 535, 536 (1803). Relying on this case and others, Harold Chesnin and Geoffrey Hazard attempted in a 1974 article to show that 'the rule that a court of equity may decide fact issues . . . was not firmly established in England until some time after 1800, at least a decade after the effective date of the Seventh Amendment'. H. Chesnin and G. C. Hazard, Jr, 'Chancery Procedure and the Seventh Amendment: Jury Trial of Issues in Equity Cases Before 1791', Yale L J 83: 999, 1000 (1974). This proposition was thoroughly exploded by John Langbein in 'Fact Finding in the English Court of Chancery: A Rebuttal', above n. 96, Yale L J 83: 1620 (1974). Langbein cited a number of Hardwicke Opinions from the 1740s (not including *Gyles v. Wilcox*) which, with other cases, demonstrated that throughout the 18th century Chancery 'had and exercised the power to resolve contested issues of fact'. *ibid.* at 1622. He pointed out that the tithe issue in *O'Connor* had, for special reasons, become the subject of 'an automatic reference to jury trial', *ibid.*, at 1624, n. 26.

Lord Eldon's generalizations in *O'Connor* about Chancery practices are nonetheless informative. In an earlier Opinion in the same case, Eldon put it this way, 'It is pretty clear, that Courts of Equity in antient times were more in the habit of taking to themselves the decision of questions of fact than they have thought wise and discreet in later times. As to the immemorial payment [of tithes], if any reasonable doubt has been raised upon it in the evidence, it has been of late thought wise and discreet to send the question of fact to a Jury. All the Judges have demonstrated their Opinion in favour of that practice, where any reasonable doubt is raised upon the fact; and I cannot suppose, there is any prejudice in a tribunal appointed according to the constitution of the country to try the fact' (*O'Connor v. Cook*, 6 Ves Jr 665, 671 (1802)).

Where there was no reasonable doubt, however, Chancery would keep the case, as shown in *Short v. Lee*, 2 Jac & W 464 (1821). There, a lessee of an ecclesiastical corporation sued for tithes, and on being urged to send an issue to the law courts, the Master of the Rolls (Sir Thomas Plummer) said there was not 'any contrariety in the evidence'; the evidence to disprove the immemorial existence of the tithes was 'entirely written, contained in thirty-six ancient Rolls in a dead language, embracing many terms of different kinds'; 'their construction has called forth the applications of learning, critical and accurate investigation and collation, frequent and useful revision, and the assistance of glossaries and antiquarian knowledge, to form a correct judgment respecting their meaning and import'. Finally, he asked, rhetorically, 'Could this be done before a jury at *Nisi Prius*, with the same effect as it may in a court, assisted by the learning and industry of the bar, during a hearing of many days, devoted entirely to this one subject, and with a knowledge of the whole of the cause to which the enquiry belongs?' *ibid.*, at 502.

that Method to determine them, but directs them to be inquired into before the Master . . . And in order that the Master may better determine the Matter, his Lordship said that he did not see but he ought to direct, that the Master should be attended by two Persons skilled in the Profession of the Law, to assist him. And Directions of this Sort have been made in Mathematical and Algebraical Inquiries. But his Lordship said he should choose, that two Persons should be agreed upon by Consent of both Parties to attend the Master in this Matter, rather than the Court should appoint them; for which Reason his Lordship said, he would direct that the Matter should stand over for a Week.[111]

One could take the view, as did the Third Circuit Court of Appeals, that as an exercise of the Chancellor's discretion not to send the case to an advisory jury, *Gyles* is not of much weight in relation to the Seventh Amendment inquiry. Instead of an action brought at common law for damages, as in *Markman*, the bill in *Gyles* was in Chancery for an injunction, and a factual issue arose. *No* case in late-eighteenth century England is known where the plaintiff sued at common law for damages, as in *Markman*, yet the common law court decided the factual issues were beyond the jury's capacity, causing the court to send the case to Chancery.

There would, however, be responses to such an argument. One could return to Lord Devlin's argument that just as the Chancellor refrained from sending complex factual issues out for advisory jury verdicts, he was willing to enjoin common law proceedings when the issues were too specialized or complex for effective jury handling. The fact that few examples of this can be found in the printed reports may be due to the simple explanation that the Chancellor was rarely asked. As Morris Arnold observed in his 'Modest Replication', 'the Plaintiff is the master of his cause of action; once it is characterized as legal by him, the ordinary attributes of a trial at law, including the availability of a jury, necessarily follow'.[112] In responding to the plaintiff's declaration, defendant was required either to demur or plead, specially or generally, and as was shown earlier with Common Pleas records, demurrers were rarely entered.[113] By the late eighteenth century, general pleas were common,[114] but if a special plea was entered

---

[111]   Barn. C. 368.

[112]   M. Arnold, 'A Modest Replication To a Lengthy Discourse', above n. 92, 128 Yale L J at 988 (n. omitted).

[113]   See n. 30, above, and accompanying text.

[114]   According to [Anon], *The Practising Attorney: Or, New King's Bench Guide*, London 1779, at 95: 'The General Issue or General Plea, is what traverses, thwarts and denies at once the whole Declaration, without offering any special Matter whereby to evade it. . . . Formerly, the General Issue was seldom pleaded, except when the Party meant wholly to deny the charge alledged against him; but when he meant to distinguish away or palliate the charge, it was always usual to set forth the particular Facts in what is called a Special Plea, which was originally intended to apprize the Court and the adverse Party, of the Nature and Circumstances of the Defence, and to keep the Law and Fact distinct . . . but the Science of Special Pleading having been frequently perverted for the Purposes of Chicane and Delay; the Courts have of late in some instances, and the Legislature in many more, permitted the

by defendant, the plaintiff would file a replication, and in either case the dispute would proceed to jury trial,[115] propelled by standard fees and filings required of the plaintiff's attorney.[116] It would be hard to imagine that a defendant, after putting himself upon the country with a general plea, would appeal to Chancery to enjoin that very process. Possibly such a request would be made by a defendant who, instead of demurring, had entered a special plea to the plaintiff's declaration. Yet if the special plea raised factual claims, the defendant would expect the plaintiff's denial by replication and request for a jury trial.[117]

To return our focus to the possibility of a complexity exception to the Seventh Amendment, if one were able to ask an eighteenth-century barrister for an example of complex civil litigation of his day, the answer would probably have been the accounting cases that customarily went to Chancery to begin with. Cases raising difficult questions of fact that could best be resolved by persons with specialized knowledge were commonly

General Issue to be pleaded, which leaves every thing open, the Fact and the Law, and the Equity of the Case, and have allowed Special Matter to be given in Evidence at the Trial.'

[115] As noted earlier (see text following n. 29), the stock expression for jury trial was to 'put oneself upon the country'. Thus, 'if the Traverse or Denial comes from the Defendant, the Issue is tendered in this Manner, "And of this he puts himself upon the country", thereby submitting himself to the Judgment of his Peers; but if the Traverse lies upon Plaintiff, he tenders the Issue, or prays the Judgment of the Peers against the Defendant, in another Form thus: "And this he prays may be enquired of by the Country."' (ibid., at 102.)

[116] The required steps were laid out in the standard practice books. One such book with graphic detail was *The Attorney's Compleat Guide In the Court of King's Bench*, London, 1773 ('By an Attorney of the Court'); e.g., the first part of 'MAKING UP RECORD FOR TRIAL' reads (at 146): 'Plaintiff must ingross record on a double half crown press of parchment. Get a King's Bench Roll from Mr *Heberden*, at King's Bench office; pay 4d.; . . . carry record Roll, and your draught of the issue to Mr *Caley*; pay him for an issue not exceeding ten sheets, 3s.6d. And for every six sheets more 1s.: This done, carry record to Mr *Tully, Holborn Court, Gray's Inn* . . .' [etc.]. The copy of this book held by the Georgetown University Law Library is a commonplace version, signed by Edward Grave, January 1778, and filled with interleaved manuscript additions. One manuscript addition that illustrates the role of the plaintiff's attorney in getting the case to trial is a 'Form of Notice of Trial where there [are] issues in Fact & in Law, to be indorsed on the back of Paper Book,' which reads as follows (at 116a):

> Messrs. G & P
> Take Notice that the several Issues joined in the Cause to be tried by a Jury of the Country will be tried at the Sittings after the present Michaelmas Term at Guildhall London. And that the Jurors of that Jury will at the Trial of those Issues inquire what Damages Plaintiff has sustained on Occasion of the premises whereof the said parties have put themselves upon the Judgment of the Court in Case Judgment shall be given thereof for the said Plaintiffs.
>
> Yours &c

[117] Special pleading was an arcane art form, and no doubt there were manoeuvres that are no longer appreciated or understood. Some techniques may have avoided a jury without going to Chancery or filing a demurrer. *The Practising Attorney* (above, n. 113) gives one example (at 98), '[I]f the Defendant in an Action of Trespass be desirous to refer the validity of his Title to the Court rather than the Jury, he may state his Title specially, and at the same time *give colour* to the Plaintiff, or suppose him to have an Appearance or colour of Title bad indeed in Point of Law, but of which the Jury are not competent Judges.'

referred to arbitration, as indeed the *Gyles* case was.[118] Arbitration referrals out of the common law courts or the Court of Chancery were done with consent of the parties, to be sure, and although occasionally a party resisted,[119] resistance was quite rare.[120]

This raises, however, another basic point. By 1791, most business cases tried in the common law courts in England were tried by special juries, not common juries, and typically the special jurors were merchants who were encouraged to use their own familiarity with relevant mercantile customs and practices in deciding upon their verdicts.[121] The special jury exists no more in England, and is a rarity in the United States.[122] This major difference between modern jury trial practices and those that prevailed in 1791 has not been identified by the Supreme Court or the lower federal courts as relevant to the ongoing application of the historical test in measuring the scope of the Seventh Amendment guarantee. Yet the special jury was available to either party in England in 1791 as a matter of *right*. As stated by Baker John Sellon in *The Practice of the Courts of King's Bench and Common Pleas* (1793), the special jury section of 'An Act for the better Regulation of Juries' (1730),[123] 'gives the subject a liberty of having a special jury in all cases whatsoever, which before that statute was only granted in certain circumstances'.[124]

The composite picture of how business litigation was handled in late eighteenth-century England argues against the proposition that, unless waived, juries are mandated by the Seventh Amendment in twenty-first-

---

[118] On referrals to arbitration in the late 18th century, see The Mansfield MSS at 151–4, and 1540–1665 (Appendix E).

[119] See, e.g., The Mansfield MSS at 154.

[120] Devlin cites a comment by Lord Campbell in an 1847 case, *Taff Vale Railway Co. v. Nixon*, 1 H.L. Cas. 111, that the judge's recommendations of references to arbitration would be accepted 99 out of 100 times. 'Jury Trial of Complex Cases,' above n. 90, at 77. I am certain that the same was true of Lord Mansfield's time on the Court of King's Bench in the late-18th-century.

[121] I have discussed the reliance by the common law courts on juries of merchants in a paper presented to the 14th British Legal History Conference held in Edinburgh in July 1999. For background about the special jury, its history and its instrumental use by the Court of King's Bench under Mansfield, see The Mansfield MSS at 94–99; J. Oldham, 'The Origins of the Special Jury', Univ. of Chi. L Rev 50:137 (1983); J. Oldham, 'Special Juries in England: Nineteenth Century Usage and Reform', J. Legal Hist. 8:148 (1987).

[122] See 'Special Juries in England: Nineteenth-Century Usage and Reform', above n. 105; J. Oldham, 'The History of the Special (Struck) Jury in the US and Its Relation to Voir Dire Practices, the Reasonable Cross-Section Requirement, and Peremptory Challenges', William and Mary L Rev 6:623 (1998). Special juries no longer exist in federal courts. It is theoretically possible to get a special jury (jurors with special qualifications) to try a complex civil case only in one state (Delaware)—although requests for such special juries appear to be seldom granted. See *William and Mary Bill of Rights Jour.* at 6: 659–62 (1998).

[123] 3 Geo. II, c 25, s. 15.

[124] B. J. Sellon, *The Practice of the Courts of King's Bench and Common Pleas*, Dublin 1793, Part II, Dublin 1795, at 444. Sellon adds that, by a 1751 enactment, the party requesting the special jury became responsible for the costs, unless the judge certified otherwise. He also spells out the steps to be taken by counsel to move for a special jury, which 'is a matter of course', such that 'no notice of the motion or affidavit of the facts is necessary' (*ibid.*).

century America in complex civil cases. This view is strengthened, more-over, by the undeniable fact that *nothing* in the eighteenth-century English legal landscape remotely approached the sheer proportions of today's complex antitrust and mass tort cases.[125] This was recognized by the Third Circuit Court of Appeals in the *Japanese Electronic Products* case[126] in hold-ing that a jury was not required for the case before it—an antitrust con-spiracy case that had been in discovery for nine years, with over 100,000 pages of depositions, and with thousands of different product models in evidence. As noted earlier, the court relied on the theory that when a case reaches a deeply complex level, the jury can no longer perform its task effectively, and if the case were forced to go before a jury, due process under the Fifth Amendment would be denied.[127]

The Third Circuit's Fifth Amendment trump of the Seventh Amend-ment jury trial guarantee did not become established in other circuits. Neither this nor a more direct 'complexity exception' to the Seventh Amendment is likely to gain a real purchase in the federal courts until a clearer endorsement emerges from the Supreme Court. In a 1990 decision extending jury trial to suits by union members for back-pay, *Chauffeurs, Teamsters and Helpers, Local No. 391 v. Terry*,[128] Justice Stevens argued in his concurring Opinion for a 'functional' approach to Seventh Amendment coverage ('whether "the issues [presented by the claim] are typical grist for the jury's judgment"'), but in the plurality Opinion, Justice Marshall stated, This Court has never relied on this consideration 'as an independent basis for extending the right to a jury trial under the Seventh Amendment.'[129]

Justice Souter in *Markman* recognized the limitations of juries in com-plex cases, but he did so as a matter of common sense and judicial admin-istration, not as a matter of constitutional mandate. He wrote that, '[s]ince evidence of common-law practice at the time of the framing does not entail application of the Seventh Amendment's jury guarantee to the construc-tion of the claim document, we must look elsewhere . . . in order to allo-cate it as between court or jury'.[130] He later added, '[w]here history and precedent provide no clear answers, functional considerations also play their part in the choice between judge and jury to define terms of art'.[131] He explained that '[t]he construction of written instruments is one of those things that judges often do and are likely to do better than jurors unbur-dened by training in exegesis'.[132] Claimant protested that a jury 'should decide a question of meaning peculiar to a trade or profession . . . because

---

[125] For a forceful demonstration of this point using reported cases, see D. King, 'Complex Civil Litigation and the Seventh Amendment Right to a Jury Trial', Univ of Chicago L Rev 51: 581 (1984).

[126] 631 F 2d 1069 (1980).   [127] *ibid.*, at 1079.   [128] 494 US 558 (1990).

[129] *ibid.*, at 565, n. 4., quoting *Tull v. US*, 481 US 412, 418 n. 4 (1987).

[130] 517 US, at 384.   [131] *ibid.*, at 388.   [132] *ibid.*

the question is a subject of testimony requiring credibility determinations, which are the jury's forté'.[133] Justice Souter agreed that sometimes there is a need for credibility determinations of expert testimony in patent cases, but he thought this rare, stating:

In the main, we expect, any credibility determinations will be subsumed within the necessarily sophisticated analysis of the whole document, required by the standard construction rule that a term can be defined only in a way that comports with the instrument as a whole . . . Thus, in these cases, a jury's capabilities to evaluate demeanor . . . to sense the 'mainsprings of human conduct' . . . or to reflect community standards . . . are much less significant than a trained ability to evaluate the testimony in relation to the overall structure of the patent . . . We accordingly think there is sufficient reason to treat construction of terms of art like many other responsibilities that we cede to a judge in the normal course of trial, notwithstanding its evidentiary underpinnings.[134]

It is unclear whether, if squarely put to it, Justice Souter would elevate these functional considerations to the constitutional level. My guess is that he would interpret the constitutional history in a way that would not require a jury in cases of extreme complexity, and were he to do so, perhaps the *Gyles* precedent would be helpful. It is doubtful, however, that the other justices would be in full agreement. The unanimity displayed in *Markman* no longer describes the Supreme Court's Seventh Amendment decision-making.

THE *FELTNER* AND *CITY OF MONTGOMERY* DECISIONS

In *Feltner v. Columbia Pictures Television, Inc*,[135] Columbia sued for copyright infringement under the Copyright Act of 1976,[136] electing to seek statutory rather than actual damages. Statutory damages were permitted under the Act 'in a sum of not less than $500 or more than $20,000 as the court considers just', or up to $100,000 for wilful violations.[137] Feltner requested a jury trial, which was denied by both the trial and appellate courts, and this was the issue before the Supreme Court. In an Opinion by Justice Thomas, a near-unanimous Court[138] held that no jury trial was granted by the Copyright Act for an assessment of statutory damages,[139] but that a jury was required by the Seventh Amendment on application of the historical test. Justice Thomas described the practice in eighteenth-

---

[133] 517 US, at at 389.   [134] *ibid.*, at 389–90.   [135] 118 S Ct 1279 (1998).
[136] 17 USC § 101, *et seq.*   [137] 17 USC § 504(c)(1) and (2).
[138] Scalia J. wrote separately, concurring in the judgment.
[139] The phrase 'as the court considers just' in § 504(c)(1) was read 'to mean judge, not jury'. 118 S Ct at 1283. Scalia J. would have read the phrase expansively to permit jury trial, which he would therefore have required as a matter of statutory construction, not reaching the constitutional question.

century England of trying damages actions for copyright infringement before juries, both those brought at common law in the form of trespass on the case,[140] and those brought under the Statute of Queen Anne—the same statute sued upon in 1740 in the *Gyles* case, discussed above. The Court rejected Columbia's argument that the statutory damages were equitable in nature, quoting a 1677 Common Pleas statement that 'by the law the jury are judges of the damages',[141] and citing other English authorities, including well-known cases from the 1760s involving John Wilkes.[142]

Nothing in the facts of the *Feltner* case invited the Court to remove an issue from the jury by declaring it a question of law or by resorting to 'functional considerations', as in *Markman*. The two decisions show unanimous and near-unanimous applications of the historical test, one denying jury trial and the other upholding it, but not inconsistently. This cannot be said of the Court's Seventh Amendment application in *City of Montgomery v. Del Monte Dunes at Monterey, Ltd.*,[143] where the plaintiff sued the city in what is termed an inverse condemnation action under Rev Stat §1979, 42 USC §1983, claiming a regulatory taking of property without providing any post-deprivation remedy for the loss. The plaintiff corporation was a developer which had been required to jump over numerous zoning hurdles in an attempt to build on its property, and after apparently clearing them all over a period of five years, was denied permission by the city council. Claimant claimed that this amounted to an unconstitutional taking, denying due process and equal protection. Over the city's objection, the trial court submitted the taking and equal protection claims to a jury, reserving to itself the substantive due process issue. The jury returned a verdict for the plaintiff, awarding damages of $1.45 million. The trial court ruled in the city's favour on substantive due process, but let the jury verdict stand. The Ninth Circuit Court of Appeals affirmed, and the principal issue before the Supreme Court was whether the trial court had properly overruled the city's objection to trial by jury.

Citing *Feltner*, the Court first decided that there was no statutory right to a jury embedded in §1983, thereby raising the Seventh Amendment

---

[140] Citing Lord Mansfield's famous Opinion in *Millar v. Taylor*, 4 Burr. 2303 (1769).

[141] *Lord Townshend v. Hughes*, 2 Mod. 150 (CP 1677).

[142] *Wilkes v. Wood*, Lofft 1 (KB 1763); *Huckle v. Money*, 2 Wils 205 (KB 1763). Another case in point from the same time period that does not appear in Seventh Amendment decisions or writings is *Grey v. Grant*, 2 Wils 252 (CP 1764). There, a jury gave £100 damages against a Member of Parliament for assault and battery, and a motion was made to set the verdict aside because of excessiveness of the damages. In rejecting the motion, the court stated, 'This was a quarrel between two gentlemen, and has been properly tried by a special jury of merchants of *London*, who are the proper judges of the damages; when a blow is given by one gentleman to another, a challenge and death may ensue, and therefore the jury have done right in giving exemplary damages; Plaintiff has been used unlike a gentleman by the defendant in striking him, withholding his property, and insisting upon his privilege, all of them tending to provoke him to seek his revenge in another way than by law, and therefore we think the damages are not excessive.'

[143] 119 S Ct 1624 (1999).

question. Five justices (Kennedy, Scalia, Rehnquist, Stevens, and Thomas) concluded that a jury was constitutionally required. Justice Kennedy wrote the lead Opinion which spoke for a majority except for the part of his Opinion finding the inverse condemnation action under §1983 to be a suit at law.[144] The dissent was written by the author of *Markman*, Justice Souter, joined by Justices O'Conner, Ginsberg, and Breyer.

Justice Kennedy, quoting from *Markman* in laying out the historical test for Seventh Amendment coverage, first concluded that claims under §1983 'sound in tort', and were actions at law. He incorporated by reference Justice Scalia's, 'comprehensive and convincing analysis of the historical and constitutional reasons for this conclusion',[145] adding his own observations that the case was analogous to the common law tort actions of nuisance, trespass, and trespass on the case, and even if viewed as closer to quasi-contract, the action would still be fairly characterized as one at law for damages. Again relying on *Markman*, Justice Kennedy then said that in deciding whether the issues in the action at law were proper for jury resolution, the Court must first look to history, and failing any clear answer, 'to precedent and functional considerations'.[146] After finding that neither history nor precedent gave a definitive answer, Kennedy turned 'to considerations of process and function'.[147] Citing a 1935 Supreme Court decision,[148] Coke's *Institutes*,[149] and *Markman* for the proposition that fact questions are typically allocated to the jury, he concluded that whether a landowner had been wholly deprived of the economic use of his property was a fact question. Whether the land-use decision advanced legitimate public interests was 'a mixed question of fact and law', but on the specific facts in the case at bar, the question of the city's justifications for its action was, as the Court of Appeals had ruled, 'essentially fact-bound [in] nature', and was properly submitted to a jury.[150]

Dissenting, Justice Souter agreed with the Court's use of *Markman* to frame the Seventh Amendment question, but the insurmountable analytical obstacle for him was the rule long established in Supreme Court cases that no jury is required in direct condemnation cases (eminent domain). That rule was, to him, inescapably inconsistent with the plurality view that a jury is necessary in inverse condemnation cases. He found unpersuasive the emphasis in both the Kennedy and Scalia Opinions on the kin-

---

[144] On that point Scalia J., writing separately, would have been more expansive, extending the ruling to all §1983 actions.

[145] 119 S Ct at 1638. Scalia J.'s historical analysis emphasized the kinship of §1983 actions to traditional tort cases, citing Blackstone's *Commentaries on the Laws of England* 3:398 (12th edn, 1796), Thomas Cooley's 1880 *Treatise on the Law of Torts*, as well as numerous modern authorities.

[146] *ibid.*, at 1643.   [147] *ibid.*

[148] *Baltimore & Carolina Line, Inc. v. Redman*, 295 US 654 (1935).

[149] E. Coke, *The First Part of the Institutes of the Lawes of England, Or, A Commentarie Upon Littleton* (London, 1628).

[150] 119 S Ct at 1644.

ship of the inverse condemnation cases to traditional tort actions for damages, pointing out that there was at the time of the Seventh Amendment nothing in English law comparable to the modern condemnation actions in American law. He also dismissed the plurality Opinion's attempt to distinguish direct from inverse condemnation cases on the basis that in direct condemnation cases, liability was admitted—the question was only how much—whereas in the indirect cases, both liability and the amount had to be decided. According to Justice Souter, 'the want of a liability issue in most condemnation cases says nothing to explain why no jury ought to be provided on the question of damages that always is before the courts'—the 'dollars-and-cents issue is about as "factual" as one can be', and '[i]f an emphasis on factual issues vigorously contested were a sufficient criterion for identifying something essential to the preservation of the Seventh Amendment jury right, there ought to be a jury right in direct condemnation cases as well as the inverse ones favored by the plurality'.[151]

These observations by Justice Souter are provocative. They invite reflection on the writ of enquiry, which was used extensively in England in the late eighteenth century to empanel juries to ascertain damages in default judgments (where there was no liability issue).[152] The relevance of the writ of enquiry to the historical test for the scope of the Seventh Amendment guarantee has scarcely been touched upon in Seventh Amendment literature,[153] and it is more than can be accomplished in this chapter. For present purposes, the Opinions in the *City of Montgomery* case show that even if all of the justices agree, guided by *Markman*, that a case is to be resolved by functional considerations, there is no clarity about the outcome. On purely functional grounds, Justice Souter's Opinion is forceful.[154] Yet both

[151] *ibid.*, at 1655. In a lengthy article in 1996, Eric Grant argues the case for juries in direct compensation cases. E. Grant, 'A Revolutionary View of the Seventh Amendment and the Just Compensation Clause', Northwestern Univ. L Rev 91:144 (1996). Souter J. cites and quotes from the article in his Opinion, but without discussion. 119 S Ct at 1650–1.

[152] As stated by Blackstone, 'But, where damages are to be recovered, a jury must be called in to assess them; unless the defendant, to save charges, will confess the whole damages laid in the declaration . . . This process is called a *writ of enquiry*: in the execution of which the sheriff sits as judge, and tries by a jury, subject to nearly the same law and conditions as the trial by jury at *nisi prius*, what damages Plaintiff hath really sustained . . .'. W. Blackstone, *Commentaries* (see above n. 145). Blackstone added, 'In like manner, where a demurrer is determined for Plaintiff upon an action wherein damages are recovered, the judgment is also incomplete, without the aid of a writ of inquiry.' Edward Christian pointed out in his notes to the 12th edn of Blackstone, however, that 'a practice is now established in the courts of king's bench and common pleas, in actions where judgment is recovered by default upon a bill of exchange or a promissory note, to refer it to the master or prothonotary to ascertain what is due for principal, interest, and costs, whose report supercedes the necessity of a writ of inquiry.' *ibid.*, at 492, quoting Wilmot CJ in *Bruce v. Rawlins*, 3 Wils 61, at 62 (CP 1770), describing a writ of inquiry after a default judgment as 'an inquest of office to inform the conscience of the court, who, if they please, may themselves assess the damages . . .'.

[153] But see P. Mogin, 'Why Judges, Not Juries, Should Set Punitive Damages', Univ of Chicago L Rev 65:179, 201–2 (1998).

[154] Souter J. further pointed out that one theory of recovery in inverse condemnation cases is, 'that the taking makes no substantial contribution to a legitimate governmental purpose';

the Kennedy and Scalia Opinions demonstrate that the traditional role of the jury in determining liability and damages in trespass or nuisance cases continues to carry strong Seventh Amendment weight, even in statutory actions which are merely analogous.

CONCLUSION

I earlier asked whether, in the light of the English trial practice of the late eighteenth century, the Seventh Amendment historical test is an American legal fiction. The answer is, yes, it is a legal fiction in application, since many more things were lodged with juries in England in 1791 than American courts, including the Supreme Court, are prepared to acknowledge. It is easy to appreciate the appeal of the test to the Court, in that it permits what many would regard as constructive change while maintaining the appearance of certainty, as well as the stability and reassurance that come from appearing to stay in touch with the historical past. *Markman* is the proof. In a unanimous Opinion, the Court removed a complex patent issue—one that arises in nearly every patent infringement suit—from the province of the jury. The Court did so by claiming and appearing to comply with Justice Story's now-venerable historical test. As to this, we might apply to Justice Souter what James Boswell once said about Lord Mansfield. In discussing a pending case with an acquaintance, Boswell predicted that Mansfield would reverse, and when asked how, he replied, 'By sleight of hand . . . He won't tell you how he does it. But he'll let you see him do it.'[155]

The *Markman* Opinion, whether right or wrong on historical grounds, might have become (and might have been intended by Justice Souter to become) a platform from which to address the 'complexity exception' in a future case, emphasizing the third prong of the *Markman* formulation—functional considerations such as the relative 'skills of judges and juries'.[156] Nothing in the *Feltner* case would have interfered with this possible development, but the Kennedy and Scalia Opinions in *City of Montgomery* cloud the prospect, especially Justice Kennedy's use of 'considerations of process and function', invoking *Markman*, to *require* a jury trial in the inverse condemnation proceeding before the Court.

The Seventh Amendment landscape now described by federal court precedent could be described as strange indeed, almost upside down. Juries are required in actions for damages no matter how complicated and

and he repeated an earlier observation from his *Markman* opinion, that '[s]crutinizing the legal basis for governmental action is one of those things that judges often do and are likely to do better than juries unburdened by training in exegesis' (119 S Ct at 1659–60; see text at n. 132 above).

[155] The Mansfield MSS at 208.　　　　　　　　　[156] 517 US, at 384.

drawn out, no matter how unrealistic it may be for a common jury to function effectively. Special juries, which might function effectively, are no longer available. Yet in construing patent claims, something juries frequently did in the late eighteenth century in England, no juries are allowed, and a new layer called a '*Markman* hearing' is inserted in patent proceedings, an innovation not necessarily welcomed by the practitioners as an improvement in case-handling efficiency.[157]

---

[157] Compare P. J. McCabe and P. M. Smith, 'Courts Order "Markman" Hearings Early in Cases', *National Law Journal*, 19 Oct. 1998 at C42, with S. Z. Szczepanski and F. R. Nation, 'A "Markman" Hearing Can Determine Case Outcome', *ibid.*, 24 May 1999, at C26.

10

The Author's Surrogate: the Genesis of British Copyright

W. R. Cornish

THE EXERCISE IN HAND

On both sides of the Atlantic Brian Simpson has done much to wean legal historians away from too great a dependence on theory. This brief appreciation of writings about the origins of modern copyright law is permeated by that teaching. So it is offered as a small tribute to his richly individual contribution to our knowledge of how our legal systems developed in the common law tradition, above all in the period since industrialization.

Scholars tend to be self-conscious authors. A good few of them, moreover, are as concerned about the commercial value of their work as they are about the style, content, and integrity of what they write, and their proper identification as author. Study of the history of copyright accordingly has its peculiar attraction. Indeed, the evolution of the modern law has now attracted the attention of theorists of many colours. At one extreme stand those who would idealize the act of 'authorship'—the creation of aesthetic works of all kinds, literary, dramatic, musical, artistic, filmic, balletic, and so on. At the other, those antipathetic to this adulation of the author strip each creative act down to a contribution to social activity which is mainly dependent on what the creator has learned—the work's significance turns upon the reactions of others to it. Authorship constructed; authorship deconstructed. At each pole, history is made to serve these higher ideological ends, as are prognostications about its future.

Do not mistake: much excellent work has been done to tease out how the modern notion of copyright emerged in Britain—an exercise of some importance, since it was the first country to have such a law in the modern sense. In this history there are two major events: the enactment of the Statute of Anne of 1710;[1] and the subsequent recognition by the courts of a common law right of property in literary and similar creations. The scope of the latter, when measured against the 1710 Statute was the great

---

[1] 8 Ann. c. 19; Ransom, *The First Copyright Statute* (1956). The Act received the Royal Assent and took effect in the regnal year 1710. Traditionally, however, it has been dated 1709: see Feather, 'The Book Trade in Politics: the Making of the Copyright Act of 1710' (1980), 8 Pub. Hist. 19, n. 3.

cause in the 'Battle of the Books', later in the eighteenth century. I do not intend to rehearse in much detail that lively and complex history, to which many have contributed, often with a fitting grace, sometimes with dedicated passion.[2] The purpose of this piece is to examine one characterization of those two events which has had considerable currency. It took a sophisticated form as the basic thesis of Lyman Ray Patterson's *Copyright in Historical Perspective* (1968):

The statutory copyright provided in the Statute of Anne was a publisher's copyright; but the Act was construed to have provided an author's copyright. The distinction between the two concepts—the one intended and the one which resulted—was fundamental. This development had little to do with the Statute of Anne itself; but because the Act provided for copyright, and the statutory copyright it provided later came to be an author's copyright, the inevitable conclusion was that the statutory copyright was originally designed to be an author's copyright.[3]

A fundamental dichotomy, then—one which presages the modern division of all such laws into the essentially economic copyright systems of the Anglo-American tradition and the more numinous *droit d'auteur* of the civilian tradition, with its equal emphasis on the author's 'moral', as opposed to economic, rights. Patterson's object, it seems, is to argue that the distinction was present in the English sources of the eighteenth century, but in such a form that no real author's right, of the civilian persuasion, was able to develop from it. In his hands at least, it is a subtle argument, and its historical basis deserves inquiry.

A WORD ABOUT ROOTS

That copyright has a history at all stems from the development of reproductive technology. The issue first surfaces with the evolution of the printing press, and in modern times it has also had to encompass not only electronic carriers, such as records and films, but also ephemeral media, such as broadcasting and cabling. Now there is the complex phenomenon of the Internet and all that lies in the digital future. But copyright law is not simply a response to technical advance. There is always a political and social dimension to it. The introduction of copyright in Britain, as in most European countries, was preceded by a period in which rulers granted privileges to printers and booksellers whom they trusted not to publish seditious, blasphemous, or scandalous material—a liaison from which those with authority made the most of their mercantilist advantage.

---

[2] Extensive bibliographies can be found in, e.g., Saunders, *Authorship and Copyright* (1992); Rose, *Authors and Owners: The Invention of Copyright* (1994); Sherman and Bently, *The Making of Modern Intellectual Property Law* (1999).

[3] At 144.

In England, certainly, the leading booksellers formed themselves into the Stationers' Company and by the mid-sixteenth century they were able to reach a satisfying accommodation with the Crown and its Church. Entitlement to publish thereafter flowed either from a royal grant of letters patent or from registration in the Register of the Stationers' Company, which was open only to its members. The Company, not untypically for its time, was furnished with direct powers of search and seizure. It could use these powers against printers and sellers of material which had not been authorized by letters patent or by registration. The chief counsellors of state, and the Church of England's figureheads, retained power to determine what should not be on the Stationers' Register, and so the censorship continued through decades of political turbulence. The Stationers, who were the substantial publisher-booksellers of London, used their power and authority as a cartel in a world of trade still dominated by local guilds and apprenticeships.[4]

As the seventeenth century advanced, and the Kingdom moved through Civil War to a Restoration of the Monarchy which it took from 1660 to 1688 to settle, the censorship became less and less easy to maintain. After 1660, it lapsed several times, Parliament refusing to enshrine it in permanent legislation. Finally in 1695 it disappeared for good.[5] By various forms of internal pressure, the Stationers could maintain exclusive rights to the Copy of books in relations between one another; and to some extent also in relation to booksellers and others who might be tempted to deal in pirate copies. Nonetheless they lacked their former disciplinary powers of search, seizure, and destruction of copies, which had enabled them to attack the actual producers of illegitimate copies. They were indeed feeling the pressures of technological advance, for new printing methods were reducing the capital costs of competitors. The old censorship had been one factor, together with the internal trade rules and understandings, which fortified the belief that a Company member held a right, unlimited in time, to publish a book of which he held the 'Copy'. The Stationers treated these rights as stemming from the registration made by a company member. The rights could then be dealt with as assignable property, often in divided shares. These were the bare elements which led the London leaders of the trade to demand legislation of the sort eventually given them in 1710.

---

[4] For the pre-history of the copyright system, see, e.g., Blagden, *The Stationers' Company: A History, 1403–1959* (1960), ch. 1; Patterson, *Copyright in Historical Perspective* (1968), ch. 1; Feather, *A History of British Publishing* (1988), Pt I; Rose (above, n. 2), ch. 2.

[5] For details, see esp. Bald, 'Early Copyright Litigation and its Bibliographical Interest' (1942) 36 P. Bib. Soc. Am. 81; Crist, 'Government Control of the Press after the Expiration of the Printing Act in 1679' (1979) 5 Pub. Hist. 49; Astbury, 'The Renewal of the Licensing Act in 1693 and its Lapse in 1695' (1978), 33 Library 296.

The Statute of Anne was undoubtedly a compromise, chiefly between the booksellers of the Stationers' Company and those—in Parliament and outside—who opposed them as greedy, monopolising 'congers'.[6] When eventually it reached the statute book, the Act provided the following: it gave to the author, or to a bookseller, printer or other assignee of the author (whether a member of the Company or not) the Copy in any book already printed for a term of 21 years from commencement of the Act. In books which were not yet published at that date, it gave the author or his or her assignees protection for a term of 14 years measured from the date when the book was published with due authorization. All this is contained in Section I, following directly upon the Preamble. By the fascinating Section XI, the Act provided that, after the expiration of this term, 'the sole right of printing or disposing of Copies shall return to the Authors thereof, if they are then living, for another term of fourteen years'.

The Act clearly characterizes these rights as property, and the author and his assigns as proprietors. It chooses authorship as the seed of entitlement and it refuses to give any privilege to the members of the Stationers' Company. Proprietors must still provide evidence of their claim by registering with the Company (Section II). But now the register is opened to authors and other non-members and, as a sanction, allows a person excluded from registration the alternative of advertising the fact in the *Gazette* (Section III). That is one anti-monopolistic thrust; another sets up a regime of control over books sold at unreasonable prices (Section IV): a threat indeed, but not one which is known ever to have been put to the test.[7]

How then does the Statute give clothing to these rights? Here, plainly, it derives a good deal from the special powers of the Company during the censorship. First, it provides that 'Offenders' must surrender infringing Copy (books, unbound sheets, etc.) for the proprietor to 'damask and make waste paper of'. Secondly, it imposes a semi-penal forfeit of one penny a sheet, one half to the Crown, the other to the claimant. For the delivery up, it prescribes no procedure; for recovery of the forfeit, it allows process by Action of Debt, Bill, Plaint, or Information, in any Royal Court at Westminster; and, for Scotland, in the Court of Session.[8] True, it does not expressly contemplate the procedures which those courts between

---

[6] One of the allegations against them was that sometimes a member registered an interest in conflict with that deriving from the author.

[7] The Act also instituted the requirement that the printer deliver 9 free copies for the Royal Library and university libraries (s.v.), a *quid pro quo* which has aroused protests from publishers ever since.

[8] Sections I and VI.

them would soon accept: for an injunction in Chancery, and for damages in an action on the case at common law.[9] But despite its split forfeit, well known as an enforcement device in criminal statutes of the day, it is much more than a statute concerned with criminal law redress. The property at its heart is a right tied neither to the author nor to the bookseller. As property it has the essential attribute of being open to assignment and so beyond the common law's general objection to assignments of choses in action as champertous.[10]

Let us for a moment dwell upon Patterson's characterization of the 1710 Act. Why does he see it as the source of a publisher's, rather than an author's, right? He (and, even more, his British follower, John Feather) have shown how the Stationers made much of the running for the new law and how, nevertheless, they had to accept more open trading rules in return for the reinstatement of remedies against pirates.[11] They appear to argue that the author found a place in the new scheme purely, and therefore in some sense incidentally, in order to give legitimacy to the booksellers' victory. If that victory had a price, it consisted mainly in the requirement that all who sought to register a book with the Company must in future trace their title back to the author. By way of demonstration, 'the author' is said to be mentioned very little in the Act.[12] But surely he or she is mentioned quite sufficiently for a momentous new principle to have been admitted: in the very first section, a property in the 'Copy' is stated to exist, and this property arises initially in the author; it may pass only by transfer or transmission from him or her—but it may pass.

The suggestive Section XI may have been accepted grudgingly as an amendment proposed in the House of Lords against the Stationers, but still it formed part of the whole. It contained the remarkable novelty that the duration of the statute's remedies was related to the author's longevity. It was thus a precursor of today's copyright laws around the world, since they measure duration by the author's life and a term of years thereafter. The section provided a reversion of title back from a bookseller-assignee to the author for a second term,[13] thereby suggesting that authors

---

[9] Instances of interlocutory injunctions being granted begin with *Taylor v. Cox* (1719) and *Burnet v. Chetwood* (1720): see Birrell, *Seven Lectures on Copyright* (1899), 101.

[10] On which issue, cf. below, text at n. 35 ff.

[11] Feather, 'The Book Trade in Politics: the Making of the Copyright Act of 1710' (1980) 8 Pub. Hist. 19.

[12] Feather claims that 'except in the preamble, authors were not mentioned at all, and indeed a series of references to authors' rights in the first draft of the Bill was removed in committee, almost certainly under pressure from the trade': above, n. 4, at 74. The first proposition is not correct; the second is curious, given that the book trade played such a significant role in proposing drafts. Cf. the more realistic assessment of Saunders, above, n. 2, 51–7.

[13] Thus Blackstone registered his *Commentaries on the Law of England* himself, then assigned the copyright for the first term; and assigned it again, after surviving for 14 years. The second assignment was 'forever', although it occurred after the Lords had cut copyright down to the statutory term: see below, n. 46.

had a distinct case for legal protection: booksellers could expect 14 years free of piracy for their investment; but authors had a larger personal association with their creations, which at least justified a second term when they were still alive at the end of the first. The Act cannot therefore be read as merely providing a publishers' right. The author had certainly been appropriated to the booksellers' ends, but that was a pattern of behaviour which would repeat itself, not one which would turn out to be at odds with later developments.

The Statute and the Judges

The great consequential issue in the Battle of the Books—explored with such heat and loquacity in and out of court—was also rooted in the inherited practices of the Stationers' Company. Its members continued to deal with the Copy-rights in their Books as indeterminate property, capable of assignment, in whole or in part. Yet soon enough the statutory periods laid down in the Act of 1710 began to expire[14] and other booksellers, many of them provincial, began rival production of books with a lasting popularity.[15] To begin with, the bookseller proprietors, often represented in court by William Murray (afterwards Lord Mansfield),[16] persuaded Chancery that the property in the Copy was a common law entitlement which would continue to attract injunctive relief even after the statutory term had expired. Assuming this to be so, interlocutory injunctions were regularly granted against alleged pirates for a term that would last until the property claim could be tried at common law.[17] Equally, books which had not yet been published were treated as subject to a common law property. Their authors or successors in title were taken to be entitled to damages at common law and so interlocutory relief was granted in Chancery.[18]

In Scotland, however, where publishing businesses were beginning to burgeon, the judges denied there was any proprietary basis in Scots law

[14] For 'old books' in 1731, for 'new books' from 1724 or 1738 onwards.

[15] There was also a growing trade in books from Amsterdam and elsewhere. The 1710 Act, with narrow intent, excluded from its benefits books printed abroad in a classical or foreign language: Section VII.

[16] See below, text at n. 40.

[17] Thus between 1735 and 1739, the 'Copy' owners secured injunctions for *The First Duty of Man* (first published c.1660) (*Eyre v. Walker*); Pope's and Swift's *Miscellanies* (including pieces published between 1702 and 1709) (*Motte v. Falkner*); Nelson's *Festiveals and Fasts* (1703) (*Walthoe v. Walker*); and, most famously, Milton's *Paradise Lost* (1668) (*Tonson v. Walker* in 1739 and again in 1751): for which, see Willes J, *Millar v. Taylor*, below, n. 25, at 2325–6. Interlocutory process did not require the common-law right first to be established by a jury trial. Just as today, the preliminary injunction was usually treated by the parties as disposing of the matter.

[18] *Webb v. Rose* (conveyancing precedents); *Pope v. Curl* (letters to Swift); *Forrester v. Waller* (notes); *Queensberry (Duke) v. Shebbeare* (Lord Clarendon's *History*)—all referred to by Willes J., *Millar v. Taylor*, below, n. 25 , at 2330–1.

for such notions; Roman law, certainly, knew no property in intangibles.[19] Beginning in the 1750s, an intense philosophical and historical debate welled up on the crest of this litigious wave. Pamphlets and essays—some deep, many opinionated, some odd—explored the essential strangeness of conferring legal protection which would prevent unassociated persons from doing something—copying the work—in ways which involved no interference with, or dispossession of, the tangible property of the rightowner.[20] The issue led inevitably to questions about the nature and value of literary creation: what was it that distinguished one book from another—its ideas or its 'style and sentiments'?[21] How original a contribution must it be? Was writing analogous to technical invention? Or to visual artistry or musical composition? In the course of the ferment appeared Edward Young's *Conjectures on Original Composition* (1759), which dignified authorship as a 'noble title' properly conferred on the work of the 'mind of a man of Genius'. It proved to be an essay of deep appeal to Herder and Goethe, Kant, and Fichte.[22] They would construct from it that supremely German theory of the Romantic author, which Coleridge would eventually press upon English consciousness.[23]

Some of these enthusiasms found their way into the language of judgments. Indeed, after various feints,[24] in *Millar v. Taylor*, the King's Bench eventually confirmed the correctness at common law of the Chancellors' assumption: copyright was unlimited in time, the Statute merely providing its special sanctions for a limited period.[25] This was unquestionably

---

[19] The London booksellers began process against the Edinburgh booksellers in 1746 (*Midwinter v. Hamilton*), which eventually reached the House of Lords (*sub nom Millar v. Kincaid*): see esp., Tompson, 'Scottish Judges and the Birth of British Copyright' [1992] Jur. Rev 18. Tompson explores the impact of increasing competition from Edinburgh, Dublin, and a few provincial cities, as well as from Amsterdam and elsewhere; and the consequent tension between the Benches in Edinburgh and London.

[20] See Rose (above, n. 2), ch. 7; Saunders (above, n. 2), 69–74.

[21] This theme would develop to give the modern dichotomy between unprotectible ideas and their protectible expression. It is stressed particularly by Blackstone in his *Commentaries* (II, 405–06), when making the case for a perpetual right to publish at common law.

[22] Kant develops an embracing theory of the innate and inalienable right of the author to publish his work. The publisher is treated as a mere agent to produce copies: *Von der Unregelmässigkeit des Büchernachdrucks* (1785).

[23] See esp. Strömholm, *Le droit moral de l'auteur* (1966) I; Woodmansee, 'The Genius and the Copyright' (1984), Eighteenth Century Studies, 425; Rose (above, n. 2), 115–24; Saunders (above, n. 2), 23–9 and ch. 4.; Strowel, '*Liberté, propriété, originalité: Retour aux sources du droit d'auteur*', in Libois and Strowel, *Profils de la Création* (1997), 141.

[24] Most evidently in the first case to be taken to King's Bench, *Tonson v. Collins* (1763) 4 Burr. 2327: a reference of the issue to all the common law judges had to be abandoned, when it become transparent that the booksellers were running a collusive action to get their hoped-for answer out of Mansfield's court.

[25] (1769) 4 Burr. 2303. The book selected for action was James Thompson's pastoral idyll, *The Seasons*, remembered today as providing the text for Josef Haydn's *Die Jahreszeiten*. The poet himself was responsible for publishing it in the late 1720s; he then assigned the rights to the bookseller, Millar, in 1730. The statutory term thus expired in the 1750s, but it continued to be reprinted most regularly.

Lord Mansfield's view and he carried two of his *puisnes* (Justices Willes and Ashton) with him; but he had to suffer the indignity of a dissent from Mr Justice Yates.[26] In the judgments, considerable learning was exhibited on both sides. To the arguments we return in a moment.

Had matters been left there, in England the judges would have trimmed the Statute of Anne to form a measure giving enhanced powers of enforcement for 14 or 28 years from publication; but common-law copyright would have been an untrimmed and abundant right flourishing without limit, just as other property. A dichotomy of undeniable significance would have been stamped on the law.

Almost immediately, however, a Chancery decision, which granted an injunction on the basis of the decision in *Millar v. Taylor*, was appealed to the House of Lords. In this great cause, *Donaldson v. Becket(t)*,[27] the English judges were consulted by the Lords. From the five questions put to them individually, it became clear that the division previously shown among the King's Bench judges existed also among the members of the other two Courts of Common Law.[28] At that time, however, the appellate chamber was still composed of the whole House and the arguments attracted unusual attention. Mansfield's great opponent, Lord Camden,[29] delivered an impassioned denunciation of the Stationers' claim to a perpetual right.[30] Intriguingly—for commentators at the time, and forever after—Mansfield did not intervene.[31] He had an astute sense that issues of high controversy should be settled by legislation, rather than by judicial decision, and that

[26] Joseph Yates, who had been counsel put up for the defendant in *Tonson v. Collins*, had not previously clashed so publicly with Mansfield. Within a year, he had taken refuge on the Bench of the friendlier Common Pleas; but he had soon to withdraw for ill health. He accordingly gave no Opinion to the Lords in *Donaldson v. Becket*.

[27] Accounts of parts of the Lords proceedings are to be found in (1774) 2 Brown P.C. 129; Supplement to *Millar v. Taylor* (above, n. 25); 17 Parl. Hist. 953; and in contemporary newspapers—for all of which, see Tompson (above, n. 19), 31–8; Rose (above, n.2), ch. 6.

[28] While there was virtual unanimity that until publication the common law gave a right to prevent reproduction, there was almost an equal division on the crucial question: did the Statute of Anne curtail the duration of any common law right after publication to its prescribed term. Though the record of the Lords' clerk is that Nares J. voted against any survival of the right, contemporary records suggest that he spoke to the contrary and some error (or possibly manipulation) occurred. In any case, there was a complication, for those who objected to a perpetual right, in that they might consider the common law right itself ended with publication, or they might hold that this right continued but was limited by the Statute—the difference was not of the first water. See Abrams, 'The Historic Foundation of American Copyright Law: Exploding the Myth of Common Law Copyright' (1983) 29 Wayne State L.R. 1119; Rose (above, n. 2), App. B.

[29] Charles Pratt, formerly, C. J. of the Common Pleas and LC 1766–70. Apsley L. C., who had granted the injunction under appeal in consequence of *Millar v. Taylor*, had no compunction in then speaking against it: cf. Burrows' explanation of Mansfield's silence: below, n. 31.

[30] 17 Parl. Hist. 992–1002.

[31] Burrows, famously, offers the view that, the case being effectively an appeal from *Millar v. Taylor*, 'reasons of delicacy' required Mansfield not to repeat his view (4 Burr. 4117); for contemporary comment, Rose (above, n. 2), 100–2, Tompson (above n. 19), 35–6.

perhaps drew him back.[32] The House proceeded to vote against Mansfield's position.[33] The Stationers did indeed promote a Bill to reverse the result of the case, but they got nowhere.[34] Britain accordingly gave not only its American and other colonies, but also the continent of Europe, the example of author-based copyright, which nonetheless would be limited in duration, so that in time a public interest in free expression and open access to knowledge would prevail over proprietary claims to a work.

Rationalizing the Outcome

The decision of the Lords was like the verdict of a jury—a resolution that the injunction against the defendant should be lifted—and not a reasoned statement of the extent, if any, to which there could be a 'property' in the reproduction of books or, indeed, in any other embodiment of intellectual activity. It has about it a blankness which nonplusses the historian of ideas. As far as legal sources are concerned, there has accordingly been a tendency to pay greater attention to the extended traverses of the battleground undertaken by the King's Bench judges in *Millar v. Taylor*. A majority of the judges in that court favoured recognizing that authors and their successors had a perpetual common law right of property in the copying of their books, and that perhaps has given credence to the proposition that the judges had converted the Statute from a publishers' protection into an author's right. The prime difficulty, however, is that the Lords' vote rejects this thesis. Much more attention accordingly deserves to be given to Mr Justice Yates's elaborate dissenting judgment in *Millar v. Taylor*, since that is the main reasoned statement from the Bench which supports the position at the end of *Donaldson v. Becket*.[35] In it, three main strands are woven: the principled, the historical, and the consequential.

The argument of principle had been the stuff of much of the pamphleteering: could the sole right to reproduce books—a right to claim against those who did so without license—ever constitute property, or was property a notion that only had meaning in relation to tangible objects? Yates

---

[32] Exhibited equally in his refusal to debate with Camden the propriety of his view that the seditious nature of a publication ought to be left to the judge, not the jury, as expressed in *Woodfall* (1770) 5 Burr. 2661; and in his refusal to rule generally on the status of slaves at common law: cf. *Somersett's Case* (1773) 20 St. Tr. 1. Tompson notes that *Millar v. Taylor* looked suspiciously like a collusion set up by the London Stationers (cf. n. 24, above) and speculates that this may have been a real embarrassment to Mansfield: (above, n. 19), at 36.

[33] Probably no formal tally of votes was taken, though one source recorded 22–11 against the injunction: see Rose (above, n. 2) at 102.

[34] The Stationers also lost their joint claim to a highly valuable prerogative patent on the printing of all almanacks: *Stationers Company v. Carnan* (1775) 2 W. Black. 1004. The Universities, together with Eton, Westminster, and Winchester, fared better with the Legislature, getting the privilege of perpetual copyrights in certain books by 15 Geo. III c. 53.

[35] We lack any verbatim record of what the judges said by way of advice to the Lords in that case. We do have the arguments of counsel and the speeches by Camden and the few other members of the Lords who spoke.

had no doubt that in the common law the concept of property could arise only in tangible things—land and movables.[36] The same conceptual constraint upon the idea of property would recur in other legal systems, forcing them into *sui generis* categorizations of those rights of protection over ideas and trading symbols which they wished nevertheless to establish. In Yates' hands the denial of intangible property is used to provide a particular explanation of the protection against the pirate copying of unpublished work which both Chancery and common law had acknowledged, and which almost all the English judges would continue to regard as a necessity.

At common law, property unquestionably existed in the physical record of the work. Yates considered it a proper attribute of that property that unauthorized copying of its contents should be regarded as wrongful. But when the owner of the manuscript authorized publication, this dedicated the work to the public as a gift. A copyist no longer had to rely on the original for a source and common law could therefore offer no protection to the author or his publisher. If any property was to be acknowledged in the expressed ideas, it would have to be created by statute or under the Royal Prerogative by letters patent. This is what had happened for 14-year terms in the case of invention patents,[37] and was also allowed for published books by the Statute of Anne.

Yates also insisted that there were no historical precedents to undermine his basic proposition.[38] He denied categorically that common law had already accepted a separate property in the Copy of a book before or after its publication. The internal trade customs of the Stationers could not be allowed to settle what the common law, as a matter of principle, could provide, and nothing in the Statute of Anne preserved any such right: certainly not Section IX when it preserved the Copy-rights of the Universities and other persons since this must be read as a reference to printing rights granted under letters patent. Pre-1710 case law likewise gave relief only for such patent rights, and not on any basis of common law property.

Yates' purpose was to deny a confection of historical reference—the first of many attempts at copyright cookery—which was undertaken with great labour for the majority by Mr Justice Willes.[39] This view was somewhat sweepingly endorsed by Mansfield from his long experience in

[36] See esp. 4 Burr at 2361–7, 2384–7.

[37] The parallel was the stronger in that the Statute of Monopolies 1624 excepted not only invention patents (s. 6) but also printing patents (s. 10): see 4 Burr. 2386–9.

[38] 4 Burr, at 2367–84.

[39] 4 Burr, at 2310–35. The historical case for a common law property from before the Statute of Anne did not die with the Battle of the Books, but tended to recur whenever a broadening of copyright was being pressed. Scrutton made much of it in his Yorke Prize essay, published as *The Law of Copyright* (4th edn. 1903) ch. 1; and it was taken up by Osterrieth, *Eine Geschichte des Urheberrechts in England* (1895), chs 1–5; cf. the even robuster attitude of Birrell, *Seven Lectures on Copyright* (1898).

acting for Stationer-plaintiffs (to which he was pleased to refer). So far as doctrine was concerned, Mansfield started at once on Yates' main weakness. All the King's Bench accepted that the common law had developed a right to protect the Copy of a book before publication—the period for which the Statute made no provision. Yet Yates' rationale—that this was an attribute of property in the physical manuscript—was insufficient. Cases were well-enough known where the copier had been given or lent the manuscript or had memorized its contents. There must, therefore, be a separate property to stop the activity of copying; and if there was a copy-property before publication, what objection in principle could there be to its continuance afterwards—indeed forever afterwards, since property at common law was by nature indeterminate?[40]

Behind all the amassing of precedent and the resort to principle, lay judgments about practical consequences. Mansfield and Yates—the old adversaries—were frank about what really moved them. Mansfield began from a Lockeian association of property and labour and therefore built up an argument about, 'the principles of right and wrong, the fitness of things, convenience, and policy as they applied to the author', starting with common law right in an unpublished manuscript:

. . . it is just that an author should reap the pecuniary profits of his own ingenuity and labour. It is just, that another should not use his name, without his consent. It is fit that he should judge when to publish, or whether he ever will publish. It is fit he should not only choose the time, but the manner of publication; how many; what volume; what point. It is fit, he should choose to whose care he will entrust the accuracy and correctness of the impression; in whose honesty he will confide, not to foist in additions; with other reasonings to the same effect.[41]

In Mansfield's view, this right, plainly admitted before publication, must equally survive it. The author's interests—in modern terms both economic and moral—remained just as important after appearance and the common law was indeed protecting the author, not the bookseller:

The author may not only be deprived of any profit, but lose the expence he has been at. He is no more master of the use of his own name. He has no control over the correctness of his own work. He can not prevent additions. He can not retract errors. He can not amend; or cancel a faulty edition. Any one may print, pirate and perpetuate the imperfections, to the disgrace and against the will of the author; may propagate sentiments under his name, which he disapproves, is ashamed of. He can exercise no discretion as to the manner in which, or the persons by whom his work shall be published.[42]

In this fine rhetoric, Mansfield deals only with the damage which a pirate might inflict. He chooses to ignore the fact that in many dealings with the booksellers of the day, the author would have no continuing pecuniary

---

[40] 4 Burr., at 2395–8.   [41] ibid., at 2398.   [42] ibid.

interest in returns. Nor would he be likely to retain legal control over disfigurements which the authorized publisher might choose to introduce into editions, if the agreement did not contain special terms of protection.

Yates takes to the same path, but with a sceptical swing to his stick:

> It is of use, certainly, that learning and science and all valuable improvements should be encouraged, and every man's labour properly rewarded. But every reward has its proper bound: and an entire monopoly for fourteen, or if the author remains alive, for twenty-eight years, seems encouragement enough for his labours: at least the Legislature have thought it sufficient encouragement to them; and have expressly declared 'they shall have it no longer'. . . . If the encouragement which the Legislature has given will not satisfy authors, it is not our province to extend it further. But I can never entertain so disgraceful an opinion of learned men, as to imagine the profits of publication of twenty-eight years will not content them.[43]

With a nice irony, he then lists the evils which might flow if *authors* were to retain an indefinite right. They might use it to suppress publication; and this could not be adequately met by any vague counter-principle of 'abandonment' (of any claim through failure to assert the right). They might use the right to fix an exorbitant price; and the price-reduction provision of the Statute of Anne would be 'totally nugatory' in face of an exclusive right in the 'authors and their assignees' (only at this point do the booksellers make their debut). The authors' claim is to a monopoly, which is counterpoised against the 'natural rights of mankind in the exercise of their trade and calling'. According to Mr Justice Yates:

> It is every man's natural right, to follow a lawful employment for the support of himself and his family. Printing and bookselling are lawful employments. And therefore every monopoly that would intrench upon these lawful employments is a restraint upon the liberty of the subject. And if printing and selling of every book that comes out, may be confined to a few, and for ever with-held from all the rest of the trade; what provision will the bulk of them be able to make for their respective families?[44]

And with his culminating cut, Yates lays bare the 'dangerous snares' in an 'ideal property' which is subject neither to notification nor registration:

> . . . so obscure a property (especially after the work has been a long while published) might lead many booksellers into many litigations: and in such litigations, many doubtful questions might arise.[45]

Though he would not himself remain long on the bench, Yates would find compelling support in the Lords' disposal of *Donaldson v. Becket*, and Mansfield's game was lost for good.[46] In what sense, then, could this

---

[43] *ibid.*, at 2391–2.   [44] *ibid.*, at 2393–4.   [45] *ibid.*, at 2394.

[46] Nonetheless, the practice among members of the Stationers Company of treating rights as perpetual undoubtedly continued into the 19th century.

outcome be said to demonstrate the attainment of an author's right, to be distinguished from the publishers' right of the Statute of Anne?[47] The cases which reached court were not, for the most part, brought by authors. They were launched by publishers who had duly secured their rights by assignment from authors and registration with the Stationers' Company. The legitimacy of the booksellers' claim to perpetual rights lay in large part in the established trade practice of dealing in rights on that assumption. The underlying issue was as clearly about the protection of their investment and trade, as had been the case for better protection against pirates in 1710. It is true that the case law added specificity to the statutory right of property by making clear that a common law action on the case lay for damages, and that in consequence equity would grant an injunction to protect that property. This was more extensive in the sense that the author might rely upon it to protect the work against piracy from the moment of its creation, and so independently of registration or actual publication.

But that is the only real sense in which the courts expanded the rights. In 1774, as in 1710, the booksellers were permitted their annexation of the creators' moral high-ground, but only on terms which gave considerable scope for countervailing interests of other writers, traders, and the purchasing public. What they secured was perhaps a mystification which veiled the relentless commodification at work. But equally there was a necessary cohesion of interest between creator and exploiter against the parasytic operations of the Copy-pirate. It was this perception of the matter which received reasonably generous, but by no means overwhelming, recognition.

The Consequences

If Lord Mansfield, and the other judges who followed him, had not lost the Battle of the Books, theirs would indeed have been a truly distinct and striking contribution and talk of a dichotomy of entitlements would have transparent meaning. Since it would have remained a controversial outcome, courts could not but have felt pressure to cut back the scope of the perpetual common law right. They might then have shown greater interest in ideas floated in the contemporary debate: should this copyright, for instance, be limited to truly serious and worthy works? Should it be infringed only by exact and directly competing reproductions? Should there be a wide notion of fair use, or of abandonment? Should price control be made into a regular system?

---

[47] Assuming, contrary to my argument above, that the Statute in essence embodied only such a right.

Thanks, however, to the Lords' vote in *Donaldson v. Becket,*, the essential issues of copyright were regarded as settled for many decades.[48] As so often with the resolution of great conflicts in law, the courts did not feel obliged to adopt all the strictures of Mr Justice Yates. They did treat the pre-publication right against copying as a distinct property, not tied to ownership or possession of the manuscript or original, and capable of being assigned in ways which would not have been possible if the right were purely personal to the author. They also continued to treat the 'Copy' during the Statute's periods as the subject of both common law and equitable remedies beyond those mentioned expressly in the Statute. In the eyes of some this represented a compromise with proper principle; but because it so substantially curbed the claims of the Stationers it was broadly accepted.

Copyright was extended in increasingly generous measure to works which fell within the term 'book' in the Statute or within the other definitions of protected works which would be later introduced by enactment. The plaintiff's work had only to satisfy a minimal level of creativity, so legal protection was available to writers all the way from Genius to Scribbler, and indeed Compiler of the most basic information. A decently opaque doctrine, drawn in terms of 'substantial copying', would allow wider protection for substantial works than for mundane productions; and it could be assumed that, when Parliament did agree to extend the duration of statutory copyright,[49] this would mainly affect great works, since they alone had long commercial lives. The extraordinary qualities of the greatest authors, in due course elevated by the mysteries of Romantic theory, thus gained a particular recognition, but the same form of protection was left open to much more ephemeral producers. The proprietary nature of the right made it endlessly adaptable to conditions of joint authorship and joint ownership, enabling the various forms of exploitation which came within the range of protection to be carved up in ever more varied ways.

THE HISTORY IN TODAY'S DEBATES

For a whole range of reasons, it remains important to understand the genesis of British copyright. In the blossoming era of digitization, the concept

---

[48] Sherman and Bently (above, n. 2), ch. 1. There is substantial evidence that members of the Stationers Company continued, for a half-century or more, to deal with copyrights amongst themselves on a basis of perpetual entitlement. The cartel had an enduring strength, given the limitations and expense of printing technology and distribution.

[49] As would occur for literary and musical works in 1842 (42 years, or the author's life plus 7 years, whichever was longer), and then, under Continental influence, in the Imperial copyright of 1911 (life plus 50 years, as required by the 1908 amendment to the Berne Convention on Literary and Artistic Works).

is as enmeshed in disputation as ever. Those who proclaim a brave new world of free, entwined communication do battle with commodity producers struggling frantically to secure returns on their promotions despite the technical difficulties of keeping copyright and contractual shackles in place. At every turn, conceptual and consequential rationalizations affect the course of legal developments.

In the eighteenth century, the author as a commercial operator was a novel being. Writers were either hacks who were paid off in a lump, or scions of the leisured class who were published without much counting of cost, let alone return. The middle-ranking author who looked to make a living from her skills was only just beginning to seek that special form of risk-taking represented by royalties on sales. Little wonder then that it was the booksellers who made all the running for greater legal protection against copy-pirates, and who annexed the moral respectability of authorship to their own interests. Indeed, what is more remarkable is the extent to which the same pattern of development has tended to repeat itself whenever copyright reform has been at issue.

Until this century, there has been no pressing cause to divide authors from their investors and each has derived a good deal from the other. Today, authors stand more evidently on their own in a triangular relationship with investors and users.

Once joint action became necessary in order to collect performing and other royalties, authors tended to form their own collecting societies and to keep publishers and producers firmly down in their ranks, if not out of them altogether. The growth of actors' and musicians' trade unions has in some countries been followed by writers', artists', and composers' unions.

In addition, modern copying technology has generated situations in which it is not sufficient for investors to rely solely on exclusive rights assigned or licensed from authors: record companies have been troubled with bootlegged tapes of music which is not their copyright; publishers have re-launched material which is out of copyright. Even those Continental systems which have leaned most definitely in favour of 'true' authors' rights have been obliged to introduce shorter-term 'related' or 'neighbouring' rights. For the most part these are conferred directly on the producer or other investor.[50] Occasionally the representatives of these industries have been tempted to argue that it is now time to abandon any reliance on rights deriving from the author, in favour of protection deriving from investment. While that might do something to undercut the bar-

---

[50] An intermediate case has been that of performers. In Britain, typically, rights in performances are now conferred not only on the performers themselves but also on investors who hold exclusive recording contracts with them: see the Copyright, Designs and Patents Act 1988, Pt II.

gaining position of authors, it could easily lead to protection for a much shorter period, such as typically has been conferred on related rights. It is not therefore a case which captures much of a following.

The proper relation of creator to investor in the development of copyright remains as much a preoccupation as ever. Consider, for instance, the need for protection of catalogues and databases.

The result of the Battle of the Books was reflected soon enough afterwards in Article 1, Sect. 8, of the United States Constitution, which gave Congress power 'to promote the Progress of Science and the Useful Arts, by securing for limited times to authors and inventors the exclusive right to their respective writings and discoveries'. Recently, the Supreme Court has found it necessary to insist that the 'writings of authors' introduces a test of substantive originality as a constitutional requisite of copyright enacted under this power.[51] Picking up the tenor of Patterson's argument, Justice O'Connor refused to allow that copyright could extend to the amassing of factual information, as in a 'White Pages' telephone book, where no intellectual discrimination was at work. 'Sweat of the brow' was not enough; copyright was not available for everyone who invested in writings expressed in language or symbols.[52]

That small insistence in the US—equivalent to the need in civilian systems to show a modicum of 'personal creativity' for there to be authorship[53]—comes at a highly inconvenient time. For digital processing has sent data collection into orbit, but not an orbit which is costless. There is therefore a case for protecting those who set up databases from the predations of free copyists. The reason is the old one: that if no protection is given the data will often go uncollected. In consequence, the European Union has had to create a new 'related' right for database producers, which, in the spirit of the times, may well prove to be positively Mansfieldian in its generosity.[54] In the United States, as in negotiations on the international stage (the two things often go hand in hand), it is proving very difficult to procure any solution at all.

For all that it was a close-run thing, the eighteenth century story teaches the virtues of practical compromise. The view which prevailed in the

---

[51] *Feist Publications v. Rural Telephone Service*, 499 US 340 (1991).

[52] In the UK, by contrast, 'sweat of the brow' copyright has long been allowed. English judges treat work as 'original' whenever it is not copied.

[53] The European Commission has campaigned steadily for the inclusion of such a concept in the emergent European law of copyright, achieving its first expression in the Software Directive (91/250), Art. 1(3); not that the British Government was moved to do anything about it by way of implementation on that occasion. It has been obliged to do so since in respect of copyright in databases (as distinct from the separate right for database producers mentioned at n. 54): see the Database Directive (9/96) as implemented by the UK Copyright and Rights in Databases Regulations 1997.

[54] Both in its definition of protectible databases and in its provision allowing for further terms of copyright protection whenever there is substantial revision of the original base—in effect a perpetual quasi-copyright.

Battle of the Books was that no great harm flows from accepting the basic linkages of interest between author and publisher as a justification for a property right of 'Copy'.

11

Due Process and Wager of Law: Judicial Conservatism in the Tudor Common Pleas

J. H. Baker

> Tombs have their periods, monuments decay
> And rust and age wear epitaphs away
> But neither rust nor age nor time shall wear
> Judge WALMSLEY's name that lies entombèd here
> Who never did for favour nor for awe
> Of great men's frowns quit or forsake the law.
> His inside was his outside. He ne'er sought
> To make fair shows of what he never thought . . .[1]

These words inscribed on the tomb of Mr Justice Walmsley (d. 1612), formerly in Blackburn Church, Lancashire, make but a transparently veiled reference to the judge's well-known qualities as a judicial conservative and habitual dissentient.[2] Walmsley was imbued with a blunt, robust common sense strongly reminiscent of Lord Bramwell. In his heyday he was the leader, and in his latter years the last surviving loser, of the intellectual struggle between his own court (the Common Pleas) and the King's Bench over recent developments in the common law. He was opposed to the use of *assumpsit* to supplant the action of debt; to other new uses for actions on the case, and (it seems) to most new-fangled things,[3] and was not too confident about the new religion. He dissented in *Chudleigh's Case* (1594),[4] *Pinnel's Case* (1602),[5] *Manning's Case* (1608),[6] *Calvin's Case* (1608),[7]

---

[1] 'Judge Walmsleys epitaph', copied by White Kennett (1724) in British Library ('BL') MS. Lansdowne 973, fo. 45v (rendered into modern orthography). Dr D. Ibbetson reports that there is a contemporary copy in the Lancashire Record Office.

[2] For his dissents, see J. H. Baker, *The Legal Profession and the Common Law* (London: The Hambledon Press, 1987), 194, 209, 412–13. Coke sometimes edited Walmsley out of his *Reports*, so it is necessary to search the better MS reports for his views.

[3] See, e.g., Were's reports, BL MS. Hargrave 7, fo. 41 (1596), where he rebuked the serjeants for not using the old forms of oral pleading when drawing recoveries at the bar.

[4] 1 Co. Rep. 120. Here Peryam C.B. (a former Common Pleas colleague) dissented with him. For this case, see A. W. B. Simpson, *A History of the Land Law*, 2nd edn. (Oxford: Oxford University Press, 1986), 218–20.

[5] 1 Co. Rep. 132 (not mentioning the dissent); *The Legal Profession and the Common Law*, 194.

[6] 8 Co. Rep. 94; Simpson, *History of the Land Law*, 221–3.

[7] This dissent was mentioned in his epitaph (n. 1, above).

and others;[8] and he registered an angry protest against *Slade's Case* (1602),[9] in which he had hoped to deliver a resounding dissent.[10] Rather more remarkably, in 1598, he was the only judge to dissent from the decision that the Chancery could not reopen judgments given at common law.[11] A biography would be very useful, since history has a natural tendency to lean towards the victors; but the losing voice deserves at least to be heard and understood.

When we find hints of an ill-tempered relationship between Walmsley and Sir Edward Coke, following Coke's appointment as Chief Justice of the Common Pleas in 1606,[12] we might well attribute the clash to strong personalities—just as we are inclined to attribute the great 1616 dispute between the King's Bench and the Chancery to the incompatible characters of Coke and Ellesmere, and the grasping opportunism of Bacon.[13] Yet this will not do. The doctrinal or philosophical differences between the two benches did not arise in the time of Walmsley, but had been inherited from the last days of the Year Books. Indeed, there is some reason for tracing them back to the long tenure of Sir Thomas Bryan as Chief Justice of the Common Pleas (1471–1500), at a time when the King's Bench under Sir John Fyneux was beginning to exploit actions on the case to expand its business.[14]

There have always been conservative as well as innovative judges. But why Westminster Hall should have divided north and south in this way remains something of a mystery. At one time it might have been convenient to regard the debate about actions on the case as a constitutional debate. The Magna Carta guaranteed that common pleas should not 'follow the King', which meant that actions of debt should not be brought in

---

[8] See *The Legal Profession and the Common Law*, 194.

[9] 4 Co. Rep. 91; A. W. B. Simpson, 'The Place of *Slade's Case* in the History of Contract' (1958) 74 L.Q.R. 381; J. H. Baker, 'New Light on *Slade's Case*', reprinted in *The Legal Profession and the Common Law*, 393–432; D. Ibbetson, 'Sixteenth-Century Contract Law: *Slade's Case* in Context' (1984) 4 O.J.L.S. 295.

[10] Popham C.J. had declined to allow the judges to deliver their individual opinions in the Exchequer Chamber. See *Wright v. Swanton* (1604), printed from 3 different texts in J. H. Baker and S. F. C. Milsom, *Sources of English Legal History* (London: Butterworths, 1986) ('Baker & Milsom'), 442–3.

[11] *Finch v. Throgmorton* (1598), as reported in Coke's MS reports, BL MS. Harley 6686, fo. 228; *The Legal Profession and the Common Law*, 208–9.

[12] See the telling interchange in *Maine v. Peacher* (1610) Cambridge University Library MS. Gg. 4. 9, fo. 38 (trans. in Baker & Milsom, 454), where Coke C.J. more or less accused him of dissenting for the sake of it. Perhaps Walmsley sometimes stayed away from court: see his letter to Coke in 1609, where he excuses himself from taking part in a prohibition case on grounds of age (Yale Law School MS. G. R24.1, fo. 83).

[13] See 'The Common Lawyers and the Chancery: 1616' in *The Legal Profession and the Common Law*, 205–29. The dispute arose from the assertion by Lord Ellesmere C. of an equitable jurisdiction to grant a common injunction *after* judgment had been given at common law, a procedure which Coke and the judges held to be illegal.

[14] This is beyond the scope of the present chapter.

the King's Bench. The use of *assumpsit* to recover debts was therefore contrary to the great charter of liberties.[15] But this will not do as an explanation either.[16] Not only is it never mentioned by Mr Justice Walmsley and his fellows, but, as we now know, the *communia placita* provision of Magna Carta had been a dead letter since the fifteenth century as a result of the fictitious bill of Middlesex. Actions of debt had been entertained by the King's Bench for at least 50 years before *assumpsit* was adapted for the purpose.[17]

How else can the phenomenon of a bipartite judiciary be explained? The judges of both benches were drawn from the same order of serjeants, and there is no obvious reason why conservatives should have been separated-out for the Common Pleas across a period of 60 years or more; nor is it easy to attribute attitudes to the influence of a strong chief justice, since the period of conservatism continued through the tenures of at least eight of them.[18] It seems more probable that it was the court which somehow made its institutional influence felt on the judges who came to it, and this may have been facilitated by the existence of two serjeants' inns: the Common Pleas judges usually joined the Fleet Street inn; while their brethren from the King's Bench went to Chancery Lane. That arrangement still obtained in Walmsley's time,[19] but went back at least to the 1530s.[20] Why the Common Pleas—or the Fleet Street inn—should have continuously inclined against innovation is not known for certain at present, but it may simply have been a natural counterbalance to the activism of the King's Bench, which needed to attract business to survive,[21] while its older sister had more than enough work to keep it busy.

[15] For explanations along these lines, but not underlining the constitutional aspect, see C. H. S. Fifoot, *History and Sources of the Common Law* (London: Stevens & Sons Ltd, 1949), 359; T. F. T. Plucknett, *Concise History of the Common Law* (5th edn., London: Butterworths, 1956), 644–5; A. Harding, *A Social History of English Law* (Harmondsworth, Middlesex: Penguin Books, 1966), 104.

[16] Cf., to the same effect, A. W. B. Simpson, *A History of the Common Law of Contract: the rise of the action of assumpsit* (Oxford: Oxford University Press, 1975), 294–5.

[17] The King's Bench was acknowledged to have a jurisdiction in personal actions (e.g. debt) over those in its custody. The bill of Middlesex was a device to secure the arrest of an alleged debtor on a fictitious complaint of a trespass, whereupon the prisoner could be sued by bill of debt and the trespass suit dropped before its falseness was tried. The trespass was laid in Middlesex so that the suit could be commenced by bill rather than by writ, the bill procedure being available for cases arising in the county where the King's Bench sat. See J. H. Baker, *Introduction to English Legal History* (London: Butterworths, 3rd edn., 1990), 49–51.

[18] There were 14 between Bryan C.J. (d. 1500) and Coke C.J. (appointed 1606). For the conservatism of Dyer C. J. (1559–82) see 109 Selden Soc., intro., xxvi–xxvii.

[19] Walmsley's only judicial colleagues known to have belonged to the Chancery Lane inn were Beaumont (1593–8), Glanville (1598–1600), and Winch (1611–25). Kingsmill J.'s inn is not known. Warburton J. seems to have belonged at different times to both inns, and it is possible that more migrations occurred. See J. H. Baker, *The Order of Serjeants at Law* (1984), Appx. IV.

[20] See *The Reports of Sir John Spelman*, vol. II (94 Selden Soc., 1978), intro., 136–7.

[21] See M. Blatcher, *The Court of King's Bench 1450–1550: a study in self-help* (London: Athlone Press, 1978).

The object of the present essay is not finally to solve the riddle, but to pin down more precisely than has hitherto been attempted the beginning of the dispute between the courts over the use of *assumpsit* in lieu of debt. That was by no means the only point of divergence,[22] but it was to be the most troublesome and has left the most visible traces. Debt has always been the largest category of civil lawsuits, and yet the action of debt was very unsatisfactory unless the creditor had the security of a deed. The principal defect in the action of debt on a contract was that the defendant was in most cases entitled to 'wage his law'—that is, to take an oath that he did not owe the money and to produce eleven 'compurgators' or 'wager-men' to support the oath. The wager-men were usually hired hands, and therefore wager of law operated as an effective bar to a debt claim without any trial of the merits. From the first decade of the sixteenth century, experiments were being made with a new form of *assumpsit* action which would enable a debt to be recovered in the guise of damages for breach of a promise to pay money.

ASSUMPSIT FOR MONEY: THE KING'S BENCH

The first judgments so far discovered in *assumpsit* on a contract to pay money are in the King's Bench rolls for 1520.[23] No less than four are found in the same year, which can hardly be a coincidence. Three of them, however, were cases where the writ of debt did not lie, and so they did not raise the problem of overlapping remedies. The first case was an action to recover damages for the value of foreign currency due to the plaintiff in exchange for English money.[24] The second case, for which there were precedents of declarations going back to the time of Henry VII, was that of the surety. *Cleymond v. Vincent* is well known, because it was reported in the Year Books and also in Port's notebook.[25] It was an action to enforce a

---

[22] An early example of divergence in another area is found in the context of defamation. In 1535 the Common Pleas refused to allow an action in respect of an accusation of heresy, as being a spiritual matter, but in 1536 the King's Bench allowed one: 94 Selden Soc., intro., 241–2; Baker & Milsom, 626–7. For Dyer C.J.'s opposition to the use of ejectment to try freehold title, see 109 Selden Soc., intro., xxvi–xxvii.

[23] The earlier precedents are of actions which did not proceed as far as judgment: see, generally, 94 Selden Soc., intro., 275–86.

[24] *Blanke v. Spinula* (1520) KB 27/1036, m. 75 (£104 recovered). The case was cited by Tanfield in *Slade's Case*, and seems to have been the earliest judgment which he could find: see *The Legal Profession and the Common Law*, 400.

[25] *Cleymond v. Vyncent* (1520–1) KB 27/1037, m. 40 (printed with trans. in 102 Selden Soc. 10–13; copied in Robert Maycote's entries, Library of Congress, MS. Phillipps 9071, fo. 37; and in Robert Catlyn's precedent book, Alnwick Castle MS. 475, ff. 52v–53v); Y.B. Mich. 12 Hen. VIII, fo. 11, pl. 3 (extract trans. in Baker & Milsom, 446–7); *The Notebook of Sir John Port* (102 Selden Soc., 1986), 10. See also Simpson, *History of the Common Law of Contract*, 265, above n. 16.

surety for the price of six barrels of salted salmon, but it was brought
against the executrix of the surety, and so there were two separate reasons
why debt was unavailable. Debt did not lie against personal representatives, unless there was a bond, and in any case the obligation of a surety
was not regarded as a debt. The King's Bench approved the action, and a
remark made by Mr Justice More shows that it may have been influenced
by the existence of similar remedies in the city of London courts.[26] The
Year Book reporter added a query whether the action would have lain
against the testator himself. That question was informally answered the
same term, when judgment was given against a surety,[27] followed soon
afterwards by a judgment in favour of a surety seeking an indemnity from
his principal.[28]

It is the fourth case which should have been reported. The plaintiff there
counted on a bargain to buy wheat, an undertaking by the defendant to
pay the price, and delivery of the wheat by the plaintiff, and then alleged
that the defendant—'scheming wickedly and maliciously to deceive the
plaintiff' of his bargain, and of the money—refused to pay.[29] In addition
to the deceit, which was now becoming a common-form allegation in all
actions on the case, the plaintiff, for good measure, added elements of consequential loss (in that he could no longer profit from the wheat which he
had delivered, and had also incurred expenses). Yet here, in reality, was
nothing more than a debt. If *assumpsit* could be brought in a case such as
this, there would no longer be any need to use debt, and wager of law
could be effectively avoided.

The plea roll does not reveal whether the fourth case prompted any
legal challenge in court in 1520, but the new incursion of *assumpsit* into the
territory of debt was certainly challenged the following year when a
slightly more elaborate declaration was made in a similar case. A vintner
complained that he had discussed the sale of some wine with the defendant's wife, that the defendant (knowing of this) requested the plaintiff to
sell and deliver the wine, promising to pay £23. 6s. 8d. within six months;
the plaintiff, trusting in the promise, delivered the wine and received 30
shillings in part payment; but the defendant, scheming to defraud the

[26] Port's notebook, 102 Selden Soc. 10 (trans. in Baker & Milsom, 447).

[27] *Grafton v. Bold* (1520) KB 27/1037, m. 88d. It is not known whether this case was discussed by the judges. *Assumpsit* against a surety was formally approved by the King's Bench,
after advisement, in *Squyer v. Barkeley* (1532) KB 27/1085, m. 32d (printed with translation in
94 Selden Soc. 253); reported by Spelman, 93 Selden Soc. 7.

[28] *Blaknall v. Pawne* (1522) KB 27/1045, m. 96. *Assumpsit* by the surety against the principal
was formally approved, after advisement, in *Holygrave v. Knyghtysbrygge* (1535) KB 27/1094,
m. 30d (printed with trans. in 94 Selden Soc. 256); *sub nom Jordan's Case*, Y.B. Mich. 27 Hen.
VIII, fo. 24, pl. 3; reported by Spelman, 93 Selden Soc. 7; noted in Simpson, *History of the
Common Law of Contract*, 266, at 291.

[29] *Snothe v. Vowell* (1520) KB 27/1037, m. 63. The defendant pleaded that there was an
indenture of sale, and traversed the informal bargain. Although the plaintiff alleged a
promise to pay £42, he recovered only £9. 10s. 4d.

plaintiff and not to fulfil his promise, and scheming 'of his evil and impudent cunning' (*ex ejus mala et proterva solercia*) to make him lose his goods and money—refused to pay, sold the wine to others, and converted the proceeds. The defendant demurred to the bill, and the court took advisement until Easter term 1525, when the action was discontinued.[30] Despite the imaginative display of invective, this was effectively an action to recover a simple debt for goods sold, and even without a report we can guess at the ground of the demurrer. The great issue was whether *assumpsit* could properly be used as a substitute for the action of debt. Further experiments were deterred during the 1520s because of this undetermined demurrer,[31] and the matter was not resolved by the King's Bench until 1532, in the leading case of *Pykeryng v. Thurgoode*.[32]

Richard Pykeryng was a London brewer with some experience of Common Pleas litigation against defaulting suppliers of malt in the years of dearth,[33] and it is tempting to guess that he had found the action of debt unsatisfactory. In 1532, having taken the advice of Robert Maycote, clerk of the papers in the King's Bench,[34] he brought a bill in the King's Bench for non-delivery of a consignment of 40 quarters of malt. He declared that, whereas for £5 13s 4d. paid in advance and another £5 13s. 4d. to be paid on delivery, the defendant had in October 1531 bargained and sold 40 quarters of malt to be delivered to the plaintiff by 2 February 1532, and had there and then promised and undertaken to deliver it accordingly; the plaintiff hoping for faithful delivery made lesser provision of malt for his brewery; but the defendant, scheming to run him into loss, did not deliver any malt, so that the plaintiff was short (of malt for his brewing) and was constrained to buy from elsewhere at a far dearer price.

The plaintiff won a verdict before Chief Justice Fitzjames at the Guildhall, and the defendant moved in the King's Bench to arrest the judgment on the ground that the proper remedy in such a case was an action of debt. The only judge who succumbed to this argument was Mr Justice Port, who observed that it was a case of nonfeasance: 'there is no act done by the defendant, but only the non-delivery, for which detinue[35] [sic] lies.'

---

[30] *Cremour v. Sygeon* (1521–5) KB 27/1041, m. 33d.

[31] Note also the demurrer in *Haymond v. Lenthorp* (1528–31) KB 27/1065, m. 77d, which may have kept the issue before the court in the interim; though it seems to have been a case where debt did not lie (since the quantity of fungibles was not fixed at the outset), and the demurrer was to the plea in bar rather than the declaration. See 94 Selden Soc., intro., *283* (which omits to mention the plea).

[32] This was first discovered by Professor Simpson: 'Spelman's Reports' (1957) 72 *L.Q.R.* at 383. See also Simpson, *History of the Common Law of Contract*, 269, 289–90, 628–9.

[33] See *Pekeryng v. Mathewe* (1529) CP 40/1063, m. 600d: a writ of debt in the *detinet* for non-delivery of malt. (The writ of debt was the appropriate action not only for money claims, but also for grain and other fungible goods.)

[34] He was the plaintiff's attorney: 94 Selden Soc. 247. Maycote may also have drawn the bill in *Cleymond v. Vyncent*, which is copied in his book of entries (above, n. 25).

[35] Presumably debt in the *detinet*, since no specific malt was set aside: cf. Shelley J. in the same sense, below, text at n. 69.

The rest of the court (Fitzjames C.J., Conyngesby and Spelman JJ.) agreed to enter judgment for the plaintiff. Their reasoning may be summarized by saying that there was both *injuria* and *damnum*—a wrong in the breach of promise, and damage flowing from the non-delivery—and that where the two concurred an action was available. Mr Justice Spelman said that Mr Justice Port's distinction between nonfeasance and misfeasance had been exploded by the earlier decisions about bailees, carpenters, and sellers of land. And the fact that another form of action was available on the facts was immaterial, since the causes of action were different—in such cases the plaintiff could elect which action to bring.[36]

Spelman's report was not printed until modern times, but the decision settled the matter as far as the King's Bench was concerned. After 1532, *assumpsit* for money blossomed in that court and soon branched into various common forms. From being unheard of in 1500, it became by the 1530s the only kind of *assumpsit* action regularly proceeding to judgment,[37] though it should be noted that it was not even then a significant threat to the Common Pleas debt business which it paralleled.[38] The action made possible the beginnings of a commercial jurisdiction in the King's Bench, chiefly in London cases tried before the chief justice at the Guildhall. At the end of the 1530s, and especially under the chief justiceships of Sir Edward Mountague (1538–45) and Sir Richard Lyster (1545–53), there was a noticeable expansion in the scope of remedies provided for the commercial litigant: *assumpsit* could now be used to enforce contracts for carriage by sea,[39] marine insurance contracts,[40] factoring arrangements,[41] partnership and joint-venture agreements,[42] and bills of exchange.[43] The expansion of *assumpsit* was not limited to the commercial

[36] *Pykeryng v. Thurgoode* (1532) KB 27/1083, m. 65 (printed with trans. in 94 Selden Soc. 247); reported by Spelman, 93 Selden Soc. 4. A similar judgment is found in *Hudson v. Webbe* (1539) KB 27/1112, m. 73 (non-delivery of wheat, so that plaintiff lost profit and had to buy elsewhere at a greater price to feed his household).

[37] In 1538 as many as 6 judgments were entered: 94 Selden Soc., intro., 279.

[38] e.g., in 1535 there were 58 judgments for the plaintiff in Common Pleas actions of debt on a contract.

[39] *Sabyn v. Toly* (1541) KB 27/1121, m. 111 (promise to pay freight; defendant refused to load ship on arrival at Bordeaux; pleads late arrival of ship); *Closter v. Cannesby* (1550) KB 27/1154, m. 126 (freight).

[40] *Mayne v. De Gozi* (1538) KB 27/1107, m. 37.

[41] *Cordell v. Crystyan* (1538) KB 27/1109, m. 24d (35s. recovered); *Saxcy v. Hudson* (1553) KB 27/1167, m. 145 (trading in Danzig; £852 recovered).

[42] *Beale v. Barnes* (1542) KB 27/1125, m. 24 (mercer and grocer; £105 recovered at the Guildhall); *Bowyer v. Rawlyns* (1544) KB 27/1132, m. 111 (grocers); *Massy v. Marten* (1544) KB 27/1133, m. 123 (grocers).

[43] *Dolphyn v. Barne* (1540) KB 27/1116, m. 35d (judgment by default); *Maynard v. Dyce* (1542) KB 27/1125, m. 110 (nonsuit); *Long v. Hunt* (1544) KB 27/1131, m. 136 (judgment for plaintiff); *Towll v. Hawkyns* (1549) KB 27/1152, m. 143; *Moreany v. Basyng* (1551) KB 27/1157, m. 40. cf. *De Grady v. De Benexia* (1539) KB 27/1113, m. 65 (*assumpsit* to pay for ducats received at 'Micena' by way of exchange, but no mention of bill); *Bonvise v. De la Sala* (1543) KB 27/1126, m. 80 (*assumpsit* that debt would be paid in gold ducats at Medina del Campo, or defendant would repay in English money; no mention of bill).

world, and we may note new types of action for marriage-money,[44] to enforce wagers,[45] and to recover legacies.[46] The action was free from some of the technicalities of debt, and thus could be brought for sums of money which were not fixed at the outset—using precursors of the *quantum meruit* and *quantum valebant* formulae[47]—and also, arguably, for instalments of a debt before the last was due.[48] By 1555 there were over 50 cases a year, in the King's Bench, of *assumpsit* to recover money.[49]

THE COMMON PLEAS REACTION

By what is probably a mere accident of reporting, a chief justice of the Common Pleas—Sir Thomas Frowyk—has appeared to posterity as the principal author of *assumpsit* for money.[50] Although there is no reason to doubt that his opinion was accurately reported, the impression given by this isolated piece of evidence is seriously misleading. His opinion was in fact a dissent, and the establishment of the action, a decade or two later, occurred in the King's Bench. By mid-century the development seems also to have been accepted in the Exchequer.[51] But the Common Pleas did not follow suit.

[44] *Andrews v. Hosyer* (1549) KB 27/1151, m. 83; *Howes v. Wolley* (1550) KB 27/1153, m. 60; *Kaye v. Kocson* (1551) KB 27/1157, m. 107; *Rokes v. Godsalve* (1555) KB 27/1174, m. 97; *Atwell v. Smyth* (1557) KB 27/1182, m. 110. Cf. Rast. Ent. 4r (promise to pay for wedding feast); *Clifton v. Molyneux* (1555) KB 27/1176, m. 74 (action for return of money under marriage agreement).

[45] *Cokerell v. Tolowrge* (1538) KB 27/1109, m. 61 (as to plight of Emperor Charles V); *Strong v. Smyth* (1543) KB 27/1126, m. 67 (whether plaintiff could shoot an arrow 300 yards against the wind; issue as to whether he was confined to one shot); *Holte v. Prycke* (1553–4) KB 27/1167, m. 134 (demurrer to declaration).

[46] *Whyte v. Batysford* (1538) KB 27/1108, m. 27d (printed with translation in 94 Selden Soc. 259); reported by Spelman, 93 Selden Soc. 8. The action seems to gain ground in 1555, when there are three examples: *Morgayn v. Mompesson* (1555) KB 27/1173, m. 27; *Nollothe v. Eyott* (1555) KB 27/1174, m. 63; *Holmes v. Warren* (1555) KB 27/1176, m. 235 (promise by executrix's husband).

[47] e.g., *Dyxson v. Bulson* (1533) KB 27/1086, m. 73d (promise to satisfy and content plaintiff for his labour); *Salwey v. Abbot of Pershore* (1539) CP 40/1102, m. 324 (promise to pay clerk of peace all fees due for the indictments of 120 defendants at quarter sessions); *Curttes v. Baron* (1551) KB 27/1157, m. 150 (promise by surety to pay English equivalent of debt in Flemish pounds if principal defaults); *Chanons v. Somer* (1555) KB 27/1173, m. 32 (promise to pay *quecunque onera et custagia* for board and tuition); *Barley v. Brett* (1555) KB 27/1175, m. 89 (promise to pay the market-price for malt at the time of delivery—*tantum pecunie quantum dicte deliberationis tempore ejusdem vendi potuerit in marcato apud Rayston*).

[48] *Pecke v. Redman* (1555) KB 27/1171, m. 106; Dyer 113a (instalments of grain; undetermined motion in arrest of judgment); *Lord Zouche v. Digby* (1557) Dyer's circuit notebook, 110 Selden Soc. 416 (Rutland assizes).

[49] Fifty-six cases were counted in the King's Bench rolls for 1555 (KB 27/1173–6). Of them, 18 proceeded to judgment, and another 27 reached the general issue (*non assumpsit*).

[50] *The Case of Barley*, i.e. *Orwell v. Mortoft* (1505) CP 40/972, m. 123 (trans. in Baker & Milsom, 406); Y.B. Mich. 20 Hen. VII, fo. 8, pl. 18 (trans. *ibid.*, 408); Keil. 69, 77; BL MS. Hargrave 105, ff. 233r, 236r; MS. Add. 35938, fo. 195v; discussed in Simpson, *History of the Common Law of Contract*, 262–4, 288–9.

[51] e.g., *Fennell v. Newyngton* (1550) E 13/232, mm. 7d, 8d (*assumpsit* for the price of goods; verdict and judgment for plaintiff).

Where *assumpsit* was brought to enforce an informal covenant, there was probably general agreement between the courts that case should lie, provided some prepayment had been made. Mr Justice Fitzherbert accepted that,[52] and it was clearly laid down by the court in his time.[53] This is probably the reason why *assumpsit* was generally accepted in surety cases in the Common Pleas,[54] since these were seen to depend on covenants to pay money rather than debts. There was likewise no overt objection to any other kind of money claim which lay outside the scope of debt.[55] Actions for the non-delivery of fungibles may also have been accepted by some Common Pleas practitioners,[56] presumably on the footing that these were essentially covenants to deliver rather than debts,[57] though doubts had been stirred before the end of the 1520s.[58]

The first reported signs of dissent come from the Year Books for 1535, when Mr Justice Fitzherbert—who evidently led Common Pleas opinion while he sat there—declared that the case of *Cleymond v. Vincent* (1520) (in which *assumpsit* for money was first judicially approved) was not only wrong but should be taken out of the books.[59] As we have noted, that was

---

[52] Fitz. N.B. 145G (94 Selden Soc., intro., *270* n. 3).

[53] *Ewer v. Elys* (1522) CP 40/1033, m. 304 (printed with trans. in 94 Selden Soc. 241); reported by Spelman, 93 Selden Soc. 3; *Anon.* (1526/36) Yorke's reports, BL MS. Hargrave 388, fo. 215r (trans. in 94 Selden Soc., intro., *296–7*; Baker & Milsom, 402–3).

[54] e.g., *Smyth v. Hylton* (1528) CP 40/1058A, m. 635 (action by surety for loan to buy wares in Iceland; judgment on *non potest dedicere*); *Tylney v. Palmer* (1535) CP 40/1085(1), m. 301 (action by surety for debt; judgment on *non potest dedicere*); *Norres v. Clerke* (1536) CP 40/1091, m. 431 (action by surety for defendant's appearance; judgment for plaintiff after verdict); *Dawson v. Smyth* (1542) CP 40/1115, m. 418d (action against surety; judgment for plaintiff after verdict); *Fulmerston v. Hussey* (1547) CP 40/1133, m. 403 (action on promise, given in return for 7s. 6d., to pay existing debt of £24 which third party owed to plaintiff; recovers £20).

[55] Note the odd cases of *Wylliams v. Jenkyn* (1547) CP 40/1134, m. 126 (undertaking to pay four marks in satisfaction of wrongs done; pleads *Non assumpsit*); *Dyve v. Chanon* (1556) CP 40/1165, m. 531 (in consideration of the grant of an office, defendant undertook to pay an annuity; imparlance; *Bradford v. Duffeld*, ibid., m. 932 (in consideration of one penny paid, defendant undertook to redeliver coins bailed; verdict and judgment for plaintiff; writ of error in 1558); *Josselyn v. Shelton* (1558) CP 40/1173, m. 532; Benl. 57 (in consideration of an impending marriage, bride's father promised to pay 400 marks to groom's father).

[56] e.g., *Fermour v. Hochyns* (1520) CP 40/1030, m. 353 (wool; writ of inquiry upon *nihil dicit*); *Cressall v. Wylson* (1521) CP 40/1032A, m. 322 (pleads arbitration); *Salter v. Walpole* (1522) CP 40/1035, m. 116d (writ of inquiry upon *non potest dedicere*); *Halle v. Bensted* (1526) CP 40/1049, m. 307 (salt; imparlance); *Jeckelove v. Meryell* (1536) CP 40/1091, m. 327 (imparlance); *Swetman v. Meyre* (1540) CP 40/1104, m. 237 (*optulit se*); *Byrkett v. Sturton*, ibid., m. 370 (sim.). Most of these were for non-delivery of grain.

[57] Some examples are clearly contracts for carriage as well as delivery: e.g., *Tuttesham v. None* (1523) CP 40/1040, m. 408 (undertaking to deliver grain sold; action against executrix); *Johnson v. Bramston* (1524) CP 40/1044, m. 267d (covenant to carry tallow from Ipswich to Bordeaux and to deliver at Bordeaux; imparlance); *Wode v. Gamon* (1533) CP 40/1079, m. 312 (undertaking to carry cargo by sea, alleging conversion as well as non-delivery); *Borne v. Grene* (1538) CP 40/1097, m. 419d (undertaking to carry and deliver successive cargoes of grain, coal and salt; pleads condition).

[58] *Colman v. Grene* (1528) CP 40/1057, m. 338 (demurrer).

[59] *Anon.* (1535) Y.B. Trin. 27 Hen. VIII, fo. 23, pl. 21 (Baker & Milsom, 447–8). See Simpson, *History of the Common Law of Contract*, 568–9.

an action against the executrix of a surety, and so it was doubly proof against the problem of duplication with debt. But Mr Justice Fitzherbert had doubts about the surety cases as well. At any rate, he favoured the resurrection of the obsolescent viscontiel action *de plegiis acquietandis*, which—if indeed it was still available, and did not require a deed—would have raised the double-remedy objection to *assumpsit* by a surety.[60] A promised indemnity was the subject of another reported Common Pleas case in 1542. This was an action of *assumpsit* on a promise to indemnify a serjeant-at-mace in carrying out his duties. The plaintiff was a serjeant of one of the sheriffs of London, who had been asked to arrest George Ferrers, MP, upon a King's Bench *scire facias* to execute a judgment in debt. The creditor had asserted that Ferrers was not a Member of the present Parliament and promised the serjeant an indemnity for the consequences; but Ferrers was in fact Member for Plymouth, and his arrest caused a stir over parliamentary privilege.[61] In the event, the serjeant was removed from office and imprisoned in the Tower by order of the Commons, and he subsequently complained that the defendant had not indemnified him. This was not an action for a fixed sum of money; but the governing principles were the same as where a surety promised an indemnity for another's debt. Serjeant Bromley objected that the action was 'based on a naked promise, and no specialty nor any money is given in covenant, but it is simply a promise'. Serjeant Hales for the plaintiff, though equipped by his Gray's Inn reading with examples where case could be brought for nonfeasance,[62] is reported as making a rather pedestrian reply. Mr Justice Willoughby thought the action would lie; but Mr Justice Shelley, having remarked that it was 'a good case, from which much learning may arise', said that he preferred to be advised. He would, 'not say precisely that the action does not lie' but only that it was 'a doubtful case'.[63] The doubt, however, related not to the use of *assumpsit* in lieu of covenant, but to what modern-day lawyers would identify as a consideration question: whether an indemnity could validly be promised to someone for performing his legal duty. Although the report does not say so, this obviously led to the more delicate question of jurisdiction over questions of parliamentary

---

[60] Fitz. N.B. 137C; and see 94 Selden Soc., intro., *282*. The action enabled a surety to recover from his principal the money which he had been required to pay to the principal's creditor. No example of the action has yet been found in the plea rolls of the benches before 1550; but see *Coxe v. Thornes* (1566) Dyer 257a; E. Coke, *Book of Entries* (London: 1614), fo. 434v.

[61] See Dyer 275a, *ad finem*; Moo. 57, pl. 163; S. T. Bindoff (ed.), *History of Parliament: the House of Commons 1509–58* (London: Martin Secker & Warburg Ltd for the History of Parliament Trust, 1982), ii. 130; Simpson, *History of the Common Law of Contract*, 266–7.

[62] Baker & Milsom, 345–8.

[63] *Taylour v. Whyte* (Hil. 1543) CP 40/1116, m. 108 (general issue; no judgment); reported *sub nom Sukley v. Wyte* (Pas. 1543) Gell's reports, Pas. 34 Hen. VIII, fo. 12v (trans. in Baker & Milsom, 404). Robert Taylour was serjeant-at-mace to Henry Suckeley, sheriff of London. Ferrers was a mainpernor of John Weldon, who owed Thomas Whyte £166. 13s. 4d. Gell's report was first noticed by Professor Simpson: *History of the Common Law of Contract*, 631–2.

privilege. But there was nothing in the report, nor in any other case from this period, to suggest Common Pleas hostility to actions on informal covenants.

The replacement of debt was another matter entirely. Here wager at law was at stake, and there was a view—shared even by those with liberal attitudes towards law and conscience[64]—that wager of law afforded a proper protection to the individual and should be defended against circumvention. In 1528 an action for non-delivery of grain was stopped in the Common Pleas by demurrer;[65] and in 1533, when another such action proceeded as far as a verdict for the plaintiff, the court took advisement and no judgment was entered.[66] In the second case there was probably a successful motion in arrest of judgment, in which case we may deduce that the court deliberately declined to accept the King's Bench decision in *Pykeryng v. Thurgoode* from the very beginning.

What is certainly known is that when another such action was brought in 1543,[67] and apparently no objection to the use of *assumpsit* was made by counsel for the defendant, Mr Justice Shelley intervened to stop the suit:[68]

It seems to me that there is another point in the case, for I believe that the action does not lie here. An action on the case does not lie in any case except where the plaintiff is without other action. But here he could have an action of detinue.[69] I perceive your purpose, however. You brought this action because he cannot wage his law in this action, as he could in an action of detinue.

This was clearly the general view of the court at least until the middle of the century, because no judgments for money in cases of simple contract are found in the plea rolls.[70] Indeed, when an attempt was made to recover

---

[64] e.g., St German, *Little Treatise on the Subpoena*, 117 (referring to the case of executors).

[65] *Colman v. Grene* (1528) CP 40/1057, m. 338 (defendant bargained and sold grain to plaintiff for £19 agreed, and promised to deliver at Whitsun, but scheming to defraud him of the bargain did not do so; demurrer to declaration). No judgment was entered.

[66] *Baron v. Wilson* (1533) CP 40/1079, m. 344 (plaintiff bought barley and beans for £24 and defendant promised to deliver by Lady Day 1532 but did not do so; no deceit is alleged). Cf. *Dalton v. Baker* (1534–5) CP 40/1083, m. 453 (promise to pay in two instalments for wool sold and delivered; confessed at assizes, and damages assessed by writ of inquiry; court takes advisement).

[67] If, as seems likely, it is identifiable as *Thwaytes v. Bealles* (Pas. 1543) CP 40/1117, m. 306, it was a less straightforward parallel than Gell's report suggests. The plaintiff declared on a delivery of malt to the defendant, who promised to sell it and pay the plaintiff 4s. 4d. for every quarter sold; the defendant pleaded a variation of the agreement, and issue was joined on the terms. This seems too uncertain to support an action of debt. No doubt that explains the absence of a demurrer by the defendant.

[68] *Anon.* (1543) Gell's reports, Library of Congress MS., Pas. 34 Hen. VIII, fo. 15r (trans. in Baker & Milsom, 415, where it is wrongly dated 1542). This case was first noticed by Professor Simpson: *History of the Common Law of Contract*, 630.

[69] More correctly debt in the *detinet*, assuming the facts as stated in the report. Cf. Port J., above, p. 276, n. 35.

[70] A judgment for £20 on a *nihil dicit* is found in *Duplake v. Glover* (1549) CP 40/1140, m. 411, but this was an action for marriage money and therefore arguably not for a debt. Occasional *optulit se* entries are also found, and a few appearances: e.g., *Homerston v. Rikkys*

the price of goods in 1550, it was firmly met by a demurrer to the declaration.[71] As a consequence, debt and wager of law remained in regular use in the Common Pleas,[72] and even an attorney might be deprived of his alleged rewards by this means.[73]

The same objection did not extend to actions against executors or administrators, upon simple contracts, even in the absence of a separate promise by the personal representatives for a fresh consideration,[74] since there was no other action in such a case and no question of waging law. Yet Mr Justice Shelley was against using *assumpsit* in these cases as well,[75] and according to Sir Robert Brooke this had always been the Common Pleas position.[76] The reason was presumably that given by Mr Justice Fitzherbert in 1535. It was that debts due by reason of a simple contract die with the person: *actio personalis moritur cum persona*.[77] Mr Justice Fitzherbert had castigated the King's Bench decision of 1520, in which he had himself as counsel persuaded the court to arrive at the wrong conclusion, saying that the court had acted unilaterally without consulting the Common Pleas judges; it was 'not law without doubt'. According to a later recollection by Chief Justice Dyer, the Common Pleas relented when Chief Justice Mountague was translated to the Common Pleas from the King's Bench in 1545 and brought with him the practice of making executors liable in *assumpsit*.[78] However, this is not borne out by the plea rolls, in which no judgments in such cases have come to light. By the 1550s, the two benches had evidently agreed to differ on these issues, though there was as yet no open conflict. In 1557 the King's Bench was invited to reverse the decision of 1520 concerning executors, given the 'great reputation' of Mr Justice Fitzherbert, whose 1535 remarks had now been published in print. But in support of the decision it was argued that personal representatives ought not to keep the assets for themselves when there were debts unpaid, and that it was for the good of the testator's soul to pay off his debts. The

(1541) CP 40/1110, m. 318 (action for price of iron sold and delivered; imparlance); *Rous v. Wychyngham* (1542) CP 40/1113, m. 331 (action for price of land sold; imparlance).

[71] *Bayly v. Davye* (1550) CP 40/1144A, m. 425 (no judgment).

[72] There are even a few stray examples in the King's Bench in the 1550s.

[73] *Predyaux v. Doble* (1558) CP 40/1176(1), m. 745 (client wages law successfully in debt for an attorney's fees and expenses).

[74] Such promises are rarely alleged: e.g., *Sandeford v. Byddell* (1555) KB 27/1174, m. 84 (promise by administrators to pay debt, in return for 20s. paid; judgment for plaintiff); *Cheyney v. Tusser* (1556) CP 40/1165, m. 627d (promise by testatrix when single to pay debt for goods delivered; *optulit se* only).

[75] *Sukley v. Wyte* (1543) Gell's reports, Library of Congress MS., Pas. 34 Hen. VIII, fo. 12v (trans. in Baker & Milsom 404–5). See also *Anon.* (1545) Brooke Abr., *Action sur le case*, pl. 4.

[76] Brooke Abr., *Action sur le case*, pl. 106 (abridging the 1535 case). Cf. *Tuttesham v. None* (1523) CP 40/1040, m. 408 (action against executrix on testator's undertaking to deliver grain sold; issue on the terms).

[77] *Anon.* (1535) Y.B. Trin. 27 Hen. VIII, fo. 23, pl. 21 (trans. in Baker & Milsom, 448). The maxim had been quoted by Fyneux C.J. in the 1520 case, when he said it did not apply to debts.

[78] *Anon* (1571) BL MS. Add. 25211, fo. 100r (trans. in Baker & Milsom, 450).

court, 'without solemn argument', affirmed its decision of 1520 and gave judgment for the plaintiff.[79]

During the mid-1550s, the Common Pleas seems to have relaxed its position somewhat, and a number of actions on the case for money are found in the rolls.[80] But full acceptance of the King's Bench position was beyond immediate reach. The conflict between the two courts was ultimately to become intolerable because of their different views as to how actions of *assumpsit* for money should be left to the jury. A short but revealing note by Dyer in 1559 shows that the difference of approach had already taken root. The King's Bench were willing to imply a promise to pay a debt, and therefore it was necessary only to prove an indebtedness, whereas the Common Pleas required proof of an express promise to pay the money at a later day.[81] Since most actions were tried on circuit by assize commissioners, who were not necessarily judges of the court where the suit was commenced, the country litigant was thereby placed in considerable uncertainty. This may account for the prevalence of London suits at the beginning of the King's Bench development.[82] But the general unpredictability of country cases would in the end result in a major clash. When the crisis came, in the 1590s, it was not a mere passing conflict between conservatives such as Mr Justice Walmsley and the more progressive King's Bench supporters. Indeed, the immediate occasion of the crisis was not personal, or political, or social, or economic, but a recent change in the legal system which gave the Common Pleas judges a louder voice.[83] The underlying doctrinal conflict, as we have seen, had been simmering for at least 70 years, certainly since the earlier part of Henry VIII's reign, and perhaps ever since the first attempts to use *assumpsit* in lieu of debt.

[79] *Norwood v. Norwood and Rede* (1557) KB 27/1182, m. 188 (summarized in Baker & Milsom, 448); reported in Plowd. 180v; discussed in Simpson, *Contract*, 569–70. Cf. *Derneley v. Rawlynson* (1555) KB 27/1176, m. 265 (judgment against an administrator); *Dyxson v. Cove, ibid.*, m. 271 (judgment against an executrix).

[80] *Harrys v. Estwyke* (1555) CP 40/1164, m. 451 (£4 awarded as the price of a gelding bargained and sold; an unsophisticated declaration, with no mention of deceit or consequential loss, and an ungrammatical *assumpsit* inserted in the *cum* clause); *Assheton v. Drewe* (1558–9) CP 40/1176(1), m. 556 (action for £36. 15s. for price of sheep; recovers £28. 11s. 8d. at Lincoln assizes). Cases pleaded to issue (*Non assumpsit*) are: *Rogers v. Bennett* (1556) CP 40/1166, m. 1051 (action for rent of sheep); *Toller v. Walter* (1558) CP 40/1175, m. 156 (action for price of malt sold); *Bachecrofte v. Roo, ibid.*, m. 411 (action for price of wool sold).

[81] *Anon.* (1559) Dyer's circuit notebook, 110 Selden Soc. 420 (Northampton assizes, before Dyer and Bendlowes, Griffin concurring). Cf., to the same effect, *Edwards v. Burre* (1573) Dal. 104 (trans. in Baker & Milsom, 416).

[82] Mr M. J. Prichard has pointed out to the writer that, since King's Bench cases from London were usually tried at the Guildhall by the chief justice of the King's Bench, the city plaintiff could be confident of a jury direction in accordance with the King's Bench philosophy.

[83] i.e. the erection of the statutory Exchequer Chamber (composed of the judges of the Common Pleas and barons of the Exchequer) to hear error from the Queen's Bench: 27 Eliz. I, c. 8. The statute was passed in 1585, but 10 years elapsed before litigants began to give the Common Pleas their new-found opportunity to trounce the superior court: see *Turgys v. Becher* (1596) Baker & Milsom, 418.

The solution to the puzzle with which we began cannot therefore be found solely in the era of Coke and Bacon, who fought the last round,[84] but must take account of a long-term divergence of judicial philosophies. It would be instructive to discover how far that divergence affected other areas of the law in the sixteenth century.[85] At least we now know that Walmsley's last stand against the spread of *assumpsit* placed him within a long tradition stretching back to Fitzherbert and possibly even to Bryan.

[84] Coke and Bacon were the principal counsel on either side in *Slade's Case* (n. 9, above), which finally ended the dispute in 1602.

[85] See n. 22, above, for two other areas of difference.

Brian Simpson in the United States

R. H. Helmholz

A. W. B. Simpson's academic career in the United States makes a pleasant and encouraging story, at least to an American who has observed it at first-hand and has benefited from it. It began without fuss. Brian first came to the States in a professional capacity during the winter of 1979.[1] He had been invited to be a visiting professor at the University of Chicago Law School, and no doubt he felt a certain degree of curiosity about life in the States. He returned to Chicago again as a visiting professor in the spring terms ('quarters') during the 1979–80 and 1981–2 academic years. The experience must have been mutually agreeable, because he accepted a professorship at the University of Chicago from the 1983–4 academic year. He stayed there as a regular member of the law faculty until 1987. In that year he was called away by a better offer, a not uncommon experience in the hunt for 'stars' that adds interest to American academics' lives and income to their pockets. In consequence, Brian became the Charles and Edith Clyne Professor of Law at the University of Michigan in Ann Arbor. He has taught there since, though not without returning regularly to the United Kingdom, as agreed at the time of his appointment.

Brian has not been idle in America. He has not been content to observe from the sidelines. Far from it. He has worked hard. At various times, he has taught contracts, jurisprudence, legal history, and criminal law at these law schools, and during the same period, compiled a record of scholarly publication that would not disgrace a younger and more ambitious man. On this account, if for no other, the editors of this volume thought it would be useful to include an account of Brian's career in the New World, and a combination of foolhardiness and affection for my subject inclined me to give it a try.

EVIDENTIARY PROBLEMS AND THE MOVE TO THE STATES

When I accepted this invitation, little did I think that accounting for his move to the American side of the Atlantic would present problems. Compared to interpreting medieval texts, making sense of Brian's American career would be (I thought) duck soup. The principal actors

---

[1] He had also served as a visiting professor at the University of Dalhousie in Canada in 1964.

were alive. He himself has left a quite full record of where he was and what he did. An impressive pile of books and articles would demonstrate what his interests were and how they had evolved since coming to American shores. Surely, writing about him would be a simple matter of collecting some facts and getting them down on paper.

Experience disappointed my expectations. There is no shortage of evidence—but what does it really mean? What motivated Brian to come to the United States? What impact did the experience have on his professional life? And what sort of relationship between Brian and his American co-workers developed out of the experience? The evidence on these questions has proved to be either conflicting or opaque (at least to my eyes). Although the bare bones of Brian's career are easy enough to discern, satisfactory answers to some of the important questions have proved more elusive. It is easier to describe what he has accomplished.

Initially I sought to discover the exact origins of the idea that Brian should came to a law school in the United States. What were the circumstances that led Brian to accept an appointment, first at the University of Chicago, and then at the University of Michigan? The profits accruing from my enquiries can only be described as meagre. The decanal records kept at the University of Chicago turned out to be singularly uninformative, and none of those who were present at the time seemed to be entirely sure how it happened.

I did have some leads. While he was still a fellow of Lincoln College, Oxford, Brian had taught Richard Epstein, who by 1979 was himself a professor at the University of Chicago. Possibly his Oxford experience had been good enough to suggest the merits of an appointment, I thought. Epstein, however, did not remember it quite that way. His experience under Brian's supervision at Oxford had been a good one, he recalled, but he modestly disclaimed having played a pivotal role in making the appointment. He pointed instead to John Langbein and Gerhard Casper, the one at the time a professor and legal historian at Chicago, the other its newly appointed dean. Speaking with them, however, proved not very helpful. Casper recalled the events surrounding Brian's departure for Michigan vividly. Losing a valuable member of the faculty leaves indelible memories. However, he did not remember much about the initial invitation to come to Chicago. His correspondence revealed only letters written before the Crosskey Lecture, delivered at Chicago in the spring of 1981, which in a much expanded form later became the book, *Cannibalism and the Common Law* (1984).[2] It seemed possible to think that the success of that lecture might have played a part in the invitation, but there was not the slightest suggestion of it in the subsequent correspondence.

---

[2] *Cannibalism* (1984); see Bibliography.

John Langbein thus seemed the most likely source of the idea. He did remember having written letters to Casper in favour of inviting Brian to come to Chicago as a visitor—Langbein had himself been in Germany when the idea first came up—but he could say no more about his reasons at the time than that Brian was a distinguished scholar and a lively person. But everyone knew that. Langbein had an inexplicable penchant for urging the appointment of legal historians to the Chicago faculty, however. Perhaps that was it. Again, however, Langbein did not remember it quite that way. What he recalled was having seen Brian on a BBC television programme. Brian was a representative of the Williams Committee on Pornography, and he looked thoroughly miserable in the role—so miserable in fact that Langbein took pity on him and initiated the visiting offer to cheer him up. An interesting story, no doubt, but it seemed quite implausible to me to suppose that pity on John Langbein's part could have been the real motive. I knew him better than that.

Well then, what caused Brian to accept the offer, once it had come his way? Here the reasons given by those who had been present at the time split basically along national lines. In general, the British respondents thought the culprit was the Thatcher government. Cuts in resources, demands for accountability, and a hostile attitude towards the universities on the part of the authorities made it unpleasant to stay at a British university in the 1980s. Brian left when he could. American respondents, on the other hand, did not think in terms of a 'culprit' or even of a 'departure'. They saw it as a matter of attraction. For them, the more likely explanation was the high quality of the intellectual life at American law schools. Maybe higher salaries also played a supporting role in persuading him to move, they said, but it was not money alone. He had not been compelled to leave England. He had been attracted to America.

It was hard to choose between such obviously interested accounts, and Brian's own explanation, when at last I approached him, did not provide any real support for either theory. I confess I found it hard to believe. He told me that he himself had come to realize that he wanted to avoid becoming an academic administrator, and that at the time he was being pushed down that path, much against his will—or at least his better judgment. The Chicago offer had come at just the right moment. It had allowed him to return to teaching and to writing. But, I objected, why not just return to teaching and to writing in the UK? I thought the impetus for the move surely must have been more than a desire to escape the burdens of academic administration. No, he said, that was pretty much it. Had he stayed, he would have had no choice but to fall into the place of a full-time academic administrator.

ACCOMPLISHMENTS OF THE AMERICAN YEARS

Whatever the reasons, Brian did shift his academic home to the American side of the Atlantic gradually but surely over the course of the 1980s, taking emeritus status at the University of Kent in Canterbury at the same time. Brian's accomplishments since arriving in the United States certainly affirm his story that he wished above all to return to active scholarship. The American years have been a productive period in his scholarly life, and throughout them he has kept his hand studiously away from all helms save those of small boats. This volume's Bibliography tells the tale, or at any rate a good part of it. His skilful development of the techniques of detailed studies of leading cases—now so closely related with him that the method is often called 'doing a Simpson'—came during his years in the United States. The scholarship of this period has been of a different character, more original in conception and style than the works of his earlier years.

Brian has not wanted for public and scholarly recognition either. He became an Honorary Fellow of the American Society of Legal History in 1994 and was elected a Fellow of the American Academy of Arts and Sciences in 1993. He has been invited to deliver visiting lectures at American universities. He was appointed an Honorary Deputy District Attorney in Colorado. But his recognition is not just a question of honours received. He has influenced American legal historians, and he has made friends.[3]

Brian has not been timid in this new location. Shortly after arriving in the United States, he published a major article sharply critical of a then recent book by one of the leaders of the Critical Legal Studies Movement, Morton Horwitz. That movement had acquired a considerable vogue at the time, and Horwitz's book, *The Transformation of American Law, 1780–1860* (1977), was widely respected as its strongest historical vindication. Although adherents of the Movement were not at one on all points, it was generally agreed among them that during the eighteenth century, American law had been dominated by notions of community and equity. Unfortunately, this peaceable regime was replaced by one based upon 'economic progress, atomistic competition, and individuality'.[4] The newer regime favoured the economic and social interests of entrepreneurs and had the by-product of encouraging exploitation of the poorer and weaker members of society.

[3] See, e.g., Cantor, Norman, *Imagining the Law: Common Law and the Foundations of the American Legal System*, xiv (Harper Collins, New York, 1997).

[4] Presser, S. B., 'Some Realism about Orphism, or The Critical Legal Studies Movement and the Great Chain of Being: an English Legal Academic's Guide to the Current State of American Law', *Northwestern Law Review*, 79 (1984) 869, at 878.

Brian examined the evidence presented in the book.[5] He concluded that its picture of legal development was more romanticism than fact. There was no reason to think, for example, that juries in the earlier period always decided in favour of the oppressed. And some of the supposedly epochal changes—rejection of the notion that courts could determine the fairness of contracts and rule accordingly, for example—turned out to rest on thin evidentiary foundations. Much narrower procedural issues were involved, and in fact in most cases very little change had actually occurred.[6] Brian doubted, moreover, that it was legitimate to make a one-to-one move from legal doctrine to social fact. There may have been an implied warranty in the sale of horses in the older law, for example, and it may have given way to a regime of *caveat emptor* in America. But this change would have had little impact upon the lives of the poor. 'The poor did not buy horses; they walked.'[7] Taking up one example after another, Brian took apart much of the argument in this award-winning book. For whatever reason, the book's author decided not to answer him.[8]

There has been an even-handedness to Brian's scholarship in the States. Horwitz was to the left of the political spectrum; the next to fall under Brian's critical eye was not. It was the man who had done so much to inspire the Law and Economics movement, Ronald Coase. In an article published in 1996, Brian took issue with the conclusions drawn from one of Coase's famous essays, 'The Problem of Social Cost'.[9] The article did this by beginning with a characteristically witty account of the life and works of one of Coase's own targets, the Cambridge economist, Arthur C. Pigou (1877–1959). It then moved to a famous English case, *Sturges v. Bridgman*, which had been featured in Coase's famous article.[10]

Pigou was one of the eccentric, misogynous Oxbridge dons of a type Simpson assured his readers was 'now almost extinct'. Pigou may (or may not have been—the point was disputed by Coase) always in favour of greater government involvement in economic affairs in order to

[5] 'The Horwitz Thesis and the History of Contracts', *University of Chicago Law Review*, 46 (1979), 533–601; reprinted in Simpson, A. W. B. *Legal Theory and Legal History: Essays on the Common Law* (Hambledon Press, London and Ronceverte, 1987), 203–71.

[6] The crucial case is *Seymour v. Delancy* 1 N. J. Eq. 320 (1831), discussed in *U. Chicago L. Rev.* 46, at 571; *Legal Theory and Legal History*, at 241.

[7] 'The Horwitz Thesis' (above n. 5), 46 *U. Chicago L. Rev.* 46, at 601; *Legal Theory and Legal History*, at 271.

[8] He did, however, go on to publish a study of later developments in American law: Horwitz, Morton J., *The Transformation of American Law, 1870–1960* (Oxford University Press, 1992).

[9] 'Coase v. Pigou Re-examined', *Journal of Legal Studies*, 25 (1996), 53–97. The original article was Coase, R. H., 'The Problem of Social Cost', *Journal of Law & Economics*, 3 (1960), 1–44, reprinted in *ibid.*, *The Firm, The Market and the Law* (University of Chicago, 1988), 95.

[10] 11 Ch. D. 852 (1877). The article also discusses liability for fires caused by railway locomotives, in particular, the case of *Vaughan v. Taff Vale Railway*, 3 H. & N. 743, 157 Eng. Rep. 667; 5 H. & N. 679, 157 Eng. Rep. 1351 (1860), but I have omitted that part of the article because it largely duplicates the issues raised in *Sturges v. Bridgman*.

compensate for whatever faults the market possessed. At any rate, there was some evidence to show this, and some of Pigou's followers were clearly in that camp. Brian identified a reaction against Pigou as one possible source of what he called Coase's, 'persistent skepticism about the merits of government intervention'.[11] The suggestion was that there may also have been a personal element to it.

Sturges, the case discussed by both men, had begun as a suit by a physician against a confectioner whose use of the tools of his trade in an immediately adjoining building made it difficult for him to carry on his practice peacefully or successfully. Coase had used *Sturges* as an illustration of the reciprocal nature of causation. In economic terms, it appears, the presence and practice of the doctor was as much a cause of the harm as the loud noises and vibrations emanating from the workrooms of the confectioner. Brian investigated the background of the case, insofar as the record allowed, and concluded that however the theoretical elegance of the Coasean approach might have assessed, it bore 'little relationship to how neighbors usually behave in real life'. Treating the case as if there could have been a 'market transaction' between the doctor and the confectioner would be of no use whatsoever in a court of law. Brian's article amounted to a frontal assault on the assumptions of the Law and Economics movement.

Unlike Horwitz, Coase did choose to reply. He largely agreed with Brian's characterization of Pigou. Indeed, he added to Brian's account of the Cambridge economist's peculiarities, although he claimed Brian had misunderstood his own views of Pigou's writing. Coase went on to disclaim any prescriptive purpose for his economic analysis of *Sturges*, chiding Brian slightly for not sharing either his interest or his expertise in pure economics. Where Coase did pointedly disagree was on the question of whether the situation in the case could sensibly be treated as a potential market transaction.[12] That important question continues to divide the Law and Economics enthusiasts from many of the rest of us. The argument on Brian's side, at least in a historical context, has rarely been stated any better than it was in his article.[13]

---

[11] 'An Addendum', *J. Leg. Studies*, 25 (1996), 99.

[12] Coase, R. H., 'Law and Economics and A. W. Brian Simpson', *J. Leg. Studies*, 25 (1996) 109: 'Simpson thinks no market transaction such as I have described would have been possible since neither of the parties would have been willing to place their rights on the market. This would have been offensive. I do not believe this. I have no doubt that had Mr Bridgman's income fallen by a million pounds if he was not able to use the mortars in the way he had been, that a bargain would have been struck.' It is as characteristic of the Law and Economics school to suppose that the question can be answered by thinking about the case in terms loss many thousands of times greater than Mr Bridgman could actually have suffered as it is—their detractors to claim that economists favour turning dinner parties into "attempt[s] to sell life insurance to fellow guests".' Simpson, '*Coase v. Pigou*' (above n. 9), 87.

[13] The best investigation of the subject in a modern context known to me is Farnsworth, Ward, 'Do Parties to Nuisance Cases Bargain after Judgment? A Glimpse inside the Cathedral', *University of Chicago L. Rev.*, 66 (1999), 373–433.

CONCLUSION

Despite these two episodes, I should not leave the impression that Brian has been a controversialist in the United States. He has not. He has done good and steady work. In terms of books and articles published and of wider influence exercised, Brian's move has been an obvious success. The Bibliography in this book tells the story well enough.

There is perhaps one caveat to the story. Despite involvement in American academic life, participation in American academic controversies, and recognition in American academic circles, Brian has not ceased to be an Englishman. This is more than a matter of his citizenship, his principal residence, and his entry in *Who's Who*.[14] Most of his scholarship has continued to be about English law. All the cases featured in his *Leading Cases in the Common Law* (1995) turn out to be English cases. He has written about the scope of civil and natural rights, but he has turned a deaf ear to the siren song of the United States Supreme Court. If the Americans who encouraged him to come to their shores feel any cause for regret— and surely they can have no just cause—their only colourable complaint must be that he has not fixed his sharp eye or exercised his archival energies on American leading cases like *Erie v. Tompkins*,[15] *Javins v. First National Realty Corp.*,[16] or *MacPherson v. Buick Motor Co.*[17]

---

[14] He has kept his entry in the British *Who's Who* up-to-date, but as of 1998 no entry at all appears under his name in the American version.

[15] 304 U. S. 64 (1938).   [16] 428 F. 2d 1071 (D. C. Cir. 1970).

[17] 217 N. Y. 382, 111 N. E. 1050 (1916).

A. W. Brian Simpson: Bibliography

Jules Winterton

This is a bibliography of the published works of Alfred William Brian Simpson, as listed in various bibliographies, library catalogues, and indexing services from the early 1950s to about February 1999. The breadth of his interests has necessitated a wide search. An attempt has been made to be comprehensive but such attempts do not always succeed, and the compiler would be glad to receive a note of any works omitted.

The works are arranged as far as possible by date of publication, earliest to most recent within four sections: books, articles and book contributions, book reviews, and selected newspaper items. I hope this arrangement is appropriate and gives some insight into the development of Professor Simpson's scholarly interests.

For those who would like to trace particular works, there is an alphabetical list by title, a simple subject index, and a list of books reviewed.

Each work has a number and the lists and indexes refer to those numbers.

A work is listed each time it was published. The title index can be used to trace all instances of publication of a work under a single title. If a work was explicitly published in revised form under a different title, a note is provided.

The bibliography is of works written by Professor Simpson but not works about him. It would have been almost impossible to include, for example, the vast number of reviews of his works. There are a few exceptions: some articles are mentioned in NOTES where they were written in reply to his articles and a few newspaper items are included where they mention him by name. Reports of official committees on which he sat are also included.

I would like to acknowledge the assistance of Professor David Sugarman and Paul Norman, Senior Reference Librarian at the Institute of Advanced Legal Studies, as well as of Professor Simpson himself.

BOOKS

1. *An Introduction to the History of the Land Law*
London: Oxford University Press, 1961
xx, 276 pp.; 22 cm
ISBN: 0 19 825150 5
NOTES: Includes bibliographies. Reprinted with corrections 1967. Second edition entitled *A History of the Land Law*, 1986.

2. *Oxford Essays in Jurisprudence: second series*
Oxford: Clarendon Press, 1973
x, 306 pp. 23 cm
ISBN: 0 19 825313 3
NOTES: Collection of essays edited by A. W. B. Simpson. Indexed. Includes: 'The Common Law and Legal Theory' by A. W. B. Simpson, 77–99.

3. *A History of the Common Law of Contract: the Rise of the Action of Assumpsit*
Oxford: Clarendon Press, 1975
xlv, 646 pp. ; 23 cm
ISBN: 0 19 825327 3, 0 19 825573 x (pbk)
NOTES: Indexed. Bibliography: [xliii]–xlv

4. *Pornography and Politics: a look back to the Williams Committee*
London: Waterlow Publishers, 1983
143 pp. : ill. ; 21 cm.
ISBN: 0 08 039156 7 (pbk)
NOTES: Cover title: *Pornography and politics: the Williams Committee in retrospect.* Foreword by the Rt Hon. S. C. Silkin Q.C. Indexed. Bibliography: 91 pp

5. *Cannibalism and the Common Law: the story of the tragic last voyage of the Mignonette and the strange legal proceedings to which it gave rise*
Chicago; London: University of Chicago Press, 1984
xiv, 353 pp., [8] pp. of plates : ill. facsim., music, ports.; 25 cm
ISBN: 0 226 75942 3
NOTES: Indexed. Bibliography: 325–44,

including list of individuals and organizations consulted, 339–44.

6. *Biographical Dictionary of the Common Law*
London: Butterworths; St Paul, Minn.: Mason, 1984
xxv, 559 pp., [16] pp. of plates: ports.; 23 cm
ISBN: 0 406 51657 x
NOTES: Edited by A. W. B. Simpson. Includes bibliographical references and references to portraits or photographs.

7. *Cannibalism and the Common Law: the story of the tragic last voyage of the Mignonette and the strange legal proceedings to which it gave rise*
(King Penguin) Harmondsworth: Penguin, 1986
xiv, 353, [8] of plates : ill.: music, facsims, ports; 20 cm, pbk
ISBN: 0 14 008381 2

8. *A History of the Land Law*; 2nd edn.
Oxford: Clarendon Press; New York: Oxford University Press, 1986
316 pp.; 23 cm
ISBN: 0 19 825537 3; 0 19 825536 5 (pbk)
NOTES: Revised edn of: *An Introduction to the History of the Land Law*, 1961. Indexed. Bibliography: [292]–5

9. *A History of the Common Law of Contract: the Rise of the Action of Assumpsit*; new edn
Oxford: Clarendon Press, 1987
xlvii, 646 pp.; 20 cm
ISBN: 0 19 825573 x (pbk)
NOTES: Indexed. Bibliography: [xiv]–xlvii

10. *Legal Theory and Legal History: Essays on the Common Law*
London; Ronceverte, W.Virg.: Hambledon Press, 1987
xiii, 432 pp.; 1 facsim., 1 port.; 24 cm
ISBN: 0 90 762883 4
NOTES: Includes bibliographical references and index. 'Collection of 16

essays originally published between 1957 and 1981 and one previously unpublished essay.'

Contents:

(a) 'The laws of Ethelbert', 1–15

(b) 'The early constitution of the Inns of Court', 17–32

(c) 'The early constitution of Gray's Inn', 33–52

(d) 'The circulation of Yearbooks in the fifteenth century', 53–66

(e) 'The source and function of the later Year Books', 67–91

(f) 'The introduction of the action on the case for conversion', 93–109

(g) 'The penal bond with conditional defeasance', 111–41

(h) 'Entails and perpetuities', 143–62

(i) 'The rule in *Wheeldon v. Burrows* and the *Code Civil*', 163–70

(j) 'Innovation in nineteenth century contract law', 171–202

(k) 'The Horwitz thesis and the history of contracts', 203–71

(l) 'The rise and fall of the legal treatise: legal principles and the forms of legal literature', 273–320

(m) 'Contract: the twitching corpse', 321–33

(n) 'The analysis of legal concepts', 335–58

(o) 'The common law and legal theory', 359–82

(p) 'The survival of the common law system', 383–402

(q) 'R. S. Rattray and Ashanti law' (previously unpublished), 403–26.

11. *Rhetoric, Reality, and Regulation 18B: a public lecture delivered by A. W. B. Simpson on Tuesday 12 May 1987*
Oxford: Child & Co., 1987
33 pp.; 23 cm
NOTES: Child & Co. Oxford Lecture 1987. Lecture jointly arranged by Child & Co. and Faculty of Law, University of Oxford. Also published as an article in 1988.

12. *Invitation to Law*
Oxford; New York: Basil Blackwell, 1988
(Invitation series)
227 pp.; 22 cm
ISBN: 0 63 114537 0; 0 63 114538 9 (pbk)
NOTES: Indexed

13. *The Judges and the Vigilant State: a public lecture delivered by Professor A. W. B. Simpson . . . on Tuesday 20 June 1989*
London: Council of Legal Education, 1989
23pp.
NOTES: The Child & Co. Oxford Lecture 1989. Lecture jointly arranged by Child & Co. and the Inns of Court School of Law

14. *In the Highest Degree Odious: detention without trial in wartime Britain*
Oxford: Clarendon Press; New York: Oxford University Press, 1992
x, 453 pp.; 24 cm
ISBN: 0 19 825775 9
NOTES: Includes bibliographical references (pp. [436]–42) and index

15. *In the Highest Degree Odious: detention without trial in wartime Britain.*
Oxford: Oxford University Press; New York: Oxford University Press, 1994 (1995 in USA). (1st pbk edn with corrections)
xxv, 453 pp.; 24 cm
ISBN: 019 825949 2 (pbk)
NOTES: Includes bibliographical references (pp. [436]–42) and index

16. *Cannibalism and the Common Law: a Victorian yachting tragedy.*
London; Rio Grande, Ohio: Hambledon Press, 1994
xiv, 353 pp., [8] pp. of plates: ill.: music, facsims, ports; 24 cm
ISBN: 1 85 285200 3
NOTES: Originally published as: *Cannibalism and the Common Law: the story of the tragic last voyage of the*

Mignonette and the strange legal proceedings to which it gave rise, Chicago: University of Chicago Press, 1984. Includes bibliographical references (pp. 325–44) and index.

17. *Victorian law and the industrial spirit: Selden Society lecture delivered in the Old Hall of Lincoln's Inn, July 13, 1994 by A. W. B. Simpson.*
London: Selden Society, 1995
35 pp.: 1 map ; 25 cm
NOTES: 'Selden Society lecture'. Includes bibliographical references (pp. 29–31)

18. *Leading cases in the common law.*
Oxford: Clarendon Press; New York: Oxford University Press, 1995.
xii, 311 pp.: [8] pp. of plates, ill., facsims, plans, ports ; 24 cm.
ISBN: 0 19 825852 6
NOTES: Includes bibliographical references (pp. [293]–302) and index. 'Three of the chapters in this book are based upon articles which have previously appeared in legal journals. I have made some modifications to enhance readability. These include reducing the bulk of footnotes; those who need fuller documentation can use the original versions.' Chapter 6 ['The beauty of obscurity'] is based on 'Contracts for cotton to arrive' 1989 *Cardozo Law Review*; chapter 8 ['Bursting reservoirs and Victorian tort law'] is based on 'Legal liability for bursting reservoirs' 1984 *Journal of Legal Studies*; and chapter 10 ['Quackery and contract law'] is based on 'Quackery and contract law' 1985 *Journal of Legal Studies*. 'Chapter 5

['A case of first impressions'] is based upon an inaugural lecture delivered in the University of Cambridge, and chapter 9 ['The ideal of the rule of law'] began life as a Selden Society lecture.
Contents:
(a) 'The study of cases', 1–12
(b) 'Politics and law in Elizabethan England: Shelley's Case (1581)', 13–44
(c) 'The timeless principles of the common law: Keeble v. Hickeringill (1707)', 45–75
(d) 'Legal science and legal absurdity: Jee v. Audley (1787)', 76–99
(e) 'A case of first impression: Priestley v. Fowler (1837)', 101–34
(f) 'The beauty of obscurity: Raffles v. Wichelhaus and Busch (1864)', 135–62
(g) 'Victorian judges and the problem of social cost: Tipping v. St. Helen's Smelting Company (1865)', 163–94
(h) 'Bursting reservoirs and Victorian tort law: Rylands and Horrocks v. Fletcher (1868)', 195–226
(i) 'The ideal of the rule of law: Regina v. Keyn (1876)', 227–58
(j) 'Quackery and contract law: Carlill v. Carbolic Smoke Ball Company (1893)', 259–91.

19. *Leading cases in the common law.*
Oxford: Clarendon Press; New York: Oxford University Press, 1996.
xii, 311 pp.: [8] pp. of plates, ill., facsims, plans, ports ; 24 cm, pbk
ISBN: 0 19 826299 X
NOTES: Reprinted in pbk with corrections 1996. Includes bibliographical references ([293]–302) and index. First published 1995 (see above for contents).

ARTICLES AND CONTRIBUTIONS TO BOOKS

(including government reports of committees on which Professor Simpson sat)

20. 'The reports of John Spelman'
Law Quarterly Review, 72 (July 1956), 334–8

21. 'Keilwey's Reports, temp. Henry VII and Henry VIII'
Law Quarterly Review, 73 (Jan 1957), 89–105

22. 'The *ratio decidendi* of a case'
Modern Law Review, 20 (July 1957), 413–15
NOTES: Comments on 'Ratio decidendi and the House of Lords' by J. L. Montrose, 20 (1957) *Modern Law Review*, 124–30

23. 'The circulation of Yearbooks in the fifteenth century'
Law Quarterly Review, 73 (Oct 1957), 492–505

24. 'The *ratio decidendi* of a case'
Modern Law Review, 21 (Mar 1958), 155–60
NOTES: Reply to 'The *ratio decidendi* of a case' by J. L. Montrose, *Modern Law Review*, 20 (1957), 587–95, which criticizes the note by Simpson, *Modern Law Review*, 20 (1957), 413–15 (see above)

25. 'The place of Slade's case in the history of contract'
Law Quarterly Review, 74 (July 1958), 381–96

26. 'The introduction of the action on the case for conversion'
Law Quarterly Review, 75 (July 1959), 364–80

27. 'The *ratio decidendi* of a case'
Modern Law Review, 22 (Sept 1959), 453–7
NOTES: Reply to 'The *ratio decidendi* of a case' by A. L. Goodhart *Modern Law Review*, 22 (1959), 117–24, which comments on the exchange of views in vols 20 and 21 (see above)

28. 'The *ratio decidendi* of a case and the doctrine of binding precedent'
In: Guest, A. G. (ed.), *Oxford essays in jurisprudence: a collaborative work*, 148–75. Oxford: Oxford University Press, 1961

29. 'The analysis of legal concepts'
Law Quarterly Review, 80 (Oct 1964), 535–58

30. 'The equitable doctrine of consideration and the law of uses'
University of Toronto Law Journal, 16 (1965), 1–36

31. 'Real property'
In Wade, H. W. R. and Lillywhite, Barbara (eds.), *Annual Survey of Commonwealth Law 1965*, 285–326. London: Butterworths, 1966.

32. 'The penal bond with conditional defeasance'
Law Quarterly Review, 82 (July 1966), 392–422

33. 'Real property'
In Wade, H. W. R., Lillywhite, Barbara and Cryer, Harold L. (eds.), *Annual Survey of Commonwealth Law 1966*, 313–43. London: Butterworths, 1967.

34. 'Rule in *Wheeldon v. Burrows* and the *Code Civile*'
Law Quarterly Review, 83 (Apr 1967), 240–7

35. 'Real property'
In Wade, H. W. R. and Cryer, Harold L. (eds.), *Annual Survey of Commonwealth Law 1968*, 375–410. London: Butterworths, 1969.

36. 'The early constitution of the Inns of Court'
Cambridge Law Journal, 28 (Nov 1970), 241–56

37. 'Real property'
In Wade, H. W. R. and Cryer, Harold L. (eds.), *Annual Survey of Commonwealth Law 1970*, 577–605. London: Butterworths, 1971.

38. 'The source and function of the later Year Books'
Law Quarterly Review, 87 (Jan 1971), 94–118.

39. 'Real property'
In Wade, H. W. R. and Cryer, Harold L. (eds.), *Annual Survey of Commonwealth Law 1971*, 210–40. London: Butterworths, 1972.

40. 'Real property'
In Wade, H. W. R. and Cryer, Harold L. (eds.), *Annual Survey of Commonwealth Law 1972*, 320–50. London: Butterworths, 1973.

41. 'The common law and legal theory'
In Simpson, A. W. B. (ed.), *Oxford essays in jurisprudence: second series*, 77–99
Oxford: Clarendon Press, 1973
NOTES: A revised version under the same title appears in *Legal theory and common law*, 8–25, ed W. Twining and in *Legal Theory and Legal History: essays on the common law*, 359–82, ed. A. W. B. Simpson.

42. 'The survival of the common law system'
In *Then and now 1799–1974: commemorating 175 years of Law Bookselling and publishing*, 51–70. London: Sweet & Maxwell, 1974

43. 'The early constitution of Gray's Inn'
Cambridge Law Journal, 34 (Apr 1975), 131–50

44. 'Innovation in nineteenth-century contract law'
Law Quarterly Review, 91 (Apr 1975), 247–78
NOTES: 'This is an amended version of a

lecture delivered in the Old Hall of Lincoln's Inn on July 3 1974.'

45. *Report of the Advisory Group on the Law of Rape*. (Cmnd. 6352) London: HMSO, Dec 1975
NOTES: Professor Simpson was a member of the Advisory Group, appointed by the Home Secretary, chaired by the Hon. Mrs Justice Heilbron, which reported in Dec 1975.

46. 'Historical introduction'
In M. P. Furmston, *Cheshire and Fifoot's law of contract*. 9th edn, 1–6. London: Butterworths, 1976
NOTES: Historical introduction forms part I.

47. 'Heraldic evidence and the early history of Lincoln's Inn'
Law Quarterly Review, 95 (Apr 1979), 201–4.

48. 'Entails and perpetuities'
Juridical Review, Apr 1979, 1–20
NOTES: 'A lecture delivered on Nov 4, 1978, at the Annual General Meeting of the Stair Society.'

49. 'The Horwitz thesis and the history of contracts'
University of Chicago Law Review, 46 (Spring 1979), 533–601

50. *Report of the Committee on Obscenity and Film Censorship*. (Cmnd 7772) London: HMSO, 1979.
NOTES: Professor Simpson was a member of the Committee, appointed by the Home Secretary, chaired by Bernard Williams, which reported in Nov 1979.

51. 'Introduction'
In Sir William Blackstone, *Commentaries on the laws of England, v.2: Of the Rights of things 1766*
Chicago: University of Chicago Press, 1979, iii–xv
NOTES: 'A facsimile of the first edn of

1765–1769' (taken from title page). Includes bibliographical references.

52. 'The rise and fall of the legal treatise: legal principles and the forms of legal literature'
University of Chicago Law Review, 48 (Summer 1981), 632–79
NOTES: 'This article originated as a paper delivered to the Fourth British Legal History Conference, held at the University of Birmingham, in 1979.'

53. 'Historical introduction'
In M. P. Furmston, *Cheshire and Fifoot's law of contract*. 10th edn, 1–15. London: Butterworths, 1981.
NOTES: Historical introduction forms ch. 1.

54. 'The laws of Ethelbert'
In M. S. Arnold, T. A. Green, S. A. Scully, and S. D. White (eds.), *On the laws and customs of England: essays in honour of Samuel E. Thorne*, 3–15. Chapel Hill: University of North Carolina Press, 1981.

55. 'Obscenity and the law'
Law and Philosophy, 1 (1982), 239–54
NOTES: Appears in a selection of papers from the proceedings of the Royal Institute of Philosophy conference on the philosophy of law, Sept 1979. Article follows and comments on 'The tendency to deprave and corrupt' by A. D. Woozley, 217–38, and is followed by 'Reply to Professor Simpson' by A. D. Woozley, 255–61.

56. '*Regina v. Archer and Muller* (1875): the leading case that never was'
Oxford Journal of Legal Studies, 2 (1982), 181–96
NOTES: n.181: 'This article is an extract from a book I have been engaged in writing on the case of *Regina v. Dudley and Stephens* and its historical background.'

57. 'The legal treatise and legal theory'
In E. W. Ives and A. H. Manchester (eds.), *Law, litigants and the legal profession: papers presented to the Fourth British Legal History Conference at the University of Birmingham 10–13 July 1979*, 11–29. (Royal Historical Society studies in history series, no. 36) London: Royal Historical Society; New Jersey: Humanities Press, 1983.
NOTES: n. at 29: 'This paper is an abridged version of a fuller study of the history of the legal treatise, and is here presented in essentially the form in which it was delivered at the Conference, without supporting notes; a fuller annotated version is available in the *University of Chicago Law Review* for 1981.'

58. 'Legal liability for bursting reservoirs: the historical context of *Rylands v. Fletcher*'
Journal of Legal Studies, 13 (1984), 209–64.

59. 'Obscenity and the law'
In M. A. Stewart (ed.), *Law, morality, and rights*, 223–38. Dordrecht; Boston: Reidel, 1983,
NOTES: The vol. contains the papers of the Royal Institute of Philosophy conference 1979 and forms vol. 162 of the Synthese Library.

60. 'Quackery and contract law: the case of the Carbolic Smoke Ball'
Journal of Legal Studies, 14 (June 1985), 345–89.
CASE: *Carlill v. Carbolic Smoke Ball Co.* [1893] 1 Q.B. 256

61. 'The common law and legal theory'
In William Twining (ed.), *Legal theory and common law*, 8–25. Oxford ; New York: Basil Blackwell, 1986
NOTES: 'A revised version of pages 77–99 of the *Oxford essays in jurisprudence* (2nd series).'

62. 'Historical introduction'
In M. J. Furmston, *Cheshire, Fifoot and Furmston's law of contract*. 11th edn, 1–16.

London: Butterworths, 1986
NOTES: Historical introduction forms ch. 1.

63. 'Rhetoric, reality, and Regulation 18B'
Denning Law Journal (1988), 123–53
NOTES: Child & Co. Oxford Lecture 1987 delivered by A. W. B. Simpson on Tuesday, 12 May 1987. Also published separately in 1987 (see books above).

64. 'Detention without trial in the Second World War: comparing the British and American experiences'
Florida State University Law Review, 16 (Summer 1988), 225–67
NOTES: 'This article derives from the Mason Ladd Memorial Lecture given at the Florida State University College of Law in Apr 1988. It represents a development of work delivered in 1987 as "Rhetoric, Reality and Regulation 18B, the Child and Co. Oxford Lecture".'

65. 'The judges and the vigilant state'
Denning Law Journal (1989), 145–67
NOTES: Child & Co. Lecture 1989 delivered by Professor A. W. B. Simpson on Tuesday, 20 June 1989. Also published separately in 1989 (see books above).

66. 'Contracts for cotton to arrive: the case of the two ships *Peerless*'
Cardozo Law Review, 11 (Dec 1989), 287–333
NOTES: *Raffles v. Wichelhaus*, 33 L.J.N.S. 160

67. 'Legal iconoclasts and legal ideals'
University of Cincinnati Law Review, 58 (1990), 819–44
NOTES: 'This address was delivered on Mar 30, 1989 at the University of Cincinnati College of Law as the Robert S. Marx lecture.'

68. 'Historical introduction'
In M. J. Furmston, *Cheshire, Fifoot and Furmston's law of contract*. 12th edn, 1–16

London: Butterworths, 1991
NOTES: Historical introduction forms ch. 1

69. 'The origins of futures trading in the Liverpool cotton market'
In Peter Cane and Jane Stapleton (eds.), *Essays for Patrick Atiyah*, 179–208. Oxford: Clarendon Press, 1991
NOTES: Forms ch. 8

70. '*Coase v. Pigou* re-examined'
Journal of Legal Studies, 25 (Jan 1996), 53–97

71. '[*Coase v Pigou* re-examined:] An addendum'
Journal of Legal Studies, 25 (Jan 1996), 99–101
NOTES: Follows the article above. This addendum is a response to R. H. Coase's article: 'Law and economics and A. W. Brian Simpson'. *Journal of Legal Studies*, 25 (Jan 1996), 103–19.

72. 'Round up the usual suspects: the legacy of British colonialism and the European Convention on Human Rights'
Loyola Law Review, 41 (Winter 1996), 629–711
NOTES: 'This paper formed the basis of the [ninth] Brendan Brown Lecture, delivered at Loyola University School of Law on Mar 17, 1995.'

73. 'The exile of Archbishop Makarios III'
European Human Rights Law Review, 1 (1996), 391–405
NOTES: History of first interstate ECHR applications arising from decision by British Governor of Cyprus to deport Archbishop in attempt to suppress colonial insurrection.

74. 'Historical introduction'
In M. J. Furmston, *Cheshire, Fifoot, and Furmston's law of contract*; 13th edn, 1–16.
London: Butterworths, 1996.

NOTES: The historical introduction forms ch. 1.

BOOK REVIEWS

75. W. Ogwen Williams (ed.), *Calendar of the Caernarvonshire Quarter Sessions Records. Vol. 1: 1541–1558.*
Law Quarterly Review, 73 (Jan 1957), 24–125.

76. Kiralfy, A. K. R., *A source book of English law*
Law Quarterly Review, 74 (July 1958), 453–5

77. Lambarde, William, *Archeion, or, a discourse upon the high courts of justice in England.* Edited by Charles H. McIlwain and Paul L. Ward
Law Quarterly Review, 74 (July 1958), 455–6

78. Bayne, C. G. (ed.), completed by William Huse Dunham Jr, *Select cases in the Council of Henry VII.* (Publications of the Selden Society, 75)
Law Quarterly Review, 75 (Oct 1959), 561–2.

79. Hall, Jerome, *Studies in jurisprudence and criminal theory*
International and Comparative Law Quarterly, 8 (July 1959), 589–90

80. Williams, Penry. *The Council in the Marches of Wales*
Law Quarterly Review, 75 (Oct 1959), 561–2

81. Sheehan, Michael M., *The will in medieval England*
Harvard Law Review, 78 (1965), 1303–5

82. Milsom, S. F. C., *The legal framework of English feudalism*
Times Literary Supplement, no. 3900, 10 Dec 1976, 1566
NOTES: Headed 'From tenure to estates'

83. Sharpe, R. J., *The law of habeas corpus.*
Times Literary Supplement, no.3915, 25 Mar 1977, 372
NOTE: Headed: 'release mechanism'. Name of reviewer given as 'A. W. R. Simpson'.

84. Toner, Barbara, *The facts of rape.*
Times Literary Supplement, no.3920, 29 Apr 1977, 508
NOTES: Headed 'With concern for the victim'

85. Smith, J. C., *Legal obligation*
Times Literary Supplement, no.3936, 19 Aug 1977, 1008
NOTES: Headed 'To do our duty'

86. Langbein, John H., *Torture and the Law of Proof*
Times Literary Supplement, no.3960, 17 Feb 1978, 194
NOTES: Headed 'The Turn of the Screw'

87. Bentham, Jeremy, *A comment on the commentaries and A fragment on government.* Edited by J. H. Burns and H. L. A. Hart
Times Literary Supplement no.3978, 30 June 1978, 737
NOTES: Headed: 'Berating Blackstone'

88. Denning, Alfred Thompson, BARON, *The discipline of law*
Times Literary Supplement, no.4002, 7 Dec 1979, 85
NOTES: Headed 'The judicial role'

89. Devlin, Patrick Arthur, BARON, *The Judge*
Times Literary Supplement, no.4002, 7 Dec 1979, 85
NOTES: Headed 'The judicial role'

90. Alderson, John, *Policing freedom*
Times Literary Supplement, no.4017, 21 Mar 1980, 337
NOTES: Headed 'May the force be with us'

91. Baker, John H. (ed.), *The reports of Sir John Spelman, vols I and II.* (Publications

of the Selden Society, 93 and 94)
American Journal of Legal History, 25 (Jan 1981), 71–3

92. MacCormick, Neil, *H. L. A. Hart*
Times Literary Supplement, no.4106, 11 Dec 1981, 1447
NOTES: Headed 'Recognizing the legal'

93. Guest, A. G. (ed.), *Anson's law of contract*. 25th (Centenary) edn
In review article: 'Contract: the twitching corpse'
Oxford Journal of Legal Studies, 1 (1981), 265–77

94. Atiyah, Patrick S., *The rise and fall of freedom of contract*
In review article: 'Contract: the twitching corpse'
Oxford Journal of Legal Studies, 1 (1981), 265–77

95. Treitel, G. H., *The law of contract*. 5th edn
In review article: 'Contract: the twitching corpse'
Oxford Journal of Legal Studies, 1 (1981), 265–77

96. Atiyah, Patrick S., *Promises, morals, and law*
American Bar Foundation Research Journal (1982), 537–41

97. McConville, Michael and Baldwin, John, *Courts, prosecution, and conviction*.
Times Literary Supplement, no.4123, 9 Apr 1982, 417
NOTES: Headed 'The criminal process'

98. Paterson, Alan, *The Law Lords*
Times Literary Supplement, no.4164, 21 Jan 1983, 66
NOTES: Headed 'Sayers of the last word'

99. King-Hamilton, Alan, *And nothing but the truth*
Times Literary Supplement, no.4182, 27 May 1983, 534
NOTES: Headed 'Ladling out the porridge'

100. Pattenden, Rosemary, *The judge, discretion, and the criminal trial*
Times Literary Supplement, no.4186, 24 June 1983, 659
NOTES: Headed 'In the judiciary's judgment'

101. Robertson, Geoffrey, *People against the press: an inquiry into the Press Council*
Times Literary Supplement, no.4201, 7 Oct 1983, 1082
NOTES: Headed 'Sleeping watchdogs'

102. Ryan, Mick, *The politics of penal reform*
Times Literary Supplement, no.4208, 25 Nov 1983, 1304
NOTES: Headed 'Emptying the prisons'

103. Cohen, Marshall (ed.), *Ronald Dworkin and contemporary jurisprudence*.
Times Literary Supplement, no.4245, 10 Aug 1984, 895
NOTES: Headed 'How do the judges do it?'

104. Leigh, David, *High time: the shocking life and times of Howard Marks*
Times Literary Supplement, no.4254, 12 Oct 1984, 1153
NOTES: Headed 'Grass and the graduate'

105. Palmer, Robert C., *The Whilton dispute, 1264–1380: a social-legal study of dispute settlement in medieval England*
In review article: 'Their litigious society'
Michigan Law Review, 83 (Feb 1985), 682–9

106. Noonan, John Thomas, Jr., *Bribes*
Journal of Legal Education, 35 (Sept 1985), 461–3

107. Arthurs, H. W., *Without the law: administrative justice and legal pluralism in 19th-century England*
American Historical Review, 90 (1985), 1198

108. Norton, Philip (ed.), *Law and order and British politics*

Times Literary Supplement, no.4278, 29 Mar 1985, 342
NOTES: Headed 'Disagreeable rhetoric'

109. Weisberg, Richard H., *The failure of the word: the protagonist as lawyer in modern fiction*
Times Literary Supplement, no.4278, 29 Mar 1985, 342
NOTES: headed 'Disagreeable rhetoric'

110. Downs, Donald Alexander, *Nazis in Skokie: freedom, community, and the First Amendment.*
Times Literary Supplement, no.4294, 19 July 1985, 790.
NOTES: Headed 'Provocatively free'

111. Rose, Andrew, *Stinie: murder on the common.*
Times Literary Supplement, no.4310, 8 Nov 1985, 1256.
NOTES: Headed 'Just, not right'

112. Unlawful sex: offences, victims and offenders in the criminal justice system of England and Wales
Times Literary Supplement, no.4314, 6 Dec 1985, 1382
NOTES: Headed 'Who, how, where, why, when'

113. Devlin, Patrick Arthur, BARON, *Easing the passing: the trial of Dr John Bodkin Adams*
In review article: 'Euthanasia for sale?'
Michigan Law Review, 84 (Feb/Apr 1986), 807–18

114. Rudden, Bernard, *The New River: a legal history*
Law and History Review, 4 (Fall 1986), 486–8

115. Ives, E. W., *Common lawyers of pre-Reformation England. Thomas Kebell: a case study*
Journal of Legal History, 7 (1986), 110

116. Beattie, J. M., *Crime and the courts in England, 1660–1800*
American Historical Review, 91 (1986), 1193–4

117. Green, Thomas Andrew, *Verdict according to conscience: perspectives on the English criminal trial jury 1200–1800*
Times Literary Supplement, no.4322, 31 Jan 1986, 120
NOTES: Headed 'Bulwarks of liberty'

118. Milsom, S. F. C., *Studies in the history of the common law*
Times Literary Supplement, no. 4353, 5 Sept 1986, 985
NOTES: Headed 'Of legal culture'

119. Kee, Robert, *Trial and error: the Maguires, the Guildford pub bombings and British justice*
Times Literary Supplement, no.4366, 5 Dec 1986, 1365
NOTES: Headed 'Bringing accusations to book'

120. Mullin, Chris, *Error of judgment: the truth about the Birmingham bombings*
Times Literary Supplement, no.4366, 5 Dec 1986, 1365
NOTES: Headed 'Bringing accusations to book'

121. Tur, Richard and Twining, William (eds.), *Essays on Kelsen*
Times Literary Supplement, no.4404, 28 Aug 1987, 920
NOTES: Headed 'Towards a legal science'

122. Atiyah, Patrick S., *Pragmatism and theory in English Law*
Times Literary Supplement, no.4406, 11 Sep 1987, 998
NOTES: Headed 'No accounting for judges'

123. Turow, Scott, *Presumed innocent*
Times Literary Supplement, no.4411, 16 Oct 1987, 1136
NOTES: Headed 'Attorney on trial'

124. Evans, E. P., *The criminal prosecution and capital punishment of animals: the lost history of Europe's animal trials.*

Times Literary Supplement, no.4412, 23 Oct 1987, 1173
NOTES: Headed 'Blaming the beasts'

125. Honoré, Tony, *Making law bind: essays legal and philosophical*
Cambridge Law Journal, 47 (July 1988), 299–302

126. Steiner, Henry J., *Moral argument and social vision in the courts: a study of tort accident law*
In review article: 'Legal reasoning anatomized'
Law & Social Inquiry: Journal of the American Bar Foundation, 13 (summer 1988), 637–45

127. Bourguignon, Henry J., *Sir William Scott, Lord Stowell: judge of the High Court of Admiralty, 1798–1828*
Lloyds Maritime and Commercial Law Quarterly (Nov. 1988), 528–9

128. Thorne, S. E., *Essays in English legal history*
American Journal of Legal History, 32 (1988), 79–80

129. Van Caenegem, R. C., *Judges, legislators, and professors: chapters in European legal history*
American Historical Review, 94 (1989), 1090.

130. Ekirch, A. Roger, *The transportation of British convicts to the colonies, 1718–1775*
American Journal of Legal History, 34 (1990), 196–7

131. Shanley, Mary Lyndon, *Feminism, marriage and the law in Victorian England, 1850–1895*
American Journal of Legal History, 34 (1990), 443–4

132. Lieberman, D., *The province of legislation determined: legal theory in eighteenth- century Britain*
Times Literary Supplement, no.4562, 7 Sept 1990, 944

NOTES: Headed 'A testing time for judges'

133. Waldron, Jeremy, *The law*
Times Literary Supplement, no.4576, 14 Dec 1990, 1344
NOTES: Headed 'Trouble with the case'

134. Cornish, William Rodolph and Clark, Geoffrey de N., *Law and Society in England: 1750–1950*
In review article: 'Legal education and legal history'
Oxford Journal of Legal Studies, 11 (Spring 1991), 106–13

135. Posner, Richard A., *Sex and reason*
Times Literary Supplement, no.4658, 10 July 1992, 26
NOTES: headed 'The economics of Eros'

136. Teeven, K. M., *A history of the Anglo-American common law of contract.*
American Historical Review, 97 (1992), 522–3

137. Conley, Carolyn A., *The unwritten law: criminal justice in Victorian Kent*
In review article: 'Law, crime, and the Victorians'
Journal of British Studies, 32 (Jan 1993), 83–8

138. Forsythe, W. J., *Penal discipline, reformatory projects and the English Prison Commission, 1895–1939*
In review article: 'Law, crime, and the Victorians'
Journal of British Studies, 32 (Jan 1993), 83–8

139. Lobban, Michael, *The common law and English jurisprudence, 1760–1850*
In review article: 'Law, crime, and the Victorians'
Journal of British Studies, 32 (Jan 1993), 83–8

140. Wiener, Martin J., *Reconstructing the criminal: Culture, Law, and Policy in England, 1830–1914*

In review article: 'Law, Crime, and the Victorians'
Journal of British Studies, 32 (Jan 1993), 83–8

141. Zedner, Lucia, *Women, Crime, and Custody in Victorian England*
In review article: 'Law, crime, and the Victorians'
Journal of British Studies, 32 (Jan 1993), 83–8

142. Anderson, J. Stuart, *Lawyers and the making of English land law, 1832–1940*
Modern Law Review, 56 (July 1993), 608–11

143. Oldham, James, *The Mansfield manuscripts and the growth of English law in the eighteenth century*
Albion, 25 (1993), 320–2

144. Thomas, Rosamond M., *Espionage and secrecy: the Official Secrets Acts 1911–1989 of the UK*
American Journal of Legal History, 37 (1993), 92–4

145. Meron, Theodor, *Henry's Wars and Shakespeare's Laws: perspectives on the law of war in the later Middle Ages*
In review article: 'The Agincourt campaign and the law of war'
Michigan Journal of International Law, 16 (Spring 1995), 653–66

146. Best, Geoffrey, *War and law since 1945*
Times Literary Supplement, no.4788, 6 Jan 1995, 7
NOTES: Headed 'The idea of restraint'

147. Spring, Eileen, *Law, land and family: aristocratic inheritance in England, 1300–1800*
Times Literary Supplement, no.4803, 21 Apr 1995, 26
NOTES: Headed 'The heiress at law'

148. Bentley, Iris and Dening, Penelope, *Let him have justice: the true story of Derek Bentley, hanged for a crime he did not commit*
Times Literary Supplement, no.4822, 1 Sept 1995, 13
NOTES: Headed 'A Tissue of Lies'

149. Hill, Paddy Joe and Hunt, Gerard, *Forever lost, forever gone*
Times Literary Supplement, no.4822, 1 Sept 1995, 13
NOTES: Headed 'A Tissue of Lies'

150. Rubin, Gerry R., *Private property, government requisition and the Constitution, 1914–1927*
Law Quarterly Review, 112 (Jan 1996), 172–5

151. Darden, Christopher A. and Walter, Jess, *In contempt*
Times Literary Supplement, no.4868, 19 July 1996, 28
NOTES: Headed 'Triumph or travesty?'

152. Dershowitz, Alan M., *Reasonable doubts: the O. J. Simpson case and the criminal justice system*
Times Literary Supplement, no.4868, 19 July 1996, 28
NOTES: Headed 'Triumph or travesty?'
'Forensic evidence': letter by Paul Collins in response to review on use of the word 'forensic', *Times Literary Supplement*, no.4870, 2 Aug 1996, 17

153. Rosenberg, David, *The hidden Holmes: his theory of torts in history*
In review article: 'The elusive truth about Holmes'
Michigan Law Review, 95 (May 1997), 2027–43

154. Cosgrove, Richard A., *Scholars of the law: English jurisprudence from Blackstone to Hart*
American Journal of Legal History, 41 (1997) 481–2

155. Brewer, John, and Susan Staves (eds.), *Early modern conceptions of property*

American Journal of Legal History, 41 (1997), 508–9

156. Gordon, Richard and R. Wilmot-Smith (eds.), *Human rights in the UK*
European Human Rights Law Review, 2 (1997) 204–6

157. O'Dell, T. H., *Inventions and official secrecy: a history of secret patents in the UK*
Law and History Review, 15 (1997), 378

NEWSPAPER ITEMS

158. 'Evidence in Camera' Letter. *The Times*, 25 Apr 1970, 9e

159. 'Oxford Aim to Debate Admission of Women.' *The Times*, 10 May 1972, 3h; 'Co–residence test plan goes ahead at Oxford.' *The Times*, 17 June 1972, 3f. News items mention submission by A. W. B. Simpson of resolution on admission of women to Oxford.

160. 'Three women appointed to inquiry on rape.' *The Times*, 2 July 1975, 2e. Membership of committee to investigate rape laws includes Prof. Brian Simpson.

161. 'Closure of law clinic opposed.' *Times Higher Education Supplement*, no. 279, 25 Feb 1977, 32e. Proposal to replace Kent University law clinic by community law centre in Canterbury meets strong opposition.

162. 'Skirting the pitfalls in "practical" legal education.' *Times Higher Education Supplement*, no. 280, 4 Mar 1977, 13d. Article by A. W. B. Simpson on closure of Kent University law clinic.

163. 'We can see the broken eggs, now show us the omelette.' *Times Higher Education Supplement*, no. 284, 1 Apr 1977, 12. Reply by Adrian Taylor and Larry Grant to article by A. W. B. Simpson.

164. 'Trades council pleads to V-C for law clinic.' *Times Higher Education Supplement*, no. 290, 13 May 1977, 2c. News item; A. W. B. Simpson maintains that Kent University law clinic's involvement in controversial cases has not affected University's decision to close clinic.

165. 'Obscenity committee.' *The Times*, 3 Sept 1977, 3d. Professor Simpson sits on Committee on Obscenity and Film Censorship; with photograph of committee members.

166. 'Parental authority and the pill.' *The Times*, 1 Aug 1983, 11g. Letter.

167. 'Learning and the learned journals: law.' *Times Literary Supplement*, no. 4211, 16 Dec 1983, 1402.

168. 'British intelligence.' *Times Literary Supplement*, no.4565, 28 Sept 1990, 1031. Letter on access to MI5's records and *British intelligence in the Second World War* by F. H. Hinsley and C. A. G. Simkins.

169. 'Detention without trial.' *Times Literary Supplement*, no.4698, 16 Apr 1993, 15. Letter clarifying activities of Prince Henry of Pless during World War II. Following publication of review by Geoffrey Best of *In the highest degree odious* in *Times Literary Supplement*, no. 4696, 2 Apr 1993, 26.

TITLE INDEX

Agincourt campaign and the law of war	145
analysis of legal concepts, The	10n, 29
beauty of obscurity	18f, 19
Biographical dictionary of the common law	6
Bursting reservoirs and Victorian tort law	18h, 19
Cannibalism and the common law	5, 7, 16
case of first impression, A	18e, 19
circulation of Yearbooks in the fifteenth century, The	10d, 23
Coase v. Pigou re-examined	70, 71
common law and legal theory, The	10o, 41, 61
Contract: the twitching corpse	10m, 93, 94, 95
Contracts for cotton to arrive	66
Detention without trial in the Second World War	64
early constitution of Gray's Inn, The	10c, 43
early constitution of the Inns of Court, The	10b, 36
elusive truth about Holmes, The	152
Entails and perpetuities	10h, 48
equitable doctrine of consideration and the law of uses, The	30
Euthanasia for sale?	113
exile of Archbishop Makarios III, The	73
Heraldic evidence and the early history of Lincoln's Inn	47
Historical introduction (*Cheshire and Fifoot's law of contract*)	46, 53, 62, 68, 74
history of the common law of contract, A	3, 9
history of the land law, A	8
Horwitz thesis and the history of contracts, The	10k, 49
ideal of the rule of law, The	18I, 19
In the highest degree odious	14, 15
Innovation in nineteenth-century contract law	10j, 44
Introduction (Blackstone's *Commentaries*)	51
introduction of the action on the case for conversion, The	10f, 26
introduction to the history of the land law, An	1
Invitation to law	12
judges and the vigilant state, The	13, 65
Keilwey's Reports, temp. Henry VII and Henry VIII	21
Law, crime, and the Victorians	136, 137, 138, 139, 140
laws of Ethelbert, The	10a, 54
Leading cases in the common law	18, 19
Learning and the learned journals: law	167
Legal education and legal history	134
Legal iconoclasts and legal ideals	67
Legal liability for bursting reservoirs	58
Legal reasoning anatomized	126
Legal science and legal absurdity	18d, 19
Legal theory and legal history	10
legal treatise and legal theory, The	57

Obscenity and the law   55, 59
origins of futures trading in the Liverpool cotton market, The   69
Oxford essays in jurisprudence: second series   2
penal bond with conditional defeasance, The   10g, 32
place of Slade's case in the history of contract, The   25
Politics and law in Elizabethan England   18b, 19
Pornography & politics   4
Quackery and contract law   18j, 19, 60
R. S. Rattray and Ashanti law   10q
ratio decidendi of a case, The   22, 24, 27, 28
Real property   31, 33, 35, 37, 39, 40
Regina v. Archer and Muller 1875): the leading case that never was   56
Report of the Advisory Group on the Law of Rape   45
Report of the Committee on Obscenity and Film Censorship   50
reports of John Spelman, The   20
Rhetoric, reality, and regulation 18B   11, 63
rise and fall of the legal treatise, The   10l, 52
Round up the usual suspects   72
rule in *Wheeldon v. Burrows* and the *Code Civil*, The   10i, 34
source and function of the later Year Books, The   10e, 38
study of cases, The   18a, 19
survival of the common law system, The   10p, 42
Their litigious society   105
timeless principles of the common law, The   18c, 19
Victorian judges and the problem of social cost   18g, 19
Victorian law and the industrial spirit   17

CASES

Carlill v. Carbolic Smoke Ball Company (1893)	**18j, 19, 60**
Greece v. UK (1956 and 1957)	**73**
Jee v. Audley (1787)	**18d, 19**
Keeble v. Hickeringill (1707)	**18c, 19**
Priestley v. Fowler (1837)	**10e**
R. v. Archer and Muller (1875)	**56**
R. v. Dudley and Stephens (1884)	**5, 7, 16, 56**
R. v. Keyn (1876)	**18i, 19**
Raffles v. Wichelhaus and Busch (1864)	**18f, 19, 66, 69**
Rylands v. Fletcher (1868)	**18h, 19, 58**
Shelley's Case (1581)	**18b, 19**
Slade's Case (1602)	**25**
Tipping v. St Helen's Smelting Company (1865)	**18g, 19**
Wheeldon v. Burrows (1879)	**10i, 34**

SUBJECTS

(Books are not indexed under legal history and jurisprudence because the terms apply to so many works. Book reviews are not indexed in this list.)

Accidents at work	**18e, 19**
Actions and defences	**1, 3, 9, 10f, 10g, 26, 32**
Archbishop Makarios III	**73**
Ashanti law	**10q**
Blackstone, Sir William	**51**
Cannibalism	**5, 7, 16, 56**
Censorship	**4, 50**
Civil rights	**11, 13, 14, 15, 18i, 19, 63, 64, 65, 72, 73**
Coase theorem	**18g, 19, 70, 71**
Colonialism	**72, 73**
Committee on Obscenity and Film Censorship	**4, 50, 165**
Contracts	**1, 3, 9, 10j, 10k, 10m, 17, 18f, 18j,**
	19, 25, 30, 32, 44, 46, 49, 53, 60, 62,
	66, 68, 69, 74
Cyprus	**73**
Defence Regulations 1939, Regulation 18B	**11, 13, 14, 15, 63, 64**
Detention	**11, 13, 14, 15, 63, 64, 65, 72, 169**
Ducks	**18c, 19**
Easements	**10i, 25, 34**
Ethelbert	**10a, 54**
European Convention on Human Rights	**72, 73**
Film Censorship	**4, 50**
Futures	**18f, 19, 66, 69**
Gray's Inn (see also Inns of Court)	**10c, 43**

Horwitz, Morton J.	10k, 49
Inns of Court	10b, 10c, 36, 43, 47
Judges	6, 13, 65
Keilwey	21
Land law	1, 8, 17, 18b, 19, 31, 33, 35, 37, 39, 40
Law and economic development	17
Law reporting	18a, 19, 20, 21
Lawyers	6
Legal literature and legal publishing	10l, 10p, 18a, 19, 20, 21, 42, 52, 57, 167
Lincoln's Inn (see also Inns of Court)	47
MI5	14, 15, 168
Mignonette (Boat)	5, 7, 16
Mosley, Sir Oswald	14, 15
Murder	5, 7, 16, 56
National security	11, 13, 14, 15, 63, 64, 65
Obscenity	4, 50, 55, 59
Peerless (Ship)	18f, 19, 66, 69
Perpetuities	10h, 18d, 19, 48
Pigou, Arthur Cecil (1877–1959)	18g, 19, 70, 71
Pornography	4, 50, 55, 59
Rape	45, 160
Ratio decidendi	18, 19, 22, 24, 27, 28
Rattray, R. S.	10q
Social cost	18g, 19, 70, 71
Spelman, Sir John	20
Torts	17, 18c, 18e, 18h, 19, 58
Trials (Murder)	5, 7, 16, 56
University of Kent at Canterbury	161, 162, 163, 164
Uses	30
War and emergency powers	11, 13, 14, 15, 63, 64
Williams Committee	4, 50, 165
Yearbooks	10d, 10e, 23, 38

BOOK REVIEWS BY AUTHOR

Alderson, John, *Policing freedom*	90
Anderson, J. Stuart, *Lawyers and the making of English land law, 1832–1940*	142
Arthurs, H. W., *Without the law*	107
Atiyah, Patrick S., *Pragmatism and theory in English Law*	122
——, *Promises, morals, and law*	96
——, *The rise and fall of freedom of contract*	94
Baker, John H. (ed.), *The reports of Sir John Spelman*	91
Bayne, C. G. (ed.), *Select cases in the Council of Henry VII*	78
Beattie, J. M., *Crime and the courts in England, 1660–1800*	116
Bentham, Jeremy, *A comment on the commentaries . . .*	87
Bentley, Iris and Dening, Penelope, *Let him have justice*	148
Best, Geoffrey, *War and law since 1945*	146

Bourguignon, Henry J., *Sir William Scott, Lord Stowell*   **127**
Brewer, John and Staves, Susan (eds.), *Early modern conceptions of property*   **155**
Cohen, Marshall (ed.), *Ronald Dworkin and contemporary jurisprudence*   **103**
Conley, Carolyn A., *The unwritten law*   **137**
Cornish, W. R. and Clark, G. de N., *Law and society in England: 1750–1950*   **134**
Cosgrove, Richard A., *Scholars of the law*   **154**
Darden, Christopher A. and Walter, Jess, *In contempt*   **151**
Denning, Alfred Thompson, BARON, *The discipline of law*   **88**
Dershowitz, Alan M., *Reasonable doubts*   **152**
Devlin, Patrick Arthur, BARON, *Easing the passing*   **113**
——, *The judge*   **89**
Downs, Donald Alexander, *Nazis in Skokie*   **110**
Ekirch, A. Roger, *The transportation of British convicts . . .*   **130**
Evans, E. P., *The criminal prosecution and capital punishment of animals*   **124**
Forsythe, W. J., *Penal discipline, reformatory projects, and the English
    Prison Commission, 1895–1939*   **138**
Gordon, Richard and Wilmot-Smith, R. (eds.), *Human rights in the UK*   **156**
Green, Thomas Andrew, *Verdict according to conscience*   **117**
Guest, A. G. (ed.), *Anson's law of contract*, 25th (Centenary) edn   **93**
Hall, Jerome, *Studies in jurisprudence and criminal theory*   **79**
Hill, Paddy Joe and Hunt, Gerard, *Forever lost, forever gone*   **149**
Honoré, Tony, *Making law bind: essays legal and philosophical*   **125**
Ives, E. W., *Common lawyers of pre–reformation England*   **115**
Kee, Robert, *Trial and error*   **119**
King-Hamilton, Alan, *And nothing but the truth*   **99**
Kiralfy, A. K. R., *A source book of English law*   **76**
Lambarde, William, *Archeion*   **77**
Langbein, John H., *Torture and the law of proof*   **86**
Leigh, David, *High time*   **104**
Lieberman, D., *The province of legislation determined*   **132**
Lobban, Michael, *The common law and English jurisprudence, 1760–1850*   **139**
McConville, Michael and Baldwin, John, *Courts, prosecution, and conviction*   **97**
MacCormick, Neil, *H. L. A. Hart*   **92**
Meron, Theodor, *Henry's wars and Shakespeare's laws*   **145**
Milsom, S. F. C., *The legal framework of English feudalism*   **82**
——, *Studies in the history of the common law*   **118**
Mullin, Chris, *Error of judgment*   **120**
Noonan, John Thomas, Jr, *Bribes*   **106**
Norton, Philip (ed.), *Law and order and British politics*   **108**
O'Dell, T. H., *Inventions and official secrecy*   **157**
Oldham, James, *The Mansfield manuscripts . . .*   **143**
Palmer, Robert C., *The Whilton dispute, 1264–1380*   **105**
Paterson, Alan, *The Law Lords*   **98**
Pattenden, Rosemary, *The judge, discretion, and the criminal trial*   **100**
Posner, Richard A., *Sex and reason*   **135**
Robertson, Geoffrey, *People against the press*   **101**
Rose, Andrew, *Stinie: murder on the common*   **111**
Rosenberg, David, *The Hidden Holmes*   **153**

Rubin, Gerry R., *Private property, government requisition* . . .   **150**
Rudden, Bernard, *The New River: a legal history*   **114**
Ryan, Mick, *The politics of penal reform*   **102**
Shanley, Mary Lyndon, *Feminism, marriage, and the law in Victorian England*   **131**
Sharpe, R. J., *The law of habeas corpus*   **83**
Sheehan, Michael M., *The will in medieval England*   **81**
Smith, J. C., *Legal obligation*   **85**
Spring, Eileen, *Law, land and family*   **147**
Steiner, Henry J., *Moral argument and social vision in the courts*   **126**
Teeven, K. M., *A history of the Anglo-American common law of contract*   **136**
Thomas, Rosamond M., *Espionage and secrecy*   **144**
Thorne, S. E., *Essays in English legal history*   **128**
Toner, Barbara, *The facts of rape*   **84**
Treitel, G. H., *The law of contract*, 5th edn   **95**
Tur, Richard and Twining, William (eds.), *Essays on Kelsen*   **121**
Turow, Scott, *Presumed innocent*   **123**
Unlawful sex: offences, victims, and offenders . . .   *112*
Van Caenegem, R. C., *Judges, Legislators, and Professors*   **129**
Waldron, Jeremy, *The Law*   **133**
Weisberg, Richard H., *The failure of the word*   **109**
Wiener, Martin J., *Reconstructing the criminal*   **140**
Williams, Penry, *The Council in the Marches of Wales*   **80**
Williams, W. Ogwen (ed.), *Calendar of the Caernarvonshire Quarter Sessions Records*   **75**
Zedner, Lucia, *Women, crime, and custody in Victorian England*   **141**

BOOKS REVIEWED BY TITLE

And nothing but the truth (King-Hamilton)   99
Anson's law of contract (Guest)   93
Archeion (Lambarde)   77
Bribes (Noonan)   106
Calendar of the Caernarvonshire Quarter Sessions Records (Williams)   75
comment on the commentaries . . ., A (Bentham)   87
common law and English jurisprudence, 1760–1850, The (Lobban)   139
Common lawyers of pre–reformation England. (Ives)   115
Council in the Marches of Wales, The (Williams)   80
Courts, prosecution, and conviction (McConville and Baldwin)   97
Crime and the courts in England, 1660–1800 (Beattie)   116
criminal prosecution and capital punishment of animals, The (Evans)   124
discipline of law, The (Denning)   88
Early modern conceptions of property (Brewer and Staves)   155
Easing the passing: the trial of Dr John Bodkin Adams (Devlin)   113
Error of judgment (Mullin)   120
Espionage and secrecy (Thomas)   144
Essays in English legal history (Thorne)   128
Essays on Kelsen (Tur and Twining)   121
facts of rape, The (Toner)   84
failure of the word, The (Weisberg)   109
Feminism, marriage, and the law in Victorian England (Shanley)   131
Forever lost, forever gone (Hill and Hunt)   149
H. L. A. Hart (MacCormick)   92
Henry's wars and Shakespeare's laws (Meron)   145
hidden Holmes, The (Rosenberg)   153
High time (Leigh)   104
history of the Anglo-American common law of contract, A (Teeven)   136
Human rights in the UK (Gordon and Wilmot–Smith)   156
In contempt (Darden and Walter)   151
Inventions and official secrecy (O'Dell)   157
judge, The (Devlin)   89
judge, discretion, and the criminal trial, The (Pattenden)   100
Judges, legislators, and professors (Van Caenegem)   129
law, The (Waldron)   333
Law and order and British politics (Norton)   108
Law and society in England: 1750–1950 (Cornish and Clark)   134
Law Lords (Paterson)   98
law of contract, The (Treitel)   95
law of habeas corpus, The (Sharpe)   83
Law, land and family (Spring)   147
Lawyers and the making of English land law, 1832–1940 (Anderson)   142
legal framework of English feudalism, The (Milsom)   82
Legal obligation (Smith)   85
Let him have justice (Bentley and Dening)   148

Making law bind: essays legal and philosophical (Honoré)   125
Mansfield manuscripts and the growth of English law. . ., The (Oldham)   143
Moral argument and social vision in the courts (Steiner)   126
Nazis in Skokie (Downs)   110
New River: a legal history, The (Rudden)   114
Penal discipline, reformatory projects and the English Prison
    Commission, 1895–1939 (Forsythe)   138
People against the press. (Robertson)   101
Policing freedom (Alderson)   90
politics of penal reform, The (Ryan)   102
Pragmatism and theory in English Law (Atiyah)   122
Presumed innocent (Turow)   123
Private property, government requisition . . . (Rubin)   150
Promises, morals, and law (Atiyah)   96
province of legislation determined (Lieberman)   132
Reasonable doubts (Dershowitz)   152
Reconstructing the criminal (Wiener)   140
reports of Sir John Spelman, The (Baker)   91
rise and fall of freedom of contract, The (Atiyah)   94
Ronald Dworkin and contemporary jurisprudence (Cohen)   103
Scholars of the law (Cosgrove)   154
Select cases in the Council of Henry VII (Bayne and Dunham)   78
Sex and reason (Posner)   135
Sir William Scott, Lord Stowell (Bourguignon)   127
source book of English law, A (Kiralfy)   76
Stinie: murder on the common (Rose)   111
Studies in jurisprudence and criminal theory (Hall)   79
Studies in the history of the common law (Milsom)   118
Torture and the law of proof (Langbein)   86
transportation of British convicts . . ., The (Ekirch)   130
Trial and error (Kee)   119
Unlawful sex: offences, victims and offenders . . .   112
unwritten law, The (Conley)   137
Verdict according to conscience (Green)   117
War and law since 1945 (Best)   146
Whilton dispute, The (Palmer)   105
will in medieval England, The (Sheehan)   81
Without the law (Arthurs)   107
Women, crime, and custody in Victorian England (Zedner)   141

Index

abandoned children 4, 12, 66–85
    adoption 68, 75, 79
    age of child 66, 67
    anonymity 76, 78, 83
    anti-anonymity approach of English
        courts 78
    Argentina 70–1
    attitudes, modern 75
    birth certificates 79, 84
    care order 75
    cautions 67
    common law 67
    concealment of birth 77
    confidentiality 76
    criminal offences 66, 67, 75
    definition 68
    development of attitudes to 67
    endangering life 66, 67–8
    fact and fiction, in 71–5
    fairytales 71–5
    finding mother 78
    folk-tales 71–5
    France 66, 78–9, 80–3, 84
    historical background 66–7, 73
    human rights: context 69–71; generally
        66; identity rights 69–71
    identity rights: access to personal files 70;
        adoption 79; anonymity 76, 78;
        Argentina 70–1; artificial insemination
        79; birth certificates 79; definition of
        identity 71; European Convention on
        Human Rights 69; fairytales 71–5;
        finding mother 78; folk-lore 71–5;
        generally 66; genetic rights, regard for
        79; human rights 69–71; illegally
        deprived, children 71; local authority
        files, access to 69; meaning 68–9;
        mother's rights and 78; public care,
        children in 69–70; survival, importance
        of 78; United Nations Convention on
        the Rights of the Child 69, 70–1;
        Victorian era, in 68–9
    infanticide 75–9, 84; concealment of birth
        77; crime of abandonment 75; history
        77; legal policy 77; offence 77;
        sentencing 77
    legal research 69
    literary background 74–5
    local authority files, access to 69
    medieval literature 74–5
    motherhood, attitudes to 78–9
    official policies 83–4
    parental responsibility 75
    Poor Law 83
    prosecutions 67
    reform of law 75
    refusal of motherhood 77–8
    reunited with mother 68
    rights of children 68–9
    secrecy 76, 83
    significance 69
    statistics 68
    terminology 76
    Thomas Coram Foundation 76
    United Nations Convention on the Rights
        of the Child 66, 69, 70–1
adoption:
    abandoned children 68, 75, 79
    birth certificates, access to 79
African Charter of Human and People's
        Rights 16
AIRE Centre 28
appeals:
    War Zone Courts 103, 106
Argentina:
    children, identity rights of 70
Atiyah 207, 211
Australia:
    common law of human rights 36, 52

Benjamin, Walter 73
Bettelheim, Bruno 72, 75
Bill of Rights:
    Hong Kong 38
    use 30
Bonnet, Catherine 82
Boswell, John 74
breaches of human rights:
    complaints concerning 13
    European Convention on Human Rights:
        Italy, breaches by 22; UK breaches 22
    UN Human Rights Commission,
        complaints to: approach to 13–14;
        consistent breaches 13–14; political
        support 14
Bronaugh 44

Campbell, Lord:
    biographer 197–8
    conclusions on 201
    early years at bar 174–8
    generally 172–3
    judge, as 192–3
    law reformer, as 195–6
    literary interests 197
    personal lives 198–200
    politician, as 184–6
    university career 174

Canada:
  common law of human rights 36, 53
cannibalism 150
capital punishment:
  United States 39–40
Central American Court of Justice 14
  abolition 15
children:
  abandoning, *see* Abandoned children
  identity rights, *see under* Abandoned
    children
  sentencing 24, 25
  social services care, in 27
China:
  common law of human rights 48–9
civil jury trial 205–24
  complex and technical matters 209
  costs 205–6, 207–8
  counterstreams to abolition 212–4
  dethronement by judicialising decision-
    making 206–12
  Dicey, A.V 209
  exclusion of jury trial 208–9
  fact-finding by court 210–11
  free-market theory and 207
  generally 205–6
  inadequacies, perceived 208
  intentional torts 207
  Judicature Acts 211–12
  malicious prosecution 214–24; control of
    jury by judge 218–21; court martial
    215; existence of jurisdiction 214–15;
    generally 213–14; hearsay 218–19;
    intent 21–4; meaning 214; *mens rea*
    214; motive 217; privilege 221–4;
    reasonable and probable cause 217;
    reasonableness 214; roles of judge and
    jury 217–21; significance 213
  malicious or wicked state of mind,
    injuries involving 206–7
  merchants 210
  pleadings and 209–10
  questions of fact 210
  reversal of decline 212
  Russia 205
  Rylands v. Fletcher 212
  special juries 210
  United Stats 205
  Victorian England, in 205–24; decline of
    jury trial 205–6
Coase, Ronald 289, 290
colonial resistance:
  engaging resistance 137–48
  legal determination and 126–48
  Papua New Guinea 127, 137–48
  responsibility of law 128–31
  terminal legality 131–5
  vibrancy, law's 135–7
common law of human rights 27, 29–65

acknowledgment of use of foreign case
  46
attribution of source 42
Australia 36, 52
binding authority 32
borrowing from other jurisdictions 36–40
Bronaugh 44
Canada 36, 53
challenges to legitimacy of adjudication
  31–2
'cherry picking' 37
China 48–9
choice of jurisdiction 37
common enterprise 52–5, 62–4
comparative jurisprudence: factors in
  using, *see* factors in using comparative
  human rights law *below*; trends
  towards 36–40
consideration of foreign law 43
criteria of relevance 48
culture of rights 41
degrees of influence 42
determination of relevance 45–6
distinguishing foreign authorities 43, 48
European Court of Human Rights,
  judgments of 33–5
explicit and non-explicit references to
  other jurisdictions 41–2
factors in using comparative human
  rights law 42, 47–59; audience 50–2;
  common alliances, existence of 52–5;
  constitution, whether transformative or
  conservative 56; differences in
  constitutional structure 59; empirical
  fact, foreign law as 57–8; generally
  47–8; identification 47; pedagogical
  impulse 49–50; perceived judicial
  competence 58–9; political regime,
  type of 48–9; Slaughter 49; theories of
  law and legal interpretation 56–7;
  Tripathi 47–8; vacuum created by
  absence of indigenous jurisprudence,
  filling 55–6
fairness 43
foreign law, use of 41–3
Glendon 36
Glenn 56
globalization of judiciary 62–4
Henkin 51
Hong Kong 37–8
India 36, 53
influence of other jurisdictions 30–1
Ireland 37
Israel 36, 37, 49
issues raised 64–5
Jacobsohn 49
Jamaica 52
kinds of authority 32
La Forest 60

McFadden 51
Mearns 55
Nelken 36
New Zealand 37, 52
NGOs, role of 62
Pakistan 52
persuasive authority 32, 33–5, 43–7
political judgments 31–2
political regime, type of 48–9
Raz, Joseph 32
reasons for decision 46
rules of relevance 45–6, 48
Schauer 44–5
significance of judicial citations 29
Singapore 37, 38
Slaughter 42, 49, 61
sources of authority 32
South Africa 36, 37, 55
Summers 47
transnational judicial conversations
59–62
Tripathi 47–8
United Kingdom 52
United States 37, 39–40, 42, 51–2, 53, 58
using transnational law 41–3
warnings, use of foreign judgments as
49–50
Weissbrodt 57
Zimbabwe 36, 53
see also National legal systems
common plea, see Tudor common pleas
comparative human rights jurisprudence
36–40
constitutions:
borrowing from other jurisdictions 30–1
contextual studies 149–69
cannibalism 150
Dudley and Stephens 150
parables, use of 151–60; interpretation
159–60; point of 156–60; texts, as 153–6
questions of fact 151–3
ratio decidendi: ambiguity 157; concept of
150; definitions 156–7; determining
156–7; interpretation 160–5; meaning
156; Prodigal Son parable, of 165–7
Rylands v. Fletcher 149–50
Simpson, Brian 149–69
testamentary capacity 151–2
theology and 168–9
Convention Against Torture:
bodies established under 15
Convention for the Elimination of all Forms
of Discrimination Against Women.
bodies established under 15
Optional Protocol 15
Convention for the Elimination of all Forms
of Racial Discrimination:
bodies established under 15
Convention for the Establishment of a

Central American Court of Justice:
international court 14
copyright 254–70
authorship 268–9
background 255–6
'Battle of the Books' 255, 259, 269
first modern copyright Act 257–67
history of 254–70
importance of understanding genesis of
267–70
investment 268
modern debate 267–70
reproductive technology 255–6
seventeenth century 256
Simpson, Brian 254
Statute of Anne 257–67; consequences
266–7; judges and 259–62; nature of
right 258–9; property rights 257;
provisions 257; rationalizing the
outcome 262–6; remedies 257–8

death penalty, see Capital punishment
Denman, Thomas:
conclusions on 200–1
early years at bar 174–8
generally 172–3
judge, as 189–92
law reformer, as 194–5
literary interests 197
personal lives 198–200
politician, as 182–4
university careers 174
Devlin 223, 241, 242
Dicey, A.V:
civil jury trial 209
Dudley and Stephens:
Simpson, Brian, 150
Dworkin, Ronald 160, 161

emergency legislation:
War Zone Courts, see War Zone Courts
European Commission for Democracy
through law 37
European Commission of Human Rights:
abolition 15
admissibility criteria 19–20
complaints to: admissibility 19–20;
individuals 15; manifestly unfounded
19, 20; merits of case 19; pre-abolition
18; rejection 19
pre-11th Protocol position 15
reference of case to Court 21
role 19
Secretariat 20
European Community:
legal system 54
European Convention on Human Rights
(ECHR):
awareness, judicial 28

ECHR (*cont.*):
  development 14
  drafting 17
  establishment 17
  individual petition: development of right
    18; UK 18
  influences of British on 17–18
  national legal systems 30
  reservations 17
European Court of Human Rights:
  access to 21
  complaints to: direct 15; generally 15;
    legal aid 20–1
  functions 15
  Human Rights Act 1998 and judgments
    of 33–5
  interpretation 20
  judges 20
  judicial pronouncements 15
  lawyers, appearance by 21
  legal aid 20–1
  questions asked by 20
  UK cases: breaches of Convention 22;
    examples 22
  work required to bring case before 21
European Court of Justice:
  comparative method 54–5
  complaints to 16
  European Convention on Human Rights
    (ECHR), interpretation of 54
  preliminary rulings 16

fascism:
  freedom of expression 23–4
Finnis 223
Fleming 223
Forsyth 206
France:
  abandoned children 66, 78–9, 80–3, 84
freedom of expression:
  fascism 23–4

Gilmore 207, 211
Glendon 36
Glenn 56
Gulf war:
  detention of Iraqis during 23

Haase 72
Hart, H.L.A.:
  international law 14
Henderson, Edith 225, 232, 235
Henkin 51
Holmes 211, 222–3
Hong Kong:
  Bill of Rights 38
  common law of human rights 37, 37–8
Horn 16–7
Horwitz 207, 288, 289

human rights:
  common law of, *see* Common law of
    human rights
  interpretation 30
  just satisfaction 23
  scope of protection 30
  use of term 13
Human Rights Act 1998:
  cause of action for breach of Convention
    rights 27
  commencement 27
  conception of human rights 33
  European Court of Human Rights,
    judgments of 33–5
  foreign case law, use of 34–5
  interpretative principle 27
  other jurisdictions, case law of 34–5
  persuasive authority 33–5
  purpose 27
  remedies 27
  universality of rights 33
  White Paper 27
Human Rights Committee:
  establishment 16
  reservations 17

India:
  common law of human rights 36, 53
infanticide:
  abandoned children 75–9, 84;
    concealment of birth 77; crime of
    abandonment 75; history 77; legal
    policy 77; offence 77; sentencing
    77
  history 77
  homicide, as 77
  offence 77
International Covenant on Civil and
    Political Rights:
  bodies established under 15
  national legal systems 30
international law:
  Central American Court of Justice 14
  Convention Against Torture 15
  Convention for the Elimination of all
    Forms of Discrimination Against
    Women 15
  Convention for the Elimination of all
    Forms of Racial Discrimination 15
  European Commission of Human Rights,
    see European Commission of Human
    Rights
  European Convention on Human Rights
    (ECHR), *see* European Convention on
    Human Rights (ECHR)
  European Court of Justice 16
  Hart, H.L.A. 14
  Human Rights Committee, *see* Human
    Rights Committee

individual's relationship with 13–28; academic's role 32; Central American Court of Justice 14; Convention Against Torture 15; Convention for the Elimination of all Forms of Discrimination Against Women 15; Convention for the Elimination of all Forms of Racial Discrimination 15; EU treaties 16; European Commission of Human Rights 15; European Convention on Human Rights (ECHR) 14–15, 17–18; European Court of Justice 16; First World War 15; Human Rights Committee 16, 17; International Covenant on Civil and Political Rights 15; League of Nations 15; reservations 17; UK 22–6; UN Human Rights Commission 13–14; UN treaty regime 15–16; Universal Declaration of Human Rights 16
International Covenant on Civil and Political Rights 15
League of Nations 15
legal positivism 14; State's intervention on behalf of individual 14
Oppenheim 14
UN Human Rights Commission, *see* UN Human Rights Commission
Universal Declaration of Human Rights 16
Ireland:
common law of human rights 37
Israel:
common law of human rights 36, 37
Italy:
breaches of Convention rights 22

Jacobsohn 49
Jamaica:
common law of human rights 52
Japan:
foreign human rights law, use of 42
judges:
training in Convention rights 28
jury trial:
civil, *see* Civil jury trial
criminal: generally 206
seventh amendment. *See* Seventh amendment right to jury trial
United States 225–53; seventh amendment. *See* Seventh amendment right to jury trial

Kanun of Lek Dukagjini 28

La Forest 60
League of Nations:
complaints to 15
establishment 15

Lurie, Alison 72
Lyndhurst, Lord:
conclusions on 202–4
early years at bar 174–8
generally 172–3
judge, as 187–9
law reformer, as 193–4
literary interests 197
personal lives 198–200
politician, as 178–82
university career 174

McFadden 51
Maitland, F.W. 212
malicious prosecution:
civil jury trial 214–24; control of jury by judge 218–21; court martial 215; existence of jurisdiction 214–15; generally 213–14; hearsay 218–19; intent 21–4; meaning of malicious prosecution 214; *mens rea* 214; motive 217; privilege 221–4; reasonable and probable cause 217–18; reasonableness 214; roles of judge and jury 217–21; significance 213
meaning 214
police 217
Mearns 55
Meyer, Jean 76
More, Sir Thomas 213

national legal systems:
Bill of Rights 30
borrowing from other jurisdictions 30–1
common law of human right, *see* Common law of human rights
development of human rights protection in 29; controversy 30; judicial role 30
distinguishing foreign authorities 43, 48
foreign law, use of 41–3
international jurisdictions and 30
motivation for development of law 29
transnational judicial conversations 59–62
using transnational law 41–3
Nazi Germany:
War Zone Courts, British, *see* War Zone Courts
Nelken 36
Nelson 207
New Zealand:
common law of human rights 37, 52
nineteenth century lawyers 172–204
Campbell, Lord, *see* Campbell, Lord
Denman, Thomas, *see* Denman, Thomas
generally 172–4
Lyndhurst, Lord, *see* Lyndurst, Lord

Paine, Thomas 28

Pakistan:
common law of human rights 52
Papua New Guinea:
colonial resistance 127, 137–48
Patterson, Lyman Ray 255, 258, 269
persuasive authority:
common law of human rights 32, 33–5,
43–7
Pigou, Arthur C. 289–90
police:
duty of care 25–6
pornography 23

ratio decidendi:
concept of 150
definitions 156–7
determining 156–7
meaning 156
Raz, Joseph 32
Redish, Martin 226
rule of law:
characterisation 128
responsibility of law 128–9
Russia:
civil jury trial 205
Rylands v. Fletcher:
civil jury trial 212
contextual studies 149–50

Schauer 44–5
Scott, Austin 232
Second World War:
freedom of expression 23
sentencing:
children 24, 25
seventh amendment right to jury trial
225–53
background 225–7
City of Montgomery decision 248–52
complexity exception 239–48
copyright 248–52
eighteenth century English trial practice
229–38; case stated procedure 231,
233–4, 235; damages 229–30; directed
verdict 233, 234–5; forms of action
230; historical test and 235–7; non-suit
231–3; pleadings 230–1; reasonable
time cases 237–8; special verdicts 231;
trespass on the case 230
Feltner decision 248–52
Henderson, Edith 225
historical test 226, 227–9, 235–7, 248–53
Markman case 226, 227–9, 235–6, 252, 253
meaning of right 225
non-suit 231–3
provisions 225
reasonable time cases 237–8
recent cases 226–7
Redish, Martin 226

scope of protection 225
Simpson, Brian:
Cannibalism and the Common law 150
contextual studies 149–69
contribution of 23–4
copyright 254
Dudley and Stephens, on 150
effective remedy, advice on right to 27
expert opinion of 24–5
historian, as 28
In the Highest Degree Odious: Detention
Without Trial in Wartime Britain 23;
European Human Rights Law Review,
contribution to 24
Legal Theory and Legal History 126
police duty of care, advice on 26–7
Rylands v. Fletcher, on 149–50
sentencing of children, advice on 24, 25
United States, in 285–91; accomplishments 288–90; evidentiary problems
with mapping career 285–7; generally
285
University of Tirana, work at 28
War Zone Courts 90, 95
Williams Committee 23
Singapore:
common law of human rights 37, 38
European Court of Human Rights,
judgments of 38
Slaughter 42, 49, 61
South Africa:
common law of human rights 36, 37, 55
foreign human rights law, use of 42
Stephen, Sir Herbert 218
Summers 47

Thayer 206
Tripathi 47, 47–8
Tudor common pleas 271–84
assumpsit 272–3, 274; common pleas
reaction 278–84; informal covenants
279; money, for 274–84; surety cases
279
bipartite judiciary 272–3
Coke, Sir Edward 272
Magna Carta 272, 273
wager of law 281
Walmsley, Justice 271–2
Turner, E.S. 105

UK:
breaches of Convention rights 22
UN Charter:
complaints under: UK, from 13, 16
signing 13
see also UN Human Rights Commission
UN Convention on the Rights of the Child:
abandoned children 66, 69, 70–1
UN Human Rights Commission:

creation 13
ECOSOC Resolution 13–14
violation of human rights: approach to
    13–14; consistent patterns 13–14;
    political support 14
United Kingdom:
common law of human rights 52
United States:
capital punishment 39–40
common law of human rights 37, 39–40,
    42, 51–2, 53, 58
cruel and unusual punishment 40
foreign human rights law, use of 42, 51–2
jury trial 225–53; seventh amendment.
    See Seventh amendment right to jury
    trial
Simpson, Brian and 285–91
Supreme Court: functions of 39
United Stats:
civil jury trial 205
Universal Declaration of Human Rights:
individual's rights 16
national legal systems 30

Venice Commission 37
Vienna Convention on the Law of Treaties
    17

War Zone Courts 86–125
accommodation: court 115; judicial 119
advantages 102
advisers 100–1
appeals 103, 106
appointments 115
assessors 114
background 86–91
caseloads 102
civil court, as 98, 100–1
clerk to the court 116
codewords 119
Commons revolt 97–8, 103–12
conclusion on 124–5
confirmation 107, 108
constitutional principle 104
constitutionalism 91
criminal procedure rules 97
death penalty 97, 101–2, 107, 109, 121
declaration of War Zone 116, 117
defensive plans, British 94–6
dismantling 122–3
emergency situations, responses to 88

establishing 104, 114–22
examination of 87–8
forcing a safeguard 101
'Henry VIII clause' 104
Home Guard 96
hybrid system 98–9
intelligence monitoring of German
    intentions 94–5
invasion 1941–1942 112–14
judges 115, 117, 118, 119
jurisdiction 102
legal press, response of 111
martial law 99, 100
military situation 91–4
military view 101
negative resolution procedure 111
newspaper reporting of 107
officials 116
Parliament and 96–112; judiciary 97;
    powers 97–112
popular imagery 89
Prerogative of Mercy 108
Presidents 118
prison governors 120–1
purpose 87
reception for 102–3
Regional Commissioners 116, 117
regulation 104, 105–6, 112
review panel 109–10
revised rules 121–2
Scotland 119–20
sentencing 107–8
setting up 114–22
Simpson, Brian 90, 95
subsistence allowances 114
support for 97–8
transport 118
Turner, E.S. 105
Victor Conference 116
warnings messages 119
winding-up 122–3
working class unreliability, justification
    of 89
Weiner, Stephen 237–8
Weissbrodt 57
White Paper *Bringing Rights Home* 27–8
Williams Committee:
Simpson, Brian 23

Zimbabwe:
common law of human rights 36, 53